EVERYMAN IN EUROPE
Essays In Social History

The Industrial Centuries

VOLUME 2

EVERYMAN IN

Allan Mitchell

University of California, San Diego

Istvan Deak

Columbia University

EUROPE
ESSAYS IN
SOCIAL HISTORY

The Industrial Centuries

PRENTICE-HALL, INC., *Englewood Cliffs, New Jersey*

Allan Mitchell and *Istvan Deak*

EVERYMAN IN EUROPE:
ESSAYS IN SOCIAL HISTORY

Volume 2   The Industrial Centuries

Printed in the United States of America

10   9   8   7   6   5   4   3

PRENTICE-HALL, INTERNATIONAL, INC., *London*
PRENTICE-HALL OF AUSTRALIA, PTY. LTD., *Sydney*
PRENTICE-HALL OF CANADA, LTD., *Toronto*
PRENTICE-HALL OF INDIA PRIVATE LIMITED, *New Delhi*
PRENTICE-HALL OF JAPAN, INC., *Tokyo*

To Four Women
Gloria, Catherine, Alexandra, and Éva

CONTENTS

PREFACE   xi

Part I

The Agony of Industrializing 1750–1850

1. THE RURAL REVOLUTION   3

Dorothy Marshall
   Rural Change in Eighteenth-Century England   *5*

Gwynn Lewis
   The Impact of the Revolution in Rural France   *11*

Jerome Blum
   Reformers, Rebels, and Abolitionists in Russia   *22*

2. THE FORMATION OF A LABOR FORCE   30

George Rudé
The City Riot of the Eighteenth Century   *32*

E. J. Hobsbawm   The Laboring Poor   *44*

P. H. Noyes
The German Working Class in the 1840s   *54*

3. THE CYCLE OF LIFE   66

Olwen Hufton
Life and Death Among the Very Poor   *68*

S. G. Checkland   The Lower Orders in England   *84*

William L. Langer   The Social Question   *98*

Part II

Acceleration and Social Conflict 1850–1914

4. OLD AND NEW SOCIAL TYPES   117

Peter Laslett
The Transformation of English Society   *119*

Peter N. Stearns   The Adaptation
to Industrialization in Germany   *128*

Arthur J. May   The Austrian "Other Half"   *145*

Lazar Volin   The Russian Peasant:
From Emancipation to Kolkhoz   *156*

5. KINDER, KÜCHE, KIRCHE   170

K. H. Connell
Catholicism and Marriage in Ireland   *172*

Robert Cecil   Childhood, Youth and Education   *187*

Theodore Zeldin   The Conflict of Moralities   *195*

6. PRIMITIVE AND CIVILIZED REBELS   207

Lewis H. Gann
Partisan Warfare in the Heyday of Imperialism   *209*

E. J. Hobsbawm
The Mafia as a Social Phenomenon   *216*

Charles Tilly
Collective Violence in European Perspective   *228*

Part III

Brave New Europe: 1914 to the Present

7. MECHANIZATION
    AND COLLECTIVIZATION   241

John Ardagh   The Slow Death of the Peasant   *243*

Hugh Seton-Watson
The Peasantry of Eastern Europe   *253*

Merle Fainsod
Controls and Tensions in Soviet Agriculture   *258*

8. FAMILY LIFE
    IN AN URBANIZED SOCIETY   278

Robert Graves and Alan Hodge
Domestic Life in Britain   *280*

Jesse R. Pitts
Continuity and Change in Bourgeois France   *291*

Richard Grunberger   The Family in Nazi Germany   *299*

H. *Kent Geiger*
What the Revolution Brought to Russia   *311*

9. THE CULT OF YOUTH   328

Walter Z. Laqueur   Young Germany   *330*

Paul Wilkinson   English Youth Movements   *341*

John Ardagh   French Youth with a Dusty Answer   *350*

Ralph T. Fisher, Jr.
The Soviet Model of the Ideal Youth   *367*

Galia Golan   Youth and Politics in Czechoslovakia   *378*

SUGGESTED READINGS   395

PREFACE

Historians ordinarily record the major events of the past. They attempt to tell us what happened, and when, and if possible why. No one would deny that these are important things to know, and few would dispute that it is a proper and necessary function of historians to be concerned with the impact of such events. Yet there has been for some time a realization among professional historians, as well as among students, that history needs to be something more than an analysis of dramatic events, however crucial they may have been. If we are really to understand the past, we ought also to know about the daily lives of the many people who endured rather than instigated the events of which we so often read in books. It is the special concern of these volumes, then, to study how most people lived rather than how a few acted.

Most men and women who populate this world have always been poor and uneducated. This is not to say that they have been altogether powerless and inarticulate. What it does mean is that they have tended to express themselves and their interests in social groups, of one sort or another, rather than as individuals. To comprehend their behavior it is therefore more useful to think in terms of social types than of personalities. In the pages that follow, proper names will consequently figure only infrequently. As important as they are, it is not Pericles, Julius Caesar, Henry VIII, and Napoleon Bonaparte who stand here in the foreground; rather it is the peasant, the worker, the woman, and the youth. In short, our chief protagonist is Everyman.

By the careful selection of articles and excerpts we have attempted to trace the changing circumstances and activities of ordinary people from Greek civilization to the present time. Our focus is Europe; and we have defined Europe as broadly as possible, drawing our examples from Ireland to Russia. Too often Europe is conceived largely in terms of what is most familiar to us and to the majority of Western historians: Britain and France. By giving the areas of central and eastern Europe their due, we hope to redress the balance and to suggest a truer picture of European society as a whole.

The attentive reader will quickly perceive that generalizations about Everyman in one area of Europe at a given time are not universally applicable. Can we nonetheless say that the various social types under consideration have something in common? Is there any constant factor among so many people in such a multitude of times and places? If so, it is certainly *not* that they have been deaf and dumb throughout European history. To the contrary, in their own way they have often and unmistakenly expressed enthusiasm, or dissatisfaction, or indifference. Even the ostensibly most random forms of violence and deviant modes of behavior have sometimes spoken eloquently as to the character of European society. Yet Everyman has hardly been the master of his own fate and what has emerged as the salient characteristic of most people's behavior is this: they usually take rather than give orders. They do not command, they obey—or at least they are expected to do so.

Is this, then, a history of the oppressed? That is a question which the reader must finally answer for himself. There is certainly much evidence to support an affirmative reply. Still, the reader cannot remain unaware of the relativity of such a notion as "oppression." What degree of consciousness must the oppressed person attain of his deprived social status before he can be considered enslaved? What degree of personal liberty is required in order to protest or to escape oppression? These are not simple issues, and they are not much clarified by dogmatic assertions of whatever political persuasion. The historian is always on the side of complexity and the social historian emphatically so; the dogmatist will therefore find little support here for his terrible simplifications.

We have kept two objectives well in view: to select essays which are adequate to the difficulty of the subject rather than to choose brief and random fragments, and to achieve a sense of variety by drawing on a representative sample of historical techniques. The reader should gain the altogether legitimate impression that social history which we believe is still its adolescence, is far from becoming a monolithic discipline.

The notion that European society was transformed in modern times by an "industrial revolution" need not be accepted without reservation. In the first place, the term "revolution" implies a rapid and thorough change, whereas the development of an industrial society in Europe has been slow, uneven, and incomplete. The transformation was, moreover, not exclusively a matter of industry; one must also take into account demographic, agricultural, and technological innovations of considerable magnitude and complexity. To separate cause from effect, or symptom from correlation, is no simple task.

Another preliminary word of caution. We are perhaps unduly conditioned to believe that history consists of winners and losers. Thus we may be inclined, without a flicker of protest, to accept the assertion that modern times were marked by the "triumph" of the bourgeoisie. Yet we would do well to recall that the results of a protracted social evolution are seldom to be measured by box scores or body counts, as if history were an athletic contest or a formal military engagement. Even if we could derive a precise definition of "bourgeois"—which would hardly hold for the entire European continent—we cannot be quite certain what "to win" really means in social terms. We know only that industrialization has meant an important alteration in the quality of life for most Europeans. A careful study of the essays in this volume should enrich our understanding of that complex phenomenon.

The preparation of this volume, as well as the preceding one, was greatly facilitated by the superb editorial care of Patricia Albano, Gloria Deak and Claire Nolte. We are also extending our heartfelt thanks to Robert P. Fenyo, Assistant Vice President of Prentice-Hall, Inc., who brings to the publishing world infinite patience and foresight.

EVERYMAN IN EUROPE
Essays In Social History

The Industrial Centuries

THE AGONY OF INDUSTRIALIZING 1750–1850

part I

1. THE RURAL REVOLUTION

Without industry, no revolution; without population growth, no industry; without more productive agriculture, no population growth. Probably most historians hold such a concatenation of assumptions to be justified. Stated more cogently they add up to this: that the industrial revolution was necessarily launched from an improved agricultural base. Although this proposition may essentially be correct, it is certainly not as simple as one might suppose. We are still left with the problem of defining what we mean by improvement; and we need to comprehend the interaction of expansion in agriculture and industry.

Dorothy Marshall begins with the earliest stages of sustained economic growth in Britain during the eighteenth century. She finds that rural England was still a slow-moving and basically medieval society until the final decades before 1800. The enclosure movement, although not the single cause of fundamental change, was symptomatic of a quickening development toward larger land-holdings and more intensive methods of cultivation. Segments of the rural population were affected differently; some grew conspicuously wealthier while others became only more impoverished. None, in any case, remained untouched.

Gwynn Lewis records the impact of the French Revolution on rural France. The peasantry already owned nearly one-third of French land before 1789. While that point is important, several qualifications are in order. The proprietorship of peasants was far from being in proportion to the actual percentage of rural labor in the total population. Also, their lands tended to be poorer and more peripheral as well as smaller than those of the higher estates. And, though few remained serfs, most peasants were still burdened with the galling taxation of the Old Regime. Thus the complaints, born both of rising expectations and bothersome restrictions, led to the rural violence of the first revolutionary months, for which the climax was the so-called Great Fear. This account considers the many ramifications and ambiguities which ensued as the nineteenth century began.

Jerome Blum draws a contrast between western and eastern Europe. While personal liberty and peasant land-holding were spreading in the West, the condition of the Russian peasantry worsened drastically. The onset of new agricultural and industrial techniques brought no commensurate social benefit to the mass of the Russian people mired in serfdom. The consequence was a growing sense of desperation and the exacerbation of long-standing grievances. Until the nineteenth century the only recourse of the peasant was an attempt to escape. But conditions grew so depressing that local insurrections began to occur with increasing frequency. The cumulative effect was to unnerve the tsarist regime and finally to open the way to formal emancipation of the serfs. Not bright ideals but sheer deprivation was, in this case, the motor force of social change.

At least one observation emerges from these discussions: that the delicate balance of an old order was everywhere being permanently upset. In some form or other the process of industrialization was spreading like an infectious disease. No aspect or area of the European social organism was completely immune. Even the most remote and backward corners of the mainland were bound to feel the repercussions sooner or later. No class and no region could maintain total stability once another was thrown into flux.

DOROTHY MARSHALL

Rural Change
in Eighteenth-Century England

It is impossible to understand eighteenth-century England, and equally impossible to estimate the effect of the economic developments which marked its closing decades without a fairly detailed knowledge of its social structure. Prominent though the merchants were in molding the policy of this country in its relations, both economic and diplomatic, with the rest of the world, England was still basically agricultural. For the greater part of the people the tie with the land remained close: the landowner was still the most potent influence in shaping its social structure.

Misled by the sophistication of so much of eighteenth-century thought and literature and by the polished elegance of its ruling class, it is easy to forget how much of the medieval foundations of society still remained, hidden, it is true, by this superstructure, but still sustaining it. Towns no doubt were growing, but, with some few exceptions where trade provided the impetus, their growth had not that staggering quality that was to mark their progress in the nineteenth century. Most of them remained small, hardly more than glorified villages except in a constitutional and legal sense. Their relation to the countryside that surrounded them also remained virtually unchanged in that their chief function was still to provide a market for the adjacent rural areas. Their population rarely numbered more than a few thousands: the great majority of people still lived in the country.

It would be a mistake to think of this rural population as being purely agricultural. By the opening years of the eighteenth century the domestic system, with its flexible organization, had scattered the possibilities of industrialization up and down the countryside. Probably by this time there were few localities where some people were not spinning or weaving for the clothier. Many it is true were only supplementing the produce of a small-holding or the enjoyment of common rights, but for others industry

Dorothy Marshall, *English People in the Eighteenth Century* (London: Longmans Green and Co. Ltd., 1965), pp. 39–40, 232–33, 236–39, 243–45. By permission of Longman Group Ltd., London.

was their main source of livelihood. But, though craftsmen, they remained essentially country dwellers, congregated in small clothing villages or living in the scattered homesteads of the North but always in intimate contact with the rural life around them. The concentration of industry, with its savage demand for hands, and still more hands, combined with an increased shortage of land as the population grew, had not yet produced that divorce from the country, which was so fundamentally to alter the structure of society in the nineteenth century. In consequence it is not surprising that though labor services and serfdom had long disappeared the whole tone of rural society was still feudal. Power was still in the hands of the man who possessed land. The merchant and the financier, important as their part in the national economy was, had still in many ways to operate within the framework of a society that had been shaped by landowners for landowners. To this extent England was still medieval in its fundamental assumptions. . . .

It is not easy to assess the extent to which economic developments had transformed the structure of rural society by the end of the eighteenth century. The greatest and most obvious break with the past was provided by the disappearance of the open-field village and the enclosure of the wastes and commons, which in 1700 still sprawled across much of the less fertile land. Neither was a rapid process. If half the arable land was still in open fields at the beginning of the century, even at its end not all of it had been enclosed, while the reclamation of wastes and commons took some hundred and fifty years before it was reasonably complete. Yet, though the process was a lengthy one, it was fundamental. The society which had grown up within the framework of the open-field village, or whose economy depended upon extensive wastes, could not survive the destruction of the agrarian shell in which it had lived.

Because these changes were definite and concrete and because there was much that the social historian could rightly deplore in the English countryside of the nineteenth century there has been a tendency to blame enclosures for many, if not most, subsequent evils. Both the destruction of the peasantry and the creation of the landless laborer have been attributed to them, and it is often emotionally implied, if not specifically stated, that in the course of a comparatively few years the peasant, happy and prosperous, was transformed into the laborer, wretched and poor. As a corollary it is often argued that misery led to rural depopulation; that the growing towns were fed by unfortunate country folk, driven from the land when it passed into the occupation of large tenant farmers, paying economic rents to greedy landlords. According to this view the manufacturers could offer mere subsistence wages to men and women who, through desperation, had no alternative but to accept. All this it is implied took place in an atmosphere of exploitation, greed and bitter injustice.

On this picture recent research into eighteenth-century agrarian history has cast increasing doubt and suggests that enclosure has been blamed for much for which it was not, in fact, responsible. Some of the confusion has doubtless arisen because of an imperfect knowledge of the complexity, and often of the misery, of earlier rural conditions; there has been an inclination to see the past as a golden age of a prosperous peasantry. In consequence, later suffering has not been balanced against previous wretchedness. Also difficulties have been created by the failure to realize that the enclosures of the century were not all of a piece and did not all produce the same effects. It seems likely that the enclosures of the earlier decades did press hardly on the smaller farmers and were a contributory factor in diminishing their numbers. It is more doubtful whether the later parliamentary enclosures had a similar effect. Indeed, if anything the agrarian re-organization that was accelerated by the pressure of the French wars and the growing population appears to have a contrary result. That enclosure eliminated the open field is obvious; its effect in reducing the number of small occupying owners and modest tenant farmers is more difficult to assess. A change in farming methods does not necessarily imply a change in either the rural population or in the acreage farmed. . . .

If enclosures did not eliminate the small farmer they at least encouraged a new type of capitalist farmer, renting a considerable acreage. The improving landlord preferred this kind of tenant and gave him every assistance. Men like Coke spent considerable sums on buildings, chose their tenants with care and gave them long leases so that they might have every inducement to put both labor and capital into their farms. The result was a new breed of prosperous farmers. Arthur Young speaks with appreciation and perhaps some envy of the way of life of the prosperous farmer with his

> large roomy, clean kitchen with a rousing wood fire on the hearth, and the ceiling well hung with smoked bacon and hams; a small room for the farmer and his family, opening into the kitchen, with glass in the door, or wall, to see that things *go right*. When company is in the house a fire in the parlour. At table great plenty of plain things, with a bottle of good port after dinner, and at least a hogshead of it in his cellar. . . . Attendance, never anything but a maid, this I consider as one of the lines of separation between different classes of people; the farmer is to have everything that yields comfort; those who chuse to give up that enjoyment for liveries or *shew* of any kind, arrange themselves with another order of mortals; no farmer who is wise will ever make the experiment of a change for he gives solidity for moon shine. . . . In the stable a good nag, for his own riding, but not good enough for hunting, a recreation too common, as it is apt to lead into a dissipated, idle, drinking and expensive life.[1]

As for his wife, she was to be allowed "a one horse chaise."

[1] A. Young: *Annals of Agriculture,* Vol. XVII, p. 152.

Not all prosperous farmers were prepared to concentrate on the substance and let the shadow go. There is a certain amount of scattered evidence that indicates that at least some of them were adopting a style of living that had previously been associated with their social superiors, and were beginning to constitute a rural variation of the middle class. Such men aroused Young's wrath. To him the wise farmer was one who, if he increases, "he does not alter his plan of life, but saves." However, he concedes that not all farmers are so wise.

> I see sometimes, for instance, a piano forte in a farmer's parlour, which I always wish was burnt; a livery servant is sometimes found, and a post chaise to carry their daughters to assemblies, those ladies are sometimes educated at expensive boarding schools, and the sons often at the University, to be made parsons but all these things imply a departure from that line which separates these different orders of beings, let all these things, and all the folly, foppery, expence and anxiety that belongs to them remain among gentlemen. A wise farmer will not envy them.[2]

Arthur Young's disapproval was mild beside the vituperation of a writer to the *Gentleman's Magazine* who, after speaking of men whom he admits are no longer mere farmers, having branched out as graziers, corn factors, mealmen, millers, maltsters, brewers and horse-dealers, described their sons as generally belonging

> to some of the numerous corps of volunteers and embodied yeomanry; these dashing bucks we see flourishing their broadswords, and exhibiting their neatly buskined posteriors to the admiration of the misses, their sisters, or neighbours, who display in their turns all the attractive graces of Grecian gesticulations and nudity. Instead of dishing butter, feeding poultry, or curing bacon, the avocations of these young *ladies* at home are, studying dress, attitudes, novels, French and musick, whilst the fine ladies their mothers sit lounging in parlours adorned with the fiddle faddle fancy work of their daughters. With as much rapidity as post horses can convey them, the fashions fly from London to the country towns, and from the country towns to the remotest villages; in so much that the *exhibitions* of girls in the country vie with those in the capitol. As the females of each class imitate those belonging to the class above them, so those below the farmers' daughters must have their white dresses as well as them, even if they appropriate to the purpose the cloth that should make them shifts.[3]

Finally he laments,

> We see not now the farmers' wives and daughters jogging to the towns for the purpose of selling the productions of the cartons and dairies; but

[2] *Annals of Agriculture,* Vol. XVII, p. 156.
[3] *Gentleman's Magazine,* Vol. LXXI (1801), p. 587.

we see them rattling in their spruce gigs to the milliners and perfumers, in order to lavish on fripperies part of the enormous gains extorted by their fathers and husbands from the groaning public.

Such tirades were obviously exaggerated distortions of the new tendencies, as any one acquainted with farming mentality must realize. In the earlier part of the letter quoted above the writer idealizes the small farmer of the past as grossly as he pillories the successful farmer of the Napoleonic era. Nevertheless, he was probably right in realizing that there was a new tendency abroad. . . .

Thus, though even the medieval village had contained a fair sprinkling of landless men, the full-time agricultural worker, living in his cottage and dependent on his wages, was not a feature of rural England until larger farms and more intensive agriculture created a need for his services. In this sense the landless laborer of the nineteenth century was the creation of changing conditions in the eighteenth. Some of these men, as tradition avers, were no doubt the product of enclosures and consolidations which deprived small tenants of their holdings and left them with no alternative but to work for wages for the big farmer who had dispossessed them. But these, for the most part, were drawn from those individual "hard cases" which always accompany large-scale economic change. It is probable that in reality the rural poor suffered more from the enclosure of the waste than they did from that of the open fields. When the waste was gone the illegal squatter, against whom the Acts of Settlement and Removal had been directed, had no other resource than to work for what wages the farmers were prepared to offer. Their livelihood had always been precarious and their standard of living low. With the loss of the waste they exchanged one kind of poverty for another, but whether they were really pushed down in the social scale may well be doubted.

Many of the eighteenth-century rural poor were neither squatters on the waste nor full-time agricultural workers but Jacks-of-all-trades, doing work for the farmers when it was available, keeping a little livestock on the waste and working intermittently at some local industry. Few counties and few districts were without their own specialities. Thus Bedfordshire, Buckinghamshire and Hertfordshire were noted for straw-plait making. At straw-plaiting women could earn from six to twelve shillings a week, and even children three or four, particularly after a change in fashion decreed the great Leghorn hats, so often depicted by Gainsborough. Lace-making was also very widespread. "The town of Bedford," wrote Young, "is noted for nothing but its lace manufactory, which employs above 500 women and girls. . . . Women that are very good hands earn 1*s.* a day, but in common only 8*d,* 9*d* and 10*d.*" [4] As a result of the demand for

---

[4] A. Young: *Northern Tour* (1770), Vol. I, p. 45.

women in these crafts it is said that maid-servants were in short supply. Not all the local crafts depended largely on female labor. In Nottingham the villages were full of stocking-frame knitters; round Northampton they made boots and shoes; in Shropshire they made garden pots at Broseley, fine china at Caughley, chains, ropes and china at Coalport, glass at Donnington, at Lebotwood there were dye works. The illustrations could be indefinitely extended to take in almost every district. Also, apart from every type of light secondary manufacture, so often forgotten or ignored as a part of the traditional pattern of the English countryside, there were very few areas that had not some branch of the textile industry. Cloth-making of every variety was probably the most widely diffused, but a good deal of linen was also manufactured, and in Lancashire cotton spinning and weaving was already a staple employment.

It is these people who have most claim to be regarded as the victims of economic change. In a world of small farmers, ample uncultivated land and scattered industry there was a place for them, though no one would describe them as well off, even at the beginning of the century, when food prices were low. Rural housing was often very bad and terribly overcrowded, food was monotonous, the hours of labor, whether in agriculture or industry, long. The value of common rights has been hotly debated, both by contemporaries and by later historians. It is easy to produce an idealized picture, where every countryman had his pig in the sty and his cow on the common. It is equally easy to pick out the idle, shiftless household that refused to bestir itself because a half-starved beast or two on the waste and a scrap of land provided a wretched minimum existence. Many poor families could not afford the price of a cow, and where they could the pasture available was often so overstocked that the beast was half-starved. Even so the most overstocked common was worth something to a poor family. If they could not afford a cow or a sheep or two for wool, at least they could keep a few geese, perhaps some hens, maybe a pig, and above all, they could gather fuel or, especially in the North, dig peat and turf. So long as the price of food was low, so long as there was some local supplement to agricultural work, so that a man was not too dependent on that for his cash earnings, so long as there was some waste available, a country family, unless it were very shiftless or unhealthy or too overburdened with very young children, could just manage. Kalm, it may be remembered, commented on the way in which, when the day's work was done, the laborers would sit drinking in the ale-house with their cronies, or would congregate round the fire, singing and telling tales. Nevertheless even this simple standard was precarious. Not one of a poor man's resources was sufficient by itself to maintain him. Any change in the delicate balance might well prove disastrous.

In the closing years of the eighteenth century that is increasingly what happened. . . .

GWYNN LEWIS

The Impact of the Revolution In Rural France

. . . The Revolution destroyed the fabric of village society, undermining the power and prestige of the nobility, questioning the basic assumptions of religious life, sharpening antagonisms within the peasant community itself. As a result of the Revolution vast amounts of property were thrown onto the open market, whetting the already keen appetite of the peasant for land. After a generation of war hundreds of thousands of peasants were never to return to their native fields. Perhaps it was the time and energy devoted to these momentous problems which helps to explain why, in the same period, no great change occurred in the cultivation of the soil.

The peasantry owned about one-third of the land, concentrated, as one might expect, mainly in the poorer and more remote regions. In Flanders, Picardy or the great granaries of the Beauce and the Brie around the capital, peasant property was not extensive. It was in the North West that Arthur Young noted during his travels through France that "the richest scenes of cultivation are to be found." It was in these same regions that the percentage of landless peasants might rise to over seventy percent. In much poorer areas like the Limousin peasant properties might account for over half the land cultivated. It was here that Young was reminded "of the misery of Ireland . . . the country girls and women do without shoes or stockings." Most French peasants were not serfs, tied to the soil and their masters: less than one million fell into this category. The great majority regarded themselves as free men, owning and disposing of their property within traditionally-defined limits. If they owned property on a noble estate, and there were relatively few who did not, the peasants paid the *cens* or *champart,* occasionally both, in recognition of the seigneur's sovereignty, for "the seigneurie represented the corner-stone of the social edifice of France." In addition to the multiplicity of feudal dues and services outlined . . . the peasant was also obliged to pay the tithe to the Church and the *taille* to the government, the latter tax being a particularly heavy load on his already overburdened shoulders.

The paradox of regarding themselves as property-owners, and yet paying dues to a lord in order to dispose of their property as they wished, had occasioned only sporadic protests among the peasantry until, in the second half of the eighteenth century, the seigneurs and the bourgeoisie began to exploit their estates more efficiently. Frequently the nobility leased their property to merchants, lawyers or even the wealthier farmers, often endowed with a more developed sense of business acumen. The property was then sublet to sharecroppers or small farmers usually on short leases of four to nine years duration. The existence of a growing number of wealthy peasants, the *laboureurs,* who provided grain for the markets, work for the landless and mortgage facilities for the impoverished, was provoking serious conflicts within the peasant community before 1789.

Such peasants, owning perhaps the only plough in the village, and acting as amateur lawyers and administrators, were far more in touch with urban life and in a good position to exploit the sale of church lands after 1789. The rich tenant-farmer who rented big tracts of land in the better agricultural regions of northern France, Normandy, the Brie and the Beauce also benefited. The vast majority of peasants, however, fell into neither of these categories, consisting of small-owners (*petits propriétaires*), sharecroppers (*métayers*) and day-laborers (*journaliers*). By 1826, over 70 percent of French peasants were farming less than twelve acres.

The sharecropping system was the most common form of agricultural labor in France, particularly in parts of the West, the Center and the Southwest. The sharecropper received the seed and occasionally the necessary farm implements in return for up to a half of the produce at harvest time. It was a miserable system, perpetuating poverty and ignorance, but it did at least provide hundreds of thousands of peasants with some sort of stake in the soil. It also raised them above the level of the day-laborer, who was often thrown out of work once the harvest had been gathered in, and left to swell the ranks of the beggars and brigands who plagued the French countryside before and during the revolutionary period.

The above résumé provides a very over-simplified picture of rural life; it reduces the complex system of landholding to its simplest terms; it takes no account of the thousands of village artisans like blacksmiths, carpenters, wheelwrights or of the violent and usually ostracised groups of woodcutters, charcoal-burners, clog-makers, who moved from region to region, often living like animals in forest huts, and frequently crossing the narrow frontier between respectability and rural crime.

One should also emphasise the importance of domestic industry in the French countryside. In Normandy, Alsace, Languedoc, wherever textile industries were based, the peasant usually supplemented his meagre income by finishing-off silk, cloth or woollen goods for a merchant-manufacturer. Arthur Young, travelling from Rouen to Le Havre, found "farmhouses and cottages everywhere and the cotton manufacture in all." In Languedoc, the great majority of peasants, particularly in the Protestant districts, grew raw silk or had a loom upon which the whole family worked during the winter months. The size of domestic industry in France, and the existence of a huge reservoir of labor, helps to explain why the country did not industrialise at the same pace as Britain in the eighteenth century.

In a way it was the conservatism of the French peasantry which swelled the rising tide of discontent in the countryside on the eve of the Revolution. It was not that the vast majority of peasants were becoming poorer; indeed, since agricultural prices rose by 60 percent in the course of the century, many were making increased profits from the sale of grain on the open market. It was the attack upon traditional customs and contracts which provoked the anger of the French peasant. More often than not peasants rioted to protect what they had, not to 'revolutionise' the system. The seizure of communal lands by the lords; the revision of old charters laying down the precise nature of feudal obligations; the increasing rapacity of the laborer class; the law of June 1787 which destroyed what remained of the old democratic village assembly, handing over effective control to the notables—all this contributed to a growing sense of unease and dissatisfaction. The disastrous harvest of 1788, occurring as it did when the textile and wine industries were still suffering from a serious slump, exacerbated an already tense situation.

It was in these circumstances that the Government asked the peasants, in February 1789, to draw up lists of grievances which would be presented to the States-General at their meeting in the following May. These lists, or *cahiers de doléances,* reflect the misery and poverty of many smallowners, share-croppers and day-laborers as well as a more general hatred of the tithe, aspects of the feudal system and the inequality of taxation. The very act of meeting to discuss the preparation of the cahiers produced a new sense of purpose and hope. In May, the States-General duly met at Versailles, but as the weeks passed in what appeared to be endless constitutional wrangling, the peasantry began to take matters into their own hands.

During the spring of 1789 there had been many isolated reports of attacks on grain convoys and peasants congregating outside the farm gates of a wealthy laborer demanding grain at "popular prices." In July and August, provoked beyond measure by soaring bread prices and political events in Paris, peasant riots assumed a new and more violent form with the burning and plundering of chateaux and monasteries and the destruction of feudal records and contracts. Some of the worst scenes of violence were enacted in the Northeast, although the repercussions of the movement were felt in many provinces. The forces of order were either too few or too sympathetic to contain the violence with the result that many noble families were obliged to flee or to promise an end to the exaction of feudal payments and service. These widespread disturbances provided an admirable pretext for the settlement of personal feuds, the renunciation of longstanding debts and, particularly in Alsace which had a large Jewish population, a renewed outburst of anti-semitism. Some property-owners organised resistance in the larger towns and villages: at the famous monastery of Cluny in the Maconnais scores of peasants were shot or strung up on hastily-erected gallows as a grim warning of middle-class susceptibilities concerning attacks on property rights.

The eruption of violence, news of the fall of the Bastille in Paris, and the very real misery of many peasants in a period of acute economic shortage, all help to explain the escalation of agrarian revolt into the "Great Fear" of 1789. With the memory of one bad harvest behind them and the wheat ripening in the fields the peasantry tended to be singularly receptive to reports of aristocratic plots and the imminent arrival of "the brigands." A cloud of dust on the horizon made by a passing carriage, exaggerated reports transmitted from village to village by travellers, the sight of a stranger in a local inn, precipitated shock waves of panic and alarm which spread in just over a fortnight from northern France to the Mediterranean. There were of course brigands roaming the countryside: a cahier from the province of Picardy referred to "poor beggars, and strangers who were becoming brigands, thieves and fire-raisers," but the traditional rural trinity of rumor, plot and fear exaggerated the truth out of all proportion. The comte des Echerolles, who owned property in the Nivernais, tells us that in his locality, "The terror was so widespread that we saw bands of peasants arriving from all parts armed with scythes and pitchforks determined to march against the brigands, but demanding to know where they could be found." *"Les brigands"* were not the less important in the spread of the Great Fear for being largely imaginary.

The famous decree passed on "the night of 4 August" 1789, which purported to abolish feudalism in its entirety, was wrung from a reluctant Assembly, partly in response to the above events. Subsequent debates, as well as the definitive decrees published in the spring of 1790, indicated that the National Assembly was determined to defend, if not the right of privilege, then certainly the sanctity of property. All forms of "personal" servitude were in fact abolished, along with the seigneurial courts, the tithe, provincial and municipal privileges. Seigneurial dues, however, were not abolished but, unless the peasant could prove that such dues had been exacted from him by force which, in the great majority of cases he could not, they were declared redeemable by purchase over twenty or twenty-five years. There is no doubt that a deathblow had been struck at the privileged nature of *ancien régime* society; there is equally no doubt that for the majority of peasants, convinced that the seigneurs had seized their lands by violence and usurpation in the irredeemable past, the solution proposed by the government was totally unsatisfactory. The logic of a revolutionary situation clashed with that of lawyers and property-owners.

Revolutionary logic triumphed. Open rebellion in a few areas, and passive resistance to the payment of any dues in many more, eventually obliged the deputies in Paris to revise their ingenious compromise. In August 1791, Arthur Young noted that "associations amongst the peasantry . . . have been formed for the purpose of refusing to pay rents." Sympathetic as he was to the peasant cause he felt constrained to comment that, "in a country where such things are possible, property of every kind is in a dubious situation": precisely the problem which had vexed the Assembly since 1789! The outbreak of war leading indirectly to the advent of a Jacobin Government in 1793 finally resolved the crisis in favor of the peasantry. In the summer of 1793, anxious to gain national support for the war-effort, the Government conceded in fact what the peasants had gained in theory in 1789—the total abolition of feudal services and payments. Although unjust in its application to many land-owners it was to be of the greatest importance in associating the mass of the peasantry with the Revolution.

The peasantry was far less fortunate in satisfying its hunger for land, despite the vast tracts of Church and émigré property placed on the open market after 1789. The decree of 14 May 1790 did provide for the sale of such land in small lots and offered the peasant reasonable time to finance the operation. Peasant syndicates were formed to purchase big estates for later subdivision amongst their members, but six months later the government applied severe restrictions, reducing the time allowed for payment and forbidding division of property into small lots. From 1793 to 1795, a certain amount of émigré property was put up for sale and it appears that in a few areas the peasantry did benefit. In certain regions of the Nord department the amount of land owned by the peasantry rose from 30 to 40 percent between 1789 and 1804. It has been estimated (although it should be stressed that such conclusions are rather tenuous) that the number of peasant small-owners increased by well over a million from 1789 to 1815, although the total amount of land cultivated by the peasantry did not substantially increase. It is true that many other factors, apart from the purchase of National Lands, were operating to produce a nation of peasant small-owners and that, compared with the gains made by the middle classes, the peasantry did not accomplish very much. Nonetheless, for the wealthier peasants at least, the early years of the Revolution had proved quite beneficial.

Only in one respect can it be said that the Revolution "capitalized" the agricultural sector of the economy. This process involved the transformation of village life from a collective to an individualistic basis. Certain laws encouraged the division of communal lands in the village; others made it far easier for the peasant to grow what crops he pleased than to be restricted in his choice by custom. This freedom could only be exercised at the cost of the poorest small-owner and landless laborer; the loss of communal rights proved to be a severe blow for the most miserable section of the peasant community. It is also true that the transformation of village life occurred very slowly. As late as 1892 it was still necessary to introduce legislation giving the municipality the right to decide on the abandonment of collective grazing rights. Revolutionary legislation, however, like the influence of the Enclosure Act on an English village, did mark a decisive stage in the breakup of the village as a community.

Released from the burdens of feudalism, the peasantry, or rather that section of the peasantry which produced food and wine for the towns, was to be imprisoned by the controlled economy of the Terror. Although many made a fortune on the "black market," the machinery of repression devised by the Committee of Public Safety brought government much closer to the peasants than at any time under the *ancien régime*. The Terror meant a detachment of the Revolutionary Army, or a *commissaire des subsistances,* poking about in the barn for hoarded grain supplies, or possibly closing down the local church. The government, faced with a critical wartime situation, did its best to requisition food for the armies and the towns but, lacking a modern bureaucracy, was only partially successful. Imprisoning or executing a farmer for hoarding was not the best way to ensure constant supplies of food and the resistance practised by many local authorities effectively frustrated all but the most energetic of the Government's Representatives-on-Mission.

Once the Government, by the decree of 29 September 1793, had fixed a ceiling, or General Maximum, on basic food supplies, the rich farmer, living on the expectation of higher prices, had the same interest as the poorest day-laborer in ensuring that grain did not leave his village. One of the major tasks of the Revolutionary Army was to break down resistance such as that encountered by the sergeant-major of the Compiègne detachment who reported that one peasant, when asked for wine had replied, "that he had plenty, but it was not for sale at the price fixed by the Maximum . . . he didn't care a damn about the Maximum since those who had thought up the idea had only done so in order to get their hands on his property."

The Terror undoubtedly sharpened antagonisms between the town and the countryside: the Revolutionary Army addressed placards to "the inhabitants of the countryside" from "their brothers in the towns," promising that unless the requisite supplies of grain were forthcoming the guillotine was only too anxious to perform its civic duties. The importance of bread supplies to the urban population is reflected in the following extract from a petition of the 48 Sections of Paris on 12 February 1793: "The people must have bread, because without bread there is no law, no liberty and no Republic." If the towns were not requisitioning grain (paid for by the assignat which the peasant, with every justification, detested) or imposing dechristianization on the countryside, they were sending out merchants, lawyers or rentiers who were eagerly buying up property which the peasant coveted for himself. In the West, as Professor Tilly has shown, "the bourgeois were the principal beneficiaries of the sales of church property." The identification of the town-dweller with the purchase of National Lands and the propagation of antireligious doctrines was one of the distinguishing features of the revolt of the peasantry against the Republic in the Year II. In the Southeast, as late as 1815, Protestant merchants were being attacked as "purchasers of National Lands at the beginning of the Revolution."

Some groups did benefit from the controlled economy introduced under the Terror: rural consumers like day-laborers, village artisans, and the army of black-marketeers or *revendeurs* waiting a mile or so outside the towns in order to purchase grain from the villages which was then sold, clandestinely, at prices above the Maximum. On the whole, however, the majority of peasants were overjoyed to learn of the fall of Robespierre and the dismantling of the political and economic system of the Terror at the end of 1794. For the richer farmers in particular 1795 was to prove an extremely lucrative year. Freed from the restrictions of the Maximum, benefiting from rising grain prices as a result of a disastrous harvest, the big farmer began to imitate the style of life hitherto associated only with the urban bourgeoisie. In the Pays de Caux district, "their houses are well-furnished . . . their wives and daughters decked with the finest jewelery. The old image of the peasant sitting by the fireside drinking his bowl of thin soup is no longer valid." The bitter hostility between rich and poor in the town aggravated by the worst famine in France since 1709, was not entirely absent in the countryside.

The famine of 1795, for all the immediate suffering it caused, did at least serve one useful purpose: it reminded the Government and the peasantry of their dependence on wheat as the basic unit of food production. The Revolution did not initiate any major changes either in the methods of cultivation or in the type of crops which the peasantry produced. Custom, collective rights and the complicated system of landholding in scattered strips outside the village all proved to be powerful brakes on agricultural improvement.

Marginal advances had been made in the course of the second half of the eighteenth century such as the introduction of root crops and fodder for animal stock, but, despite the prompting of the Physiocrats and the learned discourses delivered in hundreds of Academies, the vast majority of peasants continued to go about their labors in the time-honored fashion. The shortage of cattle helps to explain why the land was allowed to lie fallow once in every three years, even in alternate years in many regions south of the Loire; few cattle meant little fertilization and lack of fertilization meant fallow land. In 1795, the Government introduced rice and potatoes to alleviate the widespread suffering caused by the shortage of grain, but the people had very little notion of how to prepare rice, and they still regarded the potato as fit only for their pigs.

It was only under Napoleon who, like the Physiocrats, considered agriculture to be the primary source of wealth, that important, although still limited, advances were made. In a few Southeastern departments maize was introduced to offset the traditional dependence on wheat and the potato was seen more frequently, although only reluctantly, on the peasant's table. As a result of Napoleon's continental blockade and the loss of France's colonies, an attempt was made to introduce new crops liks chicory, sugar beet, tobacco and cotton. Promoted by the Prefects and various Ministers of Agriculture, the majority of these laudable schemes foundered on the resistance of the soil, the climate and the peasantry. The production of sugar beet, however, might be termed a qualified success: by 1815 there were approximately five hundred sugar-refining plants in France. Artificial fertilizers began to make their appearance on the most efficient farms. Although it is clear that these changes in cultivation and variation of crops only affected a small sector of the agricultural economy there is little doubt that they did mitigate the worst effects of the bad harvest of 1812. It was to be a long time, however, before French agriculture overcame the drawbacks of outmoded techniques, the lack of adequate credit facilities and the absence of a truly national market.

Apart from a relatively small number of affluent farmers, the style of life which characterized peasant society did not undergo any appreciable change during the Revolution and Empire.

Throughout our period the fear of famine continued to haunt the minds of both the peasantry and the government. The poor harvests of 1788–89 had precipitated a revolutionary crisis and unleashed the Great Fear in the countryside; the terrible famine of 1795 provoked the abortive risings of the spring of that year in Paris and, not only in the capital but throughout France, brought disease, a high rate of suicide and widespread starvation. In 1812 the Malet conspiracy to overthrow Napoleon was not unrelated to the serious economic situation which was partly to be explained by yet another poor harvest. Famine increased the antagonism between town and countryside. The peasant, always reluctant to see grain convoys leaving his locality, was understandably more hostile during a period of scarcity. For the villagers around the capital it was particularly galling to know that bread was being sold more cheaply in the city itself but that, owing to police regulations, it was impossible (or at least difficult) to smuggle the precious commodity through the custom-posts back to one's home. Dearth exaggerated the historic provincialism of French life: it set the landless against the landowning peasant; it awakened old animosities against the neighboring province, against the nearest town and, most of all, against Paris. In the eyes of the average peasant, the town-dweller was living off the fat of the land which he had to cultivate.

The response of the authorities to the threat of famine did not alter substantially before 1815. Increasingly laissez-faire in principle, governments, whether Monarchist, Jacobin or Napoleonic, invariably introduced the traditional mechanism of price-fixing and requisition in a crisis. Bread riots were to pose the most serious challenge to governments until the 1830s. The introduction of price-fixing laws had to be considered very carefully: too much constraint might provoke the very panic and fears which governments were most anxious to avoid. In addition, the peasantry, or at least rural producers, were bitterly opposed to such regulations. During the famine of 1812 the Prefect of the Aveyron, echoing the sentiments of the farmers in his department, told the Government in no uncertain terms that, "Price-fixing is a disastrous, unjust and impractical measure . . . in that it imposes on the profits of the farmer restrictions which are not placed on other producers. . . ."

However, since urban and rural consumers depended almost entirely on bread for their daily subsistence, governments could afford to ignore rising prices in other nonessential sectors of the economy. As one leading Physiocrat of the eighteenth century had explained: "I am all for freedom of trade, but bread is a matter for the police." Until such time as improvements in ʳgricultural yields and techniques and an increased volume of trade and industry produced a more varied diet and a wider market, governments tended to sympathise with this view. Their main problem, as the Jacobins found, was that they did not possess the bureaucratic and administrative personnel necessary to make the application of such regulations effective.

Confronted with a crisis, governments usually relied on the well-proven device of setting up soup-kitchens and workshops. *Ateliers de charité* were created in 1789 and again, in certain regions, in 1795. The Napoleonic régime, far better equipped from an administrative point of view, ran the system most effectively in 1812. During the winter months, according to a report by the Prefect of the Gard, women and children had been picking weeds and roots to eat, "not," according to the Prefect, "a completely disagreeable source of nourishment!" At the peak of the crisis in March 1812 no fewer than 89,407 individuals in the Gard alone were kept alive on bowls of soup made from rice and peas. Of course, the recipients of such charity were expected to express their gratitude in a practical way, either by weaving, spinning, or digging roads and ditches. The limited amount of food kept the mass of the population from starvation; hard labor ensured that what little energy the people still possessed would not be used for rioting. The Napoleonic régime avoided massive unrest in 1812 by maintaining a very fine balance between the provision of soup and the shovel.

Begging and brigandage were the natural heirs to famine in the eighteenth century. Both these forms of "antisocial" behavior had a long and, from the standpoint of criminality, dishonorable tradition in peasant societies. Highwaymen, salt-smugglers, child-beggars, bands of outlaws like the *Chauffeurs du Nord* are to be found as stock characters in eighteenth-century literature. The rise in population after 1750 made it even more difficult for the peasant to provide for his wife and children. In a famine year, the sons and daughters of day-laborers had no other recourse than to set out for the towns or scour the countryside in search of food and shelter. It was from 1795 to 1799 that the worst period of anarchy in the countryside occurred, although as late as 1812 reports from various local authorities speak of "armies of beggars" plaguing the more affluent farmers for food and work. This perennial problem was made more acute during the last few years of the eighteenth century by the severity of the economic crisis of 1795–6, the social and political dislocation occasioned by the Revolution and the massive scale of desertion from the Republican armies. In 1797, a Government Commission urged greater severity to counteract "the multiplicity, the audacity and the cruelty" of acts of brigandage: two years later yet another Commission begged the Government to find some answer to deal with "le torrent des assassinats."

It was in Southern France, where religious differences were superimposed on economic and political antagonisms and where the pattern of violence assumed a unique and extreme form, that brigandage was most widespread after 1795. Gangs of Catholic Royalists, like the *Compagnies du soleil* around Lyons, or, more simply, *les fanatiques* around Nîmes, accounted for hundreds of victims chosen principally on political grounds, although the distinction between political and personal crimes was always confused. A report of 1799 stated that many acts of violence in the countryside had been committed against "public officials, owners of National Lands and all those citizens attached to the Constitution of 1795." Other bands of brigands directed their activities against the wealthier farmers whose rapacity and selfishness during the crisis of 1795 was well-documented in the popular mind. Some municipalities employed shepherds or *gardes champêtres* to protect crops and property but, badly paid and recruited from the most deprived sections of the community, they were frequently responsible for the very crimes they were supposed to prevent.

Smuggling, another traditional pursuit, reached even more professional heights during the Napoleonic period as a result of the embargo on foreign imports: just as, under the *ancien régime,* entire villages had derived their livelihood from smuggling salt from one province to another, so, under Napoleon, thousands of fishermen, peasants, and rural artisans involved themselves in the contraband trade. Smugglers, poachers, brigands, the underworld of rural societies, often protected by the respectable who were not above profiting from their crimes, formed an essential part of life in the countryside.

To deal with these groups, and the deserters whose numbers increased substantially after 1812, Napoleon would have needed the Grande Armée itself. For peasants living in lonely and remote farmhouses, fear of "les brigands" was real and understandable. The threat of arson was always used, as it had been since time immemorial, to give greater force to their demands. Arson was a traditional form of protest in the countryside: it was not uncommon to hear some villager remark that one of his enemies "deserved to be grilled like a pig over a fire." Nor was it unknown for a small-holder, forced off his farm as a result of his debts, to set fire to his barn or even his cottage in order to prevent the property passing into the hands of a rival. The *chauffeurs* derived their name from the practice of "warming" the soles of victims' feet in order to obtain information of hidden sources of wealth.

The Revolution had emancipated the peasantry from the social, economic, and juridical restrictions of a decaying feudal system. It had provided, principally for the most affluent, an opportunity of acquiring property as a result of the sale of Church and émigré lands; it had also meant the assignat, the Maximum, dechristianization and, particularly between 1795 and 1799, a situation bordering upon anarchy in many provinces. Social antagonism within the peasant community itself had been increased and little or nothing had been done for the share-cropper and the landless laborer.

The Napoleonic régime did ensure that the Church and the aristocracy would never again exert, at least from an economic and legal standpoint, the same authority over the peasants. It had also restored the Catholic and Protestant cults, and mitigated the worst effects of famine by virtue of a more efficient administrative system and better cultivation. However, the Empire had created an army of petty officials—the *commissaire de police*, the customs officer, the tax assessor and, perhaps most important of all, the recruiting-sergeant. Many peasants must have wondered if freedom from feudalism had been bought at too high a price.

JEROME BLUM

Reformers, Rebels, and Abolitionists In Russia

. . . A paradoxical situation—paradoxical at least to our Western liberal ways of thinking—had developed in Russia in the era from Peter I to Alexander II. On the one hand, commerce made important advances, the factory form of production became increasingly common, and an industrial proletariat was called into being. On the other hand, during these same years the social structure of the empire retrogressed. The nobility emerged as a self-conscious class and established itself as the dominant group in society, while the mass of the people were either reduced to an unfree status, or if already in a servile condition had their positions worsened.

This mixture of modernity and medievalism seemed to provide a workable social organization. The empire expanded enormously in area and population; it became one of the major powers of the world; and it successfully withstood challenges from within and without. But as time went on, some people detected serious faults in the system that made them doubt its continued ability to survive. Above all else, they were concerned about serfdom, the central feature of the entire social order. Sooner or later, all of these people came to the conclusion that unless serfdom was reformed or abolished Russia faced certain disaster.

Selections from Jerome Blum, *Lord and Peasant in Russia From the Ninth to the Nineteenth Century* (Copyright © 1961 by Princeton University Press; Princeton Paperback, 1971), pp. 422–560. Reprinted by permission of Princeton University Press.

These critics of the existing order can be divided into three separate groups; the tsars and members of the topmost levels of the bureaucracy, the peasantry, and the intellectuals. . . .

The peasants were the second of the three groups arrayed against serfdom. Their record of opposition, of course, was far older than that of the tsars and the bureaucracy and the intellectuals. They had always been against it. But their servile status, their dispersion, and their lack of leadership, had prevented them from mounting an effective campaign to destroy it. The only way they could manifest their discontent was by flight and by sporadic outbursts of disobedience and violence. Into the nineteenth century these tactics had given the government much trouble, but had not succeeded in persuading the rulers of the empire that reform was necessary. Then, in the reigns of Nicholas and Alexander II rural unrest reached proportions that thoroughly frightened the tsars and their counselors, and convinced them that changes designed to still peasant discontent had to be made.

The peasants themselves never presented a work-out program of reform. Their protests were essentially negative. They fled from or revolted against specific injustices, such as increases in the obligations demanded by their seigniors, cruel treatment, the sale of their fellows for recruit substitutes, seizures by their masters of their personal property, or reductions in the size of their holdings. Nor was their discontent directed against the tsar and the autocracy. On the contrary, they cherished the sovereign and thought him their protector. Their enemies were the seigniors who, they believed, gave the tsar evil counsels, kept a knowledge of the true state of affairs from him, and circumvented the orders he gave to raise the peasantry from their lowly condition.

Flight continued to be the most common form of protest. Just between 1719 and 1727 the far from complete official sources showed around 200,000 fugitives.[1] Not only individuals or families but entire villages took off. Some of the runaways did not go very far, while others travelled great distances to start new lives in the Urals, Siberia, along the lower reaches of the Volga, or in New Russia. Many in the western provinces crossed the border into Poland, then still independent. According to complaints voiced by nobles at the Legislative Commission in 1767, 50,000 serfs of both sexes had fled to Poland from Smolensk guberniia alone. The serfowners of these western provinces rejoiced when the partitions of Poland moved the frontiers much farther to the west.[2]

Flight did not always bring freedom. Often the fugitives settled on the land of some other seignior and so gained nothing, except that per-

[1] Pavlenko, "O nekotorykh storonakh," p. 398.
[2] Semevskii, *Krest'iane,* I, 337–340.

haps the new master demanded less from them. Sometimes they found themselves serfs of their old master from whom they had fled, as did runaways from the Spaso-Evfimev Monastery who settled on empty land in Penza and Simbirsk. The monastery discovered their whereabouts, and instead of bringing back the fugitives preempted the land on which they had settled. Others who went to the Urals and took employment in the industries there, found themselves assigned to the plant in which they worked. Those who got as far as Siberia, however, became state peasants and never reverted to serfdom. Local officials there were supposed to return the runaways to their owners, but the need for colonists outweighed the property rights of the serf-owners. In fact, the authorities in Siberia did everything they could to help the fugitives get settled, and even went so far as to hide them when they were in danger of being apprehended and returned to their old homes.[3] Similarly, officials in New Russia, eager to populate that newly won region, protected runaways from the efforts of their masters to recover them. By far the majority of the fugitives followed agricultural pursuits in their new homes, but some took employment in industry and transportation, others became professional vagabonds, and some turned to brigandage.[4]

Nothing the government or the serfowners did seemed able to check the stream of runaways. Scores of decrees, and harsh punishment of captured fugitives and those who sheltered them, had no effect. There were more laws about runaways and their recovery than any other subject— a fact that in itself bears witness to the proportions of peasant flight. Periodically, hunts were organized to track down all the fugitives in a district or town, and return them to their owners.[5]

Peasants did not always leave their old homes at their own volition. Large proprietors continued on into the eighteenth century to abduct serfs from the lands of less powerful seigniors. Peter I tried to end this practice by imposing heavy fines on the abductors, but his efforts proved unsuccessful.[6]

Flight was a passive mode of protest. Occasionally the peasants' discontent took the more direct form of revolt against their masters. Usually these were restricted to a single property or village, and could be handled by local authorities. But every once in a while whole districts took fire as if by some spontaneous combustion, and then the central government had to use its power to crush the rising. In 1707 a revolt against the government of Peter I broke out among some of the cossacks

---

[3] Pavlenko, "O nekotorykh storonakh," pp. 398–399; Treadgold, *The Great Siberian Migration*, p. 25.

[4] Sacke, "Adel und Bürgertum," pp. 843–844; Pavlenko, "O nekotorykh storonakh," pp. 399–400; Nolde, *La Formation*, I, 96.

[5] Pavlenko, "O nekotorykh storonakh," p. 398.

[6] Kliuchevskii, *History*, iv, 333–334.

of the Don under the leadership of Kondratii Bulavin, their hetman or chieftain. In proclamations reminiscent of that earlier Don Cossack rebel, Stenka Razin, Bulavin promised freedom and a better life to all the oppressed. Word of his promises spread to the serfs of neighboring regions of the black earth, and violence directed against seigniors broke out in a number of places. The movement subsided in 1708 when regulars defeated Bulavin's forces and followed up their victory with a cruel repression. During Elizabeth's reign troops had to be used against the peasants on a number of occasions. Unrest seemed endemic on church properties, and in the factories of the Urals. Then Peter III's manifesto of 18 February 1762 that freed the nobles of their service obligation started rumors among the peasants of impending emancipation. They connected the requirement of the dvorianstvo to serve the state with their own enserfment, and reasoned that if the former was abolished then serfdom, too, must end. When their hopes were not realized some of them turned to violence. Official accounts recorded around forty outbreaks between 1762 and 1772 in the great Russian provinces, and it is certain there were many more. Between 1764 and 1769 in Moscow guberniia alone thirty proprietors—nine of them women—were slain by their peasants, and five others had attempts made on their lives.[7]

These risings gained the serfs nothing beyond the momentary exhilaration their acts of violence must have brought them. The seigniors continued to oppress them and the government did nothing on their behalf. The peasants seemed to realize the hopelessness of their position, and the first few years of the seventies were apparently free of open revolt. But the calm proved deceptive. Only a spark was needed to set off a new jacquerie. In 1773 it was provided by Emelian Pugachev, and for a few unbelievable months it seemed possible that rebelling peasants might overthrow the established order.[8]

Pugachev, who was born in 1726, was a Don Cossack. In 1773, after many fantastic adventures, he appeared among the cossacks of the River Iaik as a fugitive from justice. He found these frontiersmen, who roamed the southeast corner of the empire, and their neighbors, who included many Old Believers, full of grievances against the government's efforts to impose new restrictions on them. Pugachev saw a ready-made opportunity to make himself the leader of a mass movement. So he adopted a ruse that was not new to Russian history. He declared himself to be the tsar, namely, Peter III, husband of Catherine and rightful sovereign of Russia. The circumstances of Peter's deposition and murder in 1762 were unknown to the people. Rumors had spread among them that he had been

---

[7] Semevskii, *Krest'iane*, I, 347, 356–357.

[8] There is a large literature on this rising. The best work in a Western tongue that I have come across is Portal, "Pugačev: une révolution manquée."

driven from the throne because he had wanted to help the peasants, and that he had miraculously escaped death and was in hiding, waiting the time when he could win back what was rightfully his and carry through the reforms he had originally planned. Several adventurers found it easy to convince ignorant peasants that they were indeed the tsar, but none of the other false Peters enjoyed Pugachev's success, nor, apparently, possessed his qualities of leadership.

The Iaik cossacks took him at his word and put themselves under his command. On 17 September 1773 he issued the first of the proclamations that made his rebellion a genuine social revolution. He promised his followers freedom and the ownership of all the land. The news that "Peter III" had declared a war for liberty spread quickly to the Bashkirs, the nomadic indigenes of the borderland, who had long harbored a hatred of Moscow's domination, and to the harshly exploited workers in the factories of the Urals. These people joined Pugachev. In an incredibly short time nearly all the Eurasian frontier was in revolt.

In October 1773 the central government realized it had a full-scale war on its hands, and launched a major campaign against the rebels. Pugachev suffered reverses and retreated northward. Here he began a new stage in his rising. For the first time he raised his standard in a farming area where the peasants were serfs of private landlords. He arrived outside Kazan and took the city. The road to Moscow lay before him. But once again government forces defeated him and he ordered a withdrawal to the south. On 31 July 1774 he addressed a manifesto to the serfs of the region through which he was passing, emancipating them from their bondage and from all obligations to lord and state, and giving them possession of "the fields, forests, meadows, fisheries, and saltpans without cost and without obrok." He commanded them to seize, punish, and hang the nobles whom he called "the foes of Our rule and the disturbers of the empire and the despoilers of the peasants," and proclaimed that "after the extermination of these enemies, these criminal nobles, everyone will be able to enjoy tranquility and a peaceful life that will endure till the end of time." [9] The serfs responded with wild enthusiasm to this trumpet call. Just at the rumor of his approach thousands of them left their villages to join his columns, and to plunder, burn, and kill.

But Pugachev's odyssey was nearing its end. His rag, tag, and bobtail army of peasants could not stand up against regulars. On 24 August 1774 in a battle not far from Tsaritsyn, where a century before Stenka Razin had first proclaimed his revolt, the army of Pugachev melted away. Pugachev himself fled into the steppe, was betrayed by his entourage, and executed in Moscow on 10 January 1775.

[9] *Russkaia Starina*, XIII (1875), 441.

Official casualty lists revealed that 796 men, 474 women, and 304 children of the dvorianstvo were murdered by the rebels.[10] No records were kept of peasants who were executed in the terrible retribution visited upon the rebellious districts. The gallows put up in the villages did not come down until January 1775, and not until the end of that year was a general amnesty declared. Nor did the rising suggest to the rulers of the empire the need to improve the condition of the peasantry. In fact, in the remaining years of Catherine's reign the government followed an exactly opposite policy.

Catherine tried to stamp out every memory of the *Pugachevshchina*— as the revolt is known in Russian history. She forbad it to be mentioned publicly, and ordered that henceforth the Iaik River and the town of Iaisk should bear the names of the Ural River and Uralsk. Her efforts, of course, were in vain. The government and the nobility never forgot the threat Pugachev had presented to them, and resolved that such a crisis must never rise again. The people remembered him, too, as their only defender against oppression.

After the *Pugachevshchina* official records tell of only twenty risings between 1774 and Catherine's death in 1796, though studies based on local archives and estate records indicate the number was much larger.[11] At Paul's accession a new rash of outbreaks swept across the land. In three years of his reign there were a reported 278 disturbances in 32 different provinces.

In the quarter century of Alexander's rule official sources show a total of 281 risings. During the three decades of Nicholas's reign the frequency of disturbances steadily increased. According to data of the Ministry of Interior there were 556 risings between 1826 and 1854, but this figure included only the most serious outbreaks. A later survey that included data from other official sources showed 712 disturbances in those years and reveals, too, the unbroken upward trend in the number of risings as the years went by. Between 1826 and 1834 there were 148 outbreaks, between 1835 and 1844, 216, and between 1845 and 1854, 348. Then, from 1855, when Alexander II became tsar to 5 March 1861, the day on which the emancipation decree was published, there were another 474 disturbances. Between 1801 and 1861, then, there were a total of 1,467 peasant risings.[12]

Many of these outbreaks were purely local affairs that were put down by whippings, arrest of ringleaders, and sometimes by soothing words and promises. But some of them took on the character of mass revolts. Out of 261 risings between 1836 and 1854 for which the details of

---

[10] Semevskii, *Krest'iane*, I, 381.
[11] Rubinshtein, "K kharakteristike votchinnogo rezhima," pp. 140–141.
[12] Liashchenko, *History*, pp. 280, 370; Ignatovich, "Krest'ianskie volneniia," p. 48.

pacification are known, troops were used to quell 132. Sometimes tens, and even hundreds, of thousands of peasants were involved and whole districts affected. Frequently the disturbances were only concerted refusals to obey seignorial commands or render certain obligations—in short, strikes or collective disobedience. On occasion the serfs beat their lords and estate officials, and burned, looted, and murdered. Between 1835 and 1854 Ministry of Interior reports show that rioting peasants killed 144 seigniors (among them the father of the novelist Dostoevskii) and 29 stewards, and made unsuccessful attempts on the lives of 75 other lords and stewards.[13]

Official studies of the causes of disturbances of 423 properties indicated that rumors of emancipation were as important as the harsh treatment and inordinate demands of seigniors in inciting peasant disturbances. This bore out Tsar Nicholas's conviction that all discussions of reforms should be secret, lest the peasant become impatient and resort to violence. The belief that the tsar had abolished serfdom was found to have been the cause of outbreaks on 210 of the 423 estates. The peasants, understandably excited by the false news, rose when their owners refused to free them. On 95 properties excessive barshchina was responsible for the disturbances, on 26 burdensome obrok, on 9 it was the exacting of arrears, on 30 famine was responsible, on 17 the resettlement of peasants, and on 13 reduction in the size of holdings started troubles.[14]

Peasant unrest was not confined to serfs alone. Nonseignorial peasants, too, expressed their discontent by open clashes with the authorities. State and appanage peasants protested against demands made of them, and against corrupt and oppressive local officials; the military colonists rebelled against the regimentation of their lives; and peasants assigned to industrial enterprises rose against their compulsory employment and the conditions under which they had to work.[15]

The increase in the number of peasant risings in the first half of the nineteenth century did not mean that peasants no longer ran away. Fugitives left their old homes in a never ending stream that sometimes swelled to huge proportions, especially in the second quarter of the century. A rumor of freedom and land to be had for the asking in some frontier would sweep through a district and suddenly scores and hundreds of peasants would take off. So many runaways arrived in Astrakhan, New Russia, and Bessarabia that the government, interested in colonizing these regions, ordered that if the fugitives had lived in these places for a certain time they did not have to be returned to their owners if apprehended. The owners were to be compensated with a recruit quittance,

[13] Semevskii, *Krest'ianskii vopros,* II, 583–584, 596; Linkov, *Ocherki,* p. 271.
[14] Liashchenko, *History,* p. 372; cf. Semevskii, *Krest'ianskii vopros,* II, 596.
[15] Linkov, *Ocherki,* pp. 42–72; Tugan-Baranovskii, *Russkaia fabrika,* I, ch. IV.

or by a payment from the person on whose land the runaway had settled. Nor, apparently, were some officials in these colonial areas above issuing false papers to fugitives to protect them from being captured and returned to their old homes.[16]

Peasants also expressed their discontent with their masters by complaints to the government. The law specifically forbad this, and provided for heavy punishments of those who dared to go over the head of their owners. Yet some serfs were willing to take the chance, and a small but steady stream of petitions for protection and relief came to the throne and to the Ministry of Interior. In 1840, for example, the Ministry received three complaints, in 1842 it received seven and the tsar eight. The Ministry also reported in 1842 that local authorities received a large number of complaints from peasants about seignioral excesses, but "strict investigation" showed these charges to be unfounded. In 1844 the Ministry received 51 complaints, in 1845, 44 and the emperor 3, and so on.[17] Finally, some peasants found the only way of escape from the intolerable condition of their lives was through suicide. These were officially reported as "sudden deaths." After the emancipation a notable decline was reported in the suicide rate.[18]

The increase in rural unrest in the nineteenth century, and especially after 1825, was fearfully watched by the tsars. As earlier pages of this chapter have shown, Nicholas was certain that unless reforms were inaugurated social revolution was inevitable, even though he himself was incapable of introducing them. His successor, Alexander II, equally convinced of the dangers that peasant discontent portended, and possessed of the resolution to command emancipation, justified his act by warning that if serfdom was not abolished by legal methods the peasants would take matters into their own hands. . . .

---

[16] Engelmann, *Die Leibeigenschaft,* p. 206; cf. Kohl, *Reisen in Südrussland,* II, 24–25.

[17] Semevskii, *Krest'ianskii vopros,* II, 571–573.

[18] Masaryk, *Spirit,* I, 131 and note.

2. THE FORMATION OF A LABOR FORCE

Although the majority of Europeans remained rural well into the nineteenth century, the city always played a role disproportionate to the number of its inhabitants. This was no less true in antiquity and in medieval times than during more recent eras. Might European civilization therefore be fairly judged according to the ebb and flow of its town-life? This is an intriguing question, as the growing interest in urban history testifies. In any event, the century of early industrialization was a troubled and trying time for the populace huddled in the cities. Between 1750 and 1850 the density of the urban masses noticeably increased and the predictable consequences were material deterioration and social tension.

George *Rudé* posits that, before the mid-eighteenth century, the most frequent form of social disturbance was the bread riot. As the term suggests, this was ordinarily a short-term local protest over the scarcity or rising cost of foodstuffs. Given the lack of an adequate transportation network, these conditions were bound to recur from time to time even when harvests were relatively bountiful. Such riots remained very much a part of both the urban and rural scene, as the history of the French Revolution ("let them eat cake") illustrates. But the city of the late eighteenth century also became the forum of social disorders of which the causes were far more varied. Rudé examines the methods and motives in several of these insurrections and shows that they were something more than the indiscriminate violence of a scruffy and faceless mob.

E. J. Hobsbawm starkly poses the alternatives of the urban poor: to imitate the wealthy as best they could, to resign themselves to a degraded and demoralized existence in the slums, or to rebel. Hobsbawm gives a grim view of the impact of early industrialization in terms of urban crowding, disease, crime, alcoholism, prostitution, and pauperism. Consequently, like Rudé, he finds the rationale of rebellion both sensible and self-evident. Nothing was more inevitable, he contends, than the socialist attempts to create a labor movement as a vehicle of organized protest.

P. H. Noyes concentrates on Germany at the eve of the 1848 revolution. With political unity still lacking and industry relatively retarded, the urban proletariat was just beginning to acquire the size and shape of a coherent organization. The statistics which Noyes presents require a nuanced appraisal of the "working class," a term widely used but still in search of an unambiguous definition. In this regard it is of particular importance to note the conflict of interests between artisans, who generally resisted the advance of industry, and the new factory proletariat, whose existence depended on it. Noyes concludes that those who held factory jobs were ordinarily more secure than other laborers and thus were less inclined to revolt than artisanal and marginal workers who often lacked the employment which nascent industry could not yet provide.

If there is one impression of mid-nineteenth century Europe that we are likely to retain from these analyses, it is that of growing confusion. Yet the urban picture is not without certain apparent contours, and we can discern at least three recurrent themes: the social dislocation of the lower classes, the obvious gap between rich and poor, and the tendency toward formal association of the working population. The full consequences could not be clearly foreseen but it is easy to understand the great expectations of those who anticipated a wave of social revolution.

GEORGE RUDÉ

The City Riot
of the Eighteenth Century

If the rural riot was marked by its sensitivity to the rising price of food, the city riot was distinguished by its greater variety. Clearly urban dwellers, among whom wage earners formed so large a part, were as concerned as their fellows in the village or market town with the supply of cheap and plentiful bread. Potentially, therefore, food rioting was as constant a threat to public order in large cities as it was in the countryside; and, in many of Europe's capitals, the "lower orders" or *menu peuple* were as liable to riot in protest against famine prices at times of shortage as for any other cause.[1] But authority, which might be sanguine about periodic outbursts of popular anger in country districts, was less inclined to be so in capital cities and, in consequence, tended to limit such outbreaks by devising special measures to keep the larder stocked. In London, civic authorities and magistrates ensured that markets were well supplied, kept a close watch on the prices of wheat and bread, and reduced their fluctuations in all but the leanest years. In Paris, elaborate steps were taken to supply wheat to suburban millers and flour to the city's bakers: in fact, the preferential treatment given to Parisians was a constant source of irritation to their neighbors and provoked frequent riots among angry villagers along the capital's supply routes.[2] In addition, the policing of large cities, though grossly inadequate by nineteenth-century standards, was taken far more seriously than that of country towns. This was particularly true of Paris; so much so that a chronicler of the early 1780's

George Rudé, *The Crowd in History 1730–1848* (New York: John Wiley and Sons, 1964), pp. 47–64. Reprinted by permission of John Wiley and Sons, Inc.

[1] See E. J. Hobsbawm, *Primitive Rebels* (Manchester, 1959), "The City Mob," pp. 10–16.

[2] See L. Cahen, "La question du pain à Paris à la fin du XVIIIᵉ siècle," *Cahiers de la Révolution française*, no. 1 (1934), 51–76; and R. C. Cobb, *Les armées révolutionnaires* (2 vols. Paris and The Hague, 1961–3), II, 370–81.

wrote that, while London might be wracked by serious civil commotion, in Paris this was almost impossible to contemplate.[3]

One way or another, such measures appear to have kept food rioting in abeyance. In London, at any rate, they were remarkably successful. London was certainly not without its riots, and in them, as we shall see, concern for the price of food often played its part even when other issues were more obviously involved. But the undiluted food riot plays virtually no part whatsoever in the record of the city's popular outbreaks. There were, no doubt, minor exceptions: for example, during the Wilkite riots in 1768, a crowd besieging the House of Lords included some who cried "that bread and beer were too dear and that it was as well to be hanged as starved." [4] Yet this was in a year of strikes and general disturbance in which political factors played as large a part as concern for the price of bread.

England was, in fact, in this respect as in so many others, in a quite peculiar position. She had virtually ceased to be a peasant country, and London was, at its most vulnerable point, cut off from the countryside by the protective shield of the near-urban county of Middlesex. Paris, on the other hand, was ringed round by and exposed to the frequent invasion of peasant communities that came to sell or to buy their stocks of vegetables, fruit, grain, flour, and bread in the city's markets. So, in Paris, despite the special measures taken to supply and to police the capital, the food riot might be imported from the neighboring countryside: we have noted the case of May 1775. This, of course, could only happen in years of bad harvest, drought, hail, or frost, or when "monopolists" cornered, or were believed to have cornered, the market. But on such occasions the whole elaborate system would temporarily break down, and panic buying in the market would lead to steep rises in the price of wheat and bread and to outbursts of anger and violence by the Parisian *menu peuple*. This happened in August 1725, when the price of bread rose even higher than in the famine year 1709 and riots became so menacing that the minister responsible was compelled to resign his post. In September 1740, the price of the 4-pound loaf rose to 20 sous (equal to the daily wage of an unskilled laborer); Louis XV was assailed with cries of "Bread! Bread!"; Cardinal Fleury, his Chief Minister, was mobbed by crowds of women; and fifty prisoners at Bicêtre were shot dead after protesting against a cut in their bread ration. In December 1752, bread riots were coupled with protests against the Archbishop of Paris; and in 1775, as we have seen, Paris had its last taste of a major popular dis-

[3] L. S. Mercier, *Tableau de Paris* (12 vols. Amsterdam, 1783), VI, 22–5.
[4] See my *Wilkes and Liberty: A Social Study of 1763 to 1774* (Oxford, 1962), p. 53.

turbance due to a shortage of food before the outbreak of the Revolution.[5]

Impressive as these demonstrations were, however, even in Paris the food riot was not the predominant type of popular disturbance. There were other forms of protest in which the poorer classes, though by no means challenging the existing order, laid claim to better living standards or to a fuller measure of social justice. In July 1720, the crisis provoked by the Scotsman John Law's financial operations touched off massive riots in the business quarter: fifteen thousand people gathered in the Rue Vivienne, sixteen were trampled to death, Law's coachman was lynched, and the Palais Royal, home of the Regent, was threatened with destruction. In 1721, a succession of disturbances was caused by the severity of the punishments inflicted on domestic servants: on one occasion, a crowd of five thousand formed to protest at the whipping, branding, and exhibition in the stocks of a coachman; five were killed and several were wounded. In 1743 in Paris and nine years later at Vincennes, riots broke out in protest at the manner of balloting for the militia. In 1750, a panic followed the arrest of a large number of children, rounded up by the *archers* (armed police) on charges of vagrancy. It was widely believed (and with some justification, as this had in fact happened thirty years before) that the children of the poor were being shipped to the colonies. In the course of a week's rioting four to eight *archers* were killed; and, after sentence by the *parlement* of Paris, three men were executed in the Place de Grève amid scenes of violent disorder. There was even talk— such were the feelings aroused—of marching to Versailles to burn down the royal château.[6]

On this last occasion, the Marquis d'Argenson, who had witnessed the disturbances, deplored the fact that the *parlement,* which had ordered the executions, must now have lost all credit with the common people.[7] His fears proved to have little substance. It was, in fact, the *parlement* which, more than any other body, first drew the Parisian *menu peuple* into political agitation and taught them political lessons that they later, in 1789, turned against their teachers. Quite apart from its judicial functions, the Paris *parlement* claimed, by ancient usage, to be the guardian of the nation's "liberties" and under weak or indolent monarchs refused to register royal edicts until its "remonstrances" were satisfied. It became the firm champion of the Gallican Church against the Jesuits and Ultra-

[5] See my *The Crowd in the French Revolution* (Oxford, 1959), pp. 22–4.

[6] For Parisian disturbances of the eighteenth century, see *Journal et mémoires du Marquis d'Argenson,* vols. I-IX; E. J. F. Barbier, *Journal historique et anecdotique du règne de Louis XV,* vols. I-IV; D. Mornet, *Les origines intellectuelles de la Révolution française* (Paris, 1933), pp. 439, 444–8, 498–9; M. Rouff, "Les mouvements populaires," in *La vie parisienne au XVIIIe siècle* (Paris, 1914), pp. 263–92.

[7] D'Argenson, *op. cit.,* VI, 241.

montanes; it resolutely opposed the operation of the Bull *Unigenitus* against Jansenist heresy within the Church; and, in the name of "liberty" (a term often synonymous with "privilege"), it resisted the government's attempts to reform the finances by encroaching on the fiscal immunities of aristocracy and clergy. But the magistrates, though largely concerned to safeguard their own particular interests, were past masters at playing on popular passions in their war on Ultramontane claims or ministerial "despotism." Already in 1727, the *parlement* headed a common front, composed of the parish clergy, the Parisian *bourgeoisie,* the lawyers, and the common people of the streets, against the Jesuits. The next popular explosion of this kind came in 1752, when the Archbishop of Paris was condemned by the *parlement* and mobbed in the streets of the city for ordering the refusal of the sacrament to dying nuns and clergy who were not prepared to make formal renunciation of their Jansenist beliefs. Soon after, the political battle of the *parlement* against the royal government, largely dormant since the 1720s, began again in earnest. Having studied the "philosophers" (first Montesquieu and later Rousseau), the magistrates translated their political speculations, hitherto reserved for the more fashionable society of the *salons,* into a language intelligible to the streets and markets, and, in the course of a protracted pamphlet war, indoctrinated Parisians in the use of such catchwords as "citizens," "nation," "social contract," and the "general will." The *parlement's* remonstrances of 1753, 1763, 1771, and 1776 evoked a considerable response among the people. These years were studded with minor disturbances in support of the *parlement's* claims; they reached a climax on the very eve of the Revolution when, in 1787 and 1788, great demonstrations of city craftsmen and journeymen from the faubourgs rioted in sympathy with the exiled *parlement* and acclaimed its return to the capital.[6, 8]

In London, too, the typical eighteenth-century riot was either a form of social protest or a political demonstration; but more often it was compounded of the two. Apart from industrial disputes, the undiluted social protest without political undertones was comparatively rare: probably rarer than in Paris, at least before the 1750s. There were, however, such occasions: in July 1736, the dismissal of English workmen and the employment of cheaper Irish labor touched off violent rioting against the Irish in Shoreditch, Spitalfields, and Whitechapel; and in August 1794, "a mixed multitude of men, women, boys and children" (to quote one of the Lord Mayor's dispatches) defied the militia and Guards for three days and attacked and destroyed "crimping houses," or houses used for recruiting to the army, in Holborn, the City, Clerkenwell, and Shoreditch. On both occasions, there were sinister rumors of enemy agents at work—

[8] For the Parisian riots of 1787 and 1788, see my *The Crowd in the French Revolution,* pp. 29–33.

in the first case Jacobites, in the second Jacobins—but in neither case do the motives for rioting appear to have been any other than those that were proclaimed.

More often, however, London riots were attached to a political cause. Even if there was no such thing as a "Tory mob" (a term used by some historians), it seems evident that Tory influences were at work behind the riots of 1715 and 1716, when London crowds paraded the streets of the city, Holborn, and Whitechapel to shouts of "High Church and Ormonde," smashed the windows of government supporters, and attacked a Presbyterian Meeting House in Highgate. Yet it was not the dwindling band of Tory politicians, but the Common Council of the City of London, that most often gave the lead. The city, which prided itself on its political independence, opposed the policies of Westminster and St. James's almost continuously throughout the century, and more particularly between 1730 and 1780; and, like the *parlement* in Paris, it became the real political educator of London's "lower orders." It was the city that, in 1733, led the campaign against Sir Robert Walpole's Excise Bill and forced him to withdraw it, after London crowds had besieged Parliament and mobbed the minister to cries of "No slavery—no excise—no wooden shoes!" Three years later, a similar fate befell Walpole's Gin Act, which, though passed by Parliament, became impossible to operate. This time, riots were only threatened—in the form of mock funerals to celebrate "Madam Geneva's lying-in-state"—and actually came to nothing. The same thing happened in 1753, when a combination of City interests, country Tories, and opposition Whigs compelled the Pelham Ministry, by means of a nationwide agitation and the threat of London riots, to defeat its own Bill for the easier naturalization of alien Jews.[9]

Up to now, the City Corporation had been allied, in order to wage its political battles, with a group of opposition Tory leaders: to that extent, at least, each one of these movements, if not wholly Tory, may be said to have had Tory undertones. This was no longer the case after 1756 when, in clamoring for war with France (and later Spain), the Common Council adopted William Pitt as its champion, helped him into office, and after his dismissal in 1761 conferred on him the City's Freedom, while London's "lower orders" hailed Pitt and booed and pelted the King's favorite, the Earl of Bute. The same year, Pitt's principal lieutenant in the City, William Beckford, in standing for election to Parliament, denounced "rotten boroughs" and thereby fired the opening shot in the

---

[9] For the first of these two episodes, see my article " 'Mother Gin' and the London Riots of 1736," *The Guildhall Miscellany*, no. 10 (September 1959); and, for the second, see Thomas W. Perry, *Public Opinion, Propaganda and Politics in Eighteenth-Century England: A Study of the Jew Bill of 1753* (Cambridge, Mass., 1962).

City's campaign for electoral reform. Thus City radicalism, which challenged the principles of both parliamentary parties, came to birth.[10] From
the City's radicalism there stemmed, in turn, the wider movement that
rallied to the cause of John Wilkes; and "Wilkes and Liberty" became for
a dozen years the political slogan uniting the diverse activities of City
merchants, Middlesex freeholders, and the small shopkeepers, craftsmen,
and workmen in the London streets and boroughs. After the Wilkite riots
came the last and the most violent of London's great upheavals, the
Gordon Riots of 1780, when "No Popery" crowds held the streets of the
metropolis for a week and caused widespread destruction to both private
and public property. This last outbreak was not strictly speaking "political"; but in this case too the rioters drew their initial inspiration, though
not their mode of behavior, from a solid body of respectable City opinion.[11]

Let us now follow the same procedure as before and look more closely
at a number of these London episodes—the anti-Irish outbreak of 1736,
the Wilkite riots of 1768, and the Gordon Riots of 1780. At first sight,
they may appear to have little in common. The disturbance of 1736 began
as a dispute over the employment of Irish labor in the parishes of Shoreditch and Spitalfields, spreading later into Whitechapel.[12] In Shoreditch, a
certain William Goswell, who was in charge of the rebuilding of St.
Leonard's Church, had dismissed a number of his English workmen, who
were asking for higher pay, and employed in their place Irish labor at
one-half or two-thirds of their wages. A further grievance was that master
weavers in both Shoreditch and the adjoining parish of Spitalfields were
also employing large numbers of Irish. From this double irritation sprang
a two-day riot in the two parishes. It was graphically described by Sir
Robert Walpole in a letter to his brother Horace:

> On Monday night last (26 July), there was an appearance of numbers
> being assembled in a very disorderly manner at Shoreditch, near Spital-
> fields. Their cry and complaint was of being underworked, and starved
> by the Irish: *Down with the Irish, etc.* But that night the numbers were
> not very great, and they dispersed themselves without doing any mis-
> chief. . . . On Tuesday evening they assembled again in bodies, and
> were about 7 o'clock thought to be 2,000 in number. They now grew
> more riotous; they attacked a public house kept by an Irishman, where the
> Irish resorted and victualled, broke down all the doors and windows and
> quite gutted the house. Another house of the same sort underwent the
> same fate. By this time (those places being within the jurisdiction of the
> City), the Mayor and Deputy Lieutenant of the Tower Hamlets were as-

[10] Lucy S. Sutherland, *The City of London and the Opposition to Government,
1768–1774* (London, 1959).

[11] For a summary of these riots and further sources, see my *Wilkes and Liberty,*
pp. 13–14. For the riots of 1736, 1763–74, and 1780, see references 9, 17, 19.

[12] See my article, " 'Mother Gin'."

sembled in order to disperse them. The proclamation was read; but the mob, wholly regardless of the proclamation, increased every minute, and were thought to be about 4,000 strong. . . . Upon the appearance of the Guards the mob retired, shifted from one street and alley to another, and gave no resistance, and by break of day were all dispersed. All Wednesday things seemed very quiet till evening, when the mob rose again to as great a number; but the Militia of the Tower Hamlets being then raised, marched against them; but the mob in the same manner retired before them wherever they came, and gave not the least resistance . . . and so dispersed themselves before the morning.[13]

Walpole believed that this was "the end to this bustle," but he was over-sanguine. These earlier rioters now joined with others who, on the evening of July 30, attacked Irish dwellings and ale-houses in Goodman's Fields and Rosemary Lane in Whitechapel. By later standards, the damage done was comparatively slight: half-a-dozen victims, including Austin Allen of the *Gentleman and Porter* in Leman Street, had their houses "broke"; John Walden, publican of the *Bull and Butcher* in Cable Street, had his shutters and windows smashed; while Ann Pool was robbed of a leg of lamb and two knuckles of legs of mutton. The riots had repercussions in other districts, as we learn from a note in the *Gentleman's Magazine* of August 1 that

> Mobs arose in Southwark, Lambeth and Tyburn-road, and took upon 'em to interrogate people whether they were for the English or Irish? but committed no Violence; several Parties of Horse Grenadiers dispers'd the Mobs which were gathering in Ratcliff-highway, to demolish the Houses of the Irish.[14]

But this was virtually the end of the affair. By August 20, nine prisoners had been secured, of whom five were later brought to trial at the Old Bailey; and Sir Robert Walpole wrote to Horace that "the tumults and disorders here are quite at an end—the industry of the Jacobites was not able to improve this truly Irish incident into a more general confusion." [15]

The Wilkite riots of the 1760s and '70s, of which those of 1768 were the most substantial, were of a very different kind. They were not only political, as those of 1736 were not, but spread over a number of years and inspired by a single unifying slogan. This they owed in part to the extraordinary career and personality of John Wilkes himself, and in part to the political passions aroused in the early years of George III. It all started when Wilkes, having been committed to the Tower of London for

---

[13] Archdeacon William Coxe, *Memoirs of the Life and Administration of Sir Robert Walpole* (3 vols. London, 1798), III, 348–9.

[14] *Gentleman's Magazine*, VI (1736), 484.

[15] Coxe, *op. cit.*, III, 357.

libeling the King, was released by order of Chief Justice Pratt at Westminster Hall in May 1763; his discharge was greeted with a shout of "Wilkes and Liberty!," which for a dozen years became the rallying call of his supporters. The same year, when Parliament commanded that Wilkes's offending journal, *The North Briton,* be solemnly burned at the Royal Exchange, the "lower orders" of London's citizens pelted the sheriffs with dirt and refused to allow the public hangman to do his duty. Wilkes, however, was compelled to seek refuge in Paris, was expelled from Parliament, and was declared an outlaw. On his return in 1768, he was elected as their Member by the freeholders of Middlesex; his victory was greeted by tumultuous riots in the Cities of London and Westminster which, for two days on end, the forces of law and order were quite inadequate and unable to contain. The Austrian Ambassador was dragged from his coach; and every lamp and window of the Mansion House was smashed, as were the windows of those who, when called to do so, refused to "put out lights for Mr. Wilkes." Having surrendered to his outlawry, Wilkes was confined in the King's Bench prison; its approaches became, for two weeks on end, the scene of further riots, culminating on May 10, 1768, in the "massacre" of St. George's Fields, when the Guards shot into a vast crowd surrounding the prison, killing eleven and wounding a dozen others.

In March 1769, when Wilkes was still in prison, his supporters broke up a cavalcade of City merchants, who were trying to present a "loyal" address to George III; only a bedraggled handful were able to get through to St. James's Palace. Further noisy celebrations attended Wilkes's birthday, his defeat of Luttrell in Middlesex (after a second expulsion from Parliament), and his release from prison in April 1770. Unable to take his seat in the Commons, he now flung himself into City politics; and as a City Alderman, he played an important part in the great battle that broke out in 1771 between City and Commons over the reporting of parliamentary debates in the public press.[16] In the course of the dispute the Lord Mayor, Brass Crosby, was committed to the Tower, and huge crowds demonstrated at the approaches to Parliament, assaulted government supporters, and hailed George III himself with shouts of "No Lord Mayor, no King!" Three years later, Wilkes's election as Lord Mayor was greeted by a final salvo of broken windows in the City of London. It was the last of the Wilkite riots. The same year, he was able to take his seat in Parliament, and he gradually lost his connections with London's "inferior set of people." [17]

Four years after the last of the Wilkite disturbances, Parliament passed

[16] See Peter D. G. Thomas, "John Wilkes and the Freedom of the Press (1771)," *Bulletin of the Institute of Historical Research,* May 1960, pp. 86–98.
[17] See my *Wilkes and Liberty,* pp. 26–7, 33–4, 41–56, 62–6, 155–65, 168–71, 191–2.

the Catholic Relief Act, which repealed a number of the restrictions imposed on Roman Catholics. It was not a radical measure, and it passed through both Houses without a division. But the attempt to apply the Act to Scotland met with stern resistance; and after violent rioting in Edinburgh and Glasgow it had to be abandoned. Resistance now spread south of the Border. In London a Protestant Association was set up to conduct a campaign for the repeal of the Act. Lord George Gordon, the Association's president, launched a petition that collected 60,000 signatures; and on June 2, 1780, he addressed a vast assembly in St. George's Fields before proceeding by coach to Westminster, followed by his supporters, who marched in orderly contingents and were said to be composed of "the better sort of tradesmen." When Parliament, alarmed by the throng of demonstrators besieging its approaches, refused to consider the petition, uproar broke loose; and a part of the crowd moved off to the nearby private chapels attached to the Sardinian and Bavarian embassies, ransacked them, and burned their contents in the streets. There followed a week of rioting in the Cities of Westminster and London, and in Spitalfields, Wapping, Bermondsey, and Southwark, in the course of which Catholic chapels, schools, dwellings, and pubs, and the houses of both government and opposition supporters, were damaged or destroyed, half-a-dozen prisons were set ablaze and their inmates released, and assaults were made on Blackfriars Bridge and the Bank of England. At the height of the disorders, on the night of June 7, London appeared to onlookers to be a sea of flames. "I remember," wrote Horace Walpole on the eighth, "the Excise and the Gin Act and the rebels at Derby and Wilkes' interlude and the French at Plymouth, or I should have a very bad memory; but I never till last night saw London and Southwark in flames!" [18] It was only on the seventh day, after 100 houses had been damaged or "pulled down" to a value of over £100,000, that the military took full control. Retribution was heavy; 285 rioters had been killed and another 173 wounded. Lord George Gordon was clapped in the Tower before being tried and acquitted on a charge of High Treason. Some of his followers were less fortunate. Of 450 prisoners taken, 160 were brought to trial; and of these twenty-five were hanged and another twelve were imprisoned. Such were the Gordon Riots, perhaps the most violent and the most savagely repressed of all the riots in London's history.[19]

I have said that these movements may appear to have little in common; yet in some respects they all conform to the common pattern of the eighteenth-century city riot. First, as to the methods of the rioters. In all three

[18] *The Letters of Horace Walpole, Earl of Orford,* ed. P. Cummingham (9 vols. London, 1891), VII, 388.

[19] See my article "The Gordon Riots: A Study of the Rioters and Their Victims," *Transactions of the Royal Historical Society,* 5th series, VI (1956), 93–114.

episodes (if we limit our picture of the Wilkite riots to those of 1768), they operated in itinerant bands, marching (or running) through Shoreditch, the City of London, Westminster, or Southwark, gathering fresh forces on the way, but generally they were local men who were perfectly recognizable to publicans and other local witnesses. These bands were frequently "captained" by men enjoying temporary authority—men like Tom the Barber, who led a contingent in Goodman's Fields in July 1736; or Thomas Taplin, a coach master, who directed the collection of money "for the poor Mob" in Great Russell Street during the Gordon Riots; and similar leaders were described to the police in the Wilkite riot of March 1768. These men may also have passed on to their followers the slogans of the day: "Down with the Irish!" in 1736, "Wilkes and Liberty!" in 1768, and "No Popery!" in 1780. They may, too, have been bearers of "lists" of houses that were to be "pulled down" or whose windows were to be smashed. Whether such "lists" existed in fact (I have found none among judicial records) or were merely figments of the imagination of informants, it is certain enough that the houses of selected victims were picked out for special treatment. By such direct-action methods considerable damage was done, as we have noted; but it is also important to note that it was strictly discriminating and was directed against carefully selected targets. In the Gordon Riots, considerable care was taken to avoid damage to neighboring property,* and where the wrong targets suffered it was due to the wind rather than to the rioters' intentions. Violence was discriminating in another sense as well. It was limited to property and, of all the lives lost in 1780, it is remarkable that all were from the side of the rioters and not one from among their victims.

Nor were the rioters, on any of these occasions, the "criminal elements," social riff-raff, or "slum population" imagined by those historians who have taken their cue from the prejudiced accounts of contemporary observers. An anonymous informer of 1780 gave the following description of the Gordon rioters:

200 house brakers with tools;
550 pickpockets;
6,000 of alsorts;
50 men that . . . gives them orders what to be done; they only come att night.

But, for all its apparent authenticity, this turns out to be a largely fanciful picture. From the records of those brought up for trial at the Old Bailey,

---

* While buildings marked for destruction were "pulled down," their movable contents were burned in the street.

in Southwark, and at the Surrey Assizes we may be reasonably confident
that the rioters were a fair cross section of London's working population:
two in every three of those tried were wage earners—journeymen, apprentices, waiters, domestic servants, and laborers; a smaller number were
petty employers, craftsmen, or tradesmen. In the anti-Irish riots of 1736,
as we might expect from their nature and origins, wage earners formed an
even larger proportion; whereas in 1768 the Wilkite rioters appear again
to have been a similar mixture of wage earners, small employers, and independent craftsmen. Such elements, too, although rarely appearing on the
lists of householders assessed for the parish poor rate, were rarely vagrants,
rarely had criminal records of any kind, generally had settled abodes, and
tended to be "respectable" working men rather than slum dwellers or the
poorest of the poor. It is also perhaps a surprising fact that the most riotous
parts of London, not only on these occasions but on others, were not the
crowded quarters of St. Giles-in-the-Fields or the shadier alleys of Holborn
but the more solid and respectable popular districts of the City, the Strand,
Southwark, Shoreditch, and Spitalfields.

Other bonds in common between these groups of rioters may be found
in the motives that impelled them. Clearly, the ostensible objects of these
riots were very different in one case from another: in 1736, to prevent
the employment of cheaper Irish labor; in 1768, to celebrate Wilkes's return to Parliament; in 1780, to compel Parliament to repeal the Catholic
Relief Act; and these objects were not only overtly proclaimed but genuine
enough. But motives in such affairs are generally mixed and far from
simple: in this sense, the underlying motive may be even more worthy of
attention than that more obviously apparent. For the moment, we may dis-
count the often-repeated charge of a "hidden hand"—whether Jacobites,
High Church, or of French or American agents—lying behind such riots:
this, too, we shall have occasion to discuss more fully later. Here we are
concerned with the genuine interests of the crowd itself. Evidently, crowds
so composed would feel the pinch of hunger in times of shortage and, in
moments of social tension, might wish to settle accounts with those more
prosperous and better favored than themselves. In fact, the short-term
economic motive appears to have played a certain part in some of these
disturbances, though not in all. In July 1736, the price of the quarter of
wheat in London rose sharply to 26–36s. from 20–25s. in June; in March–
May 1768, the prices of wheat and bread were high, and had been so for
many months; on the other hand, in June 1780, prices were low, as they
had been for some time past.* So, in the first two cases, the fear of hunger

---

* Prices of wheat and bread are from the *Gentleman's Magazine.* In London,
wheat prices were high and appreciably above average (though fluctuating less
violently than in certain country markets) in 1736, 1740, 1756–7, 1766–8, 1772–3,
1775, 1777, and 1793–5.

may have been an inducement to rioting, while it seems unlikely in the third.

A more constant element, perhaps, than hunger is that of a class hostility of the poor against the rich. There is no obvious evidence for this in the riots of 1736, though it may be implicit in the observation made, a month after the anti-Irish riots, by one of Walpole's agents: "It is evident that there are great discontents and murmurings through all this Mobbish part of the Town." But it appears more explicitly in our other two examples. In March 1768, Wilkes's supporters celebrated his election to Parliament by smashing the windows of lords and ladies of opulence and fashion with gay abandon; and they made little distinction in picking out their victims between government and opposition members. This concern to settle accounts with the rich is even more strikingly displayed in the Gordon Riots. Overtly, the rioters proclaimed their hostility to Roman Catholics without distinction; but, as it turned out, the Catholics whose houses were attacked were not those living in the most densely populated Catholic districts (whether in St. Giles-in-the-Fields, Saffron Hill, or the dockside parishes of East London), but in the more fashionable residential areas of the West; and it was not the Catholic craftsmen or wage earners—men similar to themselves—that engaged the rioters' attention, but gentlemen, manufacturers, merchants, and publicans. Such evidence of social discrimination might, no doubt, be found, if it were looked for, in other city riots of the time.

Another common element among London's "mobbish" population, also noted by Dr. Hobsbawm in the case of other European cities,[20] was hostility to foreigners, or a militant type of chauvinism. "Foreigners" in this sense would include Scots and Irish as well as Frenchmen, Spaniards, Jews, and Roman Catholics. Such feelings are evident in the frequent proclamation of the free-born Englishman's "liberties" and hostility to "slavery" and "Popery and wooden shoes." Irishmen and Catholics were, of course, readily associated with each other, as they were on more than one occasion in the Gordon Riots. Frenchmen and Spaniards were, in addition to being Catholics, the traditional national enemy and therefore obvious targets of popular dislike; and in June 1780, we read of a Portuguese householder (possibly taken for a Spaniard) being assailed as an "outlandish bouger."

The case of the Scots was somewhat different, and here hostility, though intense for a time, was shorter lived. It was largely due, no doubt, to the long association of Scotland with an alien Jacobite cause: in fact, the last of the severed Scottish Jacobite heads of the "forty-five" was still grinning down from its perch on Temple Bar as late as 1772. This antipathy was particularly strong in the early 1760s, when the unpopular Bute became

[20] Hobsbawm, *op. cit.,* pp. 112–13.

the favorite of George III, and was cleverly exploited by Wilkes and the City radicals. Yet it appears to have died by 1780, for Lord George Gordon, the new popular hero of the hour, was a Scot and it was the Scots that set the English the example of "pulling down" Catholic schools and chapels. At this time, however, England was at war with France and Spain, and London's chauvinism could vent its spleen—and it was by no means confined to the riotous "lower orders"—on Catholics, whether Irish, French, or English. Although some of these antagonisms tended to diminish, others survived to serve as fuel for future riots. Francophobia was one survival: it reappears in the English "Church and King" disturbances of the 1790s and receives a fresh lease of life in the French Revolutionary and Napoleonic Wars.[21]

In brief, the eighteenth-century city riot arose over issues far more varied than those of the countryside. Yet, beneath the surface, there were common elements—no less in the methods than in the motives and "generalized beliefs" of its participants. These, even more than the issues themselves, give it its peculiar and distinct identity.

E. J. HOBSBAWM

The Laboring Poor

Three possibilities were therefore open to such of the poor as found themselves in the path of bourgeois society, and no longer effectively sheltered in still inaccessible regions of traditional society. They could strive to become bourgeois; they could allow themselves to be ground down; or they could rebel.

The first course, as we have seen, was not merely technically difficult for those who lacked the minimum entrance fee of property or education, but profoundly distasteful. The introduction of a purely utilitarian indi-

Reprinted by permission of The World Publishing Company and George Weidenfeld and Nicolson Ltd. from *The Age of Revolution: Europe 1789–1848* by E. J. Hobsbawm. Copyright © 1962 by E. J. Hobsbawn.

[21] For a fuller discussion of these and similar factors, see my article "The London 'Mob' of the Eighteenth Century," *The Historical Journal*, II, i (1959), 1–18.

vidualist system of social behavior, the theoretically justified jungle anarchy of bourgeois society with its motto "every man for himself and the devil take the hindmost," appeared to men brought up in traditional societies as little better than wanton evil. "In our times," said one of the desperate Silesian handloom linen-weavers who rioted vainly against their fate in 1844,[1] "men have invented excellent arts to weaken and undermine one another's livelihood. But alas, nobody thinks any longer of the Seventh Commandment, which commands and forbids as follows: Thou shalt not steal. Nor do they bear in mind Luther's commentary upon it, in which he says: We shall love and fear the Lord, so that we may not take away our neighbor's property nor money, nor acquire it by false goods and trading, but on the contrary we should help him guard and increase his livelihood and property." Such a man spoke for all who found themselves dragged into an abyss by what were plainly the forces of hell. They did not ask for much. ("The rich used to treat the poor with charity, and the poor lived simply, for in those days the lower orders needed much less for outward show in clothes and other expenses than they do today.") But even that modest place in the social order was now, it seemed, to be taken from them.

Hence their resistance against even the most rational proposals of bourgeois society, married as they were to inhumanity. Country squires introduced and laborers clung to the Speenhamland system, though the economic arguments against it were conclusive. As a means of alleviating poverty, Christian charity was worse than useless, as could be seen in the Papal states, which abounded in it. But it was popular not only among the traditionalist rich, who cherished it as a safeguard against the evil of equal rights (proposed by "those dreamers who maintain that nature has created men with equal rights and that social distinctions should be founded purely on communal utility"[2]) but also among the traditionalist poor, who were profoundly convinced that they had a *right* to crumbs from the rich man's table. In Britain a chasm divided the middle class champions of Friendly Societies, who saw them entirely as a form of individual self-help and the poor, who treated them also, and often primarily, as *societies,* with convivial meetings, ceremonies, rituals and festivities; to the detriment of their actuarial soundness.

That resistance was only strengthened by the opposition of even the bourgeois to such aspects of pure individual free competition as did not

---

[1] The weaver Hauffe, born 1807, quoted in Alexander Schneer, *Ueber die Noth der Leinen-Arbeiter in Schlesien . . .* (Berlin 1844), p. 16.

[2] The theologian P. D. Michele Augusti, *Della libertà ed eguaglianza degli uomini nell'ordine naturale e civile* (1790), quoted in A. Cherubini, *Dottrine e Metodi Assistenziali dal 1789 al 1848* (Milan 1958), p. 17.

actually benefit him. Nobody was more devoted to individualism than the sturdy American farmer and manufacturer, no Constitution more opposed than theirs—or so their lawyers believed until our own century—to such interferences with freedom as federal child labor legislation. But nobody was more firmly committed, as we have seen, to "artificial" protection for their businesses. New machinery was one of the chief benefits to be expected from private enterprise and free competition. But not only the laboring Luddites arose to smash it: the smaller businessmen and farmers in their regions sympathized with them, because they also regarded innovators as destroyers of men's livelihood. Farmers actually sometimes left their machines out for rioters to destroy, and the government had to send a sharply worded circular in 1830 to point out that "machines are as entitled to the protection of the law as any other description of property." [3] The very hesitation and doubt with which, outside the strongholds of bourgeois-liberal confidence, the new entrepreneur entered upon his historic task of destroying the social and moral order, strengthened the poor man's conviction.

There were of course laboring men who did their best to join the middle classes, or at least to follow the precepts of thrift, self-help and self-betterment. The moral and didactic literature of middle class radicalism, temperance movements and protestant endeavor is full of the sort of men whose Homer was Samuel Smiles. And indeed such bodies attracted and perhaps encouraged the ambitious young man. The Royton Temperance Seminary, started in 1843 (confined to boys—mostly cotton operatives—who had taken the pledge of abstinence, refused to gamble and were of good moral character), had within twenty years produced five master cotton spinners, one clergyman, two managers of cotton mills in Russia "and many others had obtained respectable positions as managers, overlookers, head mechanics, certified schoolmasters, or had become respectable shopkeepers." [4] Clearly such phenomena were less common outside the Anglo-Saxon world, where the road out of the working class (except by migration) was very much narrower—it was not exceptionally broad even in Britain—and the moral and intellectual influence of the Radical middle class on the skilled worker was less.

On the other hand there were clearly far more who, faced with a social catastrophe they did not understand, impoverished, exploited, herded into slums that combined bleakness and squalor, or into the expanding complexes of small-scale industrial villages, sank into demoralization. Deprived of the traditional institutions and guides to behavior, how could

---

[3] E. J. Hobsbawm, The Machine Breakers, *Past and Present*, I, 1952.

[4] 'About some Lancashire Lads' in *The Leisure Hour* (1881). I owe this reference to Mr. A. Jenkin.

many fail to sink into an abyss of hand-to-mouth expedients, where families pawned their blankets each week until pay-day * and where alcohol was "the quickest way out of Manchester" (or Lille or the Borinage). Mass alcoholism, an almost invariable companion of headlong and uncontrolled industrialization and urbanization, spread "a pestilence of hard liquor" [5] across Europe. Perhaps the numerous contemporaries who deplored the growth of drunkenness, as of prostitution and other forms of sexual promiscuity, were exaggerating. Nevertheless, the sudden upsurge of systematic temperance agitations, both of a middle and working class character, in England, Ireland and Germany around 1840, shows that the worry about demoralization was neither academic nor confined to any single class. Its immediate success was shortlived, but for the rest of the century the hostility to hard liquor remained something which both enlightened employers and labor movements had in common.†

But of course the contemporaries who deplored the demoralization of the new urban and industrialized poor were not exaggerating. Everything combined to maximize it. Towns and industrial areas grew rapidly, without plan or supervision, and the most elementary services of city life utterly failed to keep pace with it: street-cleaning, water-supply, sanitation, not to mention working-class housing.[6] The most obvious consequence of this urban deterioration was the reappearance of mass epidemics of contagious (mainly waterborne) disease, notably of the *cholera,* which reconquered Europe from 1831 and swept the continent from Marseilles to St. Petersburg in 1832 and again later. To take a single example: typhus in Glasgow "did not arrest attention by any epidemic prevalence until 1818." [7] Thereafter it increased. There were two major epidemics (typhus and cholera) in the city in the 1830s, three (typhus, cholera and relapsing fever) in the 1840s, two in the first half of the 1850s, until urban improvement caught up with a generation of neglect. The terrible effects of this neglect were all the greater, because the middle and ruling-classes did not feel it. Urban development in our period was a gigantic process of class segregation, which pushed the new laboring poor into great morasses of misery outside the centers of government and business and the newly specialized residential areas of the bourgeoisie. The almost universal

---

* In 1855 60 percent of all pledges with Liverpool pawnbrokers were 5s. or less in value, 2 percent 2s. 6d. or less.

[5] 'die Schnapspest im ersten Drittel des Jahrhunderts,' *Handwoerterbuch d. Staatswissenschaften* (Second ed.) art. 'Trunksucht.'

† This is not true of hostility to beer, wine or other drinks forming part of men's habitual everyday diet. This was largely confined to Anglo-Saxon protestant sectarians.

[6] L. Chevalier, *Classes Laborieuses et Classes Dangereuses, passim.*

[7] J. B. Russell, *Public Health Administration in Glasgow* (1903), p. 3.

European division into a "good" west end and a "poor" east end of large cities developed in this period.* And what social institutions except the tavern and perhaps the chapel were provided in these new laborers' agglomerations except by the laborers' own initiative? Only after 1848, when the new epidemics sprung from the slums began to kill the rich also, and the desperate masses who grew up in them had frightened the powers-that-be by social revolution, was systematic urban rebuilding and improvement undertaken.

Drink was not the only sign of this demoralization. Infanticide, prostitution, suicide, and mental derangement have all been brought into relation with this social and economic cataclysm, thanks largely to the contemporary pioneering work of what we would today call social medicine.† And so has both the increase in crime and that growing and often purposeless violence which was a sort of blind personal assertion against the forces threatening to engulf the passive. The spread of apocalyptic, mystical or other sects and cults in this period indicates a similar incapacity to deal with the earthquakes of society which were breaking down men's lives. The cholera epidemics, for instance, provoked religious revivals in Catholic Marseilles as well as in Protestant Wales.

All these forms of distortions of social behavior had one thing in common with one another, and incidentally with "self-help." They were attempts to escape the fate of being a poor laboring man, or at best to accept or forget poverty and humiliation. The believer in the second coming, the drunkard, the petty gangster, the lunatic, the tramp or the ambitious small entrepreneur, all averted their eyes from the collective condition and (with the exception of the last) were apathetic about the capacity of collective action. In the history of our period this massive apathy plays a much larger part than is often supposed. It is no accident that the least skilled,

---

* "The circumstances which oblige the workers to move out of the center of Paris have generally, it is pointed out, had deplorable effects on their behavior and morality. In the old days they used to live on the higher floors of buildings whose lower floors were occupied by businessmen and other members of the relatively comfortable classes. A sort of solidarity grew up between the tenants of a single building. Neighbours helped each other in little ways. When sick or unemployed the workers might find much assistance within the house, while on the other hand a sort of feeling of human respect imbued working-class habits with a certain regularity." The complacency is that of the Chamber of Commerce and the Police Prefecture from whose Report this is quoted; but the novelty of segregation is well brought out.[8]

† The long list of doctors to whom we owe so much of our knowledge of the times—and of subsequent improvement—contrast vividly with the general complacency and hardness of bourgeois opinion. Villermé and the contributors to the *Annales d'Hygiène Publique,* which he founded in 1829, Kay, Thackrah, Simon, Gaskell and Farr in Britain, and several in Germany, deserve to be remembered more widely than in fact they are.

[8] Chevalier op. cit. pp. 233–4.

least educated, least organized and therefore least hopeful of the poor, then as later, were the most apathetic: at the 1848 elections in the Prussian town of Halle 81 percent of the independent crafts masters and 71 percent of the masons, carpenters and other skilled builders voted; but only 46 percent of the factory and railway workers, the laborers, the domestic workers, etc.[9]

The alternative to escape or defeat was rebellion. And such was the situation of the laboring poor, and especially the industrial proletariat which became their nucleus, that rebellion was not merely possible, but virtually compulsory. Nothing was more inevitable in the first half of the nineteenth century than the appearance of labor and socialist movements, and indeed of mass social revolutionary unrest. The revolution of 1848 was its direct consequence.

That the condition of the laboring poor was appalling between 1815 and 1848 was not denied by any reasonable observer, and by 1840 there were a good many of these. That it was actually deteriorating was widely assumed. In Britain the Malthusian population theory, which held that the growth of population must inevitably outrun that of the means of subsistence, was based on such an assumption, and reinforced by the arguments of Ricardian economists. Those who took a rosier view of working-class prospects were less numerous and less talented than those who took the gloomy view. In Germany in the 1830s the increasing pauperization of the people was the specific subject of at least fourteen different publications, and the question whether "the complaints about increasing pauperization and food shortage" were justified was set for academic prize essays. (Ten of sixteen competitors thought they were and only two that they were not.) [10] The very prevalence of such opinions is itself evidence of the universal and apparently hopeless misery of the poor.

No doubt actual poverty was worst in the countryside, and especially among landless wage-laborers, rural domestic workers, and, of course, land-poor peasants, or those who lived on infertile land. A bad harvest, such as in 1789, 1795, 1817, 1832, 1847, still brought actual famine, even without the intervention of additional catastrophes such as the competition of British cotton goods, which destroyed the foundation of the Silesian cottage linen industry. After the ruined crop of 1813 in Lombardy many kept alive only by eating manure and hay, bread made from the leaves of bean plants and wild berries.[11] A bad year such as 1817 could,

---

[9] E. Neuss, *Entstehung u. Entwicklung d. Klasse d. besitzlosen Lohnarbeiter in Halle* (Berlin 1958), p. 283.

[10] J. Kuczynski, *Geschichte der Lage der Arbeiter* (Berlin 1960), Vol. 9, p. 264 ff; Vol. 8 (1960), p. 109 ff.

[11] R. J. Rath, The Habsburgs and the Great Depression in Lombardo Venetia 1814–18. *Journal of Modern History*, XIII, p. 311.

even in tranquil Switzerland, produce an actual excess of deaths over births.[12] The European hunger of 1846–8 pales beside the cataclysm of the Irish famine, but it was real enough. In East and West Prussia (1847) one-third of the population had ceased to eat bread, and relied only on potatoes.[13] In the austere, respectable, pauperized manufacturing villages of the middle German mountains, where men and women sat on logs and benches, owned few curtains or house-linen, and drank from earthenware or tin mugs for want of glass, the population had sometimes become so used to a diet of potatoes and thin coffee, that during famine-times the relief-workers had to teach it to eat the peas and porridge they supplied.[14] Hunger-typhus ravaged the countrysides of Flanders and Silesia, where the village linen-weaver fought his doomed battle against modern industry.

But in fact the misery—the increasing misery as so many thought— which attracted most attention, short of total catastrophe such as the Irish, was that of the cities and industrial areas where the poor starved less passively and less unseen. Whether their real incomes fell is still a matter of historical debate, though, as we have seen, there can be no doubt that the general situation of the poor in cities deteriorated. Variations between one region and another, between different types of workers and between different economic periods, as well as the deficiency of statistics, make such questions difficult to answer decisively, though any significant absolute general improvement can be excluded before 1848 (or in Britain perhaps 1844), and the gap between the rich and the poor certainly grew wider and more visible. The time when Baroness Rothschild wore one and a half million francs worth of jewelry at the Duke of Orléans' masked ball (1842) was the time when John Bright described the women of Rochdale: "2,000 women and girls passed through the streets singing hymns —it was a very singular and striking spectacle—approaching the sublime— they are dreadfully hungry—a loaf is devoured with greediness indescribable and if the bread is nearly covered with mud it is eagerly devoured." [15]

It is in fact probable that there was some general deterioration over wide areas of Europe, for not only (as we have seen) urban institutions and social services failed to keep pace with headlong and unplanned expansion, and money (and often real) wages tended to fall after 1815, the production and transport of foodstuffs probably also fell behind in many large cities until the railway age.[16] It was on lags such as this that the

[12] M. C. Muehlemann, *Les prix des vivres et le mouvement de la population dans le canton de Berne 1782–1881. IV Congrès International d'Hygiène* (1883).

[13] F. J. Neumann, Zur Lehre von d Lohngesetzen, *Jb.f.Nat.Oek* 3d ser. IV 1892, p. 374 ff.

[14] R. Scheer, *Entwicklung d Annaberger Posamentierindustrie im 19. Jahrhundert.* (Leipzig 1909), pp. 27–8, 33.

[15] N. McCord, *The Anti-Corn Law League* (1958), p. 127.

[16] 'Par contre, il est sûr que la situation alimentaire, à Paris, s'est deteriorée

contemporary Malthusians based their pessimism. But quite apart from such a lag, the mere change from the traditional diet of the preindustrial man to the ignorant as well as impoverished free purchase of the urbanized and industrial one was likely to lead to worse feeding, just as the conditions of urban life and work were likely to lead to worse health. The extraordinary difference in health and physical fitness between the industrial and agricultural population (and of course between the upper, middle and working classes), on which the French and English statisticians fixed their attention, was clearly due to this. The average expectation of life at birth in the 1840s was twice as high for the laborers of rural Wiltshire and Rutland (hardly a pampered class) than for those of Manchester or Liverpool. But then—to take merely one example—"till steam-power was introduced into the trade, towards the end of the last century, the grinder's disease was scarcely known in the Sheffield cutlery trades." But in 1842 50 percent of all razor-grinders in their thirties, 79 percent of all in their forties, and 100 percent of all razor-grinders over the age of fifty retched out their lungs with it.[17]

Moreover, the change in the economy shifted and displaced vast strata of laborers, sometimes to their benefit, but more often to their sorrow. Great masses of the population remained as yet unabsorbed by the new industries or cities as a permanent substratum of the pauperized and helpless, and even great masses were periodically hurled into unemployment by crises which were barely yet recognized as being temporary as well as recurrent. Two-thirds of the textile workers in Bolton (1842) or Roubaix (1847) would be thrown totally out of work by such a slump.[18] Twenty percent of Nottingham, one-third of Paisley might be actually destitute.[19] A movement like Chartism in Britain would collapse, time and again, under its political weakness. Time and again sheer hunger—the intolerable burden which rested on millions of the laboring poor—would revive it.

In addition to these general storms, special catastrophes burst over the heads of particular kinds of the laboring poor. The initial phase of industrial revolution did not, as we have seen, push all laborers into mechanized factories. On the contrary, round the few mechanized and large-scale sec-

---

peu à peu avec le XIX siècle, sans doute jusqu'au voisinage des années 50 ou 60.' R. Philippe in *Annales* 16, 3, 1961, 567. For analogous calculations for London, cf. E. J. Hobsbawm, The British Standard of Living, *Economic History Review*, X, 1, 1957. The total per capita meat consumption of France appears to have remained virtually unchanged from 1812 to 1840 (*Congrés Internationale d'Hygiène Paris 1878* (1880), vol. I, p. 432).

[17] S. Pollard, *A History of Labour in Sheffield* (1960), pp. 62–3.

[18] H. Ashworth in *Journal Stat. Soc.* V (1842), p. 74; E. Labrousse, ed. *Aspects de la Crise . . . 1846–51* (1956), p. 107.

[19] *Statistical Committee appointed by the Anti-Corn Law Conference . . . March 1842* (n.d.), p. 45.

tors of production, it multiplied the numbers of preindustrial artisans, of certain types of skilled workers, and of the army of domestic and cottage labor, and often improved their condition, especially during the long years of labor shortage in the wars. In the 1820s and 1830s the iron and impersonal advance of machine and market began to throw them aside. At its mildest this turned independent men into dependent ones, persons into mere "hands." At its frequent harshest, it produced those multitudes of the declassed, the pauperized and the famished—handloom weavers, framework knitters etc.—whose condition froze the blood of even the most flinty economist. These were not unskilled and ignorant riff-raff. Such communities as those of the Norwich and the Dunfermline weavers which were broken and scattered in the 1830s, the London furniture-makers whose old-established negotiated "price-lists" became scraps of paper as they sank into the morass of sweatshops, the continental journeymen who became itinerant proletarians, the artisans who lost their independence: these had been the most skilled, the most educated, the most self-reliant, the flower of the laboring people.* They did not know what was happening to them. It was natural that they should seek to find out, even more natural that they should protest.†

Materially the new factory proletariat was likely to be somewhat better off. On the other hand it was unfree; under the strict control and the even stricter discipline imposed by the master or his supervisors, against whom they had virtually no legal recourse and only the very beginnings of public protection. They had to work his hours or shifts; to accept his punishments and the fines with which he imposed his rules or increased his profits. In isolated areas or industries they had to buy in his shop, as often as not receiving their wages in *truck* (thus allowing the unscrupulous employer to swell his profits yet further), or live in the houses the master provided. No doubt the village boy might find such a life no more dependent and less impoverished than his parents'; and in continental industries with a strong paternalist tradition, the despotism of the master was at least partly balanced by the security, education and welfare services which he sometimes provided. But for the free man entry into the factory as a mere "hand" was entry into something little better than slavery, and all but the

---

* Of 195 Gloucestershire adult weavers in 1840 only fifteen could neither read nor write; but of the rioters arrested in the manufacturing areas of Lancashire, Cheshire and Staffordshire in 1842 only 13 percent could read and write well, 32 percent imperfectly.

† "About one-third of our working population . . . consists of weavers and laborers, whose average earnings do not amount to a sum sufficient to bring up and maintain their families without parochial assistance. It is this portion of the community, for the most part decent and respectable in their lives, which is suffering most from the depression of wages, and the hardships of the times. It is to this class of my poor fellow-creatures in particular, that I desire to recommend the system of co-operation." (F. Baker, *First Lecture on Co-operation,* Bolton 1830.)

most famished tended to avoid it, and even when in it to resist the draconic discipline much more persistently than the women and children, whom factory owners therefore tended to prefer. And, of course, in the 1830s and part of the 1840s even the material situation of the factory proletariat tended to deteriorate.

Whatever the actual situation of the laboring poor, there can be absolutely no doubt that every one of them who thought at all—i.e. who did accept the tribulations of the poor as part of fate and the eternal design of things—considered the laborer to be exploited and impoverished by the rich, who were getting richer while the poor became poorer. And the poor suffered *because* the rich benefited. The social mechanism of bourgeois society was in the profoundest manner cruel, unjust and inhuman. "There can be no wealth without labor" wrote the *Lancashire Co-operator.* "The workman is the source of all wealth. Who has raised all the food? The half-fed and impoverished laborer. Who built all the houses and warehouses, and palaces, which are possessed by the rich, who never labor or produce anything? The workman. Who spins all the yarn and makes all the cloth? The spinner and weaver." Yet "the laborer remains poor and destitute, while those who do not work are rich, and possess abundance to surfeiting." [20] And the despairing rural laborer (echoed literally even today by the Negro gospel-singer) put it less clearly, but perhaps even more profoundly:

> If life was a thing that money could buy
> The rich would live and the poor might die.[21]

[20] Quoted in A. E. Musson, The Ideology of Early Co-operation in Lancashire and Cheshire; *Transactions of the Lancashire and Cheshire Antiquarian Society,* LXVIII, 1958, p. 120.

[21] A. Williams, *Folksongs of the Upper Thames* (1923), p. 105 prints a similar version that is rather more class conscious.

P. H. NOYES

The German Working Class
in the 1840s

The thirty-eight states of the German Federation stood on the threshold of the Industrial Revolution in the years before 1848. Predominantly agricultural, with economies based on the peasant and the farm, the guild and the artisan, Germany was "in many ways medieval and in many places less vigorous than it had been in the days of Dürer and Holbein." [1] But a variety of factors—the freeing of the serfs, the break-up of the guild system, the campaign for internal free trade and the foundation of the *Zollverein*—was transforming the old system. Industries slowly began to appear, in the Rhineland, in Saxony and Silesia, around Berlin. By 1848 there did exist in Germany a "working class."

The working class of 1848 was not, however, a unified, self-conscious body; the radicals and democrats of 1848 were to note to their sorrow that there was no "ideal proletariat" to carry out the revolution.[2] Rather the working class was of mixed origins: failed or failing master craftsmen, journeymen frustrated in advancement by the guild system, skilled tradesmen put out of work by the new techniques of production, casual and day laborers and that mass of economic misfits Marx called the *Lumpenproletariat*. Factory workers, where they existed, often considered themselves to be superior to the common run of workers; the machine builders were held to be the "aristocrats" of the Berlin labor force.[3]

Nor was the line between the working class and the lower middle class, the *Kleinbürgertum,* one which could be drawn with any precision. Indeed

"The Condition of the Working Class in Germany in the 1840s" in P. H. Noyes, *Organization and Revolution: Working Class Associations in the German Revolution of 1848–1849.* (Copyright © 1966 by Princeton University Press), pp. 15–33. Reprinted by permission of Princeton University Press.

[1] J. H. Clapham, *The Economic Development of France and Germany, 1815–1914,* Cambridge, 1936, p. 82.

[2] See the report of the Central Committee to the second Democratic Congress, held in Berlin in October 1848, quoted by Gustav Lüders, *Die demokratische Bewegung in Berlin im Oktober, 1848,* Berlin, 1909, pp. 152–156.

[3] Stephen Born, *Erinnerungen eines Achtundvierzigers,* Leipzig, 1898, p. 122.

it has been argued that "there was strictly speaking, in Germany, neither a powerful bourgeoisie nor a powerful working class [4] but only an industrial lower middle class which began to release certain groups upward and downward." [5] The poor journeyman who failed to obtain advancement in his trade guild and joined the ranks of the factory workers and the rising manufacturer were both initially members of the same social group and both products of the same crisis—the collapse of many of the old artisan trades.

The difficulty in defining the working class of 1848 lies partly in the drastic and complex changes which were occurring in the very concept of "class" and the vocabulary of social description. The emergence of the working class coincided with the emergence of the idea of class itself as distinct from status or estate: *Klasse* began to replace *Schicht* or *Stand* in contemporary nomenclature. The old German states had been regarded as static societies composed of estates. The economic forces which produced a working class saw the destruction of the medieval ideal of hierarchic or corporative estates which were equated with society, though many, from Frederick William IV of Prussia to the members of the entrenched guilds, still clung to it. The concepts of "state" and "society" separated; the individual's rights in one were not to be determined, fixed or limited by his function or position in the other. Liberals demanded political rights for all; socialists preached class war. Both were ready for revolution; neither realized the true nature of the conditions under which the revolution would take place.[6]

---

[4] *Vierten Stand*—literally "fourth estate." There is no adequate translation in English for this phrase and therein lies the problem of discussing the German working classes in 1848.

[5] Stadelmann, *Soziale und politische Geschichte*, p. 156.

[6] For the distinction between "state" and "society," "status" and "class," see the two highly illuminating articles by Werner Conze, "Staat und Gesellschaft in der frührevolutionären Epoche Deutschlands," *Historische Zeitschrift*, vol. 186 (1958), pp. 1–34, and, more importantly for the study of the working class, "Vom 'Pöbel' zum 'Proletariat,' Sozialgeschichtliche Voraussetzungen für den Sozialismus in Deutschland," *Vierteljahrschrift für Sozial- und Wirtschaftsgeschichte*, vol. 41 (1954), pp. 333–364. The first of these articles has now been published in an expanded version along with essays illustrating the topic by a number of Conze's students in Werner Conze, ed., *Staat und Gesellschaft im deutschen Vormärz 1815–1848*, Stuttgart, 1962. On the older conception of German society, see Leonard Krieger, *The German Idea of Freedom, History of a Political Tradition*, Boston, 1957, pp. 8ff.; Franz Schnabel, *Deutsche Geschichte im neunzehnten Jahrhundert*, Freiburg im Breisgau, 1933, vol. 1, p. 13. The distinction between *class* and *status* is a fairly common one among sociologists; see Max Weber, *Essays in Sociology*, trans. H. H. Gerth and C. Wright Mills, New York, 1946, pp. 180–185. A discussion of similar developments in England may be found in Asa Briggs' article, "The Language of 'Class' in Early Nineteenth-Century England," *Essays in Labour History*, ed. Asa Briggs and John Saville, London, 1960, pp. 43–73; see also Raymond Williams, *Culture and Society, 1780–1950*, New York, 1959, introduction.

The growth of population was in Germany, as in Britain, "the dominant event of the nineteenth century." [7] Between 1800 and 1850 the population of the German states swelled from 23 million to 35 million, an increase of over 50 percent; two thirds of this increase occurred in the period after 1820. The rate of increase varied considerably between the different states. The Prussian population grew by 60 percent from 1816 to 1846; that of Austria-Hungary rose by only 25 percent between 1818 and 1846.[8]

The mass of population was still overwhelmingly rural. In 1850 approximately 70 percent lived in the country or in villages of less than one thousand inhabitants; the figure had been 90 percent at the beginning of the century.[9] The rural situation was thus far from static. Improvements in agricultural techniques such as deep plowing, the planting of a greater variety of crops and the use of artificial fertilizers had rapidly increased the productivity of German agriculture. More importantly, the movement to free the serfs, beginning with the Prussian decree of October 9, 1807, sweeping through the smaller states in the 1820s and 1830s and culminating with the abolition of the last labor dues, especially the Austrian *robot,* in 1848, both stimulated production and created a considerable problem of overpopulation in the rural areas. The dangers and difficulties of the "agrarian proletariat," the *unterbäuerliche Schicht* of the German villages, were much discussed in contemporary pamphlet literature. The villages themselves, the leading feature of German agricultural life which once could be said to "hold the people together, fostering a spirit of association," [10] were plagued with excess labor, with large numbers of landless peasants or those with holdings too small to support themselves. Faced with unemployment in the villages, with the decline of the smaller agricultural holdings and the breakdown of home industries, especially of weaving and spinning, the workless peasant moved whenever possible to

[7] So it was called by J. H. Clapham, *An Economic History of Modern Britain,* vol. 1, *The Early Railway Age,* Cambridge, 1926, p. vii.

[8] Jürgen Kuczynski, *Die Geschichte der Lage der Arbeiter in Deutschland von 1789 bis in die Gegenwart,* vol. 1, pt. 1, *1789 bis 1870,* Berlin, 1954, p. 34. Britain in the same period (1800–1850) showed a population increase of nearly 70 percent, France of but slightly more than 30 percent. Georg von Viebahn, ed., *Statistik des Zollvereinten und nördlichen Deutschlands,* Berlin 1862–1868, vol. 2, p. 251; Jerome Blum, *Noble Landowners and Agriculture in Austria, 1815–1848,* Baltimore, 1948, p. 43.

[9] Viebahn, *Statistik,* vol. 2, p. 147; Gustav Schmoller, *Zur Geschichte der deutschen Kleingewerbe im 19. Jahrhundert, Statistische und nationalökonomische Untersuchungen,* Halle, 1870, pp. 189–190; Friedrich Lütge, *Deutsche Sozial- und Wirtschaftsgeschichte, Ein Ueberblick,* Berlin, 1952, p. 307.

[10] Thomas Banfield, an Englishman who visited Germany in 1845, spoke in praise of the German villages as a force for order and improvement. In them, he declared, "the first attempts at association have been made." (*Industry of the Rhine,* London, 1846–1848, vol. 1, p. 83.)

the towns and cities, seeking employment in the new industries or swelling the ranks of the handicraft workers.[11]

The growth of the towns was perhaps the most marked feature of the period. Berlin grew by 110 percent between 1819 and 1846, Vienna by 81 percent in the same period, so that by 1848 they each had a population of over 400,000. Apart from these two there were few cities of any great size; only Hamburg and Breslau exceeded 100,000 in 1848, while four other cities (Munich, Dresden, Königsberg and Cologne) were approaching that mark.[12] It was not the larger cities so much as those of middle size that grew most. Partly because of the difficulties of traveling from one state to another and partly because of the lack of industry, the peasant or day laborer turned often as not to the nearest town of any size in his search for employment.[13]

In Germany the existence of cheap labor came first and was followed, all too slowly in many areas, by the development of industry. By the time of the 1848 uprisings the beginnings of industry were present, but only the beginnings. There were few industrial centers in the modern sense. Mining, for example, was carried out in rural areas; the miners were peasants who farmed small holdings at the same time that they worked the mines. In the Ruhr the Krupp factory employed only 122 workmen in 1846. Though the Borsig works on the outskirts of Berlin beyond the Oranienburger Tor had 1,200 employees, the average number of workers in the machine building factories in all of Prussia was only 58. There were only 1,261 steam engines for industrial purposes in Prussia and only 1,631 in the whole of the *Zollverein*.[14]

Manufacturing was most often carried on by master craftsmen, together with their journeymen and apprentices, working at home or in small workshops, either individually or as the employees of some entrepreneur who

---

[11] On the peasant proletariat in the 1830s and 1840s, see Conze, "Vom 'Pöbel' zum 'Proletariat,' " pp. 348–349.

[12] For the population of Berlin, see E. H. Müller and C. F. Schneider, *Jahresbericht des statistischen Amtes im königlichen Polizei-Präsidio zu Berlin für das Jahr 1852*, Leipzig, 1853, p. 7; the other figures are cited by Namier, *Revolution of the Intellectuals*, pp. 5–6, n. 2.

[13] For example, Stettin, the chief Baltic port for Prussia, increased its population by some 77 percent between 1819 and 1847, although in the later year it still contained only some 45,000 inhabitants. *Mittheilungen des Centralvereins für das Wohl der arbeitenden Klassen*, Aug. 15, 1849. Also Banfield, *Industry of the Rhine*, vol. 2, p. 235.

[14] Banfield, *Industry of the Rhine*, vol. 2, p. 75; Clapham, *Economic Development of France and Germany*, p. 92; Pierre Benaerts, *Les origines de la grande industrie allemande*, Paris, 1933, *passim; Die Verbrüderung, Correspondenzblatt aller deutschen Arbeiter*, Apr. 2, 1849; Hermann Müller, *Die Organisationen der Lithographen, Steindrucker und verwandten Berufe*, Berlin, 1917, p. xx.

hired out the work and the materials. This held for a variety of trades and areas, ranging from the cutlery industry of Solingen to the textile trade of Saxony and Silesia. A few factories did exist in these areas, but they were regarded as exceptions and often treated as unwanted interlopers by the craftsmen. "Germany in general could in no sense be called capitalistic." [15] The artisan or handicraftsman provided the basis of German industry.

The predominance of artisans may be seen from an examination of the figures compiled by the Prussian Statistical Bureau under the direction of Friedrich Dieterici.[16] In 1846 the Prussian industrial class may be divided into the following groups:

master craftsmen	10.0
journeymen and apprentices	9.0
independent handicraft workers	33.0
servants and day workers	28.5
factory workers	12.5
trade and commerce	7.0
total	100.0

The first three groups constitute the class of handicraftsmen; taken together they represent some 52 percent of the industrial class. On the other hand, the figure of 12.5 percent given for factory workers must be modified; Dieterici included in this group all workers employed in the weaving trade and many of these worked not in factories but in their own homes under a putting-out system. Excluding the master craftsmen, the industrial working class comes to 27.2 percent of the total male population of Prussia over fourteen years of age; the factory workers (in Dieterici's sense) constitute only 4.2 percent. Such was the Prussian working class on the eve of 1848.

Contemporaries did indeed refer to this group as a "working class" and even as the "proletariat," though they were often somewhat hazy as to just what they meant by these terms. The anonymous author of a pamphlet entitled *Reflections of a German Proletarian* which appeared in Munich at the outbreak of the revolution offered the following definition: [17]

> The proletariat is that class which does not have sufficient property to feed itself on the proceeds of the same but must support itself through

[15] Clapham, *Economic Development of France and Germany*, p. 85.
[16] F. W. C. Dieterici, *Mittheilungen des statistischen Bureaus in Berlin*, Berlin, 1849, pp. 68–80.
[17] *Betrachtungen eines deutschen Proletariers*, Munich, 1848, p. 19.

manual labor, which however only exists during the periods of well-ordered government and political stability. Also to be counted as proletarians are those small property owners or artisans whose income is no sooner affected by some small event in the life of society than it does not suffice to support them.

Another anonymous pamphleteer spoke of the working class which "consists of the just—since propertyless—classes, the proletarians, the mass of the workers who are despised as a 'mob' and mistreated by the bourgeoisie, debased by money, or [by] the aristocracy, proud of its family tree." In this class the author included small master craftsmen, their journeymen, apprentices and assistants, factory workers and manual laborers, daily wage earners as well as students, artists and writers! [18] And the city chronicler of Nuremberg referred to the "proletariat" simply as "a new word for people who have no money." [19] The idea of a "working class" had thus gained considerable currency, though the workers to whom the term was applied were a very mixed group indeed.

The existence of a working class at this time is a denial of the proposition that such a class is the product of the Industrial Revolution, a refutation of the dictum that "the proletariat follows the capitalistic form of production as its shadow." [20] Rather in Germany the process seems to have been reversed: the growth of the proletariat, or what contemporaries regarded as a proletariat, preceded the full development of capitalism. Indeed the extension of the factory system was regarded as a partial solution to the problem of an underemployed working class otherwise dependent on the old trades and hampered by guild regulations. "The sickness for Germany," wrote Peter Reichensperger in 1847, "lies not in the excess of population, not in the machine system nor in the superfluity of industrial factories in general; rather it lies precisely in the lack of those machines and factories which ought to create work and employment for *our* workers instead of the English." [21] A contemporary Englishman explained the quiescence of German factory workers in the face of low wages and long

[18] *Contre-Revolution in Berlin oder Bürger und Arbeiter,* Berlin, 1848. The pamphlet ends with the stirring declaration, typical of the time: "The intelligentsia and the workers: they are one!" This attitude is not so farfetched however; actors and artists, for example, both thought of themselves as members of the working class—superior ones to be sure—and petitioned the Frankfurt Assembly to be included in the regulations for workers' guilds. *Akten des volkswirtschaftlichen Ausschusses,* vol. 10, minutes for committee meeting, Apr. 28, 1849; vol. 17, petition of artists in Paderborn in Westphalia.

[19] Quoted by Ludwig Brunner, *Politische Bewegungen in Nürnberg im Jahre 1848 bis zu den Herbstereignisse,* Heidelberg, 1907, p. 37.

[20] Werner Sombart, *Socialism and the Social Movement in the Nineteenth Century,* New York, 1898, p. 9.

[21] Quoted by Conze, "Vom 'Pöbel' zum 'Proletariat,'" p. 361.

hours by this "excess of supply over demand for labor." [22] The factory workers were relatively secure, relatively well off, and they knew it: this accounts to a large extent for the conservative role the factory workers were to play in the coming revolution.

The members of the old established handicraft trades and the medieval guilds constituted the largest section of the working class. In Prussia in 1846 this group came to some 14 percent of the entire population; moreover, it was an expanding group, having increased in size by some 87 percent since 1816, that is, at a rate substantially greater than that at which the total population was growing. Elsewhere, in Bavaria, for example, and Baden, and most of all in Saxony, the guild handicraftsmen formed an even more dominant element in the working class. [23] This growth in size runs counter to the general picture of decline; indeed the declining position of the artisans was partly a result of their increased numbers.

Moreover the artisans as a group were changing in composition. Master craftsmen still exceeded their assistants in number but, whereas at the end of the Napoleonic Wars there were in Germany nearly twice as many masters as there were journeymen and apprentices, the proportion in 1846 was something like ten to nine. The increase in the number of journeymen and apprentices was an accelerating phenomenon, largely confined to the years after 1830. [24] The change led to a severe conflict of interest between the journeymen and the masters. The latter, fearing competition and overcrowding of the market, attempted to increase the difficulties of entering a trade, raising the standards of the entrance examinations or even establishing arbitrary limits on the numbers to be admitted. The journeymen found their way blocked, their hope of achieving the rank of master foiled and themselves condemned to a lower standard of living. [25] Opposition between masters and journeymen was not a new feature; many examples can be found in the eighteenth century and before. But then the journeymen remained among the strongest supporters of the guilds. Now they were ready to ignore, perhaps because they were forced to, the fixed course prescribed by guild regulations; they began to look for revolutionary remedies

---

[22] Banfield, *Industry of the Rhine*, vol. 2, p. 41.

[23] Schmoller, *Geschichte der deutschen Kleingewerbe*, pp. 65, 71, 139–140.

[24] Schmoller, *Geschichte der deutschen Kleingewerbe*, pp. 168–169. Stephan Born noted that the most important division in the German working class was between the masters and the journeymen. "There were," he remarked, "two age levels, not two classes." *Erinnerungen*, p. 136.

[25] One symptom of the increasing gap between masters and journeymen was that the latter now found it more difficult to find wives among the daughters of the former, who came to regard a mere journeyman as beneath their social position. E. F. Goldschmidt, *Die deutsche Handwerkerbewegung bis zum Siege der Gewerbefreiheit*, Munich, 1916, p. 12; Veit Valentin, *Frankfurt am Main und die Revolution von 1848–49*, Berlin, 1908, p. 104.

and lent an eager ear to the socialist agitators they met abroad, in Paris or Switzerland, during their *Wanderjahre*.[26] The masters were themselves divided. A few were prosperous, employing large numbers of journeymen or at least as many as the guild regulations would allow them, achieving a substantial income and enjoying a position of considerable importance in their communities, retaining only nominally the position of artisan.[27] Most, however, worked without assistants and had a standard of living little if any better than the mass of journeymen. There was great fear among the master craftsmen of sinking into the working class, of being, in the words of the petition the guilds of Eschwege in Electoral Hesse were to send to the Frankfurt Assembly, "forced into the abyss of the proletariat." [28]

In fact it seemed to some that the *Handwerkerstand* could itself be divided into two "classes." Gottfried Kinkel, the radical professor of history at the University of Bonn, summed up the position of the artisans in 1848 in the following words: [29]

> In the handicraft trades the struggle of capital and labor, the angry opposition of the aristocracy and the proletariat, rages more deeply than in the other estates. Half the artisans belongs to the bourgeoisie and visits the casinos . . . ; the other half sends its children to the poor house and lives a mean and miserable life on its daily earnings. Among the artisans themselves an aristocracy has arisen—namely, *the aristocracy of the better coat.*

The crisis of the handicraft trades was a complex one, going beyond the impoverishment of the artisans. A simple picture of decline is inadequate. Indeed the crisis did not hurt all artisans nor was it evident at all times. The years following the end of the Napoleonic Wars were ones of relative stability and even prosperity for the small trades; the decline set in only in the late 1830s, perhaps not until the financial crisis of 1839, and then more markedly in the 1840s, producing the unrest that broke out with the Silesian weavers' revolt of 1844 and fed into the revolutions of

[26] Rudolf Stadelmann, Wolfram Fischer, *Die Bildungswelt des deutchen Handwerkers um 1800, Studien zur Soziologie des Kleinbürgers im Zeitalter Goethes,* Berlin, 1955, pp. 70ff.

[27] Stadelmann and Fischer give biographical sketches of several such figures, *Bildungswelt,* pp. 117ff., 158ff., 168ff.

[28] *Akten des volkswirtschaftlichen Ausschusses,* vol. 12. The petition noted that those already belonging to the "proletariat" came "in large part . . . from the sick stem of the artisan class."

[29] *Handwerk, errette Dich! oder Was soll der deutsche Handwerker fordern und tun, um seinen Stand zu bessern?* Bonn, 1848, pp. 5–6. Kinkel dedicated his pamphlet to the Economic Committee of the Frankfurt Assembly and called for legal protection from the state for the handicraft trades together with direct material aid and the granting of the right of free association. These were in essence the demands of the German workers of 1848.

1848. Even then not all trades were affected. The blacksmith in the village, the mason and carpenter in the city, were still needed for local work. But tailors, shoemakers, printers, weavers and even cigar makers (the groups that were to be most active in 1848)—all of these could be and were hurt by competition from other cities and other countries and by the improvement in methods of production.[30] At the same time, the use of machines created new opportunities for mechanical artisans.

Two factors in particular undermined the position of the traditional handicraft trades: the foundation of the *Zollverein* in 1834 and the growth of the railways, which expanded rapidly from the first line in 1835 (five miles of track from Nuremberg to Fürth), so that by 1848 there were 3,000 kilometers and the railway age for Germany could be said to have begun.[31] Schmoller indeed saw the railways as the chief cause of the collapse of the small handicraft trades. For the competition of trade from the farthest reaches of the German states as well as increasingly cheap goods from Britain and Belgium attacked the position of many of the handicraft trades before industrial production was of great importance in Germany itself.[32]

The importance of trade accounts for the intensity and the particular focus of debates on laissez-faire in Germany. The interests which fought against free trade in Germany were different from those in England. There the controversy centered on the protection of agriculture. In Germany a greater range of positions could be found. Many acecpted Friedrich List's arguments for internal free trade and protection abroad. But the problem was complicated by the question of the protection of the handicraft trades and the preservation of the guild system. Indeed two concepts were involved though they were not always clearly separated by contemporaries. The German word *Gewerbefreiheit* means literally "trade freedom" and is perhaps best translated as "free entry into trades." This, for the workers and artisans, was a far more important issue than simply *Freihandel* or free trade in the English sense.[33] For many observers the troubles of the artisans started with the introduction of trade freedom, or free entry into trade, in the Rhineland by the French during the Napoleonic Wars and the subsequent reforms of Stein and Hardenberg, particularly the laws of 1810–1811 which sought to establish this free entry through-

---

[30] Among the collapsing trades was also that of the wig makers, a direct casualty of the decline of the fashions of the old regime.

[31] Jürgen Kuczynski, *Die wirtschaftlichen und sozialen Voraussetzungen der Revolution von 1848/49*, Berlin, 1948, p. 15.

[32] Schmoller, *Geschichte der deutschen Kleingewerbe*, p. 166; the railways changed in particular the pattern of the *Wanderjahre* of the journeymen, cf. Stadelmann and Fischer, *Bildungswelt*, p. 74.

[33] The German economic historian Lütge treats *Handelsfreiheit* as simply a subdivision of the general problem of *Gewerbefreiheit*. *Sozial- und Wirtschaftsgeschichte*, p. 329.

out Prussia. "From this time," declared one pamphleteer of 1848, "dates the impoverishment of the industrial class." [34]
The French and Prussian efforts to reform the guild system were in some respects not new; indeed they may be seen as the culmination of eighteenth century attempts at codifying guild laws, attempts which date back to the instructions of the Imperial Diet of 1731, calling on all the German states to reform the regulations of the guilds. And in spite of the French and Prussian reforms the guild system remained intact throughout most of Germany. Even in Prussia the laws of 1810–1811 were never thoroughly applied nor were they extended to the portions of Saxony acquired in 1815.

A fixed period of apprenticeship under a qualified master, several years of travel and work as a journeyman—the *Wanderjahre* much extolled by German poets of the period—and the passing of a set of stiff examinations were required for entry into most trades. There were a number of anomalies: often simple articles, a lock, a table, a loaf of bread, were made by guild members, supposedly the more skilled among the workers, while complex ones, a piano, for example, or scientific instruments, were not. Guild and nonguild workers were joined in similar or related jobs. Masons and carpenters belonged to guilds, but architects, construction workers and shipbuilders did not; the ironsmiths belonged but the machine builders did not. The Prussian regulations were codified in the industrial ordinance of January 17, 1845, which marked a further advance toward industrial freedom and was put through over the protests of many of the handicraft workers. The rights of guilds to limit the number of apprentices were abolished; their power of examination and control over the entry into trades was limited; the requirement of *Wanderjahre* for journeymen (and with it their guaranteed support) was dropped. Still the guilds remained in forty-two different trades, some new guilds were founded where none before had existed, and police permission was often substituted for guild membership as a requirement for the practicing of a trade. [35]

Elsewhere the guilds were in an even stronger position than they were in Prussia. The whole effect of the French reforms in Electoral Hesse was counteracted with the restoration of the guilds there in 1816. A Württem-

[34] C. F. Wesenfeld, *Beschränkte oder unbeschränkte Gewerbefreiheit, Eine Zeitfrage,* Berlin, 1848, p. 3. The laws of 1810–1811 are analyzed in detail in Kurt von Rohrscheidt, *Vom Zunftzwange zur Gewerbefreiheit, Eine Studie nach der Quellen,* Berlin, 1898, bks. 2 and 3; Hugo Roehl, *Beiträge zur Preussischen Handwerkerpolitik vom Allgemeinen Landrecht zur Allgemeinen Gewerbeordnung von 1845,* Leipzig, 1900, pp. 107–155.

[35] Goldschmidt, *Die deutschen Handwerkerbewegung,* pp. 10–11, 14–15; Schmoller, *Geschichte der deutschen Kleingewerbe,* pp. 83ff.; Roehl, *Beiträge,* pp. 251ff.; Hugo C. M. Wendel, *The Evolution of Industrial Freedom in Prussia 1845–1849,* Allentown, Pa., 1918, pp. 8, 23–47.

berg ordinance of 1838, while freeing thirteen trades from the requirement of guild membership, retained this requirement for some fifty others, including many of the most common. In Bavaria, with the exception of the Rhenish Palatinate which had been occupied by the French, the guild system remained and a law of 1834 limited the previously existing privileges of officials in granting exceptions to the entry regulations. In Saxony, in spite of its growing textile industry, guild regulations and compulsory guild membership were strictly enforced under a law of 1840, and the country retained the highest proportion of artisans to total population among the members of the *Zollverein*.[36]

Yet legal protection was probably inadequate to preserve the position of the guilds. The problem was not simply the impoverishment of the artisans. Beyond economic grievances lay the devotion of many of the members of the guilds to an entire way of life, a culture with deep roots in the past, an ethos which had established the guild members as men of status and stature in the community. Contemporary literature paid considerable attention to the moral effects of the collapse of the artisan guilds as well—the undermining of the restraint and educational benefits which a respected master provided for apprentices and journeymen. The 1840s saw the breakdown and threatened destruction of a system which had grown up in the later Middle Ages and survived largely untouched at least until the beginning of the nineteenth century.[37]

There was also throughout Germany more than ample cause for the workers to demand simple, physical improvement in their standard of living. Many were hungry; many lived in abject poverty.[38] Long hours (12 per day was a minimum and 14 or even 16 quite usual) and low wages were a common and constant complaint. In Berlin, for example, wages ranged from less than 1 thaler per week (approximately 84 cents at the contemporary exchange rates) to 5 or 6 thaler in the most skilled and exclusive trades. Printers, who were considered to be well off among the handicraft workers, received 3 thaler, 15 silbergroschen per week, and this

---

[36] Hamerow, *Restoration, Revolution, Reaction*, pp. 26–29; Rudolf Bovensiepen, *Die kurhessische Gewerbepolitik und die wirtschaftliche Lage des zünftigen Handwerks in Kurhessen von 1816–1867*, Halle, 1907, p. 13; Richard Lipinski, *Die Geschichte der sozialistischen Arbeiterbewegung in Leipzig*, Leipzig, 1931, vol. 1, p. 46.

[37] For a description of guild ethos and guild customs, see Stadelmann and Fischer, *Bildungswelt*, ch. 2, "Das Ethos des Handwerkerstandes"; also Rudolf Wissell, *Des alten Handwerks-Recht und Gewohnheit*, Berlin, 1929, 2 vols.

[38] Horror stories abound: one mother in Vienna was reported to have cooked her dead baby and served it to her starving children. At the same time the Viennese press reported a dinner for the wealthy with strawberries imported from Italy at £1 apiece. C. Edmund Maurice, *The Revolutionary Movement of 1848–9 in Italy, Austria-Hungary and Germany*, London, 1887, p. 210.

at a time when the barest minimum upon which it was possible to live for a single worker with neither wife nor family was estimated at upward of 2 thaler per week. Many were attempting to exist below this minimum.[39]

The working class of Germany was thus faced with genuine grievances but with a system of work and organization in the various trades which hampered any efforts at improvement. It was the artisan far more than the factory worker that was hurt by this system. Moreover the guild structure was in part a bar against efforts at self-improvement. The master stood in a semipatriarchal relationship to his journeymen and apprentices and it was considered almost a sign of ingratitude for the latter to complain against his regime.[40] This spirit of servitude extended to the state and went back to the days of Frederick the Great and Joseph II. Indeed the workers looked primarily to the state to regulate their position, to maintain the old trades and guilds. Yet the state, as the Prussian industrial ordinance of 1845 indicated, was increasingly unable or unwilling to do this.

Such was the position of the workers when faced with the economic crisis of the mid-1840s. The potato famine of 1845 was followed by grain failures of 1846 and 1847. By the middle of the latter year the price of wheat in the Rhineland was 250 percent higher than it had been in 1845; rye was up by 300 percent and potatoes by 425 percent.[41] Wages did not keep pace with prices but remained roughly constant. State aid, though immediately sought by the workers, was slow in coming. When it came it consisted mainly in the alteration of tariffs in favor of imports and the prohibition of the exportation of foodstuffs, together with such question-ably beneficial measures as the publication of recipes for baking bread from grass and the holding of public barbecues to encourage the eating of horse-meat. The bad harvest of 1847 coincided with a considerable financial and trade crisis which began in England and spread throughout the con-tinent. From August 1847 through January 1848 some 245 firms and 12 banks failed in Germany alone.[42] To high prices and low wages was added the threat, and often the reality, of unemployment.

The workers responded with a flood of petitions for government pro-tection, with increased interest in the workers' associations and at least the slogans of socialism, and with a readiness for revolution.

---

[39] Ernst Dronke, *Berlin,* Berlin, 1953 (first published in 1846), pp. 229ff.; Born, *Erinnerungen,* pp. 123–124; Hermann Meyer, *1848, Studien zur Geschichte der deutschen Revolution,* Darmstadt, 1949, p. 80; Wilhelm Friedensburg, *Stephan Born und die Organisationsbestrebungen der Berliner Arbeiterschaft bis zum Ber-liner Arbeiterkongress,* Leipzig, 1923, p. 5.

[40] Born, *Erinnerungen,* p. 124.

[41] Oscar J. Hammen, "Economic and Social Factors in the Prussian Rhineland in 1848," *American Historical Review,* vol. 54 (1949), pp. 828–830.

[42] Max Wirth, *Geschichte der Handelskrisen,* Frankfurt am Main, 1858, p. 457.

5. THE CYCLE OF LIFE

The daily living conditions of the poor deserve to be observed in greater detail. For many Europeans the onset of industrialization meant, as one writer has put it, a time of "grave social damage." We need to know precisely how they were affected by changing societal conditions and why. The basic demographic fact was a general increase of the European population, due both to a rising birthrate in the latter half of the eighteenth century and to a declining deathrate thereafter. But this meant, among other things, that more people were born to poverty and condemned to live in poverty. Even when there was plenty of food, it was often poorly distributed; and even where there was ostensibly enough housing, it was usually crowded and unsanitary. In general terms this may be familiar to us. Yet the details should be no less unsettling to anyone who reads the following accounts with concern, and who remembers that most of the world's population has never passed beyond the confines of poverty.

Olwen Hufton reconstructs what she gloomily calls a "hierarchy of wretchedness." It is encouraging to note that the eighteenth century was somewhat less distressed than the seventeenth; the population was better protected from plague and famine than before. But if a minimum of subsistence became more certain after 1700, the hardships of everyday life were little diminished. The squalid conditions which Hufton describes were all the more keenly felt by those who endured them because of the ostentatious wealth of the few who knew no deprivation. All in all, it is a pitiless tale of unrelieved labor, shared alike by men, women, and children from early childhood to the crippling humiliations of disease or advanced age.

S. G. Checkland confines his inquiry to the changes wrought by industry on the fertility patterns and living conditions of the English. Whereas workers often married young, the combination of long hours, female labor, contraception, and urban crowding kept the birthrate from spiraling, and the deathrate remained relatively high in the cities. Still, despite the steady accumulation of filth and refuse, the industrial towns continued to attract the rural population, and the problems of physical and mental hygiene were further compounded. For the first time, as a result, there occurred a major exodus of "respectable" people from the inner city, leaving the congested streets and alleyways of certain quarters to those who wallowed in poverty. The magnitude of this migration confirms how serious the problems created by pauperism had become by the mid-nineteenth century.

William L. Langer stresses that working conditions had always been bad; industry only made them more visible and, in some cases, increased the hectic tempo of labor. He finds one important new factor introduced by mechanization: the instability of urban employment. On the European mainland, he estimates, well over half of the entire industrial labor force might be left unemployed at certain times. The easy availability of cheap labor, in turn, kept wages depressed and held the mass of population at a level of bare subsistence. Langer's account corroborates those of Hufton and Checkland in most particulars, and it suggests that European society had reached its nadir before the second half of the nineteenth century.

The only possible comfort which one might derive from reading such a lamentable record is the thought that sometimes things must get worse before they get better. While this view may mollify our own feelings, it would have been of precious little value to the generations of humanity who lived through the beginning phases of industrialization. We can never know, of course, just how much of the misery described here was in some sense necessary and how much was simply the consequence of negligence or insensitivity. But it is small wonder that some of those who lived through these times asked themselves whether it was all worthwhile.

OLWEN HUFTON

Life and Death Among
the Very Poor

The economist Malthus, concerned in the nineteenth century with the problem of maintaining the precarious balance between population and supply, saw as the only answer the two natural checks, famine and disease, which rising at intervals applied a ruthless shears to a growing populace whose demands were rapidly outstripping food production. He might well have chosen the latter half of the seventeenth century and the first decade of the eighteenth as classic crises of the type he delineated. Indeed, so general was harvest failure in almost all the countries of Europe that historians have conjectured a change in climate, have noted the growth of glaciers— a little ice age—and attributed the hardship to a meteorological upheaval. The debate remains undecided but certainly the closing years of the century did see an extraordinary run of disasters for European food supplies from Castile and Sicily in the south to Finland in the north; striking alike Alpine villages, the cornlands of Poland and even the chestnut crop of the Tarn. In the north the enemy was damp—rain which caused the corn to rot in the fields before it reached fruition or which brought the grain weevil, the *hanneton* of Normandy, to consume the crop; in the Mediterranean lands the enemy was drought, which—ironically—produced a bumper wine harvest but which reduced corn production to one of the lowest recorded levels and brought with it to Spain and France plagues of grasshoppers which descended like locusts and stripped the fields. In the train of famine came disease. It is almost a truism to point out the enhanced susceptibility of an undernourished population to epidemics, to typhus, enteric fevers, influenza and so on; but as well as these, the food crisis of the late seventeenth century was accompanied by the killer of all killers, the bubonic plague, a disease which could strike the nourished as well as the under-

From *The Eighteenth Century* by Alfred Cobban, 1969. Copyright © Thames & Hudson, London. Used with permission of McGraw-Hill Book Company.

nourished and which had a devastating effect upon town populations in particular. The coincidence of serious plague outbreaks with protracted harvest failure leaves no doubt that these two events were in some way associated. But whether this was because at such times the rat hosts of the fleas which carried the plague migrated to towns and granaries in search of food, or whether the plague fleas multiplied most rapidly in the same climatic conditions which caused harvest failure is still not known. Great Britain was last struck by plague in 1665 and though the years immediately after 1693 were known as the "seven ill years" because of the heavy death toll from typhus, France and Spain suffered far more from plague in the 'nineties. Then in 1708 came the outbreak in Poland which spread through Silesia, Brandenburg, the Baltic countries and Scandinavia, halving the population of Danzig, fractionalizing those of Copenhagen, Königsberg, Prague, Cracow, Stockholm and Helsinki, leaving eleven thousand vacant farms in East Prussia alone and pressing west through northwest Germany in 1712, to Austria, Bohemia and Bavaria in 1713 and there petering out mysteriously before making its route southwards to Italy.

The combined effects of dearth and disease arrested population growth and in some areas led to decline. The impact was nowhere quite the same. Most probably the population of Europe was slightly higher at the end of the seventeenth century than it was at the beginning though it was differently distributed. By 1700 Spain had 932 *despoblados*—deserted villages —mostly gathered in the arid interior whilst the littoral, healthier and better watered, bore a relatively prosperous air. After 1640 the population of England either remained static or experienced an increase, slight in comparison to the estimated growth of the previous century, and the same could be said of Italy and France though that tentatively in the light of very defective figures. But beyond doubt, the food shortage and the great epidemics both checked population growth and caused a severe dislocation in the economic life of Europe.

A CENTURY OF SUFFERING

One can do scant justice in a few sentences to the effects of famine and epidemic upon the lives of the European populace. The small landowner was forced to consume seed needed for the next sowing and to borrow in order to plant the next crop; his mounting indebtedness to the large landowner from whom he had to borrow corn at interest until repayment of the debt might even force him to part with his land. This is only one aspect. Women rendered infertile by starvation, an increase in the number of still births, and family units cut down by quite minor diseases in face of lowered resistance are others. Nor did the countryside alone suffer, for local industries were seriously affected by the shrinkage of rural markets in times of dearth when the small peasants, forced to spend their entire income on food, simply ceased to buy other goods. Small towns in affected areas found themselves flooded with the starving and destitute from the surrounding countryside who came hoping to draw attention to their plight. The towns of the plain of Languedoc, for example, became the burial ground of the mountain dwellers of the Massif Central who, disease ridden and weak from lack of food, swarmed out of the barren hills and perished, mere names and a date in a death register.

The effects of plague or virulent epidemic were no less terrifying—indeed perhaps they were more so for no one knew where and who they would strike, the flea being no respecter of persons—and if the rat-ridden hovels of the poor rendered them the most susceptible, the rich were not guaranteed immunity. The best account of the psychological aspects of an outbreak remains Defoe's imaginative *Journal of the Plague Year*. It depicts the rich fleeing, panic stricken, from the scene of the outbreak, the suspension of trade, the inadequacy of the attempts to seal off the victims, the carelessness of the poor who did not hesitate to invade abandoned houses for loot and deal in old clothes and objects which may well have been contaminated. He also touches on another point of relevance—the revival of religious intensity in face of impending death. One of the strange ironies about the late seventeenth century is that at a time when intellectuals were taking their first tentative steps along a road that was to lead them to disbelief, the larger part of the populace was moving in the opposite direction. Processions of penitent sinners, barefoot and sometimes indulging in self-flagellation, led by bishops and clerics, were designed to wring mercy from the deity; and when the plague had passed, splendid ceremonies brought together dignitaries of the Church, town officials and magistrates in flowing robes, with *Te Deums* and orations to offer humble thanks for delivery.

It is certainly not surprising that every country in Europe between 1660 and 1685 found it necessary to reconstitute its methods of according poor relief—a fact we shall examine more closely later—and that it is from this period that date the foundation of many of the great European *hospices,* for example of Dijon and Lyons, whilst in Spain the Hospital de la Caridad in Seville serves as a good instance, decorated by Murillo with scenes to recall the love of God for the destitute, his infinite mercy towards the poor and afflicted and the shelter offered by the Church to those in need. Splendid buildings, founded on private philanthropy yet insufficient to cope with the extent of the misery with which they were designed to contend, remain as the expression of yet another paradox—that for all its magnificence, at root *le grand siècle* was a century of poverty, human suffering and squalor.

THE PLAGUE RELENTS

The eighteenth century proper presents a different picture. The hardship of the late seventeenth century and the first decade of the eighteenth is without parallel thereafter in western Europe. There were, it is true, occasional years of shortage scattered at intervals through the period but the cumulative effect of year after year of scanty harvests had vanished forever. This factor provides the single most cogent explanation of the sudden upward movement of population in the eighteenth century. Throughout Europe the mortality rates declined rapidly not in normal years but because of the abatement of the great crises: "the peaks rather than the plateau of mortality were lowered." Secondly, with the mysterious dying out of the plague—the last outbreaks were in Marseilles and Provence in 1721–22 and Messina in 1743 and both were strictly localized— the greatest killer of adults and children alike had vanished. Other epidemics struck with less virulence and were predominantly infantile often leaving the family unit reduced but essentially capable of repairing the breach.

One would wish to create the impression of a population that breathed more easily for its liberation from famine and plague without overstressing the extent of that liberation. The population of Europe and especially the poorest sections remained a prey to typhus, enteric fevers (typhoid in particular), small pox, measles and diphtheria; the first two reigned perennially in all large European cities—indeed in London they killed a minimum of one thousand people a year and perhaps only a small proportion of those afflicted died: and in Sweden ten to twelve thousand people of a population of under two million perished annually from typhus and smallpox. Known as putrid, malignant or intermittent fever, depending on the severity of the outbreak, typhus, transmitted by the bite of a body louse, was predominantly the disease of the poor and associated with the depths of human misery, undernourishment and infestation with body lice. Gracious as doubtless were the public buildings of the great European cities, the streets remained filthy with refuse, and drainage was totally inadequate. Berlin could be smelt six miles away: Linnaeus compared the stench of Hamburg to an open sewer. In Stockholm, Amsterdam and Venice stagnant water and damp dwelling houses offered an open invitation to typhoid and malaria. Every city had its share of ramshackle dwellings, cramped together in medieval confusion, sometimes spilling over the still present medieval town walls. In continental Europe all except the rich let out the upper parts and the cellars of their houses to the poor. Whole families lived within the confines of one room, sleeping on straw, their only possessions a few blankets and battered cooking pots. Hygiene in rural areas was if anything even less apparent. Dwelling in one-roomed cottages where light and air were secondary considerations to warmth, and huddled together often with their animals for the heat their bodies afforded, the laboring poor lived in habitations that were an abnegation of all standards of cleanliness. To read Bishop Berkeley on the cabin of the Irish peasant filled with pigs, stinking children and animal excrement, or Doctor Bagot on the odors that issued from the Breton farm laborer's cottage, is to understand why if the winters were in any way prolonged and the family longer confined than usual the death toll was heavy, for these tiny dwellings were breeding grounds for disease. But though perhaps more perished from typhus than ever before, and though mortality rates in many large cities exceeded the birth rate, in no way did they approach the numbers annihilated in the previous century. Only one French province, Brittany, suffered a demographic setback from *la maladie de Brest,* typhus, which originated in the ports and spread rapidly through the hinterland of chronically underfed beings, whilst in England only the great towns were seriously affected.

A DEMOGRAPHIC PUSH

Indeed, to explore the conditions of extreme misery in which the population expansion of the eighteenth century took place is to render yet more horrible the demographic stagnation of the late seventeenth. Every child that was born jeopardized the life of its mother, and the female relatives or the village wise woman who assisted at the labor, were powerless to save her if the presentation of the fetus was in any way abnormal. The entry for "accouchement" in the *Encyclopédie Méthodique de la Jurisprudence* gives at least one explanation for the larger number of crippled and deformed who counted among the poor in the eighteenth century:

> One sees men who are blind, crippled or physically handicapped from birth owing to the ignorance of the midwife who pulled or pressed too hard bones still soft and membraneous with the result that many are mentally or physically damaged for life.

French doctors, given the opportunity in the 1770s, inveighed against midwives who were in fact well-meaning murderesses of mother and child, their only knowledge based on observations, their only implements farm tools. Small wonder that the hazards of birth and infantile proneness to disease caused the young baby to be regarded with a singularly dispassionate eye by its parents who reserved affection for the older children who had survived the rigors of infancy.

If disease and conditions of reproduction make the phenomenon of expansion remarkable, the quality of the diet in the eighteenth century makes it more so. In spite of the improvements in agriculture the Lancashire cotton worker and the Yorkshire woollen worker lived largely on a monotonous diet of potatoes and oatcake, and could count themselves amongst the best fed in Europe. Even if meat and protein foods were conspicuously lacking from their food they lived substantially better than the peasant farmer of central France who lived largely on boiled chestnuts or the Breton with his *bouillie*—a form of gruel made largely from buckwheat, a cereal now reserved for feeding poultry—or the Spaniard on his grease-soaked rye bread. In any country meat appeared only on the table of the relatively wealthy.

Yet in spite of the circumstances, the population growth of the eighteenth century was unprecedented not so much because of the rate of increase as for the fact that the upward movement started from a higher level and that this was *maintained*. It was also markedly uneven. To point out that Europe as a whole sustained a growth of 20 percent between 1700 and 1750 and 30 percent between 1750 and the end of the century is to overlook a variety of regional changes. Broadly speaking the demographic push showed itself first in southern not northern Europe, in Spain, Italy and the Mediterranean littoral of France, west of Marseilles —Catalonia, for example, doubled its population between 1718 and 1788 —but the growth had slackened by the 1780s when that of northern Europe was accelerating and indeed was very rapidly to overtake it. From 1750 to 1800 Scandinavia, the Low Countries, Russia, England and Wales, Ireland and Germany underwent an annual growth of about one percent (higher in Russia and Ireland) whilst Spain, Italy and France sustained one of less than one-half percent per annum. By the end of the century the population of Britain had risen from about 5,500,000 in 1700 to 9,200,000, and that of France from 18,000,000 in 1715 to over 26,000,000, to quote only two examples. But population figures alone are meaningless; the significant question to ask is how European society responded to this protracted growth.

THE DEMAND FOR FOOD

Very evidently the fate of Europe hinged upon the two basic factors of feeding and employing this rapidly growing population. For unless the supply of food could be increased sufficiently then the periodic devastation caused by famine would eventually be replaced by long term malnutrition and even before that stage had been reached the price of food would have risen in view of the greater demand. If potentialities of employment were not enlarged, either by bringing under cultivation new land or by developing new industrial resources, then the result would be underemployment, a ridiculous subdivision of existing holdings, and a surplus labor force whose wages would not rise to counteract the rise in prices. Put another way, the population explosion made more efficient and intensive farming essential everywhere and, in many cases, industrialization crucial to the well-being of the state concerned.

Moreover, though one should perhaps not overstress this, even in those countries which were developing most rapidly and which could provide a solution to the problems presented by population growth, economic gains were often secured at the expense of those displaced in the course of change—the artisan in an industry rendered uncompetitive or redundant in a world of larger scale industries and the rural worker, both male and female, when domestic industry dried up, or those turned off the land by enclosure in the pursuit of agrarian progress. In Great Britain especially, this period might be regarded simply as one of painful adjustment to changing circumstances: the gradual transition, for example, from the family as the basic unit of production to larger scale manufacturing which took production out of the home and hence disrupted the whole pattern of the family economy. Moreover each country had special problem areas: those which were chronically overpopulated in relation to their resources and disgorged their excess into adjoining areas—often with the effect of universalizing poverty. The Irish, for example, refugees from misery, were already beginning to pour into London and the larger English cities to infest the cellars and attics with their tubercular lice-covered bodies, creating their own ghettos of poverty where the rich never set foot.

France had the problem nearer to hand. The north and northeast, the wealthy cornlands of the Beauce, the great areas of viticulture of which Bordeaux and Marseilles were the ports must be balanced against the infertile Massif Central, the Alps and the Pyrenees all of them reservoirs of men and human suffering where available land was only too readily saturated by increased demand. Something under a fifth of the destitute of the Mediterranean littoral were actually indigenous: the rest were drawn from the desolate hills to the north. In Marseilles it has been estimated that a settled population of 106,000 supported a floating population of 30,000 who reserved the profits of their efforts to buttress a minute holding more likely than not in the barren Dauphiné.

"THE COMMON SORT"

Such circumstances make more readily understandable an apparent contradiction: that it was fully possible for progress and relative emancipation from famine and plague to produce a greater number of poor than ever before. A starving population generally speaking cannot reproduce itself, an undernourished one has no difficulty in so doing. In the hierarchy of wretchedness there is a world of difference between the man who is literally starving—even for a short period—and he who is merely undernourished all the year round. To understand this particular subtlety of the problem of poverty is to understand something of the difference in many European countries between the early eighteenth century and the end. For if by the end of the period the number of those fitting into the first category had almost vanished, the other had multiplied beyond all proportion. Indeed, the most significant consequence of the population explosion was the broadening of the base of the social pyramid more widely than ever before and this was to endow the eighteenth century with its most distinctive feature: proliferation of those whom contemporaries referred to in a vocabulary of distaste as "the meaner kind," "the common sort," the "mob," "rabble" or *canaille*. They were in reality the laboring poor but with a crucial difference for not only were they now scattered throughout the countryside, docile peasants whose occasional *jacqueries* burnt themselves out beyond the pale of civilization, but increasingly they were gathered in towns. All European societies, both at the beginning and end of this period, were predominantly agrarian and moreover in every country the population expansion, as far as it has been analyzed, appears to have been a rural phenomenon. Certainly in the large cities, and often in the less considerable towns, mortality rates continued to be higher than the birth rates but if urban growth was not self-generated it occurred notwithstanding because of the heavy rural influx. London perhaps provides an extreme case: there the number of deaths seems to have surpassed that of births annually until 1790, yet the population rose from about 674,500 in 1700 to 900,000 in 1801. Nevertheless smaller cities like Strasbourg, Montpellier, Nottingham or Leghorn would provide equally good examples. Flooded by immigrants from the surrounding rural area and often almost totally without the means to employ them, they were impotent to arrest the process. Driven thither in a search for employment, attention, relief or because of the enhanced possibilities of criminal pursuits, the intensely mobile poor swarmed into the cities and small towns; teeming humanity gathered together, depressed, emotionally unstable, volatile, potentially dangerous, something for governments to fear or repress. Between the peasant risings of distress in the wake of the great famine of the later seventeenth century and the vicious vindictiveness of the Gordon Riots lies something of the difference. It is expressed eloquently in the works of the Le Nain brothers on the one hand and Hogarth on the other. The first, in the 1640s, saw the poverty of the small French peasant and painted exactly what they saw, without pausing to moralize: they saw suffering and patient resignation, acceptance of starvation, pain and deprivation. The other, unparalleled as the painter of the urban poor, caught an element of the times. He depicted the poor as vicious, cruel and immoral: his subjects were alive struggling beings responding vigorously to the hardship of their surroundings, anaesthetizing themselves to the ugliness of their lives with cheap alcohol or eking out a pitiful income with prostitution or pilfering or both. Often what he saw as the causes of poverty were perhaps the results, but no one conveyed better than he the conglomeration of human misery that made up the back streets of London, "the great wen." That in Europe in the eighteenth century the working classes became the dangerous classes is a meaningful juxtaposition, and 1848, when urban revolutions shook Europe and brought down governments, is perhaps the most natural corollary of events started in our period. Nor is it insignificant that Hogarth's harlot like Cleland's Fanny or Restif's *La Paysanne Pervertie* is a country girl corrupted by the evil influences of the city—a common enough literary device but one which became increasingly frequent in works of this period —for to begin to discuss the condition of the people in the eighteenth century one must inevitably begin with the victims of changing conditions in the countryside: with the subsistence farmer, those of whom Arthur Young remarked in his "Travels in France" they "marry on the *idea* of an inheritance," a tiny unit fractionalized by each generation; and with the even commoner figure, the day laborer looking for work in an overcrowded market; and with their wives and sons and daughters and perhaps even their grandchildren. However else one sees the problems of the eighteenth century one must see them as family problems and begin with the recognition that the family economy of the working classes was their natural economy—the family needed the work of each of its component members to support the whole. Hence, broadly speaking, the man who had sufficient land to provide for the wants of his family had sufficient to employ that family. In the event of his not having enough, he or his family or both must seek an alternative source of income. In the case of the day laborer or the wage earner this was doubly true for nowhere in Europe could the wage earner expect to earn more than he needed for his own personal maintenance. Indeed, at the beginning of our period this factor was an integral part of current economic theory, an aspect of mercantilism in which the wage was allied with the costs of production and hence must be kept low if goods were to remain competitive. But laying theory aside, one does not need to look any further than the state of the labor market, overcrowded to an unprecedented extent, to appreciate that one did not need to pay the laborer more than a minimal personal subsistence rate and that he was lucky if he could command even that. To do so he had perhaps uprooted himself, travelled vast distances, possibly leaving his family behind to fend for themselves and his situation became less and less tenable as more and more joined his ranks.

Indeed, one can almost make the generalization that nowhere in Europe did any section of the working class stand a chance of bettering their condition in their lifetime and in southern Europe at least an actual deterioration in living standards took place between 1750 and the end of the century. The remark must be qualified, however, because in certain industries at certain times—good instances would be the English weavers in the period immediately following improvements which accelerated spinning output, and the building workers of expanding Barcelona who could command the best salaries of their kind in Spain—temporary demand made an exception to this rule.

WOMEN AND CHILDREN

If one takes as a point of departure the limited earning capacity of the working man, one must then consider not only his potentialities for employment but also those of his wife and children. In most societies the young unmarried man was not a real problem for poor law administrators, he could make out—perhaps not with ease—but he was one of the most mobile sections of the population in his search for work, and he was the one whom uprooting caused the least trouble and who had the least to restrain him. The same could not be said of the married man or of the wives and daughters of laboring men. Marriage and procreation brought a whole series of new problems; there was certainly no spirit of academic dispassion behind the demand, reiterated throughout the French *cahiers* of grievances of 1789, that extra taxes should be placed on bachelors for the support of the children of large families.

In any society in the eighteenth century, women of the working classes were expected to work to support themselves both when single and married: "Consider, my dear girl," runs *A Present for a Serving Maid* (1743) "that you have no portions and endeavor to supply the deficiencies of fortune by mind. You cannot expect to marry in such a manner as neither of you shall have occasion to work and none but a fool will take a wife whose bread must be earned solely by his labor and who will contribute nothing towards it herself." In fact they had no option but to do so. Generally speaking female employment fitted into three main categories. The first, restricted to the unmarried, was domestic service, perhaps the most highly sought after employment by the unmarried girl because it made her independent of the family and she needed little skill or tuition —though Irish women in London and the Savoyardes in Paris were considered too barbaric to perform even the most menial tasks in the home.

Secondly, domestic industry of several kinds which could be carried out either by the unmarried or the married but which, in the latter case especially, was of crucial significance to the family economy. The commonest forms of this were, of course, spinning wool or cotton and the manufacture of lace. The first might or might not form part of an integrated family manufacture—the children helping in the initial stages of washing and carding the raw material, the women in spinning, the men in weaving. In this case the woman was not paid a wage as such: rather was the whole family awarded a single sum for the completed cloth and the family, it should be remembered, was up to the end of the period the commonest unit of production.

Elsewhere domestic industry formed a useful supplement to work in the fields for the women of the household. To textile spinning should be added the production of lace which in northern France, Belgium, Holland and parts of southern England came a very close second to spinning in the numbers it occupied. The value of the lace lay almost entirely in the handiwork, for the quantity of linen or silk thread involved was slight. Sometimes this was a skill taught by religious orders with the express purpose of making the wives and daughters of the poor self-supporting, and in France and Belgium often the profits from the sale of the work went in large part to the religious who used it to train more workers whilst the lacemaker herself earned a pittance for her labors. Domestic industry was essentially for women *at home* and herein lay much of its value. The baby could lie in the cradle and the smallest children play on the floor whilst the mother kept to her wheel or attended to her lace bobbins. If she fell behind in her tasks they could be completed late into the night, whilst the children slept. But changes were taking place which were to threaten the continuance of this situation—at least as far as spinning was concerned. For the distribution of the raw material and collection of the finished product an elaborate network of travelling merchants was involved, a lengthy and irregular process. Little wonder that spinning was the first process to be subject to industrial change, an important point for no changes were to disrupt more the family economy. They were to take the spinner out of the house and destroy the family as a unit of production and hence to render employment in some cases very difficult for married women. Early town factories in England in fact accorded preference to the unmarried.

By far the commonest kind of female labor throughout the world at this time was simply the lowest kind of heavy and distasteful tasks such as load carrying. Nothing in fact was too menial. They carried soil, heavy vegetables to market, water, coal—anything. The terraces cut into the steep mountain hillsides of Spain, France and Italy were kept watered by thousands of women who daily made the steep ascent with buckets— in the Auvergne it was estimated that the climb could take anything up to three hours and often they performed as many as three a day. The Scottish miners employed their wives as "fremd bearers" to carry coal from the face. The mines at this period had no winding gear and the women had to climb with their burden up a spiral staircase winding around the walls of the shaft. Sometimes the return journey could take up to four hours. The man was of course paid a single wage and if unmarried, had to find a girl to act as his beast of burden to whom he paid a part of his earnings. Irish women, unable to sew or clean who found their way to London acted as load carriers or helped their husbands work as navvies. Elsewhere women found employment as rag sorters, cinder sifters, refuse collectors, assistants to masons and bricklayers and so on.

Easily the most mobile section of the population in their search for work, women, especially unmarried ones, would travel many miles in the hope of finding employment. Annually women from North Wales left their homes to work on the fruit harvest in Middlesex; carrying a load on their backs into the London markets and sometimes walking anything up to fifteen miles a day during the fruit season. Moreover they had walked from Wales. One must imagine the wives and daughters of the poor condemned to a lifetime of drudgery in an attempt to keep themselves and their offspring fed. Women enclosed in tiny airless rooms, poring over lace bobbins, working late into the night by the light of candles until their eyes would serve them no more. Blindness was the likeliest fate of the lacemaker. Even those who worked at home and delivered the fruit of their labors to a wandering merchant could not afford to be irregular in their production of work. Washing and mending, cooking and cleaning had to be done afterwards and childbirth had to be accomplished with the minimum of disruption. It is not surprising that they were old women by their late twenties.

The question of child labor was perhaps of even greater importance than that of female labor. The wage of the average working man was enough for his personal upkeep and perhaps, if his wife was employed, for that of two young children. Keen social observers were quick to point out that real trouble started for families with the advent of the third child. This consideration alone entitled the silk and diamond workers of Antwerp to some slight relief, but the situation was too common for the funds of public assistance to allow help to every man in this state.

The advent of child labor has often been depicted as the outstanding evil of the factory system and of the tragic plight of many children in the early factories there can be no doubt. But to approach the question from this angle is to view it with twentieth century eyes, for life was hard for the children of laboring men in all European countries in the eighteenth century. They were expected to become self-supporting *as soon as possible* so as to relieve the strain on the family budget. Indeed, the children of the poor were committed as soon as they left the cradle to an unremitting struggle for survival in a hostile world. It is possible that children in areas of domestic industry were singularly privileged. The tasks they performed were unskilled and demanded little physical strength. In manufacturing areas of England and Belgium and Normandy children of seven and upwards were relatively self-supporting. Even four-year-olds were capable of certain jobs. Samuel Crompton's eldest son, George, has left a telling account of the kind of work performed by weavers' children.

> I recollect that soon after I was able to walk I was employed in the cotton manufacture. My mother used to bat the cotton wool on a wire riddle. It was then put into a deep brown mug with a strong ley of soap suds. My mother then tucked up my petticoats about my waist and put me into the tub to tread upon the cotton at the bottom. When a second riddleful was batted I was lifted out, it was placed in the mug and I again trod it down. This process was continued until the mug became so full that I could no longer safely stand in it when a chair was placed besides it and I held on by the back.

The cotton was then dried and carded by the grandmother and mother.

In Belgium children earned enough to support themselves after the age of seven by emptying silk cocoons. But in most communities and especially heavily agrarian communities child employment was almost totally lacking. Bishop Berkeley might fulminate against the Irish peasant who left his eight-year-old child idle in his nakedness and poverty and point out the glowing example of the Protestant Dutch who were held to make a child self-supporting at the age of five, but unless rural industry was in any way developed or the family holding large, there was little to employ women and children apart from a few days' work at hay-making and harvest. When such circumstances prevailed the question of how the family eked out a living assumes complex proportions, unanswerable in simple terms and demanding recourse to hosts of specific examples.

MIGRANT LABOR

The poor did not sit back and let starvation overtake them: amongst the laboring poor there had always been a tradition of mobility, of temporary or seasonal migration into areas offering short-term work prospects and during the period under review they were to assume important proportions. The most extensive migrations doubtless took place from the most mountainous regions of Europe: the Pyrenees, the Alps, the Massif Central, the Ardennes, Dolomites, Snowdonia and parts of Ireland, for several reasons of which the most cogent was that climatic conditions made all-the-year-round work impossible and secondly a limit was sooner reached on the amount of land that could be brought under cultivation. The mountain dweller was a traditional migrant though a temporary one; what was new was the extent of these migrations and what was striking was the extent to which they served to buttress an uneconomic unit which on the surface would not have appeared to afford the owner or exploiter enough to live. But if the adult males could earn something extra during the dead season, or for a part of the year, then the family income could be stretched a little further. Hence the small peasant of the Campine or the Ardennes, in Belgium or Luxembourg was prepared to make a weary biennial walk to Hungary or a shorter but less lucrative one to serve as a navvy in Amsterdam: the Pyrenees emptied annually in the winter of men who went into Spain or to Bordeaux offering themselves as rough laborers. The Irish wended a rowdy way into London or the large English cities: men and women worked as navvies or—more commonly in the case of women—as load carriers of water or coal or groceries. These people embarked with none of Dick Whittington's illusions that the streets of the capital were paved with gold. The step was one of distress, a recognition that they could not earn a living at home. A perfect example of how initiative and ingenuity could together keep families alive under the most adverse circumstances is afforded by the Massif Central. Every year thousands of men left the villages leaving their wives behind to care for the holding which often meant merely picking up chestnuts as they fell, one by one from the trees. Some walked to Spain; others to the Midi to work on the grape harvest; some to Portugal as woodcutters, a winter occupation; some to Normandy and Brittany as pedlars of pins and needles; some to Paris and indeed almost every part of France as chimney sweeps. Some stayed away for a few years—the levellers of hills (*terrassiers*) and tinkers who made the long trek to Spain. Wages were perhaps lower in Spain than France but the high metallic content of the Spanish currency gave it a peculiarly high value in France where there was an acute shortage of *specie*. Others only stayed away a few months. Each village had a traditional destination, traditional employments, traditional times for departure and return and traditional routes and stops which were closely followed. The degree of organization involved was impressive. Those who returned from a four or five year stay in Spain perhaps hoped never to leave again and to use the capital they had amassed to eke out a miserable living. Those who merely spent five months in Normandy or Paris perhaps hoped to do no more than keep themselves and pay their taxes and spend the rest of the year on their meager land. In whole villages in the Auvergne taxes were paid in *pesos* and significantly this was one of the first areas to be depopulated in the nineteenth century.

THE BRINK OF RUIN

The family economy was very obviously a frail edifice from which no one stone could be removed without jeopardizing the continuing existence of the whole. Again, this is best illustrated by example: Davies (*The Case of the Labourers in Husbandry*) cites the case of a family of seven persons whose yearly income was £ 39 17s. 4d. and whose yearly expenditure on basic necessaries was £ 39 14s. 4d. Although the mother of the family earned only 4½ d. a day, without the meager sum the family would have lacked basic essentials. In her own words "the earnings of her husband and boys maintained the family in food and that what she herself and the girls (aged respectively 7 and 5 years) earned by spinning and at harvest, found them in clothes, linen and other necessaries."

However convincing figures may be, they remain strangely inadequate to convey the full human consequences attendant upon economic change: nor do the annals of the poor, though numerous, often throw much light on how economic questions conditioned the attitude of a man and wife to each other and their children or how the family coped with the failure of the wage of the working man or woman to keep pace with rising costs, a problem felt most nearly in the home and in one's immediate relationships. It meant that one lived daily from hand to mouth without provision for old age, sickness, incapacity to work, or disasters such as harvest failure or even the arrival of a baby. It affected one's attitude toward one's aged parents and made one's own advancing years something to fear; it presented the working man with the demoralizing experience of toiling all day only to return home with a pittance inadequate for the decent maintenance of his family; it made theft and violence, drunkenness, vagabondage and prostitution constant features of this society and understandably so, for it was only too easy to cross the narrow boundary between poverty and destitution. It needed only some everyday occurrence, a sickness of the main earner, his death, the drying up of domestic industry, the birth of a third or fourth child, to plunge the family into difficulties from which recovery was almost impossible. The ease with which the boundary between poverty and destitution could be crossed provided the century with its most cogent social problems. The sick or crippled who could earn nothing and the aged who were enfeebled might form a relatively small part of the population but the same could not be said of the family that could not manage because of its restricted earning capacity. In France probably something like a third of the population teetered on the fringes of destitution whilst something like a tenth had already crossed that boundary, and an extensive survey made by the French government in 1791 revealed that young children spelt disaster for the family economy. The corollary of this was that in many areas begging children plagued the street crying for alms, begging bread, serving as decoys for pickpockets or as little tinkers peddling pins and ribbons. "Babies" a sub-delegate of the Auvergne moaned, "have scarcely left the cradle before they are taught how to beg so as not to be a burden to their families." In Paris groups of children made a poor living by selling bundles of firewood or working for rag and bone merchants. Elsewhere they acted as water carriers, sellers of flowers or melons or anything that they could gather together by their own labor and sell for a few pence. . . .

The lesson of the eighteenth century was that there was no quick or simple solution to the problem of poverty; that appeals to "submission" and "contentment" were of little avail and that pity and *noblesse oblige* were outworn attitudes. But the poor remained stranded somewhere between two concepts: as the children of God and the test of a Christian State on the one hand and as the enemies of society .on the other. They were left an amorphous, ill-defined mass of men, women and children, old and young, able-bodied and sick and as such they were destined to remain until, caught up in the momentum of a rapidly industrializing economy, economic progress carried sufficient of them above the most precarious subsistence level. That achieved, the problem of poverty was reduced to such manageable dimensions that gradually an eighteenth-century ideal could be realized and the poor indeed legislated away.

But this is to look far into the future. The student of social history is drawn to the eighteenth century in part at least because of its infinite variety. The elegant town houses and public buildings caught in the earlier pages of this volume bear witness to the refined tastes and new wealth of substantial sections of the community but they are only one side of the coin. It is hoped that these pages have shown something of the other. Whilst the merchants of Liverpool grew rich on an amalgam of slaves and cotton, Irish immigrants perished in the cellars of the city; whilst the profits of the wine trade built a new and beautiful Bordeaux, the garrets of the old town were crammed with the influx from the Pyrenees.

Our period is *par excellence* one of contrasts in which, to an unprecedented extent, European society was sharply divided into rich and poor, a dichotomy which became more and more apparent as urbanization intensified and the two dwelt closer together—indeed we are not far from the day when Disraeli would speak of the "two nations" between whom there was no contact and even less understanding. The road from the conquest of plague to the welfare State and social security was long, circuitous, uncharted and if by 1800 a way-stage had already been passed, for the most part the journey was still only beginning.

S. G. CHECKLAND

The Lower Orders In England

BIRTH, MARRIAGE, AND DEATH

The general trend of population growth though clear enough in outline, was the result of many forces operating upon the birth, marriage, and death behavior of these many groups of men and women, so diverse in the way in which they lived and sought the means to live.[1]

Fertility varied markedly between various occupational categories.[2] The highest birth rates appeared among the agricultural laborers, the miners, the less skilled building workers, the general laborers, and the submerged of the great cities, especially in the East End of London. With the exception of the last group, these were the sections of the community in which physical exertion was greatest and skill least. But other aspects of their lives varied widely, including the level and stability of their incomes.

The procreative power of the farm workers was strong, and was little affected either by ideas or techniques concerned with birth control: it was normal to marry and beget children. Moreover the countryside was continuously disembarrassed of its excess numbers by the movement to the towns and abroad. Housing shortage seemed to have little effect upon the birth rate in the countryside, even in the case of the close parish where control lay with one or two landowners who could strictly regulate the supply of cottages, a device operated down to the Union Chargeability Act of 1865. This high birth rate was reinforced by a lower than average child mortality rate. But though the farm worker might continue to be prolific, his loss of relative importance in the population as a whole was bound to reduce the nation's rate of increase.

S. G. Checkland, *The Rise of Industrial Society in England 1815–1885* (New York: St. Martin's Press, 1964), pp. 222–25, 251–53, 263–66, 272–79. Also by permission of Longman Group Ltd., London.

[1] For much interesting material see William Farr, *Vital Statistics,* N. A. Humphreys, ed., London, 1885.

[2] T. H. C. Stevenson, 'Fertility of Various Social Class . . . ,' *J.R.S.S.,* 1920; J. W. Innes, *Class Fertility Trends in England and Wales, 1876–1934,* Princeton, 1938.

The miners, like the farm workers, reached their peak earnings early, with the result that the age of marriage was low and the period of child-bearing was long. Mining, however, was not the kind of occupation in which the worker enjoyed alternatives. Miners were by the nature of their job ill suited for other employment; their children too were bred to their ways. But in contrast to agriculture, mining was an expanding industry. It seized eagerly upon the sons of miners over successive generations, making it possible for them to marry young and thus aid the process of expansion.

In building many of the rapidly growing labor force were of a low order of skill. But their earnings were often protected by effective combination, both among themselves, and among their masters who could thus keep the rewards of the industry higher than might have been the case if unregulated competition had prevailed. This could often occur in spite of the great number of small enterprises in building.

The general laborer represented that range of society that had no effective means of combining for the protection of earnings. Some could do well, where tempting piece-rates were offered to accelerate the tasks to which machinery could not be applied (as with railway navvying), but on the whole the unskilled worker was on a casual, ill-paid basis. Yet his numbers increased at a startling rate. At the bottom end of the skill-less scale came the slum-dweller. For him all elements of life were adverse: poor housing, low incomes, and unemployment destroyed the potential for improvement in successive generations. Yet the result was not to reduce the birth rate; on the contrary. In terms of the death rate, however, these factors were effective, carrying off slum children in great numbers, especially the very young.

Just as textiles lost ground in terms of the growth of employment, so textile workers failed to maintain their fertility. In the first decade of the century they had helped to swell the expansion; by the mid-century they were beginning to lose their power to propagate; in the third quarter of the century its decline was marked. It was in the textile areas of Lancashire and Yorkshire that female employment was highest. The effect of this upon child-bearing was much stressed by observers, for the physical problems of raising a family were made much more difficult. Increasing money earnings, especially in a house with a dual income, might further reduce the disposition to have children, especially as the earning capacity of the latter was reduced by the Factory Acts.

The skilled artisans also showed signs of producing smaller families, though for different reasons. With such men the timing of earnings could be important, for virtually alone among the workers they did not attain maximum rewards until after a considerable apprenticeship and educational delay, thus causing postponement of marriage and the adoption of control measures within it. There is evidence of the spread of birth control in the towns of the north from 1870 onward. The new education and the increased aggregation in towns made contraceptive information and sale easier to arrange. The inhibitions involved in the older view of family life were weakening, especially as the church lost ground. It was the skilled operatives of the wool towns, like Halifax and Huddersfield, and the shoe workers of Northampton, who received the particular attention of neo-Malthusian propagandists like Annie Besant and Charles Bradlaugh. This factor became more powerful as the need for skill and technical education was increasingly felt.

The death rate was constant for thirty years down to 1870. The first reduction in the early part of the century had been achieved in relatively easy conditions. But the whole pace and scale of change from the forties onward was greater. Even to keep the rate constant required that amelioration should go forward. Urban death rates were well above the national rate of 22.4 in the early forties: at least a dozen of the largest towns had rates of 26 or more.

The new challenge was not the traditional one of food supply, but pestilence. Formerly the two had been closely related in that food shortage both reduced resistance and made people indiscriminate about the condition of the things they ate. But now pestilence had taken on an independent existence. Great numbers of people in close proximity with no official intervention to serve their common needs meant trouble, even though real wages might be rising. A full private purse was no insurance against impotent public bodies.

In the late thirties, for 100 persons per thousand who died in the home counties, 164 died in London. The great problems were to cleanse and purge: to do this involved a clear and copious water supply, and efficient drainage. At last, in the seventies, equipoise between deterioration and improvement was effectively disturbed and the death rate, stationary for thirty years, resumed its downward trend. Thus, coincident with the redundancy of labor power appeared the new capacity to preserve it. Yet infectious diseases were still responsible for one-third of the total deaths at all ages, with respiratory, nervous, and digestive diseases a formidable second.[3]

The great reduction in urban death rates, especially among infants, beginning in the seventies, was apparent particularly among those who had suffered most from the earlier deterioration of urban conditions. But it was among these receivers of low incomes and occupiers of inferior houses that there was least response in terms of diminishing births. The effect was to induce rapid increase among families with the poorest pros-

---

[3] W. P. D. Logan, 'Mortality in England and Wales from 1848–1947,' *P.S.*, 1950.

pects. For those of the middle classes whose philosophy was liberal this posed a most serious problem. . . .

THE CONDITIONS OF LIVING

The industrial cities of England came into being almost by inadvertence: they were merely the places where factories, offices, depots, and warehouses were built and to which the new industrial population was attracted.[4] The long tradition of town planning and regulation going back to the middle ages had largely passed into abeyance.[5] In the newer cities it had never been operative. The urban revolution was so great in scope and scale as to obliterate the older sense of responsibility.

Problems accumulated steadily. Down to the forties no real attempt at solution was made. Learning about cities had to be imposed by experience; deterioration had to be well advanced before the necessary response could be evoked, for the immensity of the effort required to regulate an industrial city was so great that it was only forthcoming as an inescapable imperative. Moreover, the form and content of the new kind of city represented the attempts of its myriad of members to find the formula that allowed of the implementation of their individual plans, either as masters or men. Until the nature of the resulting complex could be perceived it was impossible to plan to control it. There was thus a paradox: for the morbid aspect of urban growth to be treated it had to be allowed to develop until it carried irresistible conviction.

By the forties a state of affairs had been reached in which three great dangers threatened. There had long been fear of the great mysterious masses accumulating in the areas that were unknown and unpenetrated by the middle class. This could lead to a politically explosive situation. Even more imminent was the danger of epidemic. The cholera outbreak of 1832 and subsequent visits in the forties brought terror to the towns.[6] Every middle-class family relied upon its servants; they con-

---

[4] For a general view see Asa Briggs, *Victorian Cities*, London, 1963. For particular places see Conrad Gill and Asa Briggs, *History of Birmingham*, Oxford, 1952; Arthur Redford and I. S. Russell, *The History of Local Government in Manchester*, London, 1939–40; T. C. Barker and J. R. Harris, *A Merseyside Town in the Industrial Revolution: St. Helens, 1750–1900*, Liverpool, 1954; Sidney Pollard, *A History of Labour in Sheffield*, Liverpool, 1959; W. H. Chaloner, *The Social and Economic Development of Crewe, 1780–1923*, Manchester, 1950; A. Temple Patterson, *Radical Leicester; a History of Leicester, 1780–1850*, Leicester, 1954; *The British Association Handbooks* provide valuable studies of the cities visited by the Association. For general bibliography, W. H. Chaloner, 'Writings in British Urban History,' *Vierteljahrschrift für Sozial- und Wirtschaftsgeschichte*, 1958.

[5] W. Ashworth, *Genesis of Modern British Town Planning*, London, 1954.

[6] Asa Briggs, 'Cholera and Society in the Nineteenth Century, *P. and P.*, 1961; Charles Creighton, *A History of Epidemics in Great Britain*, 2 vols., Cambridge, 1891–94.

stituted an almost instantaneous channel along which disease travelled from slums to residential squares. In the fifties it was discovered that the Royal apartments at Buckingham Palace were ventilated through the common sewer. Outbreaks of disease were predicted by the opponents of the Great Exhibition; before 1851 it was thought unreasonable that the Queen should visit Liverpool and Manchester, and when she did so in that year it was "almost a matter of wonder." [7] Finally, the growth and deterioration of the cities was very damaging to efficiency and therefore an obstacle to the lowering of production costs. British industry and trade were doing well in the third quarter of the century, but it was becoming apparent that the conditions of living of the workers would soon become a seriously limiting factor.

The dangers of dirt were the first to provoke thought and action. The system of natural liberty could provide the food and raw materials required to maintain the population of vast cities; indeed the philosophically minded marvelled how the grand design of the Deity was thus demonstrated. But it could not purge its wastes. It was as though the organs of sustenance were efficient but the organs of elimination were defective.

Men, women, and children, in varying degree, were wearing, breathing and drinking refuse. Old garments moved down the social scale and passed from peer to pauper at its nether end. The air was defiled with industrial and human effluvia. Water-courses became open sewers. Tipping and dumping were uncontrolled; there was a lack of depots for night soil. The sewage system was largely on the surface, courts were unpaved, the movement of air was blocked by crowded buildings. The builder might place the primitive privy where he wished, inside or outside the houses: when indoors the smells in winter were dreadful in houses tightly closed to keep them warm, when outdoors women and children, unwilling to visit them in exposed places, became habitually constipated. Cemeteries gave off noxious smells and polluted the water supplies; tanneries, breweries, dyeing works, chemical plants, slaughter houses, and manure driers were uncontrolled in their disposal of waste matter, as gas, liquid, or solid. The cesspool, "that magazine of all the contagions" as Farr described it, was still general. [8] The children were the heaviest casualties. In the sixties about twenty-six out of every hundred died under the age of five; in the best districts the number was eighteen, in the worst it was thirty-six. The first great task of the urban improvers was to deal with the toxic refuse of urban life. . . .

[7] 'Loyalty in the Workshops,' *Econ.*, 18 October 1851, p. 1147.
[8] William Farr, 'Mortality of Children,' *J.S.S.*, 1866, p. 9.

THE IMPACT ON PERSONALITY

Even more fundamental to happiness than monetary rewards and living conditions was the state of mind of men, women and children who needed to be able to find comfort and even pride in their relations with one another and with the productive tasks upon which their livelihood depended. Each was obliged to seek his identity and self-expression in terms of some basic human group, usually the family, and in terms of the larger group or class to which he belonged. Within these he needed a working concept of the function he discharged.

Preindustrial society had over very many generations solved these problems. The closely knit, though often very extended, family was the fundamental unit within which personalities, loves and loyalties were formed. The general divisions of society were so obvious and irrefragable that most men lived their lives in the class into which they were born, itself related to others by well-established conventions. As to function, most men, women and children worked on the land, directly engaged in the primary task of producing food or raw materials—preparing nature for her yield and gathering and storing the product. Application to these tasks was the condition upon which the continuance of life itself depended —there could be no futility here. Even the village craftsman was half a farmer and half a provider of the simple tools of a farming community.

The new industry disrupted and eventually destroyed this ancient pattern within which the individual could find assimilation. The new structure of society, instead of minimizing individual assertion, put a premium upon it.

The result was grave social damage.[9] A family dwelling in an industrial town found itself not only divorced from nature and from the particular place of its origin, but cut off from other families. To isolation were added serious stresses within the family. Not all its members were engaged, as formerly, as a group, doing essentially farming tasks, and sharing the benefits on the basis of a family communism administered by the senior members. Instead, the members of the family might well be employed in different occupations, with a premium placed by the wages system upon youth and vigor, so that the rights and authority by which the older generation traditionally maintained their status and self-respect into old age were impaired or destroyed. The new mobility made possible by the railway operated to disperse families as their more enterprising members sought new opportunities. Many of these became lodgers in the houses of others, or servants living in dingy conditions in the lesser middle-class families. So there developed an element of the population

---

[9] Neil J. Smelser, op. cit., *passim.*

with a kind of substatus, neither heads of families nor true members. Others of the unassimilated were the growing hordes of homeless children, the street-arabs who became a kind of nomad class in the heart of the great cities.[10] The disruption of the family was not arrested by official policy, but, rather, furthered. The Poor Law caused many families to be broken up upon admission to the Poor House so that even for those in this extremity there was no official thought of providing support for personality through the family.

The new conditions of work imposed further psychological strains. There were many men whose skill, once an important element in community life and a source of personal pride, was now wanted by no one. Much of the new employment involved long repetitive hours doing jobs that were meaningless in themselves, a mere portion of a process that ended in a product the worker would not consume. Many tasks now involved the worker in tying himself to a machine powered by a great engine, the whole controlled by managers. The latter would probably be of their own kind, caught up in the same new situation, but distinguished in their ability to manipulate the new system. Divisions of interest thus came within the family as some rose and others did not.

Fissures also appeared between classes of men in the same community, depending upon differences in skill, income, and respectability. Added to this was the growth of distinctions between communities. By the forties the Lancashire collier had sunk to an appalling degradation. For though the family had maintained its solidarity, with man, wife, and children acting as one productive unit, the man taking payment in a lump sum, this had involved a debasement of outlook and living that caused the colliers to be wholly isolated from other sections of society. The mill workers and the colliers maintained, in close juxtaposition, communities that were absolutely divorced. Other families found it difficult if not impossible to assimilate to the rest of society. By the seventies the bargees were a sizeable group: no less than 44,000 adults, more than half of them unmarried, with some 72,000 children, about 40,000 illegitimate, were floating up and down the country, innocent of sanitation, religion, or education.[11] Economic breakdowns had not only sent Englishmen abroad; they had brought foreigners in—men and women to whom England offered opportunities for improvement on eastern European conditions that combined oppression, poverty, and military conscription. From 1870 onward came Jewish immigrants, settling especially in the East End of London and the other great cities, with their Yiddish newspapers, *chevras* or conventicles, some to fall victim to, and some to operate, the sweating system.[12]

[10] Benjamin Waugh, "Street Children," *C.R.*, Lancashire, 1888.
[11] Escott, op. cit., vol. I, p. 258.
[12] Lloyd P. Gartner, *The Jewish Immigrant in England, 1870–1914*, London, 1960;

The natural models upon which conduct might be based withdrew themselves from the sight of those who might have accepted them as mentors. The middle class, who had always dwelt in the centers of the towns at or near their places of business, had taken, by the thirties if not earlier, to abandoning the old setting. The incentives to do so were usually some combination of three factors. There was a desire for landed space, and the ways of the landed. Profits could be realized by urban sales: property values rose steeply in town centers of business (Cobden reckoned in 1832 that the house he had bought for 3,000 guineas in Manchester had become worth 6,000 within some four years).[13] Finally there was serious deterioration of amenity, for old town centers were often made unsavory by the masses who had been brought to being by the new business initiative—especially those who had sunk furthest and who constituted the growing mass of idlers, importuners, and disturbers of the peace. The centers of the towns, as places to live, were abandoned to the petty shopkeepers, the publicans, the laborers, the "dangerous classes," and the police. Not for another fifty years were the English middle class to resume contact with the workers in their sordid streets, and then only in charity.

But for all this, the worker was not crushed.[14] Indeed humanity was able to demonstrate its extraordinary adaptability in a more dramatic form than ever before. For as urban living became typical, men and women, taking the city as a datum, developed new attitudes, new entertainments, and new ways of mutual assimilation. Many indeed subsided into dirt and fecklessness, seeking the oblivion of drunkenness. But even these could often find pleasures and loyalties. The vitality of the countryside was a kind of hidden reserve upon which the Englishman at the nether end of the social scale could draw during the worst decades of the first half of the century. A new birth brought its worry, but also brought its joy; as Sam Laycock, the Laureate of the Cotton Famine put it:

> But tho' we've childer two or three,
> We'll mak' a bit o' room for thee
> Bless thi, lad
> Th'art prettiest bird we have in t'nest
> So hutch up closer to mi breast;
> Aw'm thi dad.[15]

V. D. Lipman, *A Century of Social Service, 1859–1959; The Jewish Board of Guardians,* London, 1959, chapter II; *Social History of the Jews in England, 1850–1950,* London, 1954.

[13] John Morley, *The Life of Richard Cobden,* London, 1893, p. 22, n. 2.

[14] For some aspects of adjustment see W. A. Abram 'Social Condition and Political Prospects of the Lancashire Workmen,' *F.R.,* 1868, p. 426.

[15] George Milner, ed., *The Collected Writings of Samuel Laycock,* Oldham, London and Manchester, 2nd ed., 1908, p. 3.

The genetic miracle of the renewal of life continued to manifest itself so that dilapidated parents produced babies capable of responding anew to the challenge of their situation. The children who survived the dreadful infant death rate learned to play on the inches of paving that separated them from the earth, and to develop their games in the enclosing streets and alleyways. Youth renewed its spirits with each generation as errand boys and apprentices took to ribaldry and larking. As kinship groups were established, usually through mothers and grandmothers, there came a new security, confirmed by gathering together for celebrations of christenings, marriages, and funerals. . . .

THE RESIDUUM

The pauper and the criminal had been objects of experimentation in England at least since the sixteenth century. No really satisfactory treatment had emerged. Now industrializing society was producing unassimilated men and women on an immense scale.[16] They suffered greatly.[17] But a new humanitarianism had developed in the Britain of the nineteenth century, from which the greatest gainers were "the poorest, the most dependent, and the most defenseless."[18] This urge to help the casualties of society had to come to terms with human dilapidation in the urban, industrial, society.

Men had to be coerced into changing their jobs if the national product was to rise rapidly enough to make possible the support of the mounting population. Some, especially the young and vigorous, might do so voluntarily, in response to the incentives of higher wages. But most had to be subjected to persuasion. This typically took the form of falling wages in obsolescent jobs, or absolute loss of employment. If the goad was to be effective there had to remain no alternative but to seek new employment. Any Poor Law that provided an income, however minimal, would arrest the essential process of adjustment, and, as the authors of the Report of 1834 argued, place the nation in a parlous state, if, while committed as it was to industrialization, it so acted as to forestall the operation of an essential mechanism.[19]

But to the poor the matter looked quite different. Most of them could not adjust to new tasks as the reformers wished—they did not know

[16] Henry Mayhew, op. cit., vol. IV, 1862, 'Prostitutes, Thieves, Swindlers, Beggars.'

[17] See the illustrations by Doré in Gustave Doré and Blanchard Jerrold, *London. A Pilgrimage*, London, 1872, chapters XVII and XVIII.

[18] Macaulay, *Works*, vol. I, p. 332.

[19] *Report of the R. C. for Inquiring into the Administration and Practical Operation of the Poor Laws*, 1834.

where to go geographically, they were offered no means of retraining, they had no reserves to cover the transition period, and if they left their houses it was very unlikely that they would find a dwelling place elsewhere. Finally, there was the new instability of the system: prosperity came and went; in bad times jobs were not to be had anywhere. The problem of the Poor Law thus became: how far should the workers be subjected to the discipline of starvation and exposure; how far should compassion be expressed through public policy?

In the countryside, before the enclosure movement culminating during the Napoleonic wars, there had been scope for the poor to scrub along with tiny parcels of land and casual jobs. In addition there was the Poor Law, steadily relaxed after Gilbert's Act of 1782 and especially after the general spread of the system adopted by the Justices of the Peace in the Parish of Speenhamland, in Berkshire, in 1795, whereby relief was related to the cost of living as measured by the price of the quartern loaf, and need took account of all children, legitimate or otherwise. In the same year, by the Settlement and Removal Act, a poor person, formerly removable if thought likely to become a public charge, could only be ejected from the parish if he had actually become chargeable.[20]

As a result all rigor went from the system. The municipal workhouses were in a very bad state by the early thirties. The paupers within them were often dissolute, depraved, and promiscuous, and many of those outside showed an alarming tendency to accept their dependence upon the parish. The parish officers could no longer, as they had done since Tudor times, hurry new arrivals back onto the road as soon as they appeared.

But this easy permissiveness ended with the new Poor Law of 1834.[21] The decision was taken that the nation could no longer permit its poor to be in receipt of incomes without working for them, free of poorhouse discipline. Poverty was to be made painful; the state was to provide no incentives to idleness, but was rather to discipline those at the nether end of the income scale. The principle of "less eligibility" was the keynote of the Report, whereby no one maintained by the parish was to be as well off as the poorest paid laborer in work. Outdoor relief was to be cut to a minimum, and segregation of the sexes, with consequent breaking up of families, was to be carried out wherever possible. Parishes were to be grouped in "unions" so that a more viable unit of administration became available, more effectively answerable to the central government, though each parish still remained responsible for its own poor.

[20] Sidney and Beatrice Webb, *English Local Government,* 9 vols, London, 1906–29, vols. VII, VIII, IX, *English Poor Law History.*
[21] Maurice Bruce, *The Coming of the Welfare State,* London, 1961, chapter IV.

The three Commissioners for the enforcement of the Act, with Edwin Chadwick as their energetic and uncompromising Secretary, went about the task of implementing the policy of the Report. They did so with such vigor as to be quickly execrated as the "three bashaws of Somerset House," their workhouses damned as bastilles.[22]

The new policy was understandable enough. The farming parishes, especially in the south, were indeed producing a frightening pauper population. But many such, if not most, had no alternative but to seek parish aid. The farmers, still suffering depression and in any case wishing, in the larger enclosed fields, to economize on labor, could not employ them. There was, moreover, a struggle between the landlords and farmers whose interest lay in the "close" parishes, and those concerned with the "open" ones.[23] In the former the land was owned by a few, making possible, through the control of the supply of cottages, the control of the number of poor likely to become chargeable. If cottages were allowed to fall into decay, and new building was not undertaken, the parish population diminished, families removed to open parishes, and walked to their work in the close ones, and thus were able to sustain their birth rate. Though some landlords of close parishes took great interest in their workers, the double system was liable to grave abuse, with the laborer the victim. The alternative for the farm laborer was movement to the towns. But many, especially those of mature years, could not face such an upheaval; moreover the generative power of the countryside produced, in many parishes, new lives in excess of the emigration. The result was great suffering.

In the new industrial towns of the north the Poor Law encountered not the relatively passive resentment of the farm laborer, but urban militancy. This disciplinary piece of legislation was bitterly resented by men and women who were without jobs, and who found their pleas to a reformed Parliament for an employment policy left unanswered. Good harvests in the years immediately after the Act made possible an apparent reduction in pauperism, but in 1836 depression returned and with it bitter hostility.

In 1847 with famine and bad trade disturbing the nation, the duties of the Poor Law Commissioners of 1834 passed to the President of the Local Government Board, who was an M.P. and often a Cabinet member. A steady succession of inspectors produced invaluable Reports. By this time Poor Law Unions authorized by the 1834 Act covered most of the country, with their new and imposing workhouses. Strict segregation of the sexes had proved impossible because of building costs. The new

---

[22] G. R. W. Baxter, *The Book of Bastilles,* London, 1841.
[23] Clapham, op. cit., vol. I, pp. 467–70.

Board was obliged in 1852 to recognize that resistance in London and in the north had made a flat refusal of outdoor relief impossible. Policy differed between regions; by the seventies refusal of relief was a reality only in some of the rural areas. Yet there was still enough rigor in the system to contribute to the conversion of laborers and their sons from agriculture to other tasks. In addition, the bad times caused a further relaxation in the Settlement Law; by the Act of 1846 those who had resided in a parish for five years without receiving relief acquired a "settlement" there, that is to say became irremovable.

Though the country was gaining in prosperity in the sixties, the poor remained a serious problem. The cotton famine brought general unemployment in south Lancashire, causing the passage of the Public Works Loans Act of 1863 whereby parish unions and local authorities could raise loans for public works. The housing conditions of much of the agricultural population, as described by Dr. Hunter in his Report to the Lords of the Privy Council in 1864, were very bad. The Union Changeability Act of 1865 sought to improve the Poor Law by making the Unions more effective. The old distinction between the fund for common purposes and the parochial fund, used for relief, was done away with, so that the Union and not the parish administered the aid to paupers. Settlement was to pertain to the Union, so that the pauper was now entitled to relief in any constituent parish. This went some way to obviating the old distinction between open and close parishes, and was strongly resisted by a powerful landed group on this account.

By 1871 the case for bringing the Poor Law, Public Health, and local Government affairs under a single government department provoked an Act assigning to the Local Government Board this triple responsibility. The inspectorate of the Board, together with the Union Poor Law Guardians, launched a campaign against outdoor relief, and, in general, sought to return to the principles of 1834. The number of paupers fell, so that in 1884–86 they reached a new low as a proportion of population, constituting only 2.8 percent. Though the strict meaning of this figure is difficult to determine, it would seem to suggest real diminution. On the other hand there was a concession to the poor under an Act of 1876, whereby the period of residence required to obtain a settlement was reduced to three years. Thereafter, with the accelerated mobility of persons, the idea of settlement gradually became a nullity, with the poor relieved in the parish in which they found themselves. Though the vagrancy laws still made it possible to award three months' hard labor for rogues and vagabonds, there was a formidable number of mendicants moving about the countryside, begging in the towns, and even mapping out the new suburbs for begging purposes. Thousands of doorways sheltered " 'appy dossers," and the Embankment shortly after its completion in the seventies became a national dormitory for the down-and-outs. Prostitution was an ever-present problem.[24]

Yet the idea was still strong in the eighties that there was no way of separating the workers from the worthless, other than by test labor, that is, their reaction to arduous physical work in the stone yard, the parish saw pit, or even the treadmill. Men who showed themselves willing thus reassured the Guardians they were not parasitic, and so could make a relaxation of rigor possible. For as the desire to behave in a humane way toward the deserving poor grew, so grew the fear of making the nation vulnerable to the crime and social disturbance of the worthless. For the peace of mind of those responsible it was essential to have a test of worthiness; it is impossible not to feel sympathy for them in their bafflement. And though fear of excess population in a general sense had largely passed away, there was very real concern about increase among the least fit, for among the lowest class it was often the case that the more incompetent the parent for work, the larger his family, as if the one reason for his existence was to multiply incapables.[25] Finally, the Poor Law was very difficult to interpret, being in need of codification. It also contained many anomalies; those in receipt of relief in Battersea got 5s. 6d. per week while those in the adjacent union of Rotherhithe received only 2s. 4d.

Between pauperism and crime there was the army and the navy, for a high proportion of recruits, especially to the army, were men not otherwise employable. The effect on character was very bad: in the sixties nearly one-third of the soldiers stationed in the United Kingdom were admitted to hospital, each year, for venereal disease.[26] Army reform in the seventies had among its aims that the nation should no longer depend upon the waifs and strays of the population.

The prisons contained those who were total liabilities to society, men and women who had become wholly parasitic; with them were immured many who were more unfortunate than vicious but who, under such conditions, often changed for the worse. They were in the charge of a prison system that was sunk in promiscuity and squalor, jailers' tyranny and greed, and administrative confusion. Many of the worst were confined in the hulks, the decaying carcasses of ships moored in the Thames

[24] For a bibliography see O. R. McGregor, "The Social Position of Women in England, 1850–1914," *British Journal of Sociology,* vol. IV., no. 1; Wm. Acton, *Prostitution considered in its Moral, Social and Sanitary Aspects,* 2nd ed., 1870; Wm. Logan, *The Great Social Evil,* London, 1871.

[25] Francis Peek, "The Workless, the Thriftless, and the Worthless," *C.R.,* 1888.

[26] *Report of the Registrar General,* 1875, Supplement, p. lxix; *Report of R.C. on Contagious Diseases,* 1871.

adopted as an emergency expedient in 1776.[27] Some were more fortunate in being placed in ships still capable of seagoing, which bore them as deportees to the colonies of Australia, a practice continued as late as 1853. It was ended by the Penal Servitude Act of that year.

The ending of deportation led to two developments: the provision of gaols [jails] and the reorganization of prison administration, and the ticket-of-leave system. The enormous new prisons of Millbank and Pentonville were built, and eventually a national responsibility for all prisons was accepted in 1877, under the Prison Commissioners. Though the new system bought a new administrative order, it brought also rigor and regulation, with the purging away of elements of tolerance formerly present at least in some places, and the adoption of close regulation, solitary confinement, and the rule of silence.[28] But in the direction of clemency and redemption the experiment was tried of allowing provisional remission of one-sixth to one-third of the sentence, with the prisoner released on ticket-of-leave. The garottings and violence which rendered the London pavements unsafe in quiet streets after or even before sunset were blamed by the frightened upon such men and their premature freedom.

Just as Victorian England, under the impetus of a few devoted men and women, was trying to amend its penal system, changes were going forward also in the criminal law, reducing brutality and severity. In 1800 there were 220 capital offenses, in 1837 there were fifteen, in 1870 there were two only, murder and high treason.[29] The use of the pillory was restricted in 1816 and abolished in 1837, with the treadmill often a substitute. Dissection of murderers' bodies, formerly obligatory, was made optional for the judge in 1834, and was abolished in 1861. Hangings as public entertainments ended with the Act of 1868.

Greater compassion entered into the treatment of the insane.[30] But though the Lunatics Act of 1845 required all English counties to provide themselves with asylum accommodation, the lunatic often continued to share the poorhouse with the other inmates. The national police system was greatly strengthened. Peel's new force in London formed in 1830 was very effective; the result was a migration of criminals to other cities, with the consequent need to establish real forces over the country.

[27] W. Branch-Johnson, *The English Prison Hulks*, London, 1957.

[28] D. L. Howard, *The English Prisons*, London, 1960; Gordon Rose, *The Struggle for Penal Reform*, London, 1961; Henry Mayhew and John Binney, *The Criminal Prisons of London*, London, 1862.

[29] A. B. Dicey, op. cit., p. 29; Elizabeth Orman Tuttle, *The Crusade against Capital Punishment in Great Britain*, London, 1961.

[30] Kathleen Jones, *Lunacy, Law and Conscience, 1744–1845: The Social History of the Care of the Insane,* London, 1955; *Mental Health and Social Policy, 1845–1959*, London, 1960.

But in spite of prison reform, the development of new criminal law, and the institution of a national police system, crime, far from being purged from industrial society, became a confirmed and permanent problem. As general wealth increased, the element of decay at the lower end of society became more obvious. Crime for many had become a kind of hereditary occupation; something approaching a criminal caste had appeared in all the large cities by the eighties, involving society in a heavy burden, and creating a sense of insecurity. Retribution rather than the reform of the criminal remained the basis of policy.

WILLIAM L. LANGER

The Social Question

THE STANDARD OF LIVING

In the decades preceding 1848 Europe was deluged with literature discussing the "social question" or, as it was called in Britain, the "condition of England question." Everywhere thoughtful people were appalled not so much by the existence of poverty, hunger and disease, for they had been familiar social afflictions since the beginning of time, as by the alarming increase of what came to be known as "pauperism" and by what seemed like the further deterioration of the lower classes. "Such is now the accumulation of misery endured by thousands of skilled and industrious laborers, that no conceivable alteration for the worse can take place," wrote an English journal in 1826, while Thomas Carlyle, in his *Past and Present* (1843), could declare: "I venture to believe that in no time since the beginnings of society, was the lot of those same dumb millions of toilers so entirely unbearable as it is even in the days now passing over us." [1]

Since the deterioration in the condition of the working classes was

From pp. 181–98 ("In the decades . . . day of retribution.") in *Political and Social Upheaval 1832–1852* by William L. Langer. Copyright © 1969 by William L. Langer. By permission of Harper & Row, Publishers, Inc.

[1] Sidney Pollard: "Nineteenth Century Coöperation" (in Asa Briggs and John Saville, eds.: *Essays in Labour History,* London, 1960, 74–112); David Daiches: *Carlyle and the Victorian Dilemma* (Edinburgh, 1963).

most striking in the cities, it was natural that it should have been linked by many contemporary writers to the concurrent progress of industrialization. The question was often raised whether the price being paid for greater and cheaper production of goods was not, in terms of human suffering, disproportionately high. Goethe, among others, saw industrialization as a slowly gathering storm, soon to break over the land, bringing with it, along with obvious benefits, social calamity.[2]

Actually it was a mistake to attribute the greater woes of mankind to the coming of the machine, for the frightening growth of pauperism was fully as great in nonindustrialized areas as in the new manufacturing centers. The basic fact, increasingly so recognized by modern scholars, was the unprecedented growth of the European population after 1760. This led to overpopulation, "that condition of a country in which part of the inhabitants, although able-bodied and capable of labor, are permanently unable to earn a sufficiency of the necessaries of life." [3] There were, according to Edward Gibbon Wakefield, simply "too many competitors for a limited fund of enjoyment." [4] Everywhere, on the Continent as in Britain, there were just too many people for the available jobs, and the surplus (or "redundant") population was the great ulcer of European nations, "the master evil," to borrow Francis Place's description.[5]

It was inevitable that so great and sudden an increase in the population should have entailed major dislocations in European society. Agrarian laborers unable to find work were reduced to utmost destitution or forced to migrate to the nearest towns in the hope of finding employment, if possible in the new factories, or at any rate in some menial occupation. In the cities many of them were no better off than they had been before, to put it mildly. The new machine industry provided a precarious existence for some, but at the same time proved ruinous for many engaged in the traditional home industries, which were unable to compete with the new methods of production. Taken all in all, it would seem that in Europe the lowest classes, the "poor," those who lived on the brink of starvation and who in the sixteenth century had comprised about one-fifth of the population, had come in the nineteenth to number a third or more.[6]

[2] *Wilhelm Meisters Wanderjahre* (1829).

[3] William A. Thornton: *Overpopulation and its Remedy* (London, 1846), I.

[4] *A View of the Art of Colonization* (London, 1848), 66.

[5] Quoted by James A. Field: *Essays on Population* (Chicago, 1931), chap. iii.

[6] Wolfram Fischer: "Soziale Unterschichten im Zeitalter der Frühindustrialisierung" (*International Review of Social History*, VIII, 1963, 414–435). In 1844 Friedrich Harkort estimated that one-third of the Prussian population was hardly able to earn a living, and it has been asserted that in the 1840s fully a third of the Paris population lived in a "precarious condition." See Max Quarck: *Die erste deutsche Arbeiterbewegung* (Leipzig, 1924), 11; Adeline Daumard; *La bourgeoisie parisienne de 1815 à 1848* (Paris, 1963), 8–9.

Among present-day British writers there has existed for some time a school of so-called "optimists," who hold that industrialization brought at least some rise in the standard of living; in other words, that the workers shared to some extent, however modest, in the benefits of the new economy. This was certainly not the impression of contemporary writers and indeed it is a view that has been vigorously challenged by adherents of the "pessimist" school, who think that the lower classes were for a time worse off than they had ever been. The question is obviously one of prime importance, but unfortunately one that can never be "solved," for lack of adequate statistical data. The debate has been complicated by the fact that different students have taken different periods for their analyses, and that the term *workingman* has frequently been loosely used. In the cities as in the country there were endless gradations of labor, from skilled technicians and specialized craftsmen, through artisans, journeymen and apprentices, to the homeworkers of the putting-out system and factory workers, among whom again there were gradations from foremen to the younger child workers. Lowest of all was what Karl Marx was to term the *Lumpenproletariat,* the riffraff consisting of nondescript workers, mostly unemployed and often driven by desperation to vice and crime.

Although the standard-of-living debate has proved inconclusive, it has brought at least some measure of agreement. There was undoubtedly an aggregate rise in real wages, but this benefited the skilled, well-paid worker rather than the lowest class. It may be that even the poorest element experienced some improvement, for while wages remained fairly unchanged, prices declined. However, all seem to be agreed that if there was a change in the standard of living, it was not a significant one. Furthermore, the actual condition of the poorest class depended at any time largely on the availability of work, about which reliable data are meager and unsystematic.[7]

While it is true that aggregate prices declined in this period, food prices remained high, reflecting the pressure of population, and fluctuated greatly according to the state of the harvest and the general economic situation.

---

[7] The literature on the standard of living in England is so rich that it cannot be listed here. Among important recent items are the debate between R. M. Hartwell and E. J. Hobsbawm: "The Standard of Living during the Industrial Revolution" (*Economic History Review,* Ser. 2, XVI, 1963, 119–149); E. J. Hobsbawm: "The Standard of Living Debate: a Postscript" (in his *Labouring Men,* London, 1964, 120–125); J. E. Williams: "The British Standard of Living, 1750–1850" (*Economic History Review,* Ser. 2, XIX, 1966, 581–589); Phyllis Deane: *The First Industrial Revolution* (Camridge, 1965), chap. xv; E. P. Thompson: *The Making of the English Working Class* (London, 1963); Sydney G. Checkland: *The Rise of Industrial Society in England, 1815–1885* (London, 1965), 225 ff.; and, on the general problem: W. Woodruff: "Capitalism and the Historians" (*Journal of Economic History,* XVI, 1956, 1–17); A. J. Taylor: "Progress and Poverty in Britain, 1780–1850" (*History,* XLV, 1960, 16–31); J. Potter: " 'Optimism' and 'Pessimism' in Interpreting the Industrial Revolution" (*Scandinavian Economic History Review,* X, 1962, 245–261).

Meanwhile, wages certainly did not rise substantially, if at all, until after the depression of 1841–1842. The matter is one difficult to generalize about, for the data, which are abundant, are often contradictory or at least widely divergent. Regional differences were important. Wages were markedly higher in Britain than on the Continent and might vary greatly within any country. Furthermore, wages differed according to the type of work and might fluctuate significantly according to the supply and demand for labor. Finally, any discussion of actual wages must take account of the changing values of money, of the fact that family income was more important than that of the individual male worker, and that the extent of unemployment was often the crucial factor in deciding the fate of the worker and his family.

Certain general statements can, however, be ventured. Everywhere in Europe workers in the traditional skilled handicrafts and trades, as also foundrymen and the new mechanics, ordinarily earned a wage that enabled them to live in relative comfort, with decent lodgings and an adequate diet that might include meat two or three times a week. In England such workers might earn thirty shillings to two pounds a week, and in France twenty-five to thirty francs. British coal miners could earn fifteen to twenty shillings and so could the average cotton mill "operative." The French journeymen or factory workers had about the same wage, but the rate was distinctly lower in Belgium, Switzerland and Italy. In Germany the average worker had a money wage of about nine to ten marks a week, which was somewhat more than he could earn in Austria. Everywhere in Europe, in Britain as on the Continent, the hardest hit were the handloom weavers, particularly in the cotton industry. In their case the population pressure made itself keenly felt, for the handloom weavers were not exposed to the competition of the machine until the 1830s in Britain and the 1840s elsewhere. Their problem derived from the fact that ever more unskilled and unwanted laborers resorted to the handloom in the hope of earning at least a pittance, with the result that they achieved that and nothing more. While in 1815 they were still earning thirteen shillings and sixpence a week, their wages had fallen to six shillings in 1833 and never again rose much above that figure. In Germany, where handloom weaving was still the most important industry, the wages had fallen to two and a half marks per week and in Silesia even to one and a half marks. The position of framework knitters and ribbon makers was hardly better.[8]

[8] The movement of wages is, of course, discussed in all economic histories. Thornton: *Overpopulation*, 26 ff., gives a useful contemporary survey, based largely on government reports. For the Continent, see Carl von Tyska: *Löhne und Lebenskosten in West Europa im 19. Jahrhundert* (Munich, 1914); Paul Louis: *Histoire de la classe ouvrière en France* (Paris, 1927), 58 ff.; Ernest Labrousse: *Aspects de la crise de l'économie française, 1846–1851* (Paris, 1956), 93–141; Jürgen Kuczynski:

The figures in themselves are fairly meaningless unless taken in conjunction with the cost of living. The evidence is quite conclusive that the average worker (for example, the millhand) could barely earn enough to support a family with three children when he was fully employed. It was estimated that in London in 1841 a family could live in reasonable comfort on thirty shillings a week; that it led a tight existence on twenty-one shillings; and that it could barely survive on fifteen shillings. Another study demonstrates that in Switzerland a textile worker could earn only a little more than half of what was required to support a family, while in the mountainous region of Saxony, one of the poorest sections of home industry in Europe, most families could not make a living and were therefore dependent on relief or charity.[9]

This consideration if no other explains the widespread employment of women and children, who were welcomed in the textile mills because they could do the work as well as men, were far more tractable, and required respectively only one-half or one-quarter of the man's wage. To be sure, women and children had always been employed in home industries, but now they were subjected, even at tender ages, to the long unbroken hours and strict discipline of the factories. Besides, during the first half of the nineteenth century there was a vast increase in this type of labor, so that in most mills less than half the employees (sometimes only one-quarter) were adult men, while another half consisted of boys and girls under eighteen. The same was true of the industrial labor force in France, Belgium and Germany.[10]

European workers had been accustomed, long before the Industrial

---

Darstellung der Lage der Arbeiter in Deutschland von 1800 bis in die Gegenwart (6 ed., Berlin, 1954); P. H. Noyes: *Organization and Revolution* (Princeton, 1966), chaps. i and ii; M. Peeters: "L'évolution des salaires en Belgique de 1831 à 1913" (*Bulletin de l'Institut de Recherches Economiques et Sociales,* X, 1939, 389–420); Antonio Fossati: *Lavoro e produzione in Italia* (Turin, 1951), 135 ff.; Luigi Bulferetti and Raimondo Luraghi: *Agricoltura, Industria e Commercio in Piemonte dal 1814 al 1848* (Turin, 1966), 118 ff.; and in general, John Burnett: *Plenty and Want* (London, 1966), chap. iii.

[9] Burnett: *Plenty and Want,* 45; Jürg Siegenthaler: "Zum Lebensstandart schweizerischer Arbeiter im 19. Jahrhundert" (*Schweizerische Zeitschrift für Volkswirtschaft und Statistik,* CI, 1965, 423–444); Heinrich Bodemer: *Die industrielle Revolution mit besonderer Berücksichtigung der Erzgebirgischen Erwerbsverhältnisse* (Dresden, 1856), 99.

[10] For contemporary accounts, see Peter Gaskell: *The Manufacturing Population of England* (London, 1833), chap. vii; John Fielden: *The Curse of the Factory System* (London, 1836), 2 ff., 40; Edouard Ducpétiaux: *De la condition physique et morale des jeunes ouvriers, etc.* (Brussels, 1843). Further, I. Pinchbeck: *Women Workers in the Industrial Revolution* (Chicago, 1959); Jürgen Kuczynski: *Geschichte der Kinderarbeit in Deutschland* (Berlin, 1958); Gustav Otruba: "Zur Geschichte der Frauen und Kinderarbeit im Gewerbe . . . von Niederoesterreich" (*Jahrbücher für Landeskunde von Niederoesterreich,* n.s. XXXIV, 1958–1960); Karl-Heinz Ludwig: "Die Fabrikarbeit von Kindern im 19. Jahrhundert" (*Vierteljahrschrift für Sozial- und Wirtschaftsgeschichte,* LII, 1965, 63–85); Valerie Castronovo: *L'Industria cotoniera in Piemonte nel secolo XIX* (Turin, 1965), chap. iv.

Revolution, to stay at their tasks from dawn till dusk. This traditional workday, long in summer and shorter in winter, was taken over by the factories, though there was soon a tendency to extend it as gaslighting became available. Everywhere in Europe the normal workday was twelve to fourteen or fifteen hours, with about an hour and a half out for lunch and afternoon refreshment. This stiff regimen applied not only to women as well as men but also to the children, many of whom tended to doze off unless prodded to continue at their task. The factory system, unlike that of home industry, did not permit variations in the work tempo. The inexorable demands of the machine therefore taxed the endurance of mankind to the very utmost.

The worst feature of the new industrial system was its instability, no doubt natural under the circumstances but nonetheless puzzling, even to the economists. Good and bad times alternated every four or five years, the depressions coming with great suddenness and the periods of recovery tending to be long and unsteady. This meant that the factory workers were liable at any time and without warning to find themselves without work, while the home-industry workers likewise could not dispose of their product. If the crisis continued for several years, like that of 1838–1842, all business would stagnate to the point where even skilled workers were obliged to accept any kind of work, with miserably low wages. At Bolton in 1842 the earnings of handloom weavers were down to three shillings and sevenpence hapenny a week. Masons, who ordinarily made thirty-four shillings a week, were lucky to earn ten shillings and sixpence. In Bath 150 skilled workers were obliged to content themselves with five shillings and eightpence per week.[11]

It is unfortunate that statistics on unemployment in this period are lacking in all countries, but British government reports and private analyses provide enough evidence to indicate that it was extensive and that its consequences were often disastrous. Karl Marx estimated in 1845 that one in ten of the European population was a pauper, that is, dependent on relief. This figure was probably too high for the Continent and too low for Britain, where at times one in six was destitute. Reliable investigations showed that in Manchester 50 to 75 percent of all workers were idle in 1841–1842. In Stockport, out of a population of 15,823, only 4,070 were even partially employed, while the remainder were totally unemployed or unemployable.[12]

---

[11] Thornton: *Overpopulation,* 30 ff.; R. S. Neale: "The Standard of Living, 1780–1844: a Regional and Class Study" (*Economic History Review,* Ser. 2, XIX, 1966, 590–606).

[12] W. Cooke Taylor: *Tour in the Manufacturing Districts of Lancashire* (2 ed., London, 1842), 38, 113, 220; Friedrich Engels: *The Condition of the Working Class in England* (1845, new ed. by W. O. Henderson and W. H. Chaloner, Oxford, 1958), chap. iv; Thornton: *Overpopulation,* 30 ff.; Hans Stein: "Pauperismus und Assoziation" (*International Review for Social History,* I, 1936, 1–120).

On the Continent as many as 60 or 70 percent of the workers might be idle at certain periods. In the large cities they made a pathetic sight as in winter they stood around in the public squares, shivering and hungry, hoping for something to turn up. Many were dependent on public relief (which was meager) or on private charity (which was hard to come by). In Paris 85,000 were on relief in 1840; in all Belgium 400,000, the figure rising to 530,000 in 1845 and to 691,000 in 1847. In one district of Silesia, where destitution reached unprecedented dimensions, 30,000 were in need for relief in 1844 out of a population of 40,000. In many parts of Europe the problem of relief had become so formidable that local authorities were unable to cope with it.[13]

Under the circumstances, the food consumption of the workers was absolutely minimal. Their diet consisted of bread, potatoes, a little milk or cheese, an occasional turnip or cabbage, and very rarely a bit of bacon or meat. In some places bread was reported to be a luxury, the population subsisting almost entirely on potatoes, like the Irish peasants. The evidence is conclusive that the lower classes were obliged to spend 60 to 70 percent of their income on food and drink, this in itself an indication of a very low standard of living. Careful studies leave little doubt that the worker in 1850 could buy far less food for his wages than he could in the year 1500. The decline was most striking in the item of meat consumption. In 1500 the per capita meat consumption in Germany was in the neighborhood of 2000 pounds per annum; in the early nineteenth century, in both Germany and England, it was thirty-five to forty pounds.

Budgets of workers' families are had to come by. In 1825 an English family of five required per week twenty-four pounds of grain stuffs (at three shillings and sixpence); roughly two pecks of potatoes (one shilling and twopence); six pounds of animal food (two shillings and threepence); and coal (one shilling and ninepence). Three shillings and sixpence were spent on clothing and two shillings and threepence on rent. In Paris a carpenter's family of four, of which the father could earn 1,200 francs a year if he had 300 days of work, required 1,050 to 1,300 francs to live decently. In Belgium a poor linen weaver, together with his wife and two children, could earn only 12.90 francs a week, while his living expenses (including two younger children) required 14.20

[13] Ferdinand Dreyfus: *L'assistance sous la Séconde République* (Paris, 1907), 13 ff.; Ernest Labrousse: *Aspects de la crise . . . de l'économie française, 1846–1851* (Paris, 1956), 104 ff.; Laurent Dechesne: *Histoire économique et sociale de la Belgique* (Paris, 1932), 411 ff.; J. Dhondt: "De sociale kwestie in Belgie" (in *Algemene Geschiedenis de Nederlanden,* Utrecht, 1955, X, 314–349); Kuczynski: *Lage der deutschen Arbeiter,* 233 ff.; Karl Obermann: *Die deutschen Arbeiter in der Revolution von 1848* (2 ed., Berlin, 1953), 40.

francs. Fortunately, in this case the deficit could be met by cultivating a little home garden.[14] Obviously, wages and cost of living were such as to leave the worker without a margin even in good times. When out of work he was reduced to relief and even to starvation. It was the plight of the urban workers that inspired Thomas Carlyle to write his impassioned *Past and Present* (1843) and produced throughout Europe a landslide of literature on the shocking social question.[15]

THE ROOKERIES OF THE POOR

The problems of modern city life appear to be unending, for two centuries after the onset of the Industrial Revolution the great cities of Europe and America are still grappling with the problems of unemployment, poverty, congestion and sanitation. But so much is certain: that in no European city of the late twentieth century are conditions comparable to those of the first half of the nineteenth, when the importance of sanitation was little recognized and almost nothing was known of the causes of disease. The surplus population was streaming into the cities—into the old centers as well as into the new industrial towns—and creating conditions of unprecedented complexity. A large part of the European population was being uprooted. Society was in a state of disruption.

Some idea of the magnitude of the changes can be derived from a few representative figures. In the decade 1831–1841 London's population grew by 130,000, Manchester's by almost 70,000, Birmingham's by 40,-000. The rate of increase in the British industrial centers was of the order of 40 to 70 percent in each decade.[16] The statistics for Continental cities are much the same. Paris gained about 120,000 souls between 1841 and 1846 and reached one million population before 1848. Vienna grew by

[14] There is some discussion of workers' budgets in Gaskell: *Manufacturing Population,* chaps. iv and v, and in Edouard Ducpétiaux: *Budgets économiques des classes ouvrières en Belgique* (Brussels, 1855). See also Frances Collier: *The Family Economy of the Working Classes in the Cotton Industry, 1784–1833* (Manchester, 1964), 49 ff.; Burnett: *Plenty and Want,* 42; E. H. P. Brown and Sheila V. Hopkins: "Seven Centuries of Prices of Consumables Compared with Builders' Wage-rates" (*Economica,* n.s., XXIII, 1956, 296–314); Wilhelm Abel: *Der Pauperismus in Deutschland am Vorabend der industriellen Revolution* (Dortmund, 1966), 17 ff.

[15] On the voluminous German literature, see Jürgen Kuczynski: *Bürgerliche und halbfeudale Literatur aus den Jahren 1840 bis 1847 zur Lage der Arbeiter* (Berlin, 1960); Carl Jantke and Dietrich Hilger: *Die Eigentumslosen* (Munich, 1965) is an admirable anthology of these writings.

[16] Arthur Redford: *Labor Migration in England, 1800–1850* (London, 1926), chap. iv; H. A. Shannon: "Migration and the Growth of London, 1841–1891" (*Economic History Review,* Ser. 2, V, 1935, 79–86); Leon S. Marshall: "The Emergence of the First Industrial City: Manchester, 1780–1850" (in Caroline F. Ware, ed.: *The Cultural Approach to History,* New York, 1940, 140–161).

125,000 in the years of 1827–1847 and became a city of 400,000. Berlin, which in 1848 had a comparable population, had grown from 180,000 in 1815, chiefly through immigration from the eastern provinces.[17]

It was hardly to be expected that adequate housing could be found for this influx of new people. On the contrary, new construction lagged far behind the population increase. In Vienna, for example, where the population rose by 42 percent between 1827 and 1847, the increase in housing was only 11½ percent (900 new houses). The newcomers were therefore obliged to crowd into the old, already congested central sections of the cities, while the more well-to-do inhabitants moved into new sections on the outskirts. "The difficulty of finding lodgings," wrote a contemporary historian of Paris [18] "is for the worker a constant ordeal and a perpetual cause of misery." In Paris some 30,000 workers (mostly unmarried men and women immigrants) lived in lodginghouses, where they were housed eight and nine to a room, without discrimination of sex.[19]

Sources describing the living conditions of the lowest classes in the mid-century are legion. Most workers lived in single rooms, not infrequently two or three families in one room, with a few ragged curtains for partitions. The Irish laborer of Manchester or Glasgow was, according to Carlyle, "the sorest evil" the country had to contend with, for "he lodges in any pig hutch or doghutch, roosts in outhouses, and wears a suit of tatters the getting off and on of which is said to be a difficult operation, transacted only in festivals and the high tides of the calendar." The Irish immigrant was apt to add a pig, a goat or a donkey to the family circle. In St. Giles, the Irish quarter of London, 461 persons were living in twelve houses in 1847, each having only 175 cubic feet of space. In Liverpool and Manchester the lowest class, chiefly Irish, lived in cellars, which were a popular abode in Continental as well as British cities because they were less leaky than the garrets and warmer in winter. Few of the workingman dwellings had heat, for fuel was expensive. In cold weather six or more individuals of both sexes and all ages would lie huddled on a pile of dank straw or

---

[17] On Paris, Louis Chevalier: *La formation de la population parisienne au XIXe siècle* (Paris, 1949), 45, 48, 183; on Vienna, Friedrich Walter: *Wien: die Geschichte einer Gross-stadt an der Grenze* (Vienna, 1944), III, 105 ff.; on Berlin, Richard Dietrich: "Berlins Weg zur Industrie- und Handelsstadt" (in Berlin: *Neun Kapitel seiner Geschichte*, Berlin, 1960, 159–198).

[18] Théophile Lavallée: *Historie de Paris* (Paris, 1852), 205.

[19] Etienne Laspeyres: *Der Einfluss der Wohnung auf die Sittlichkeit* (Berlin, 1869); Honoré-Antoine Frégier: *Des classes dangereuses de la population dans les grandes villes* (Paris, 1840), I, 22; Louis Chevalier: *Classes laborieuses et classes dangereuses à Paris pendant la première moitié du XIXe siècle* (Paris, 1958), 216 ff., 271 ff. On the German cities, see Ernst Dronke: *Berlin* (Frankfurt, 1846), chap. vi. The situation in England was discussed in the famous report by Edwin Chadwick on *The Sanitary Condition of the Laboring Population of Great Britain* (London, 1842; new ed. with intro. by M. W. Flinn, Edinburgh, 1963), 411 ff.

rotting potato peels with nothing but a ragged hanging for a cover. In her novel *Mary Barton* (1848) Mrs. Gaskell, who lived for years in "dull, ugly, smoky, grim, gray Manchester" as a parson's wife, has left a heart-rending account of lowest-class life.[20]

The problem of congestion was aggravated by the hopelessly inadequate sanitation. The great cholera epidemic of 1832 had struck particularly in the slum areas and had convinced many physicians that the incidence of disease depended largely on filth and polluted air. In France much attention was given to studies of public as well as private hygiene. Boards of public health were established in most large cities and important books were published on the relations of indigence and disease.[21] Chadwick, in planning and drafting his famous report on sanitary conditions among the working class, was much influenced by these studies. His painstaking investigations constitute one of the most important public documents of the nineteenth century, for they prepared the way for the passage of the Public Health Act of 1848.

The evidence collected by Chadwick was fully corroborated by contemporary writers such as Engels, Gaskell, Beames and others, to say nothing of those great pioneers, James Kay, Neil Arnott and Southwood Smith, all of them devoted physicians and humanitarians. They pictured the main streets of the cities as paved, cleaned and frequently lined with trees as well as with elegant shops and imposing residences, while behind or near them were often slums—narrow lanes and courts, many with alluring names such as Angel Court or Paradise Court, but unpaved, littered with garbage and other refuse, and invariably so noisome as to offend even those whose olfactory sense had already been dulled. Add to this the smog and smoke, the "inky panoply" that hung over the cities. Flora Tristan, the French labor leader, visiting the St. Giles district of London in 1840,

[20] The Chadwick report, cited in the previous footnote, is the most important single source for working-class conditions. Its record is well borne out by the classic account of Friedrich Engels: *The Condition of the Working Class in England in 1844* and by such contemporary studies as Gaskell: *The Manufacturing Population of England*, chap. v; Taylor: *Tour in the Manufacturing Districts*, 13. The classic French account is that of Louis R. Villermé: *Tableau de l'état physique et morale des ouvriers* (Paris, 1840), 361 ff., which may be supplemented by Chevalier: *Classes laborieuses*, 216 ff. Conditions in the Belgian cities are recounted in Armand Julien: "La condition des classes laborieuses en Belgique, 1830–1930" (*Annales de la Société Scientifique de Bruxelles*, LV, 1935, Ser. D, 247–302). For the German cities, see Johannes Scheer: *Deutsche Kultur und Sittengeschichte* (1860, new ed., 1938), 586; Alfons Fischer: *Geschichte des deutschen Gesundheitswesens* (Berlin, 1933), II, 500 ff. An excellent anthology of English source materials is E. Royston Pike's *Hard Times: Human Documents of the Industrial Revolution* (New York, 1966).

[21] Such as A. J. P. Parent-Duchâtelet: *Hygiène publique* (Paris, 1836) and Michel Lévy: *Traité d'hygiène publique et privée* (Paris, 1844–1845). See Erwin H. Ackerknecht: "Hygiene in France, 1815–1848" (*Bulletin of the History of Medicine*, XXII, 1948, 117–155).

was appalled by the sight of women in tatters, of children playing naked in the filth, lean and feverish, with looks of stupid ferocity: "The dreams of a delirious imagination would fall short of this frightful reality," she exclaimed.[22]

No city in Europe had at this time an adequate or sanitary water supply. In England water was supplied by private companies which, in the poorer sections, turned on the local pumps or standpipes only for a few hours on three days a week (never on Sundays). Workers were obliged to store water, which had at least the advantage of allowing the dirt to settle. For the water was taken mostly from rivers which received the street drainage. Paris had better water than London, for Napoleon had constructed a purification plant on the Seine above the city, and had begun to bring in water from the Ourcq River. In 1823 the opening of the Ourcq-Marne Canal had made possible the tapping of Marne water also. Furthermore, a great deal was done during the July Monarchy. The number of street fountains and standpipes was increased from about 500 to 1,850. Yet even in Paris the water supply was inadequate, being sufficient only for two baths per capita per annum.

Worse even than the water supply was the sewage system, for the existing sewers were intended only for drainage of the surface water and were, therefore, not connected with the houses. In all but the best sections of the city the refuse was thrown into the streets or courts, while human excrement went into cesspools under the houses. In London there were still 250,000 of these cesspools in 1850. At best they were emptied only once or twice a year. What is more, there were far too few of them for the requirements of the burgeoning population. In Manchester in 1832 a third of the houses had no privy. In many cities there was only one convenience for several hundred people. It stands to reason that in the congested areas the streets were full of "stagnant pools, ordour and heaps of refuse." In 1838 Chadwick could report from London on the "pondings of ordourous liquids as made one universal atmosphere of filth and stink." Much of this waste was ultimately washed into the sewers and carried to the rivers from which the water supply was taken. Friedrich Engels, in his classic account of the condition of the working classes, has left an all too vivid description of the River Irk, which, flowing through Manchester, gave off such a miasmic stench that it was all but impossible to cross the bridge. Even the great Thames was, at London, little more than a vast pool in which millions of tons of sewage were washed to and fro with changing tides. In London, Paris and other cities the work of extending and modernizing the sewer system had gotten under way

---

[22] Flora Tristan: *Promenades à Londres* (Paris, 1840), chap. x. Thomas Beames: *The Rookeries of London* (London, 1851), 48 ff., describes the same area in much the same terms.

by 1850, but the task was a Herculean one, requiring years of effort.[23] The great manufacturing towns, "reeking with lean misery and hungry wretchedness," (Dickens) were perfect breeding grounds for disease, as the medical profession was coming to realize. The rate of mortality was much higher than in the rural areas; indeed the cities would have become depopulated except for the constant influx of immigrants. Half the children born failed to survive the fifth year and the general expectancy of life was at birth still less than forty years. The horrible cholera epidemic of 1832 aroused interest in public health, but in terms of mortality the chronic illnesses, mostly pulmonary or dietary, were far more important than this novel affliction. Tuberculosis (consumption) was endemic, and was accepted as inevitable. It accounted for about 30 percent of all deaths and seems to have been at its worst in the decade from 1837 to 1847. In Paris 42,614 people died of it between 1839 and 1848. Typhus, loosely classed as one of the many "fevers" (asthma, catarrh, etc.), was epidemic as well as endemic, serious outbreaks occurring every five to ten years. By 1840 it was recognized as a disease of destitution, a product of slum conditions. Smallpox had been brought under a fair measure of control through the introduction of vaccination, but its place as a fatal disease of children was being taken by measles. Add to these afflictions rheumatism, constipation and dysentery and one can readily understand the weakness and apathy of many workers. Dr. Southwood Smith kept preaching that what was needed was not more charity but a better water supply, good drainage and pure air. The work of the physicians, like that of administrators such as Chadwick, was to culminate in the Public Health Act of 1848 and the inauguration of serious sanitary reform.[24]

Considering the appalling conditions under which the proletarian elements lived, it is not at all surprising that they should have become

[23] Chadwick's classic *Report* puts all other studies in the shade, but see also S. E. Finer: *The Life and Times of Sir Edwin Chadwick* (London, 1952), especially Book V, chap. i. On Paris there is a wealth of information in Henri Meding: *Essai sur la topographie médicale de Paris* (Paris, 1852), 250 ff., and in David H. Pinkney: *Napoleon III and the Rebuilding of Paris* (Princeton, 1958), 8 ff. On the German cities, the authoritative treatment is that of Alfons Fischer: *Geschichte des deutschen Gesundheitswesens* (Berlin, 1933), II, 500 ff.

[24] M. W. Flinn, in the introduction to the new edition of the Chadwick *Report,* 8 ff.; Meding, *Essai,* 122 ff. There is rich material in Charles Creighton: *A History of Epidemics in Britain* (Cambridge, 1894), II, 598 ff. On cholera, see R. E. McGrew: "The First Cholera Epidemic and Social History" (*Bulletin of the History of Medicine,* XXXIV, 1960, 61–73); Asa Briggs: "Cholera and Society in the 19th Century" (*Past and Present,* July 1961, 76–96). On tuberculosis, S. L. Cummins: *Tuberculosis in History* (Baltimore, 1949); René and Jean Dubos: *The White Plague* (Boston, 1952). In general, B. L. Hutchins: *The Public Health Agitation, 1833–1848* (London, 1909), chap. iv; M. C. Buer: *Health, Wealth and Population in the Early Days of the Industrial Revolution* (London, 1926), chaps. vii and viii; Richard A. Lewis: *Edwin Chadwick and the Public Health Movement, 1832–1854* (London, 1952); William M. Frazer: *A History of English Public Health, 1834–1919* (London, 1950).

demoralized. Whenever they had a little pay they were apt to escape from the discipline of the factory and spend "blue" Monday at some popular amusement place, whence they would return dead drunk and penniless. Or more likely the entire family would resort to the café or pub, in winter about the only refuge from the cold and the dark. All cities were well supplied with pubs. In 1836 there were 8,659 in London and 1,200 in Manchester. In Whitecross Street (London) there were twenty-three in 300 yards. That they were prosperous is beyond doubt. In one large London establishment 3,146 men, 2,189 women and 686 children entered in one day, by actual count. In Manchester one pub was entered by 412 persons within the space of an hour. In Glasgow, where conditions were at their very worst, it is recorded that nearly 30,000 persons would be in a "state of brutal intoxication" on a Saturday night.[25]

Extreme want also drove many into crime. In times of unemployment juvenile delinquency, as depicted in Dickens' *Oliver Twist* or Eugène Sue's *Mysteries of Paris,* became alarmingly widespread. A London police official estimated the number of thieves in London alone at 70,000. In all large cities organized gangs prowled the streets at night, breaking into bakers' and grocers' shops, attacking pedestrians and generally terrorizing the well-to-do.[26]

Especially ominous was the rapid spread of prostitution and the growing rate of illegitimacy. "We verily believe," wrote a London police commissioner in 1829, "that there are fewer conscientious scruples entertained respecting sexual intercourse than at any former period." [27] There was apparently no marked increase in the number of registered prostitutes, of whom there were about 9,000 in London and 3,600 in Paris, lodged either in brothels or in private rooms of varying degrees of elegance. These professionals were not the problem. It was the unknown number of poor women—factory workers, laundresses, seamstresses, domestics—who were driven to supplement their meager earnings through at least occasional prostitution. It was thought at the time that in London there were some 80,000 regular and occasional prostitutes. In the Waterloo Road district a French visitor was shocked to see them sitting in doorways or at the windows, nude to the waist and in most provocative postures. At night they would invade the West End in groups, as starving girls did in Vienna

---

[25] The contemporary accounts of Gaskell, chap. iv; Engels, 142; Taylor, 256 ff. Further, Wade: *A Treatise on the Police and Crimes of the Metropolis* (London, 1829), 223 ff., 305; James S. Buckingham: *History and Progress of the Temperance Reformation* (London, 1854), 28 ff.; Meding: *Essai,* 97 ff.; A. Baer: *Der Alcoholismus* (Berlin, 1878), *passim.*

[26] Wade: *Treatise,* 158 ff.; Beames: *The Rookeries of London,* 119 ff.; Chevalier, *Classes Laborieuses,* introd. and Book I; Scheer: *Deutsche Kultur- und Sittengeschichte,* 587 ff.

[27] Wade: *Treatise,* 148.

also, some of them carrying old mats as an added inducement to prospective customers. Recent researchers leave little doubt that Victorian sexual morality was largely a myth. Immorality was everywhere prevalent, but was not discussed in polite society.[28]

In the days when advocacy of contraceptive methods was just beginning, widespread prostitution inevitably resulted in a high rate of illegitimacy, especially among the lower classes. In the large cities a third to a half of all babies born were illegitimate. Since their mothers were unwilling or unable to support them, they were quietly disposed of by smothering or simple neglect. Dr. Edwin R. Lankester, the biologist, is reputed to have stated that in London alone there were 16,000 mothers who had murdered their offspring.[29] Certain it is that infanticide was widely practiced everywhere and that the abandonment of newborn children in doorways and on the streets had reached alarming proportions. In France and other Latin countries foundling hospitals accepted infants without asking questions, with the result that large numbers of children were so disposed of, many of them through professional *sages femmes*. In France not fewer than 127,507 children were so abandoned in the year 1833 alone. Since many of the babies were already in poor condition and the hospitals were unable to care for such large numbers, the majority of the children died within a few weeks or en route to the provinces, where they were sent to be nursed. Small wonder that the entire system was denounced as "legalized infanticide." [30]

The "barbarians" or "savages," as the Parisians called them, were utterly ignorant and brutalized. Gaskell was shocked by the profanity and obscenity of their language, even within the family. Disraeli, in turn, thought them different from the brutes only in their inferior morality.[31]

---

[28] The pioneer classic of the subject, A. J. G. Parent-Duchâtelet: *De la prostitution dans la ville de Paris* (Paris, 1836), falls squarely into this period. On the situation in England, see Wade: *Treatise,* 152 ff.; Flora Tristan: *Promenades à Londres* (Paris, 1840), chap. viii; Michael Ryan: *Prostitution in London* (London, 1839); Gordon R. Taylor: *The Angel-Makers* (London, 1958), chap. iv; Steven Marcus: *The Other Victorians* (New York, 1966), 6 ff. On France, see also Frégier: *Des classes dangereuses,* 49, 97, and chap. iv; Meding: *Topographie médicale,* 94 ff.; Chevalier: *Classes laborieuses,* 334; on Vienna, Adolf Schmidl: *Wien und seine nächsten Umgebungen* (Vienna, 1847), 141; Ernst Violand: *Die sociale Geschichte der Revolution in Oesterreich* (Leipzig, 1850), 45 ff.; and on Berlin Scheer: *Deutsche Kultur- und Sittengeschichte,* 587.

[29] Quoted by Annie Besant: *The Law of Population* (London, 1878), 25 ff.

[30] See the two excellent articles by Alphonse Esquiros: "Les enfants trouvés" (*Revue des Deux Mondes,* XIII, 1846, 211–242, 1007–1044). Further, Alexander von Oettingen: *Die Moralstatistik* (3 ed., Erlangen, 1882), 236 ff.; F. S. Hügel: *Die Findelhäuser und das Findelwesen Europas* (Vienna, 1863), 137 ff.; Léon Allemand: *Histoire des enfants trouvés* (Paris, 1885), 205, 276; Arthur Keller and C. J. Klumper: *Säuglingsfürsorge und Kinderschutz in den europäischen Staaten* (Berlin, 1912), I, 441 ff.

[31] Gaskell: *Manufacturing Population of England,* chap. v; Disraeli: *Sybil.*

Certainly religion played no part in the lives of the vast majority. The construction of churches was far from keeping pace with the population increase, and in any case the workers would hardly have been welcome in the houses of the Lord, dirty and ragged as they were. Many of them admitted to investigators that they never prayed and in fact had never heard of Jesus. A census of church attendance taken in England in 1851 revealed that the working people of the cotton and coal towns were "as utter strangers to religious ordinances as the people of a heathen country." Few of them attended church or chapel; indeed, in one of the poorest sections of London, only about 6,000 out of a population of 90,000. The workers made no secret of the fact that they regarded religion as a luxury of the upper classes, that they thought the churches indifferent to the sufferings of the poor, that they were excluded from the pews rented by the rich, and that, besides, they had no decent clothing to appear for public worship.[32]

The situation in France was much the same. The urban laborers were indifferent if not actively hostile to religion. In many districts of Paris only about one in ten of the men observed Easter Communion. According to prominent churchmen, there were in Paris only about 50,000 to 100,000 practicing Catholics in a population of almost a million, and of these most were women.[33] In religion as in other respects the working-man had become socially alienated, degraded, ostracized. Eugène Sue compared his famous *Mysteries of Paris* to James Fenimore Cooper's Indian tales: respectable Parisians were likened to the American settlers, living among dangerous savages. European society was indeed, as Disraeli asserted, becoming divided into two nations, one of which was increasingly moved by resentment and hatred, while the other was becoming more and more frightened by the sight of its sullen and at times ferocious neighbors. Carlyle, writing in his *Chartism* (1839) of the "wild, inarticulate souls," spoke emphatically of their sense of social injustice, which was harder to bear than even material want. Mrs. Gaskell, too, in her novel

---

[32] J. L. and B. Hammond: *The Age of the Chartists* (London, 1930), chaps. xii and xiii; George Kitson Clark: *The Making of Victorian England* (London, 1962), chap. vi; Kenneth S. Inglis: *Churches and the Working Classes in Victorian England* (London, 1963), 1 ff.; Owen Chadwick: *The Victorian Church* (New York, 1966), I, 332 ff., 363 ff. Thomas Cooper's *Wise Saws and Modern Instances* (London, 1845) is a collection of stories by a self-educated worker which throw light on the attitude of the workers toward the churches.

[33] Thomas W. Allies: *Journal in France in 1845 and 1848* (London, 1849), 41, 112 ff., 257, 278; M. H. Vicaire: "Les ouvriers parisiens en face du catholicisme de 1830 à 1870" (*Schweizerische Zeitschrift für Geschichte*, I, 1951, 226–244); Monique Vincienne and Hélène Courtois: "Notes sur la situation religieuse en France en 1848" (*Archives de sociologie des religions*, No. 6, 1958, 104–118); François A. Isambert: *Christianisme et classe ouvrière* (Tournai, 1961); 180 ff.; Yver-Marie Hilaire: "La pratique religieuse en France de 1815 à 1878" (*Information historique*, XXV, 1963, 57–69).

Mary Barton (1848), noted the rising antagonism of the workers to the propertied classes and had one of them say: "They'n screwed us down to the lowest peg in order to make their great fortunes and build their great big houses." In Germany many eminent writers such as Franz Baader and Robert von Mohl warned of the coming crisis, while the Swiss pastor-novelist Jeremias Gotthelf declared: "A new spirit has arisen among the workers. Their hearts seethe with hatred of the well-to-do; their eyes lust for a share of the wealth about them; their mouths speak unblushingly of a coming day of retribution. . . . ."[34]

[34] Franz Baader: *Ueber das Missverhältnis der Vermögenslosen oder Proletairs zu den Vermögenbesitzenden Klassen der Sozietät* (Munich, 1835); Robert Mohl: *Ueber die Nachteile der fabrikmässigen Industrie* (1835); Jeremias Gotthelf: *Die Armennot* (1841). These writers are all excerpted in Carl Jantke and Dietrich Hilger: *Die Eigentumslosen* (Munich, 1965).

ACCELERATION AND SOCIAL CONFLICT 1850–1914

part **II**

4. OLD AND NEW
SOCIAL TYPES

One of the most significant results of industrialization was to deepen the fissure between western and eastern Europe. This gap was already apparent long before the industrial era began; by the end of the nineteenth century it was very pronounced. Reduced to its simplest terms the difference was that in the West the common man had, in the majority, become an urban dweller while in the East he remained a peasant. Yet the simplicity of this proposition is deceptive. Industrialization did not immediately elevate the life of the common man in the West. Even in Britain it was still far from eliminating poverty and misery which was often all the more degrading in city life. Russian society, on the other hand, despite its oppressive backwardness, was by no means completely agrarian or static. Thus everywhere in Europe the new was mingled with the old.

Peter Laslett treats the unique case of England, the single fully industrialized society in Europe by the year 1900. Although farm labor may still have busied more persons than any other single occupation, most Britons had by then become urbanites with a salaried income. For the first time in history, it was appropriate to posit the existence of an urban proletariat which was conscious of its social disadvantages. Yet the course that Britain would take was uncertain since the welfare state was only a glint in the eye of a few reformers. One thing was clear: here was an emerging society which was different from any the world had ever seen.

Peter N. Stearns considers the other most rapidly industrialized European society, that of imperial Germany. There the real wages of labor were advancing, but their distribution was inequitable and the effect was often a serious social dislocation. The forced march of industry, spurred on by credit-banking and the formation of joint-stock companies, forced a progressive breakdown of traditional artisanry and required an adaptation of workers' skills to perform new tasks. Stearns provides illustrations of the transition from countryside to city: shifting family patterns, the creation of entirely new trades, participation in union and wildcat strikes, changing styles of consumption and fashion. In these and other ways, the factory system extracted a price from those who were drawn into the demanding pace of industrial life.

Arthur J. May scans the territories of the Hapsburg monarchy and finds them lagging behind the social transformation of the West. Even though industry was achieving phenomenal progress in the latter decades of the nineteenth century, rural labor remained predominant and the conservative influence of the Church was much in evidence. Still, Austrian society was becoming mobile. To the familiar types of the past—the peasant, the parish priest, or the provincial noble—were added new ones who were virtually indistinguishable from their counterparts in the West: the bourgeois merchant, the professional man, the salaried worker in large enterprises, and the urban Jew for whom economic prominence and acquired social status were seldom identical.

Lazar Volin explains why formal emancipation from serfdom provided no drastic solution to the social problems of the Russian peasantry. One obvious factor was the retardation of industry and hence the absence of any major outlet from the countryside. This outer fringe of European society remained overwhelmingly rural. It is impossible, in fact, to overlook the similarities between the lot of the Russian peasants in this period and that of the French before the Revolution of 1789. One important difference, however, was the *mir*, that communal organization of the peasants which was peculiarly Russian. As Volin demonstrates, a "chronic rural distress" was still the primary fact of Russian history and afforded a somber backdrop for the revolutions of 1905 and 1917.

Benjamin Disraeli was moved to write of the "two nations," by which he meant the upper and lower classes. It would seem equally appropriate to speak of the two Europes, one rapidly advancing to an industrial society and the other only gradually yielding the coveted terrain of tradition. Yet, for reasons amply explained, such conceptions are largely rhetorical. In its social structure, Europe was developing toward complexity rather than simplicity. The geographical bifurcation, quite apart from exceptions and qualifications, had nothing immutable about it. In hindsight we know that the twentieth century was to provide much different circumstances than one might have imagined on the eve of the First World War.

PETER LASLETT

The Transformation
of English Society

THE WORKING CLASS SINCE 1901

Rattle his bones, over the stones
He's only a pauper whom nobody owns

When Queen Victoria died at the very outset of the twentieth century one person in five could expect to come to this, a solitary burial from the workhouse, the poor-law hospital, the lunatic asylum. On the whole the first year of our century, 1901, was a prosperous time for the English, one of the twenty good years not marked by depression or by war to the death which they were to have in the fifty which followed. There was a war going on, it is true, the South African War, which, if men had but known it, was the beginning of the end of the English as a people of commanding world-wide power, but its social effects at the time did not go very deep. The huge coalfields of Yorkshire and Lancashire, the great shipbuilding towns, the acres and acres of factory floor given over to textiles, were made busier by the demand for armaments and uniforms and machinery. Nevertheless something like a quarter of the whole population was in poverty.

Poverty, we must notice, was no vague condition then, nothing like as uncertain as the state of "decreasing wealth of the kingdom" has to be for the historian looking back to England in 1688 through the eyes of Gregory King. Families were in poverty "whose total earnings were insufficient to obtain the minimum necessary for the maintenance of mere physical efficiency."

Those precise syllables come from Seebohm Rowntree's book called *Poverty* which appeared in 1901 and which published the somber results of a house-to-house survey carried out with monumental thoroughness in his native city of York, a railway center, where the family firm of Rown-tree manufactured chocolates as it has ever since. Confectionery is per-haps as representative a light industry of the twentieth century type, as railways were of the heavy industry of the nineteenth century, which had given England and especially the north of England her world-wide manu-facturing supremacy. Young Mr. Rowntree had done his work in order to find out whether a reasonably typical provincial city was like London. He had discovered that 27.84 percent of the citizens of York were living in poverty according to his definition. In London 30.7 percent of the people were in poverty as his predecessor and mentor, Charles Booth, had already shown, London, which was the richest city in the world and a fifth of the whole kingdom.

Englishmen in 1901 had to face the disconcerting fact that destitution was still an outstanding feature of fully industrial society, a working class perpetually liable to social and material degradation. More than half of all the children of working men were in this dreadful condition, which meant 40 percent of all the children in the country.

These were the scrawny, dirty, hungry, ragged, verminous boys and girls who were to grow up into the working class of twentieth-century England. This was the generation which was to man the armies of the First World War, although they were inches shorter and pounds lighter than they would have been if they had been properly fed and cared for. Those who were left of them became the fathers and mothers of the working people who endured the Depression of the 1920s and the Great Depression of the 1930s, and who saw at last the squalid streets in which they made their homes luridly lighted up by Hitler's bombs. They were also the men and women who nurtured the Labor Party, the working-man's party, and brought it to maturity in the 1920s, and to overwhelming, if somewhat short-lived, political victory in 1945. They are still, it could be claimed, the most easily neglected element in English political and historical consciousness even today.

We might take a very well-known example to demonstrate this fact, though the tenacious memory of labor politicians and labor voters for the terrible days of not so long ago might seem to prove it straightaway. Young Beatrice Potter was an assistant in Booth's survey, as gifted and extraordinary a member of the governing minority as ever took to "Social Reform" as the Edwardians called it. But she did not go as far as a year or two with the Charity Organization Society, and then marry one of her own set, compounding for a series of subscriptions to worthy causes as so many of her fellows seem to have done. She became the wife of Mr. Sidney Webb, of the London County Council and the Fabian Society, and the two of them founded the London School of Economics as well as the New Statesman. As Lord Passfield and Mrs. Webb—for the aristocratic Beatrice would have nothing to do with Sidney's silly title—they visited Russia in the early 1930s. Hence the title of their final book, the last of a long series, *Soviet Communism, a New Civilization.* Irreducible poverty, that of London in the 1890s and of all the English unemployed forty years later, had helped to turn them from liberal socialism and the most successful movement of gradual reform that the world perhaps has ever seen, into prophets of communism.

In this final mood, and perhaps only then, they ceased to be typical of the attitude taken up by their countrymen to what was ordinarily known in their youth as the "condition of England question," one question amongst the many others that the eminent English political leaders had to deal with. The exact percentages in Booth's and Rowntree's figures make uneasy reading in our generation, when statistics are so much more cautiously handled that two places of decimals almost never appear in sociological percentages. An attempt at a scientific, a physiological definition of poverty, one graduated in terms of the biological needs of an ordinary man in performing his day's physical work, would never be attempted today. It will, therefore, perhaps be doubted whether the shift from 1688 to 1901, from counts of parishioners and Gregory King, to house-to-house surveys, Mr. Booth and Mr. Rowntree, makes much difference as to reliability. Can we really be so certain that the problem of poverty was still so urgent after a century and more of miraculous economic growth and change? Our traditional picture of England in 1901, the first year of the golden Edwardian age, is altogether lighter than this.

What about the countryside, and the country towns? What about the really prosperous manufacturing areas, which were to make the England of Edward VII more expansive economically than it ever was to be again until George VI was on the throne and Mr. Attlee became his Prime Minister? The actual condition of the population as a whole of course will never be known, though in the succeeding two generations many cities were submitted to the treatment given to London and York, using an evermore realistic criterion of prosperity and poverty. But Rowntree had thought of agricultural England.

Some years were to pass before his analysis of agriculture was to be completed, but in his book on York he pointed out that in 1899 over three-quarters of the population of England lived in "urban areas." The time in fact had already almost arrived which we talked of when discussing the village community of the traditional world, when the balance between town and country would be completely reversed, and the typical Englishman would be brought up amongst bricks and mortar, and only the exceptional amongst trees and fields. Moreover Rowntree was probably right to assume that those who had remained in the country after three or four generations of steady emigration from it lived rather below the standards endured by their grandchildren, great-nephews and cousins in the city streets.

In 1903 the little village of Ridgmont in Bedfordshire, over the wall from the great park at Woburn, the seat of the Duke of Bedford, was investigated according to the principles of Booth and Rowntree. The Dukes of Bedford were doing very well in that year, with income tax at elevenpence in the pound and death duties at a maximum of 11 percent. Like most noble families they had urban as well as rural property, industrial and commercial wealth as well as landed. In fact the Fabian Society alleged that the Bedford Estate was receiving £15,000 a year from Covent Garden at the time that Professor Higgins met Eliza Doolittle outside the Royal Opera House. Still the estate was managed in an exemplary way and Ridgmont was being rebuilt cottage by cottage; the tall red-brick roofs of that time of expansive if cumbersome domestic architecture are still to be seen in the village. Yet the investigator found that 41 percent of the population living there were in poverty, the sort of poverty which left biological need unsatisfied.

We cannot linger long in Ridgmont, though the facts about countryside and town, about inequality in income and about the persistence of the country house as the political instrument of a very different society are all very important to our subject. In October, 1900, the Marquess of Salisbury submitted the name of the Duke of Bedford to Queen Victoria when he was reconstructing the Cabinet, and his Grace declined because of his interest in estate-management; Woburn remained a center of political power nevertheless. Perhaps the annual income of this great noble family was some £100,000 and it must have ranked with the largest in the country, even with the huge industrial and commercial fortunes, though an English duke might already find it advantageous to marry an American heiress, as the Duke of Marlborough had done in 1895. Here was a splendid contrast with an income of about £50 which was what was earned by a farm laborer in Ridgmont. In Gregory King's time the average nobleman had £3,000 a year and a laborer £15, which was a similar disproportion if a Duke then possessed double the ordinary noble income.

But though agricultural labor was still the biggest occupation in England in the early 1900s, it cannot have been any longer true that the country could be divided, as King divided it, into a large minority receiving six times the income of the bare majority. We cannot tell how the £6 10s. a year which King reckoned to be the resources of that quarter of the people in his day whom he called cottagers and paupers compared with Rowntree's £100 a year, or rather less, which he reckoned to be what a family needed to be above the poverty line in 1899. Still it is clear that the traditional, agricultural society as it had survived in Ridgmont was not more prosperous than the commercial and manufacturing society of the city of York. Nothing went on in this part of Bedfordshire except the tilling of the soil and the keeping of beasts; rural industry was already almost entirely dead. A few cottagers still plaited straw, but lacemaking had disappeared completely. The making of hats had gone off to the factories of Bedford and Luton. Not so much as a loaf of bread was baked in the village; it all came in horse vans from the towns. And every single village child was living in poverty.

To the historian of an earlier England it is a gross and telling contrast that Ridgmont should have belonged in 1901 to a residual area of rural society within an expanding industrial whole, an area already not much more than a fifth and still getting smaller. This made English society different in order from anything which had ever gone before, in Europe or in the whole world. It means that the process of social and economic transformation which we call *industrial revolution* was already virtually complete in our country. This distinguishes the society of England as it now is, very sharply from other societies. English social experience since the death of Victoria is the only lengthly experience any country has ever had of really mature industrialization.

It has been in fact experience not of a state of things exactly, but of a perpetual tendency towards continuous change. For industrialization is not a once-for-all process and it is an English error to suppose that it is. Since 1901 our country has tended to fall somewhat behind others in the race to reindustrialize with every new technique, but our history since 1901 has been a history of successive transformation all the same. The question of importance for the contrast we are trying to draw in this essay is the question of welfare. In so far as the industrializing process is to be described above all as a change in the scale of living, . . . only in England does it seem to have been virtually complete by 1901. What has happened since then has been a matter of the levelling up of standards, the lengthening of life, the diminution of poverty, the universalization of education. This may not have been the result of what became so suddenly and shockingly apparent after Booth and Rowntree had done their work. But since that time, intentionally or not, the spread of the benefits has gone on both by political compulsion and perhaps also of itself.

This may seem an easy and too comforting a generalization, since the contemporary world is even now discovering that in rich societies great hidden areas of poverty go on persisting. The conclusion that we shall reach about the Welfare State which arose in England out of the attitude which Rowntree represents will not be that it was completely successful in abolishing want in an industrial society, rather perhaps that it was just the last and most effective way of convincing the conscientious that it had been abolished. But when all this has been said there is a difference between Rowntree's revelations and those which shocked the 1960s about the condition of the old in Britain and of the colored in the United States. It is difficult for us now to realize what it meant in 1901 for England to have to recognize that after a century of leading the world in economic matters, when she was still undoubtedly the world's greatest political and military power, still in many ways the world's wealthiest power, a quarter of her population was living in poverty, in something like destitution.

If King's figures are comparable with Rowntree's, and if both are somewhere near the truth, then the growth of wealth brought by industry did succeed in reducing dependency and destitution by more than half in two hundred years, from the 1690s to the 1900s. If this was so, then it accomplished a great deal, especially when we remember how little sign has ever been found that progress of this sort was ever possible in the world we have lost, where the text "The poor ye shall always have with you" was a truth not worth the disputing. But the difference in standard between these two observers, the Stuart pursuivant-at-arms and the Edwardian industrialist with a conscience, is so enormous that this most challenging and difficult of questions must be left on one side for the present as unanswerable.

Unfortunately the same objection, that of a difference in standard, can be urged against the known facts about the subsequent history of poverty in the England of the twentieth century. The truly remarkable thing about Seebohm Rowntree was that he lived long enough to satisfy himself by personal investigation that poverty of the hopeless sort had virtually disappeared. In 1936, thirty-seven years after his first survey of York, he examined the city again. This time he used a much more sophisticated method of survey, impelled as he was by the disaster of unemployment which made him expect rather less of a reduction of poverty by 1936 than he had hoped for. Things were even worse than he feared, for on his new and more realistic standard 31 percent of the working class of York were still in poverty in the late 1930s, as against 43 percent in 1899, on the cruder standard he was then using.

But there were other differences between the two years. The greatest individual cause of poverty in 1899 had been insufficient wages, and no more telling indictment of industrialism could be imagined: but by far and away the greatest cause of poverty in York in 1936 was unemployment. When he was eighty years old in 1961, Rowntree was able to publish his last, and, it must be said, his least satisfactory, survey of poverty in the city. Using a new and still more sophisticated poverty line, he found that only 3 percent of the population were in destitution, and that the great cause of poverty was old age. From being a predominant feature of our social life, poverty, so Rowntree tended to think at the very last, had been reduced to insignificance.

We must notice that the abolition of poverty, if abolition it was, came about not gradually over the years, but suddenly, between the late 1930s and the late 1940s, as part of the foundation and functioning of the Welfare State. Within half a generation of that time, in spite of the warnings of Rowntree's successors as investigators of poverty in our country, we have now begun to think of the problem of industrial society as a problem of affluence, of having too much leisure and too many goods.

This attitude may not survive for long. There are signs that the remainder of the twentieth century may also interpret its social mission as the equalization of wealth between every citizen, whatever his color and his history. This time the redistribution will have to go on not only within so-called rich societies, but between "rich" and "poor" areas of the globe as a whole. But gross and familiar contrasts between our country as it was in 1901 and as it is now are quite immediate nevertheless. If any such superficial attempt as this one to describe the twentieth-century English working class is to be successful it must rely for the most part on the reader to make the comparisons from his own experience. Here is some of the obvious material.

In 1901 people in the upper class could expect to live for nearly sixty years, but those at the very lowest level for only thirty: paupers were still, in fact, as short-lived as the whole population in Stuart times. In 1901 you could tell at sight whether a man belonged to the upper or the working classes—bearing, dress and speech, size, attitude and manner were noticeably different. Some are still alive who remember seeing the Victorian farm laborer in his smock. School teachers then had an average of seventy children in every class. Only two-fifths of the population had the vote, and no women at all. Shop assistants worked an average of eighty hours in every seven days, and many of them lived in dormitories above their work, compulsorily unmarried. Since those who had no separate room were excluded from the franchise, a shop assistant living in voted only if the partitions between the beds in the dormitory reached the ceiling. So conscious indeed was this earlier England of social class that the bath-houses of London displayed the following notice:

Baths for working people, 2d. hot and 1d. cold.
Baths for any higher classes, 3d. cold and 6d. hot.

Of course such a crude method as this cannot convey anything like an accurate idea of what we are trying to show and the choice of poverty as a starting point for our survey has grave disadvantages. It distorts our picture of the working people because it leaves out prosperous workers. A wrong twist may have been given to the evidence a little while ago. It was not those who were sunk in hopeless misery who founded and ran the trade unions, who organized the Labor Party. The submerged tenth, as they were sometimes and too hopefully called, were not pre-eminently the people who created and transmitted the traditional culture of the working men which interests our own generation.

We must never forget that well over half of the workers were above the poverty line at any one time, though we are at the great disadvantage of knowing very little from first hand evidence of how they lived. Poverty was on the consciences of our fathers and grandfathers and it was poverty which they described for us. The working-class family, said Rowntree, pursing up his lips, spent 6s. a week on beer, a whole sixth of their income—hence a very great deal of secondary poverty, which the people could have avoided, and which less sympathetic people blamed them for. Now for 6s. you could get 36 pints of beer in 1901, and a working family in the clear can get a great deal of fun out of 36 pints of beer, even if it did sometimes finally lead to the workhouse.

Nevertheless, as has been said, the most important cause of poverty at the turn of the century was low wages. "The wages paid for unskilled labor in York," Rowntree concluded, "are insufficient to provide food, clothing and shelter adequate to maintain a family of moderate size in a state of bare physical efficiency." Here, then, was the proletariat of Marxian theory and the Marxian law of increasing misery under capitalism seemingly demonstrated for all to see, in the only mature industrial society then known.

The great puzzle about the English working-class may therefore seem to be why it was that the active, intelligent and well-paid amongst them did not all draw the correct Marxian inference, why it is that there has been no violent social revolution in England in the twentieth century. It cannot be said that geographical and personal propinquity has been lacking in anything like the way that it was lacking amongst their ancestors in the Stuart countryside. Working-classness has existed since well before 1901. It should become clear as we go on that the issue of revolutionary action was never quite as simple as this might make it seem, and that critical social change has in fact occurred without it. . . . The problem of the acquiescent attitude of English workers in the twentieth century goes beyond the limits of this essay. Let us turn our attention to the cyclical character of poverty in recent times, not so much the alternation of periods of prosperity and depression as the succession of events in the lifetime of an individual working man. This is one of the interesting points of resemblance between his situation and that of his predecessors in traditional society. Rowntree tells us,

A laborer is in poverty and therefore underfed:
In childhood, when his constitution is being built up.
In his early and his middle life, when he should be in his prime.
In old age.
And
The women are in poverty for the greater part of the time when they are
bearing children.

This is how the life cycle of working people went. Very few manual laborers in York in 1899 could have been without neighbors, friends, relatives struggling for subsistence. Infantile mortality was 94 in a thousand in the middle class, but no less than 247 amongst those in poverty. Again the resemblance with Clayworth in the 1670s comes to mind. One baby in every six died in the working class generally—the small coffin on one of the family beds, or on the table, or under the table when the family had a meal. This was a sight every working man must have seen and every working woman grieved for.

The discovery of the cyclic descent into the area of poverty was the most interesting sociological discovery which Seebohm Rowntree ever made, and has too often been forgotten. It meant that everyone in the working class had at some time in his life had personal experience of people living below the poverty level, even if he himself had never been so unfortunate. It meant in fact that the fear of poverty, the insecurity which that fear brought with it and the resentment against the system, all these things went deep down into the character of the English working man. It is not entirely fanciful to think of them as an inheritance from the traditional world of peasant, craftsman and pauper.

Those amongst us who now talk of the bourgeoisification—the horrid word they use—of the working class should take due note of this. Those who look for a center for the sense of community in the working class should note it as well, the sense of community which is forever being stressed as the heart and soul of the Labor movement. The positive urge to remake the world in a way which would abolish poverty has its spring in a negative attitude, the fear which dominated the lives of grandfathers, fathers, uncles, aunts and cousins. To call the prosperous working family of the later twentieth century simply bourgeois or middle class is a superficial historical misconception. It is rather the working family of the 1900s, of the 1920s or the 1930s with something of the horror of poverty removed. "Working-classness" in the social development of England in the twentieth century has, therefore, an obvious justification in attitude, in instinctive response, though of course it has many other defining characteristics. It has an immemorial history too.

So much for the English working class since 1901. For all the oversimplification which the developing story of our own century had brought with it, it must be obvious that no such phenomenon could ever have existed in the world before the coming of industry. . . .

PETER N. STEARNS

The Adaptation to Industrialization in Germany

. . . The issue that has dominated historical consideration of working classes—material conditions and their trend—need not delay the student of German workers too long. Real wages rose fairly steadily for factory workers from the beginning of industrialization. They certainly were rising between 1890 and 1914, despite rapid inflation, though the rate of their increase diminished.[1] Conditions were still bad, far worse than in France or Britain. Housing was cramped, diet still rather meager. Yet there was improvement in most consumption items. This being reasonably well established for the 1890–1914 period, we can more readily turn to questions of adaptation to industrial life which many historians, in their preoccupation with material conditions, have only touched in passing. We must in fact broaden the scope of "material conditions" to include pace of work or transportation time from home to job. For material conditions were obviously part and parcel of adaptation. German workers' adaptation may have been facilitated, vis-à-vis Britain at least, by the improvement in living standards over accustomed levels; but we must be sure that the quality of material life did in fact improve, that modest gains in consumption do in fact allow us to judge this quality.

Peter N. Stearns, "Adaptation to Industrialization: German Workers as a Test Case," in *Central European History*, vol. III, no. 4 (December, 1970), 304–23. Reprinted by permission of the publisher, Emory University. Copyright 1971 by Emory University.

[1] Jürgen Kuczynski, *Darstellung der Lage der Arbeiter in Deutschland von 1871 bis 1900* (Berlin, 1962), and *Darstellung der Lage der Arbeiter in Deutschland von 1900 bis 1917–18* (Berlin, 1967); these volumes chart a substantial increase in real wages between the 1880s and 1900, though more limited for craftsmen than for factory and building trades workers, and a slower rise after 1900. Ashok V. Desai, *Real Wages in Germany 1871–1913* (Oxford, 1968), is more detailed but not contradictory.

Many aspects of German manufacturing suggest the transitional character of the labor force even after 1900. Of course, given the constant change which industrialization imposes, a social group is always in transition. And a comparative framework for the German economy needs to be more carefully worked out than has been done heretofore. Nevertheless, it can be suggested that from the standpoint of the working class the German economy was not so uniformly advanced as national production figures imply and that some categories of workers were touched by traditions that had long been forgotten not only in Britain but also in France.

Take, for example, the German merchant marine. A large percentage of the sailors were still from sea villages and owned land there. Sailors were given holidays for harvest work—and this was true not only in small ports like Flensburg, but in Bremen as well. It is true that the peasant-sailor type was giving way to the thoroughly urban, propertyless worker, particularly in Hamburg. But the German merchant marine cannot yet be compared to the floating port population of Britain or the semiconscripted, professional marine in France. Relatedly, it was far less prone to agitation.[2]

The factory labor force was also less urbanized than its counterparts in the older industrial countries. Only 7 percent of the workers in one concern in the center of Magdeburg lived in the city; the rest were scattered in suburbs and villages up to 23 kilometers away. Metal workers commuted from the countryside and did occasional agricultural work in many areas.[3] Obviously, the railroad in Germany tended to retard the complete separation of workers from the country in comparison with France as well as Britain.

The character of many German firms themselves reflected the relative newness of industrialization. Leave aside the fact that there were still four million workers in the rural putting-out system.[4] The typical unit of factory employment was still not overwhelmingly large. The average mining company had 163.5 workers in 1907 and was only a fifth the size of its French counterpart. The average metal firm had six workers, the average textile company eighteen. These figures admittedly conceal the existence of some huge units, but they usefully point to a vast manu-

[2] E. Fitzer, *Die wirtschaftliche und technische Entwicklung der Seeschiffsfahrt* (Leipzig, 1902), and M. Pappenheim *et al., Die Lage der in der Seeschiffsfahrt beschäftigten Arbeiter* (2 vols., Leipzig, 1902). On France, André Sayous, *Des Grèves Maritimes* (Paris, 1910).

[3] Hermann Beck, *Lohn- und Arbeitsverhältnisse in der deutschen Maschinenindustrie* (Dresden, 1902); Otto Homme, *Die Entstehung und Tätigkeit des Deutschen Metallarbeiterverbandes* (Berlin, 1912).

[4] W. H. Dawson, *Industrial Germany* (London, 1912), p. 204; see also his *The Evolution of Modern Germany* (London, 1908).

facturing economy beneath that level.[5] Nor was German mechanization invariably at the forefront. By 1914, 3 percent of German coal output was produced by the new mining machines, compared to 10 percent in Britain. German printing and shoe manufacture lagged behind French technology. Most important, for understanding German workers and the labor movement, workers in urban industries dominated by small units and fairly traditional methods vastly outnumbered those in factory employment. There were, in 1907, 221,679 metallurgical workers, compared to almost a million metal workers. There were a million and a half construction workers, but only 700,184 workers in the engineering trades. There were almost as many wood workers (571,549) as miners (649,-277).[6]

Within this framework, two types of adaptation were being forced on or offered to workers in the decades before the War. The first was within the crafts. It was not new—there are signs of it before 1848—but it reached new levels in this period. This was an adjustment by artisans to employee status and a substantial increase in the size of unit of production. The average construction concern employed 2.3 workers in 1895, 7.5 in 1907, a rate of increase nine times that of mining and several times more shocking to the workers involved. Everywhere there are signs of disruption of artisanal traditions. Bakers—over 47 percent still housed and fed by their employers—began to be forced out of their dependence by employers and simultaneously to grow restive under it.[7] Overlying all of this was the introduction of new machinery and materials, from kneading machines to metal scaffolding. Similar developments were occurring in other industrial countries, but there artisans had made more of a previous transition to new ways. German artisans were unusually accustomed to small units of employment, to contact with the countryside—over one-half of German masons lived in villages and many did some agricultural work, continuing traditions of apprenticeship and *Wanderzeit*.[8] And any changes forced on German artisans were automatically important because of their predominance in the manufacturing labor force.

The majority of factory workers were first- or second-generation even in 1914. Census figures reveal this clearly. Between 1895 and 1907 the

[5] Georg Neuhaus, *Die deutsche Volkswirtschaft und ihrè Wandlungen im letzten Vierteljahrhundert*, II (Berlin, 1913). On France, Office du travail, *Résultats statistiques du recensement général . . . de 1911* (Paris, 1914).

[6] Kaiserliches Statistisches Amt, *Berufsstatistik*, 1907.

[7] Verband der Bäcker und Berufsgenossen Deutschlands, *Jahrbuch*, 1906.

[8] Franz Habersbrunner, *Die Lohn-, Arbeits- und Organisations-Verhältnisse im deutschen Baugewerbe* (Leipzig, 1903); Bernhard Adeling, *Sein und Werden* (Offenbach, 1952). The wandering of German artisans, both informally from east to west in the summertime, and formally through the two-years' travel that followed apprenticeship in many trades, is comparable to the situation in Britain in the mid-nineteenth century. See E. J. Hobsbawm, *Laboring Men* (New York, 1964).

mining labor force almost doubled, as did that in metallurgy. Textiles grew more slowly and chemicals advanced only 60 percent, but the machine-building industry almost tripled its employment. More specific studies confirm this pattern. In the wool hat industry in Luckewalde, where the industry began in the 1870s and grew only modestly, only 30 percent of the workers had had fathers in the textile industry and only 24 percent had had grandfathers who were factory workers of any sort. Of the fathers 23 percent had been artisans, 9 percent peasants, 11 percent members of the higher professions; of the grandfathers 38 percent had been peasants.[9] In the Ruhr mines in the mid-nineties only 37 percent of the workers were children of miners, and a few years later only 40 percent of the miners' children of working age were in the mines—and this in an industry where stability was usually high aside from outright increments to the labor force.[10] In one Mönchen-Gladbach textile firm only 14 percent of the workers had peasant fathers, though in the city as a whole large numbers of the new semiskilled workers came directly from the countryside.[11] In clearer contrast, a Berlin machine-building giant had only a small core of workers whose fathers had been in the industry; a large number of the new workers were from East Prussia while many of the unskilled had previously been handworkers in textile or shoe manufacturing, many of the skilled former smiths. Everywhere machine building,[12] including automobile production, drew in massive numbers of locksmiths from the villages and small towns.

Despite Germany's ranking as an industrial power, industrialization in the literal sense was new to most of its workers around the turn of the century. It was drawing in peasants. It attracted servant girls, following a common pattern in relatively early industrialization in which servant status constituted a transition from rural life to factory life.[13] It attracted many small-town artisans, even though none of the large artisanal groupings was declining in size. This, too, reminds us of an important aspect of early industrialization which had largely ceased in Britain.[14]

[9] Elise Hermann, *Auslese und Anpassung der Arbeiterschaft in der Wollhutindustrie* (Munich, 1912).

[10] Franz Schulze, *Die polnische Zuwanderung im Ruhrrevier und ihre Wirkungen* (Munich, 1909).

[11] Ernst Bernhard, "Auslese und Anpassung der Arbeiterschaft," *Jahrbuch für Gesetzgebung, Verwaltung und Volkswirtschaft im Deutschen Reich* (1911), p. 1407; Marie Bernays, *Auslese und Anpassung der Arbeiterschaft der geschoossenen Grossindustrie* (Leipzig, 1910); Max Morgenstern *et al., Auslese und Anpassung der Arbeiterschaft* (Leipzig, 1912).

[12] Heinz Reichelt, *Die Arbeitsverhältnisse in einem Berliner Grossbetrieb der Maschinenindustrie* (Berlin, 1906).

[13] Bernays, *Auslese*, p. 166, and *passim*.

[14] Artisans were still being displaced in Britain, of course, but there is no significant trace of the village smithy in the composition of the engineering labor force by 1900.

We can, then, learn something about the nature of adaptation to new artisanal forms and to factory industry by studying German workers. Adaptation to new residence and to new work is a massive subject, and I cannot pretend that what follows is an exhaustive treatment. The role of religion, for example, is not directly examined. Some questions that are germane to earlier industrial situations cannot be followed up for Germany at this point. There was little overt resistance to machines. When a Bremen shipbuilding company introduced riveting machines, manned by semiskilled labor, older workers angrily curtailed their production,[15] but in general the reaction to machines was subtle. Obviously machines were too well entrenched for Luddism to be conceivable, nor was this the truly brand-new industrial labor force from which Luddism stems.

The most basic subject to raise is whether the work itself was found pleasant or unpleasant. A study of the modern British working class bases its claim that a distinctive class exists primarily on workers' distaste for their jobs.[16] Can this be applied to an earlier industrial situation? Immediately after this we must ask what the wage meant and the extent to which consumption was viewed as a compensation for unpleasant work. The big question here is the extent to which a traditional view of both work and the wage gave way to a market or progressive view that related production to wage incentives and insisted on steady improvements in living standards off the job.[17] Changes in family structure were naturally forced by industrialization; what did they mean to workers? What was the workers' general outlook? Insofar as adaptation involved stress, what remedies did they seek? Finally, in all these questions, to what extent were workers united in their reaction? Were they developing, as E. P. Thompson suggests for British workers as early as 1832, not only common institutions but a common structure of feeling and a collective culture? [18]

Unskilled workers who came into the factories from the countryside worked hard without complaint. There is overwhelming evidence on this point. Silesian miners who came to the Ruhr thought it was evil to miss a shift. Amazed at the laxness of the Ruhr miners, they thought, "We Silesians are better than this crummy crew." [19] In metallurgical factories

---

[15] Niedersächsiches Staatsarchiv (Hannover) 70, police reports received on strikes, 1898–1905.
[16] John H. Goldthorpe *et al., The Affluent Worker in the Class Structure* (Cambridge, 1969).
[17] Hobsbawm, *op. cit.,* pp. 406–13.
[18] E. P. Thompson, *The Making of the English Working Class* (New York, 1963), pp. 194 and 423.
[19] Leo Uhen, *Gruppenbewusstsein und informelle Gruppenbildungen bei deutschen Arbeitern im Zeitalter der Industrialisierung* (Berlin, 1963).

in Hanover Poles and Germans of rural origin were noted as zealous workers. In a Mönchen-Gladbach textile plant workers from small towns and the countryside earned up to 12 percent above the company's average because of their high production.[20] Key groups of workers were loath to strike for a reduction of hours. Dockers did not mount the pressure for a limitation of their long workday that their counterparts in French ports began in the 1890s. Many were proud of their ability to work round the clock periodically, if only because their extra earnings contributed to their family's well-being. German miners rarely raised questions of hours of work in their strikes, though their working day was two hours longer than that in France and Britain. Their docility in this matter was due to the fact that over half of them were freshly in from the countryside.

There were several reasons for the new arrivals' zeal for work. They were grateful for regular employment. German unemployment rates were quite low for unskilled workers according to official figures, but there was substantial seasonal unemployment, at the least, in the countryside and the small towns.[21] Satisfaction with what seemed to them high pay was another obvious factor. Miners from eastern Germany thought that pay in the Ruhr was splendid. They delighted in daily meat and butter and were happy to be allowed to work hard, accepting overtime on top of their long shifts.[22] Accustomed to hard work anyway, many of them found nonmaterial satisfactions in working with machines. Some were entranced by the sheer power of machines.[23] Others were lured by the prestige of a big company; a worker took pride when it could be said of him, "He is with Daimler." Perhaps most important, they found factory work exciting or at least not boring. Women were particularly pleased with the bustle and camaraderie of factory work, when contrasted to their rural traditions or their work as servants.

How much did the ardor for work mean beyond the willingness to put in long hours? In the one study of the Mönchen-Gladbach textile factory, the above average production of workers from the countryside contrasted with the up to 30 percent below average production of city-bred workers. Rural masons and bricklayers also seem to have outproduced their urban

[20] Walter Timmerman, *Die Entlohnungsmethoden in der Hannoverschen Eisenindustrie* (Berlin, 1906); Beck, *op. cit.*

[21] Zentralverband der Maurer Deutschlands, *Jahrbuch,* 1909; *Der Arbeitsmarkt,* 1912 and 1913. In 1913 1.1 percent of the total work force was unemployed; Germany was remarkable for its low unemployment rate among groups like dock workers.

[22] George Werner, *Ein Kempel. Erzählung aus den Leben der Bergarbeiter* (Berlin, 1930).

[23] Waldemar Zimmermann, *Die soziale Verhältnisse der Angestellten im preussischen Staatsbahnbetriebe* (Altenburg, 1902); Heinrich Herkner, *Probleme der Arbeiterpsychologie* (Leipzig, 1912).

counterparts.[24] But in general it seems likely that the rural workers accepted long hours in part because their pace was rather leisurely. They were not usually highly skilled and therefore were not subjected to the most intense pressure to produce at maximum. Comparative studies revealed that German workers despite their longer hours were less productive than British; textile workers, for example, handled only a half to two-thirds the machinery per worker that their British counterparts managed. There is some indication that German workers took more breaks during the day than workers in France and Britain. The unusually high ratio of foremen to workers in Germany reflects the leisurely pace that many workers sought to adopt. Production fluctuated more during the week in Germany than was common elsewhere, with productivity on Mondays particularly low.[25] And workers, including some of rural origin, had habits of job-changing that reduced both their productivity and the work they actually put in during a given year. Much of this evidence admittedly is hard to apply to the newly arrived workers specifically. But it does suggest that the zeal for work had yet to be harnessed to an industrial pace, that it consisted mainly of plodding through a long day.

German workers generally had a different view. Some of the contrast has already been suggested. Big-city workers and miners established in the Ruhr did not seem to work as hard as the new arrivals. Skilled workers found the *Arbeitsfreude* of the unskilled proof of their unintelligence. Adolf Levenstein's survey gives us a statistical picture of sorts. In textiles, 75 percent of the workers found no joy in their work; 60 percent of the miners agreed, while 15 percent enjoyed the work if the pay was good, and 18 percent professed indifference.[26] Of the metal workers surveyed, 57 percent found no pleasure in their work. Levenstein probably had a biased sample, for he elicited responses from an unusual number of convinced socialists. A survey of workers in Mönchen-Gladbach textile plants, while not focusing on attitudes toward work specifically, revealed that 44 to 50 percent of the workers were "satisfied" with their position, though only 29 percent said that they really wanted to be textile workers.[27]

There were workers, then, who enjoyed their work. A weaver wrote

[24] Beck, *op. cit.;* B. Quantz, "Über die Arbeitsleistung und das Verhältnis von Arbeitslohn und Arbeitszeit im Maurergewerbe," *Jahrbücher für Nationalökonomie* (1912), p. 644.

[25] E. D. Howard, *Causes and Extent of the Industrial Progress of Germany* (London, 1907); Richard Ehrenburg, *Regenerativ-Ofen und Arbeiterbewegung in der deutschen und englischen Grünglas-Industrie,* in *Thünen-Archiv* (1909), pp. 18–139; R. M. R. Dehn, *The German Cotton Industry* (Manchester, 1913); Marie Bernays, *Untersuchungen über die Schwankungen der Arbeitsintensität während der Arbeitswoche und während des Arbeitstages* (Leipzig, 1912).

[26] Adolf Levenstein, *Aus der Tiefe. Arbeiterbriefe* (Berlin, 1905), p. 120 and *passim;* Adolf Levenstein, *Die Arbeiterfrage* (Munich, 1912).

[27] Bernays, *Auslese, passim.*

that he could get through the day quite pleasantly thinking about other things, particularly astronomy. A miner said, "There is no work so interesting as that of the miner." [28] Many skilled workers remained proud of their work, even when new machines were introduced. Printers who switched to the new composing machines resisted any return to manual labor, partly because this involved longer hours but partly because, though the skill required on the machines was reduced, they were able to read more manuscripts.[29] Still other workers took pleasure in working for a piece rate, because it increased their freedom and made the job more interesting. This was particularly true of the highly skilled, including some who had been artisanally trained in small towns.[30]

But majority sentiment was against these positions, even if some groups of workers, in metals particularly, had to surrender their opposition to piece work. Textile workers complained of exhaustion: "My eyes burn so—if I could only sleep." [31] Metal workers worried more explicitly about their health. Both complained of noise and boredom, one noting that his work was so dull that "wild longings" tormented him.[32] A miner in the Ruhr, Max Lotz, wrote an impassioned lament about the dangers and hardships of his work, which he found beneath human dignity. Even in the mines he found that "The work is becoming increasingly mechanical. No more incentive, no more haste, we muddle along wearily, we are worn out and mindless." [33]

The outlook of the majority of German workers, particularly among the skilled, was revealed in strikes and in the trends of per capita productivity. Construction workers cut their production dramatically as more and more construction shifted to the big cities, perhaps by as much as 50 percent. In 1913 Berlin masons set 300 stones a day, compared to 600 in Göttingen. Their production had begun to drop in the 1890s and by 1912 had reached British levels—suggesting that urban construction workers could catch up to the patterns of advanced industrial countries rather quickly, a point to which we shall return. In mining, productivity which had more than doubled in the second half of the nineteenth century fell slightly between 1900 and 1913; in one Silesian company it dropped from 368 tons per worker in the 1890s to 340 tons between 1901 and 1910. Technical factors undoubtedly contributed to these developments, par-

[28] Levenstein, *Arbeiterfrage,* p. 154.

[29] J. Zitzhoff, *Arbeitsgliederung in Maschinenbau-Unternehmungen* (Jena, 1913); Hans Hinke, *Auslese und Anpassung der Arbeiter im Buchdruckgewerbe* (Berlin, 1910).

[30] Reichelt, *op. cit.;* Paul Göhre, *Drei Monate Fabrikarbeiter* (Leipzig, 1913); Carl Fischer, *Denkwürdigkeiten und Erinnerungen eines Arbeiters* (Leipzig, 1904).

[31] R. Broda and Julius Deutsch, *Das moderne Proletariat* (Berlin, 1906), p. 173.

[32] Levenstein, *Arbeiterfrage,* p. 50.

[33] Levenstein, *Tiefe,* p. 57 and *passim.*

ticularly in mining as shafts deepened, but there is evidence here of genuine worker reaction. Both mining and construction were of course loosely supervised industries in which workers could indulge their resistance to hard work with some freedom.[34]

Thirty-two percent of all German strikes between 1899 and 1914 raised demands concerning hours of work. This contrasts vividly with the situation in France, where only 15 percent of the strikes involved hours of work. To this should be added many of the 21 percent of German strikes directed against foremen or other workers, though this rate was not so unusual.[35] Many German strikes that seemed to stem from other issues actually concerned the intensity of work. Miners in Barsinghausen, for example, struck for a raise because this seemed a safe demand, but the real cause of their strike was a new foremen who was driving them to work harder.[36] Construction workers and metal workers pushed hard for an eight-hour day—far harder than their counterparts in France or even in Britain. And the strikes for hours reduction were justified in different ways in Germany. In France, workers who struck for shorter hours generally talked of the desirability of cutting unemployment; some also wanted to seize the opportunity for more overtime pay. These factors were present in Germany. Unemployment rates among skilled workers ranged around 5 percent in normal years—much higher than the rates among urban unskilled, ironically—and this undoubtedly encouraged strikes for shorter hours. But workers also talked directly about the need to curtail their fatigue and the dangers to their health. The key grievance in the great

---

[34] Quantz, *op. cit.*, p. 644 and *passim;* Hobsbawm, *op. cit.*, p. 413.

[35] The French rate of "personal-issue" strikes was in fact a bit higher. The whole question of worker-employer relations is obviously vital for this stage of industrialization; we shall return to it in discussing socialism in Germany. On the surface relations were bad. A German worker with experience in England noted how formal worker-employer relations were in his own country in contrast, how sycophantic the worker had to become. (Ernst Dückerstoff, *How the English Workman Lives*, trans. C. H. Leppington [London, 1899].) But not all workers were sycophants—many felt free to criticize their foremen (Fischer, *op. cit.*, p. 386). And not all relations were so formal. Even in the factories, skilled workers were often treated more as journeymen-comrades than as workers by foremen, who used the pronoun "du" with them. The relatively high rate of collective bargaining and strike victories in Germany suggests that in most industries relations may not have been completely strained. Finally, insofar as there was unusual formality it may have reduced tensions in some situations. When *Kalkulationsbüros* replaced foremen in setting piece rates many workers professed satisfaction at the reduction of whimsical treatment, though not at the increased pace of work that often resulted. More generally there is no correlation between size of company and worker radicalism—the most radical German workers, judging by their strike rate at least, were in small-unit industries. See Göhre, *op. cit.;* Clemens Heiss, *Auslese und Anpassung der Arbeiter in der Berliner Feinmechanik* (Leipzig, 1910). Office du travail, *Statistique des grèves* (Paris, 1899ff.).

[36] Niedersächsiches Staatsarchiv (Hannover), 71.

Crimmitschau strike was chronic fatigue.[37] Shoemakers in Pirmasens struck for nine hours because new machines had made the work more intensive. Doubtless socialist influence helped workers articulate their resistance to intense work, but labor movements in France and Britain tried the same arguments with far less success among their constituents.[38] Finally, skilled workers in Germany began to seek annual vacations. Far more strikes—though still only a handful—involved this issue than was true in other countries, and far more workers won the point. In 1908 75,591 metal workers (particularly in machine building) had gained regular vacations; in 1912 the figure had risen to 233,029.[39]

The German strike movement was not, as a whole, nearly as sophisticated as that in France or Britain. Strikes were smaller, longer, and for the most part raised less advanced demands. So the attention to relieving the intensity of work stands out strongly.

The reaction to factory work was unquestionably intensified by the speed-up devices manufacturers everywhere were introducing around 1900 —such as the *Kalkulationsbüros* which appraised piece rates—and by the relatively advanced technology. Even so, the German workers' reaction may tell us something of the difficulties new workers experienced in comparable stages of industrialization elsewhere. We can speculate about English workers' first exposure to the din and pace of factory labor, but we know that many German workers were appalled. It took a generation for unskilled workers to shake off their rural-bred resignation, but the workers born in the cities *and* the large contingent of artisans entering factories or larger craft units for the first time had real problems of adjustment. Their vigorous resistance may have alleviated the problems, of course, as hours of work declined and in some cases as productivity itself leveled off. At the same time it can be suggested that this stage in the adjustment to industrialization was just that, that contentment with work might grow as experience increased and job conditions improved. A survey of German workers in the 1920s revealed that 67 percent of the skilled workers and 44 percent of the unskilled felt more pleasure than distaste for work.[40]

[37] Historische Kommission zu Berlin, Sammlung Schaarschmidt Nr. 32; *Schumacher-Fachblatt,* 1911–1912; Joh. Croner, "Die Folgen der Berliner Bauarbeiterbewegung," *Jahrbücher für Nationalökonomie* (1908), pp. 371–78.

[38] These points about France are explored more fully in Peter N. Stearns, *Revolutionary Syndicalism and French Labor: A Cause Without Rebels* (New Brunswick, 1971), *passim.*

[39] Deutsche Metallarbeiter-Verband, *Arbeiterferien* (Stuttgart, 1913).

[40] H. De Man, *Joy in Work* (London, 1928). This would qualify the conclusion in Goldthorpe *et al., op. cit.,* that modern workers take no pleasure in their work, though the comparison with the extent of middle-class pleasure would still stand. I must agree with Hobsbawm, *op. cit.,* p. 411, that workers' enjoyment of their work is commoner than outsiders may imagine.

Even before 1914 the labor force was deeply divided in its reactions to work. Probably very few felt as strongly as Max Lotz. How many, at the other extreme, agreed with the miner who thought his work the most interesting in the world? We cannot know precisely, but the existence of strong minority enthusiasm for work and the piece rate is undeniable. Differences in personality and health from one worker to the next make any generalization suspect. One can discern certain industrial patterns. Variations in discontent with work among textiles, mining, and metals were considerable even in Levenstein's poll. Textile workers, at least males, were least happy with their work because they were physically weak—their rate of military rejections was extremely high—and because their pay was low. Metal workers worried about the intensity of their labor but they found some interest in it. And they were better-fed and healthier to begin with. Metallurgical workers were more satisfied still, despite the fact they worked twelve-hour shifts. Their piece rates were rarely altered, partly because labor costs were a low percentage of the total, and so they could earn more as they worked harder or more skillfully. In machine building piece rates fluctuated, if only because the nature of the work changed so often; this created a tension in which the worker could easily feel unfairly paid and therefore overworked.[41]

Variations of this sort could be endlessly refined. I think that, for general purposes, three sets of reactions to industrial labor can be marked off. The first is of course the traditionalist approach brought in by the unskilled, to work long hours but not usually very intensely; traditionalism was sometimes abetted, particularly among women, by a sense that the factory was a diverting place. The second reaction was one of shock and resistance, as with male textile workers. The third embraced workers who found some genuine interest in their job, or whose resistance paid off sufficiently, in shorter hours for example, to remove any fundamental grievance, or who learned to compensate for unpleasant work by other enjoyments. The second group set much of the tone for the period, as was reflected in the polls that were taken. But we cannot determine the importance of each group by reaction to work alone. The outlook toward wages varied widely also, exacerbating the despair of some of those who detested their work—like Max Lotz, who could scarcely imagine being paid enough to compensate for his arduous labor—but aiding the adjustment of others to new methods and a new pace.

The outlook of the new, unskilled workers toward the wage has already been suggested. They seemed content, even delighted with the pay and living standards they won in the factories. As a skilled worker noted scorn-

---

[41] Otto Jeidel, *Die Methoden der Arbeiterentlöhnung in der rheinischwestfälischen Eisenindustrie* (Berlin, 1907); Morgenstern, *op. cit.;* Timmerman, *op. cit.*

fully, they were "satisfied when they are able to buy cigarettes." [42] They concentrated particularly on improving their diets, recalling a rural childhood of potatoes and milk. Silesian workers in the Ruhr, particularly the women, adopted local styles, but in most factories a hierarchy of dress persisted in that the unskilled wore simple garb. In Stuttgart factories the unskilled wore no overcoats and professed to find this appropriate. Perhaps the key was the attitude of the women, who were used to plain clothes and did much of the family sewing.[43] Housing—which was quite exiguous in the cities—seemed satisfactory. The unskilled complained of rents but not of housing directly. Here, obviously, the bad quality of rural housing set low expectations. The unskilled were generally satisfied with two rooms. They were not the ones who pressed out to surrounding villages to seek their housing; what they found in the cities sufficed.[44] There was little interest in other items of expense. Medical care was feared. As one East Prussian woman said, "God is the best doctor. If he wishes, I'm healthy; otherwise not . . . I would rather die than let them cut." [45] It is, I admit, always presumptuous to talk of satisfaction among poor people, but this seems to be accurate here. Traditionally low standards which factory work exceeded in terms both of pay and of regularity of work, plus the hope of some that factory life was only temporary, a basis for a return to the countryside with enough money to buy land, make this outlook understandable.

The traditionalists were a large group, but probably not a majority of the labor force. What of the rest: the textile workers and others who hated their work, the skilled workers in factories and shops who faced changing conditions on the job?

To what extent were German workers eager to improve their wages? As the outlook of the traditionalists indicates, such eagerness cannot automatically be assumed. The question can be further refined. To what extent did workers become aware of the wages as a market item, as an incentive which should be increased when production increased? [46] Did they transfer

---

[42] Levenstein, *Tiefe,* p. 120.

[43] Göhre, *op. cit.;* W. J. Ashley, *The Progress of the German Working Classes* (London, 1904); Schulze, *op. cit.;* Fritz Schumann, *Auslese und Anpassung der Arbeiterschaft in der Automobilenindustrie* (Leipzig, 1911).

[44] Oskar Mulert, *Vierundzwanzig ostpreussische Arbeiter und Arbeiterfamilien* (Jena, 1908); Eugen Jaeger, *Die Wohnungsfrage,* 1 (Berlin, 1902); Kurt Seidl, *Das Arbeiterwohnungswesen in der Oberschlesischen Montanindustrie* (Kattowitz, 1913). The preference for small housing units was not only a matter of tradition; it also saved on heat, which was understandably of great concern in Germany.

[45] C. Moszeck, ed., *Aus der Gedankenwelt einer Arbeiterfrau* (Berlin, 1909), pp. 44, 111.

[46] Hobsbawm, *op. cit.,* pp. 406–13. Hobsbawm implies a rather sophisticated notion of the relation between work and the wage, without considering the wage from the consumer's viewpoint; yet in traditional labor protest workers more often seized on consumption (price) grievances than on pay grievances—and they were likely to make the transition to a new view of the wage through this same channel.

some of their dissatisfaction with their work to the wage? Or did they view the wage more as consumers, in which case the question is less involved in the work situation, more in the degree to which improvements in the standard of living were sought? Both of these approaches are useful, but I find the latter more applicable to the situation of most German workers in this period.

Again, even aside from the traditionalists, German workers were divided in wage matters, but let us begin with some general points. Compared to workers in older industrial countries, German workers were not avid for wage gains. It is true that their real wages continued to increase, though slowly, in contrast to trends in Britain and France after 1900. It is also true that one must not exaggerate French and British eagerness for material progress. But there is a difference, clearly related to the stage of industrialization.

If German workers were able to transfer their grievances about changing work conditions to wage demands, one would expect a massive wave of strikes in this period. Such was not the case. Despite Germany's much larger labor force, fewer German than French workers went on strike between 1899 and 1914—25 percent fewer in absolute terms, over 100 percent fewer per capita of the manufacturing labor force. Relatedly, the average strike—with 119 workers—was unusually small. Wage strikes were still smaller than this average, the reverse of the pattern in more advanced industrial countries. Few German workers could be roused over this issue, and often those who were found themselves a minority among their immediate colleagues. Hence a French manufacturing worker was almost two and half times more likely to strike over wage issues than his German counterpart.[47]

It is true that 71 percent of all German strikes did raise pay demands, a percentage higher than that in France (where the figure was under 65 percent) and much higher than that in Britain. Without doubt, a minority of workers were capable of seeking wage gains. But a surprising number of major wage strikes were actually defensive, against a reduction of pay. Unfortunately it is difficult to be very precise in comparisons. Between 1899 and 1914, 8 percent of all German wage strikes were listed as defensive—about the same figure as in France. Even here, it is noteworthy that the French defensive strikes were much smaller than average and that they were bunched around the 1901–1902 slump, declining sharply thereafter. In contrast German defensive strikes were of about average size and their rate increased. Furthermore, the official figures underrepresented defensive wage strikes. Metal workers had to strike repeatedly against price-rate reductions that cut their take-home pay. So did shoe workers

---

[47] Kaiserliches Statistiches Amt, *Statistik über Streiks und Aussperrungen,* 1899–1914; Office du travail, *Statistique des grèves.*

and textile workers—like the Cunewalde weavers who struck against an 18 percent cut in 1901.[48] Again, essentially defensive strikes were far more important in other countries than official figures convey,[49] but they were less common than in Germany and usually less direct reactions to a pay cut. In many of their wage strikes, German workers argued simply in terms of poverty. Masons in Gelsenkirchen asked for a raise so that they could earn enough "that we can regularly feed our families."[50] Arguments of this sort almost never appeared among workers in older industrial countries.[51] They suggest that many German wage strikes and the high rate of wage strikes overall reflected no new attitude toward the wage but rather the marginal conditions in which many German workers lived.

Miners in France and Britain were in the forefront in the development of progressive material expectations. There were hints of a similar evolution in Germany, as in the Barsinghausen strike where miners asked for a raise to compensate for the rising pace of work. But the great Mansfeld strike stemmed simply from misery. Miners in the Ruhr in 1905 ultimately asked for a raise, but the strike initially broke out in pits where pay had been falling, and miners in the whole basin had for two years been subjected to periodic losses of earnings—and great physical discomfort—during hospitalizations for the worm disease. The strike actually illustrates the amazingly elaborate set of causes necessary to rouse large numbers of German miners and to produce even limited wage demands.[52]

Working-class budgets confirm the judgment that German workers found it difficult to envisage major improvements in their living standards. Overall, German workers spent a low percentage of their income on rents and recreation—the two items most revealing of rapidly rising material expectations. This, of course, is partly a statement of their relative poverty. More important for our purposes is the fact that when incomes went up, workers did not alter their budget allocations greatly. Metal workers earning under 1200 marks a year spent 56 percent of their budget on food and drink; those with incomes of 1200 to 1600 marks dropped this only to 55 percent; those with incomes of 1600 to 2000 marks dropped it yet another two percentage points; those with incomes of 2000 to 2500 marks dropped

---

[48] Münster Staatsarchiv, Regierung Arnsberg I 76 (police reports); Generalkommission der deutschen Gewerkschaften, *Correspondenzblatt,* 1904.

[49] Stearns, *op. cit.*

[50] Münster Staatsarchiv, Regierung Arnsberg I 76.

[51] The poorest workers who struck in France, for example, generally referred to past wage rates or to inflation, but not to absolute poverty. See, for an example, Léon de Seilhac, *Les grèves du tissage de Lille* (Paris, 1910), and *Le Lock-out de Fougères* (Paris, 1907).

[52] Niedersächsisches Staatsarchiv (Hannover), 71; Münster Staatsarchiv, Regierung Arnsberg I 84; Johann Leimpeters, "Der Kampf in Mansfeld," *Sozialistische Monatshefte* (1909), pp. 1545–52; *Aus Mansfelds Ehrentagen* (Halle a. S., 1910); Robbe Waltrand, *Die Knappschaftsfessel von Mansfeld* (Berlin, 1958).

it to 52 percent. Conversely the percentage spent on rent rose from 12 to 14 to 15 percent in both the higher income groups. All this suggests a desire to use higher earnings mainly to improve existing levels slightly, with particular stress on a better diet including more meat; yet metal workers had more advanced expectations than most German workers. Textile workers actually increased their percentage expenditure on food with higher earnings, while cutting the rent percentage. Recreation and health expenditures were very low generally.

Only in clothing were there signs of hopes for rather rapid improvement, as Ruhr miners and others awakened to possibilities of new fashions. Correspondingly this was the only nonfood budget category where German workers led those of the older industrial countries. The interest in clothing is characteristic of workers in many early industrial situations. Possession of respectable clothing for walking about the city on Sundays was extremely important. Along with some improvements in diet it seems to be the first new consumption interest to emerge. Why? Obviously clothes are cheap; perhaps an interest in them is naturally human, an extension of the skin as Marshall McLuhan would have it. But students of consumption habits can beware of calling anything "natural." Only by indirection were many workers led to want better housing; as we shall see, changes in family life rather than a virgin birth of the modern economic man were often involved. The early interest in clothing was a reaction to change, a desire to prove one's place in fairly well known terms, for even in the countryside differences in dress were known marks of status. For some of the small-town artisans and others who had status anxieties as well as a general sense of uneasiness in the factories stylish clothes may have been particularly important. By the same token the interest in clothes was not immediately part of a desire for more material goods generally. Workers could be satisfied with better dress. And clothing was cheap enough that it did not prompt elaborate wage demands.[53]

Three factors add to this impression of limited expectations; at least two of them, like the limited expectations themselves, flowed naturally from the early industrial setting. German workers were filled with a longing for the countryside. "I believe that every city resident, as soon as time permits, should go to the countryside, go to nature, and fill his lungs with

[53] Deutsche Metallarbeiter-Verband, *320 Haushaltsrechnungen von Metallarbeitern* (Stuttgart, 1909); Carl von Tyszka, *Die Lebenshaltung der arbeitenden Klassen* (Jena, 1912), p. 42; (British) Board of Trade, *Report of an Enquiry into Working Class Rents, Housing, and Retail Prices* (London, 1908); Board of Trade, *Report of an Enquiry into Working Class Rents, Housing and Retail Prices . . . in the Principal Industrial Towns of France* (London, 1909) and . . . *of Germany* (London, 1908); Elisabeth Gottheimer, *Studien über die Wuppertaler Textilindustrie und ihre Arbeiter* (Leipzig, 1903).

pure, unspoiled air." [54] Workers acted on this sentiment. An overwhelming majority listed walks in the country and gardening as their favorite recreations; pastimes that cost more money and might have induced higher expectations—including books and education—could not compete. Miners and then textile workers particularly relied on nature and gardening, but the interest was general. Longing for nature reflected the rural origins of many workers and the grievances about work that many felt. One may speculate that the walks and gardening not only inhibited material expectations but also, for the millions of workers who still could enjoy them, provided some genuine satisfaction. [55]

Drink was another carry-over from tradition that was also fed by discontent with work while inhibiting higher expectations. Many German workers were frequently drunk. They spent 6 to 11 percent of their budget on alcohol—an allocation that was not matched by higher segments of German society until the level of university professors. Articulate miners deplored their fellows' penchant for drink, which retarded their education and limited their goals. When polled, a fifth of the miners admitted their dependence on drink. Less than a tenth of textile and metal workers made a similar admission, but their budgets too revealed high rates of spending on alcohol which tended to rise as incomes went up. [56]

Skilled German workers showed a marked interest in cleanliness. (The unskilled did not, so I think we can dismiss sheer Germanness as a cause of the characteristic.) They carefully washed and changed clothes before leaving the worksite and they often struck for improved wash facilities. Their concern stands out among workers of other industrial countries. It suggests some of the tension and status anxieties of workers from small-town and craft environments. It is related, obviously, to the interest in clothing. [57] It may also have distracted workers from more elaborate consumption expectations because so many German companies provided excellent wash facilities and because agitation for further improvements took up energies that might otherwise have been used for wage gains. As one group of Ruhr workers noted when they won new rules on bathroom conditions in their factory, "These rules are worth much more to us than a pay raise." [58]

[54] Heiss, *op. cit.*, p. 222.

[55] Levenstein, *Arbeiterfrage*.

[56] Dückerstoff, *op. cit.*; L. Rexhäuser, *Haushaltungs-Rechnungen Nürnberger Arbeiter* (Nuremberg, 1901); Levenstein, *Arbeiterfrage*. On the university professors, see Kaiserliches Statistisches Amt, Abteilung für Arbeiter Statistik, *Zwei Wirtschaftsrechnungen von Familien höherer Beamten* (Berlin, 1911).

[57] Franz Schulte, *Die Entlöhnungsmethoden in der Berliner Maschinenindustrie* (Berlin, 1906); Schumann, *op. cit.*

[58] Gerhard Adelman, *Die soziale Betriebsverfassung des Ruhrbergbaus vom Anfang des 19. Jahrhunderts bis zum Ersten Weltkrieg* (Bonn, 1962), 1, 247.

In contrast to the general hesitancy about advancing wages, a minority of workers were committed to expanding prosperity. Some were in factories, like the metallurgical workers who shunned company housing and moved into towns distant from concentrations of lower-paid workers. Far more were still in the crafts. At an extreme, artisans like printers adopted an essentially bourgeois consumption pattern, even though their wages might be in the middling range. They cut the percentage they devoted to food—down to 39 percent in one case. They drank little and sometimes had their wives make their clothes. But they valued housing, spending up to 28 percent on rent, and they saved for the education of their children.[59] Still more workers kept a rather proletarian expenditure pattern but strove for steadily advancing wages. Skilled construction workers led the way. Their wage strikes resembled those in France and Britain in frequency and in the arguments used, which means they sharply departed from the norm in Germany. They conducted 32 percent of all strikes between 1899 and 1914, though they numbered only 18 percent of the manufacturing labor force, and their offensive wage strikes were almost 30 percent more frequent among all their strikes than the rate for strikes in general with construction strikes excepted.[60] They led the way also in wage movements that did not result in strikes; in 1905, for example, masons conducted 507 such movements affecting 106,761 workers. These workers, along with printers, brewers, and others, had a "modern" idea of the wage and of advancing living standards. They were not for the most part new to their trade. Though many of them faced radical changes in business organization and substantial changes in working methods in this period, they could adjust through the wage. And, minority though they were, their numbers were not small.[61]

Examination of adjustment to work and the wage yields three groups of workers—an assortment that is not surprising but one that is decidedly hard to unify. At one end were the traditionalists in work habits and consumption expectations. At the other end craftsmen and metallurgical workers either found enjoyment in their work—remember the printers on the composing machines—or compensated by seeking higher wages, or, most commonly, both. This leaves the group in the middle, the reasonably skilled factory workers, many from small-town craft backgrounds. Most of them had not made a full transition to a progressive view of the wage and consumption. Some of them were content with their work—the middle group of the work-aggrieved was smaller than the middle group

[59] Walter Abelsdorff, *Beiträge zum Sozialstatistik der deutschen Buchdrucker* (Tübingen, 1900); August Busch, *Preisbewegungen und Kosten der Lebenshaltung in Frankfurt am Main* (Munich, 1914); Jeidel, *op. cit.*

[60] Kaiserliches Statistisches Amt, *Streiks*, 1899–1914.

[61] Habersbrunner, *op. cit.;* Zentral-Verband der Maurer Deutschlands, *Bericht des Verbandsvorstandes*, 1905–1906.

of consumption-conservatives. But there was a mass of workers, in textiles, mining, machine building, and shoe manufacture, who disliked their work without finding full compensation in a new view of the wage. These workers were not yet capable of making the basic bargain that industrialization required, to admit new work methods, sometimes unpleasant ones, in return for advancing earnings. . . .

ARTHUR J. MAY

The Austrian "Other Half"

Well over half of the Austrian population at the outset of the twentieth century earned a living from soil and forests, a somewhat smaller proportion than in 1870. Conditions of rural life and labor varied considerably across the empire, for climate was not the same everywhere, terrain was diversified in character, great disparities in land tenure prevailed, and social habits and customs diverged widely. During the revolutionary storm of 1848, encumbrances upon the peasantry, lingering on from medieval times, were removed and many rustics acquired full proprietary rights over pieces of ground while retaining traditional privileges of pasturage in common meadows and of gathering firewood in the common forests. It was unlawful to divide a peasant holding under sixty acres; when a proprietor died, his land normally passed to the eldest son, who was obligated to compensate other children appropriately. That custom often put the inheritor of a property hopelessly and permanently in debt.[1]

At first the abolition of serfdom brought agricultural and social gains. The material lot of the rustic population showed some improvement, and great proprietors, who had been compensated by the state for the property rights of which they had been deprived, tended to have their estates cultivated more carefully, so that many doubled and even trebled their

Reprinted by permission of the publishers from pp. 165–67 and 171–79 of *The Hapsburg Monarchy, 1867–1914*, by Arthur J. May (Cambridge, Mass.: Harvard University Press). Copyright 1951 by the President and Fellows of Harvard College.

[1] In the archduchy of Austria this practice was abolished in 1868.

incomes in the space of a single generation. Land values shot up over a hundred percent, even more in some districts.

In sections of the Austrian empire, peasant holdings adequate to provide sustenance for a family, though rarely producing an appreciable surplus for the market, predominated. This was the case in the provinces of Upper Austria, Styria, and Carniola, and in the Alpine areas. In Lower Austria there was a marked tendency toward independent proprietorships on which gardens and vineyards were cultivated to satisfy the requirements of Vienna and other populous centers. Ownership of landed property in Carniola was especially widespread, a heritage of the land redistribution effected while the province belonged to the Napoleonic kingdom of Illyria. As of 1870, small Austrian farms were not, as a rule, heavily mortgaged; it was exceptional to find a little holding mortgaged to as much as half its value, and on the independent farmsteads there was considerable material comfort and contentment.

In certain areas of the empire peasants supplemented their incomes in special ways. Tourist traffic, for example, in the Austrian Alps, in the health spas of Bohemia, and on the Dalmatian coast created seasonal employment; in one Styrian district, peasants turned amateur veterinarians and traveled far and wide over eastern Europe doctoring animals by rule-of-thumb techniques; many a Bucovinian rustic was hired as a "beater" on a large game preserve. Work in forests and in timber industries was an important source of revenue for some poor peasants; and almost everywhere household handicrafts were carried on in cottages when the weather was inclement and in the winter months when the ground could not be worked. Womenfolk spun and wove, made lace and embroidery, or plaited straw articles, while the men turned out baskets and pots or worked up articles of wood and leather; wages for this toil were invariably small, miserably small.

The growth of factory production, which had ruinous consequences for cottage industries, and competition from mechanized agriculture both at home and abroad seriously affected the economy of the small proprietor of Austria. Service of mortgages reduced some peasants in time to the living standards their fathers had known in the serf period, when they were obligated to turn over part of their harvests to noble lords. Many a small owner sought escape from his economic plight by moving into factory centers or to a new home beyond the Atlantic. Increasing pressure of population in the countryside likewise swelled the exodus to cities and overseas.

In some mountainous districts of Austria wealthy townsmen bought up peasant holdings, planted them with trees, and used them as hunting preserves. What happened was poetically depicted by the novelist Peter Rosegger in *Jacob the Last,* a tale of rural Styria. In the novel many peasants sell their properties to a rich city chap, who allows trees to grow up on land that once had been tilled. Ravenous deer ruin the crops of those peasants who linger on in the community. So the peasants, with one solitary exception, part with their holdings and move off to cities, where they find living drab and unsatisfying. But the obdurate Jacob clings tenaciously to his good earth, though conditions of existence grow progressively more harsh. He is caught killing a deer for food; imprisoned, and in terrible misery of mind and spirit, he takes his own life. To his memory an old friend raised a rude tombstone, into which was cut: "Jacob Steinruther, the last peasant of Altenmoss."

Except in the Adriatic region, there was not much farm tenantry in the Austrian empire and where it existed the landowner commonly supplied seeds and fertilizers. The tenant's share of the produce was as little as a third, though in the least fertile districts his portion might reach as much as four-fifths. So long as a tenant cultivated the land properly he could not lawfully be evicted, and if he desired he might purchase the property. There was a distinct trend toward the conversion of tenant farmers into independent proprietors.

The conspicuous features of rural economy in the provinces of Bohemia, Moravia, and Silesia were the large estates of the aristocracy and the dwarf properties of the peasantry. Census reports of 1896 disclosed that more than a quarter of the land of Bohemia belonged to a fewer than 2 percent of the landowners, while in Moravia a third was owned by fewer than 1 percent. Huge properties in Bohemia, extending over more than five thousand acres, covered more than a quarter of the province; the largest of the holdings, belonging to the powerful Schwarzenberg clan, reached almost five hundred thousand acres, a veritable kingdom. In Moravia and Silesia the proportion of big estates was almost as great, and properties of thirty thousand acres were not unusual. A considerable part of these latifundia was forested and much of the arable soil was leased to peasants. On the big estates agricultural machinery was increasingly the vogue and there was a tendency to grow crops that required a minimum of labor.

In the northern provinces peasant holdings capable of supporting a family were relatively rare, by no means typical. As of 1896, 45 percent of the farms were under an acre and a quarter and 58 percent were smaller than two and one-half acres; owners of these drawf properties often rented additional land from the great estates. Similar conditions of land tenure existed in Galicia, where three-fifths of the productive soil belonged to big estates and many peasants owned only an acre or two. In the Cracow district, for each big property there were thirty to forty dwarf farms, and a like situation prevailed in the heavily wooded province of Bucovina.

The insufficiently landed rural class, wherever found, depended heavily for livelihood upon employment on the large estates, while the wholly landless class, an enlarging company, lived entirely on their pay as farm laborers. Treated with scant consideration, illiterate and inefficient, paid poorly and worked long hours in the busy seasons, the Austrian rural proletariat resembled that of Hungary, Russia, and sections of Italy. On the wide Schwarzenberg domains, the workers, some Germans, some Czechs, lived in a feudal environment, subject to eviction from their rented huts if, for instance, they married without the sanction of their lord. . . .

It is a truism that none but a peasant can really penetrate the peculiar psychology, the distinctive mentality, of the European countryfolk. Ignorance, stupidity, and habit combined to make them, particularly if they were owners of property, incredibly patient and industrious, extremely conservative, cautious and mistrustful. The range of peasant interests was confined to the necessary and the traditional: the exacting routine of land labor, the satisfactions and consolations afforded by mother church, the simple diversions of the countryside, and reluctantly, under duress, a term of service in the conscript army, and the payment of taxes.

A peasant's overarching pride was his land; his loftiest ambition, if he was landless, was to obtain land. Both the soil and the tools that turned the soil were sacred, the very stuff and staff of life. However few his acres might be, the peasant clung to them tenaciously and cultivated them in keeping with the time-tested customs and methods that his forefathers had followed century upon century. Normally not much affected by the economic ebb and flow of the wider world, the tiller of the soil was content to remain brother to the ox, to walk where his fathers had trod, willing to labor from dawn to dark for a bare subsistence, happy if his money income sufficed to procure homely necessities such as matches, oil, and salt, and to meet dues to state and church. Farming for the authentic peasant meant the raising of enough food to supply the wants of his family, and his wealth was reckoned, not in terms of money, but in foodstuffs to feed so many mouths from grandparents on down. Without the spur of capital accumulation, the peasant had little conception of labor value and small regard for efficiency in work. If his land was decently productive, if he was diligent and frugal, if the exactions of government and clergy did not weigh too burdensomely upon him, he and his family somehow managed. Let the big estates produce the surpluses required to feed the teeming populations of the industrial towns and cities.

Apart from the good earth, mother church bulked largest in the concerns of the peasant as she had done in bygone centuries. With the church and her divine services he associated the interpretation of the mysteries of existence, if any was required, and the explanation of the good and ill in the daily and seasonal round, as he engaged in the everlasting struggle with the elemental forces of nature. In the peasant beliefs, there was a large admixture of superstition, of notions and customs handed on by his pagan ancestors; woven into the rustic creed were strands of old, old earth worship. Belief in spirits, ghosts, fairies, and the like were prevalent, and soothsayers were often called for advice. The peasant felt that he, his family, his cattle, and his crops were somehow kindred phenomena. The good earth bore them, the good earth would reclaim them, when their life's task was done. Wayside shrines scattered generously about the countryside, and crowds of peasants marching in procession to hallowed pilgrimage places, such as Maria Zell in Styria, testified to the active interest of the Austrian villagers in the world beyond this world.

For the typical peasant, the voice of the priest was the voice of the Almighty. If the priest condemned "progress," it stood condemned; if the priest inveighed against city-bred innovations, they were anathema; if the priest said think this way and vote that way, thus the peasant thought and, if an elector, voted. Priest and great landed proprietor, exalted personages indeed, knew about these matters and deserved to be respected and obeyed, as they had been for century after century.

The Austrian rural masses were taught, and few doubted, that Francis Joseph was their divinely appointed guardian and peasant affection and loyalty for the ruler were impressively vast. It was almost pathetic to observe the enthusiasm with which the villages celebrated the name day, the birthday, and other days associated in any fashion with events in the career of their sovereign.

Marriage for the peasant was a transaction of the utmost importance, for a wife meant another pair of hands, a new piece of farming equipment, possibly an acre or two of land as dowry. Bachelor peasants were rarities. No doubt the round of the rural woman was even more prosaic and exacting than that of the man. By old established custom she started the fire and fetched the water, cooked the meals, made the clothes with primitive spindle or loom out of flax or wool, washed garments at the water's edge, mended, endlessly mended, and cared for cow or goat. She and her children performed such field tasks as their strength permitted; in the winter months many worked away at cottage handicrafts. Often the peasant woman gave birth to as many as ten children, usually without benefit of professional medical care, and a couple of days after childbirth she was back at her accustomed household tasks; quite likely half the children would die in infancy. Inability to bear children was the supreme disgrace for a country woman and sterility was legitimate ground for separation.

As a rule the woman was treated coarsely by her husband, considered inferior in value to a cow, for a cow after all cost money. Now and then the drab routine of drudgery was interrupted by folk festivals with colorful costumes, songs and dances; wild, boisterous affairs those peasant dances, requiring great physical endurance and expressing all facets of feeling and passion. The peasant woman, wrinkled and unattractive before she reached middle life, was "aged before she was old." But the really old woman—the chronologically old—was very often an austere matriarch, occupying a place of dignity and respect in her family and community.

Apart from the occasional folk festival and parties in the winter, from low-thatched cottage to low-thatched cottage, such social life as the peasantry knew centered on the village tavern. There dances were held on Sundays and holidays; there was staged part of wedding pageantry. Weddings were no doubt the most thrilling rustic social functions, accompanied by an elaborate peasant etiquette, with guests attired in their peculiar national costumes. After the church ceremony, guests assembled in the tavern and spent days drinking, roystering, dancing, and singing, to the neglect of their homework. One chronicler comments ruefully that as the nineteenth century moved along only the customs of drinking and boisterousness at weddings were honored. Christenings and funerals were also occasions for drinking and hilarity.

Illicit love was rife in Austrian countryside and there was much illegitimacy, more in some districts than in others, to be sure. Children born out of wedlock ranged (1910) from under ten in a hundred in Dalmatia to more than thirty-seven in a hundred in Carinthia; but the peasant attitude toward unblessed unions diverged from that of the American farmer, with his heritage of Puritanism and his generally higher standard of living and education.

Peasant codes concerning crime such as robbery and murder varied a great deal, but it may safely be asserted that the peasants distinguished between misdeeds committed against the government and the well-to-do and similar wrongs against their own fellows. A peasant who outwitted the tax-gatherer or the shopkeeper was likely to be thought of as clever, while he who fleeced one of "God's poor" merited and received the condemnation of the rural community; thievery seems to have been the largest source of trouble in the villages. Changes were introduced in traditional morals as schools brought some enlightenment and therewith a deeper sense of social responsibility and greater opportunity for personal improvement.

This or something like this was the way of life of the Austrian peasants, sowing and reaping, toiling and spinning, with little thought of gain or plan for profit, but rather so that they and their households might dwell in peace, close to the level of subsistence, and be allowed to worship in freedom.

For centuries Austrian society was composed essentially of nobility, clergy, and land workers, but in the very modern age a new element intruded, or rather a small older category was greatly enlarged: the town-dwelling burghers and wage earners. This social grouping expanded in proportion as trade and banking, transportation and industry progressed. Accumulation of wealth afforded greater leisure in Austria as elsewhere; the arts of civilized living could be and were more thoroughly cultivated, and the more widely culture was diffused, the larger the educational opportunities, the weaker became the fixity of classes. The Austrian bourgeoisie, thrusting forward in economic affairs, disputed the monopoly in politics and learning which the aristocracy and the clergy had so long held. The city of Vienna was the home of one of the most cultivated and subtly civilized middle classes to be found anywhere in the world.

Like their counterparts in other countries, the bourgeoisie of Austria prized diligence, creative work, and self-reliance as virtues. They heartily believed in the religion of progress, in the optimistic faith that there was an iron law of inevitable human improvement. They cherished the belief that, with the help of applied science and the growing prestige of reason, humanity was proceeding to a social paradise on this earth. They tended to substitute happiness in the here and now for eternal bliss or everlasting torment beyond the grave. Many Austrian middle-class spokesman rallied round the banner of anticlericalism, when indeed they were not unsympathetic to organized religion in any form.

As possessors of wealth or culture or both, the Austrian bourgeoisie disputed the monopolistic pretensions of the aristocracy to political power. Yet underneath, middle-class folk—or some of them—secretly envied the "bluebloods" and in their social attitudes and appetites paid them the most flattering variety of flattery—imitation. Plutocratic bourgeois families built splendid residences in the hope of forming social friendships with patricians and they allied with them against the haunting specter of socialism.

In actuality, the bourgeoisie of Austria was a heterogeneous grouping with very real gradations, just as was the case with the aristocracy and the rural population. The wealthiest bankers and manufacturers ranked above the owners of small shops and independent mechanics, who endeavored to safeguard their interests by supporting the Christian Socialist party, as did well-to-do peasants.

Also in the petite bourgeoisie were the salaried public servants and "black-coated" private employees; both of them had advanced educational training, often of university grade. There were, too, the members of the "free professions," physicians, lawyers, university professors, and others. Practitioners of the liberal professions spent long years in study and training and earned next to nothing before they were thirty years of age. The Austrian lawyer, for instance, after completing his university studies at about twenty-three, served seven years as a sort of apprentice before he was fully qualified to engage in practice. The economically more successful professional men enjoyed incomes and had living standards comparable to the plutocratic among the banking and industrial gentry.

There was a growing class of citizens, beneficiaries of higher education, who, on completion of their studies, found only inadequate opportunities to apply their talents—which were not always equal to their ambitions. Among this element there was a feeling of frustration and therewith, not infrequently, the conviction that the prevailing social and economic order required far-reaching transformation. From their ranks issued some of the leaders of the vigorous Austrian Socialist movement. Part of the middle class, too, was the "labor aristocracy," that is, well-paid skilled artisans, and some officials of trade unions and coöperative societies.

In the bourgeois society of Austria, Jews occupied a peculiar, and as time went on, a powerful position. According to the census of 1910, the empire contained 1,314,000 professing Jews, or just under 5 percent of the whole population. Apostasy, intermarriage with Christians, and Christian baptism, growing in volume among the educated Jews in the western cities of Austria, made heavy inroads into Jewish ranks. It is probable that Jews and "non-Aryan" Christians formed, as of 1914, the greater part of the cultivated and well-to-do classes of Vienna.[2]

Children of Israel actually resided in the realm of the Hapsburgs before the arrival of the Hapsburgs themselves, and it may be that Jews were dwelling in Vienna when the community was still a military outpost of the Roman empire. But most Austrian Jews lived in the province of Galicia, which was finally incorporated in the Hapsburg Monarchy in 1815. After about 1870, when legal limitations upon Jewry were removed, many migrated from Galicia to the west, and their numbers were swollen by impoverished newcomers who streamed in from Hungary, Russia, and Rumania to find better economic and cultural opportunities or to escape discrimination, abuse, and persecution. The wandering Jewish peddler was a familiar figure in all sections of the Austrian empire. By 1914 there was scarcely a village without its Jewish shopkeeper or tavern proprietor, many of whom combined moneylending with their other business, and many great landed estates employed Jewish stewards. Thousands upon thousands of Jews crowded into Vienna, Prague, and other cities. To the Jews, Austria was indebted for many pioneer industrial undertakings, such as leather and silk manufacturing, the processing of tobacco, and the large-scale distillation of spirituous beverages.

<hr />

[2] Standard works on Vienna's Jewry are Sigmund Mayer, *Die Wiener Juden . . . 1700–1900* (Vienna, 1917); Max Grunwald, *History of Jews in Vienna* (Philadelphia: Jewish Publication Society, 1936).

Vienna was the focal point of Jewish migration and concentration. One district of the capital, the *Leopoldstadt,* an island between the Danube canal and the river, was formally assigned to the Jews as a place of residence in 1622. At the middle of the nineteenth century only a few thousand Jews actually resided in Vienna, and there were only sixty-three officially authorized Jewish traders; yet many shops and stores were operated by Jews and they were supreme in the wholesale textile trade. In the years after 1870, Viennese Jewry increased rapidly, and by 1900, 146,926 residents were classified as Jews.

Down through the Christian centuries, Vienna's Jewry experienced the typical and familiar cycle of favoritism, discrimination, persecution, and then toleration again. Welcomed at times as valuable for the economic welfare of the community in general, or as financiers and counselors of rulers and princes, on other occasions Jews were the victims of destructive pogroms, wholesale pillage of property, and banishment.

During the reign of Emperor Joseph II, many traditional limitations upon the Jewish population were revoked or relaxed; Jews were allowed, for example, to engage in almost any trade, and to make loans on real property, though they might not buy it. Ancient regulations obliging Jews to wear distinctive costumes and debarring them from public places of entertainment were abolished. Those who lacked hereditary names were required to adopt them, so no longer were they designated simply as Jew Isaac, Jew Sara, and so forth. And Jews were made liable for military service on the same conditions as Christians. On the other side, special taxes upon Jews went untouched, and until 1823 the privilege of building a synagogue in Vienna was withheld. Down to 1848 Jewish residents were obliged to report to a Jewish Bureau every three days and to pay a tax every fortnight; they were not allowed to acquire land, nor to enter the civil service or the legal profession. As a result, they concentrated mainly in finance or handicraft industry, or became tutors or physicians.

Certain energetic and thrifty Jews pressed into prominent positions in the financial and banking affairs of the country. All other Jewish banking houses were eclipsed or crowded aside by the Vienna branch of the ramified and powerful financial dynasty of the Rothschilds. Solomon Rothschild, who arrived in the Hapsburg capital about 1820, quickly forged to the front in the banking world and, aided by his international connections, remained until his death in 1855 the most influential figure in the financial affairs of the empire. Befriended by Prince Metternich, he was particularly active in the flotation of government bonds, in the building of the early railways, and in lending to impecunious nobles.

Solomon's son, Anselm, a shrewd and cautious banker, launched the famous Viennese *Creditanstalt* on its fabulous career, and his heir, Albert, carried the fortunes of the Viennese House of Rothschild to dizzy heights.

Albert and his brother, Nathaniel, whose preferences followed artistic rather than business lines, built palatial mansions in Vienna, frequented exclusive social circles, and even gained admission to court society; they were the admiration of their coreligionists and the envy of many a Gentile. The Rothschilds were merely the most conspicuous representatives of the culturally refined Jewish moneyed aristocracy of Vienna.

Equality of rights was formally extended to Austrian Jewry in 1867, but deviations from the law were frequent in places. Allowed greater freedom of movement and in choice of vocations, Jews after about 1870 penetrated the learned or "free professions" and went into journalism in large numbers. In time a large percentage of the physicians and lawyers of Vienna and a predominant portion of the newsmen, even on papers notorious for their anti-Jewish proclivities, were Jews. They forged to the front rank in literature, in the theater, and in intellectual affairs, broadly, and pressed into lower positions in the civil service. And Jewish participation in the commercial and financal affairs of the empire increased prodigiously, with by far the greater proportion of Jews in the category of the small operator in wholesale or retail trading. Though no statistics on which reliance may be placed are available, it is safe to say that by 1914 the industry and trade of Vienna were to an overwhelming extent in Jewish hands. Not uncommonly Gentiles filled conspicuous offices in business concerns, where they were known to the general public, while Jews, who were the real directors, kept behind the scenes.

After restrictions on Jewish landownership were fully removed in 1867, some prosperous Jews commenced to purchase real property and by 1902 they owned something like 7 percent of the cultivable area of Galicia. A few wealthy Jews managed to secure titles of nobility, and some who accepted Christian baptism were able to marry into the bottom levels of the Austrian aristocracy. Among the Jews dwelling in the western cities, Vienna and Prague particularly, there was a distinct tendency to abjure the faith of their fathers, to accept Christian baptism, and to merge pretty thoroughly with the rest of the population. Assimilated Jews frequently discovered that they were regarded by conforming orthodox Jews as traitors and renegades, and that they were looked upon by the enemies of Jewry as undesirable and unwelcome intruders.

Deeply ingrained social prejudices persisted against all but the most polished and most affluent children of Israel. Old, insurmountable barriers kept Jews out of the Hapsburg diplomatic service, out of responsible positions in the army and in the bureaucracy (with rare exceptions), and denied them top rank in the universities of Austria. Dr. Sigmund Freud, the world-famed pioneer in psychoanalysis, was only the best-known Viennese scholar whose Jewish antecedents debarred him from a full professorship.

Very modern anti-Judaism in Austria, serious, open, organized agitation against Jewry, first assumed importance after the financial crash of 1873. The prosperity of a handful of Jews in a time of general hardship was strummed upon by adroit demagogues in whipping up popular passions and latent emotional prejudices, and Jewry entire was condemned as the author and the beneficiary of the economic distress. Thereafter suspicion, distrust, and hatred of the Jew were constant forces in the public and private life of the empire.

Competition of small Jewish tradesmen, competition of Jewish artisans, the displacement of handworkers by machine industry in which Jewish business men played a part—all furnished fuel for anti-Judaism. Not untypical of the antipathy toward Jewry on economic grounds was the comment of the clerical *Reichspost* on the death of Albert von Rothschild: "The state has long been the productive milch cow of a syndicate at whose head stands the firm of Rothschild, and some of the most recent profits pocketed by it might be considered anything but justified."

The fires of anti-Judaism were fed by the steady migration of *Ost Juden* from Galicia and other East European sources into the Austrian cities, especially Vienna. Small islands in the broad Christian-Slavic sea, the *Ost Juden* had largely preserved their medieval outlook on man and the world and cherished the belief that they were, peculiarly, the chosen of God. By choice as well as by social pressure they insisted on exclusiveness in marriage and in other ways, to a degree unmatched by Gentiles. Consciously and deliberately they were a folk apart and that was conducive to unpopularity.

Down to the minutest details of everyday living, the way of life of the eastern Jew was regulated by religious dogma and moral rule. Attempts to acquaint the Galician Jewry with modern ideas by innovations in education and in synagogue service met with small success, and efforts at cultural and intellectual reformation fell pretty flat; eastern Jewry, for the greater part, preferred to walk in the conservative paths which the fathers had followed.

Poverty-stricken ghetto dwellers for the most part, victims of hazardous living and inequalities and misunderstanding across the centuries, restricted and exploited by officialdom, subjected to recurrent physical attacks, despised and mistrusted by their Gentile neighbors generally, the Galician Jews were, by and large, unappealing specimens of humanity, uncouth, tricky, penny-grubbing, cringing. These tendencies, as well as their exotic costumes and their outlandish speech, wandering Jews carried to new homes in Vienna's *Leopoldstadt* and other centers of settlement.

Given time in their new and freer environments, the *Ost Juden* abandoned something at least of their medieval heritage, just as they shed their traditional garments, but in the interval they encouraged dislikes and suspicions among Gentiles that affected the whole Jewish community. Critics echoed the shrill warning of the German savant, Treitschke, that "year after year there pours in from the inexhaustible Polish reservoir a host of ambitious pants-selling youngsters, whose children and children's children will some day control . . . the stock exchanges and the newspapers." Westernized, assimilated Jews in Austria, or some of them, greatly resented the steady influx of *Ost Juden* and, out of fear for their own position, tried to prevent immigrants from settling in and about Vienna and Prague. . . .

LAZAR VOLIN

The Russian Peasant: From Emancipation to Kolkhoz

The very selection of the year 1861 as the starting point of this inquiry is symptomatic of the importance attached to the peasantry in the Russian social fabric. This is, I am sure, not due to a mere physiocratic bias or predilection. For 1861 is associated with a great milestone in the historic fate of the Russian peasant—the Emancipation Act of February 19. It decreed the abolition of what the great Russian historian Kliuchevsky characterized as the worst form of serfdom in Europe.[1] By the same

Reprinted by permission of the publishers from Cyril E. Black, ed., *The Transformation of Russian Society* (Cambridge, Mass.: Harvard University Press). Copyright 1960 by the President and Fellows of Harvard College.

[1] V. O. Kliuchevsky, *Kurs russkoi istorii* (5 vols.; Moscow, 1910), I, 434. For a discussion of the Russian servile system, see also: G. T. Robinson, *Rural Russia under the Old Regime* (New York, 1932), chs. 3–4; Lazar Volin, "The Russian Peasant and Serfdom," *Agricultural History,* XVII (January 1943), 41–61, reprinted in Herman Ausubel, ed., *The Making of Modern Europe* (2 vols.; New York, 1951), II, 709–31. Of the voluminous Russian literature on the subject re-

token, 1861 became a great national landmark, ushering in a new era justly remembered in Russian history as that of the Great Reforms of the early reign of Alexander II. Following in the wake of a severe jolt administered to the Russian autocracy by the humiliating defeat in the Crimean War of 1854–1855, these reforms revitalized national life after the sterile reactionary regime of Nicholas I. Despite the abolition of serfdom, the dictum of Gustav Schmoller, that in Europe "from 1500 to 1850 the great social question of the day was the peasant question," [2] continued to be applicable until much later in Russia. For in one form or another, it has never disappeared as a central political-economic issue at every critical juncture in modern Russian history, even after the peasantry ceased to be the predominant element of population.

Half a century after the emancipation, the peasant question or, as it was then called, the land or agrarian question was again in the foreground during the 1905 Revolution, and it emerged as an explosive issue a decade later during the revolution of 1917. It was central in the transition from War Communism to the NEP in 1921 under Lenin and, of course, in the collectivization crisis of the early 1930s under Stalin. After Stalin's death this question came back to plague the heirs of the late dictator.

This cursory review should make it clear that the peasant question in Russia was not settled by the emancipation in the 1860s as it was in Western Europe by the French Revolution and the subsequent agrarian reforms, and the industrial revolution in the nineteenth century. On the contrary, the historic contest between the Russian peasant and the landlord, shielded by the Tsarist state, continued until a complete victory was apparently won by the peasant in 1917. However, this was a Pyrrhic victory followed by a new conflict, this time between the peasant and the Communist state, bent on collectivization of agriculture and a rapid but lopsided industrialization. Throughout this period, while the institutional agrarian structure underwent significant changes, the peasant continued to be the Cinderella of the body politic, except for some transitory and sectional improvements.

The period between 1861 and the revolution of 1917 poses a crucial question: why, having begun with a promising agrarian reform, did it end

---

ferred to in the above publications, there must be singled out the monumental *Velikaia reforma: Russkoe obshchestvo i krest'ianskii vopros v proshlom i nastoiashchem,* ed. A. K. Dzhivelegov and others (6 vols.; Moscow, 1911). The first four volumes are devoted to a description and analysis of various aspects of serfdom.

[2] *Volkswirtschaftslehre,* I, 520, quoted in J. H. Clapham, *The Economic Development of France and Germany, 1815–1914* (Cambridge, Eng., 1921), 1.

with a peasant revolt resembling in many respects Pushkin's celebrated "Russian mutiny—terrible and senseless"? Certainly Alexander II recognized the dilemma—agrarian reform or eventual revolution—when he warned the serf-owning landlords in the beginning of his reign that it is better to liberate serfs from above than to wait until they liberated themselves. He saw the handwriting on the wall and hoped to forestall a possible peasant uprising, a rumbling of which was to be heard in frequent local mutinies of serfs, keeping alive that nightmare of the serf-owner—the *Pugachevshchina*.[3] When the government's intention to abolish serfdom became known about a hundred years ago, it was greeted with immense enthusiasm by the Russian intelligentsia of all shades of opinion: from the Slavophiles at the right, to liberals like Kavelin and (at that time) Katkov at the center, to Herzen at the left of center, and even Chernyshevsky at the extreme left.

This enthusiasm, however, faded as the emancipation legislation, which was to affect so profoundly the life of the liberated peasantry, began to take shape.[4] Not only did radicals like Ogarev and Chernyshevsky damn the emancipation reform, but even Ivan Aksakov, the conservative Slavophile, was critical. For a strong impact was exerted on the new legislation by the landowning nobility, which was strongly entrenched at the imperial court and in the governing bureaucracy. The landowners were bent on making the liberation process economically as painless as possible to themselves when they realized its inevitability. The pressure of the landlord interests, though in some respects divergent (as between different geographic regions), resulted in many a compromise unfavorable to the liberated peasants.[5]

To be sure, the peasant ceased to be legally what Herzen called "baptized property." And, what is equally important in view of the attachment of the Russian peasants to their land, they were not liberated as landless proletarians. This was the fate of the peasants freed from bondage much earlier in the Baltic provinces (1818), and the idea was

---

[3] A term for a peasant revolt derived from the name of Emelian Pugachev, the leader of a formidable peasant rebellion in the 1770s during the reign of Catherine the Great.

[4] For a detailed treatment of the emancipation legislation, see: Robinson, ch. 5; George Pavlovsky, *Agricultural Russia on the Eve of the Revolution* (London, 1930); P. I. Lyashchenko, *History of the National Economy of Russia to the 1917 Revolution* (New York, 1949), ch. 21; *Velikaia reforma*, V, 4–5; A. A. Kornilov, *Krest'ianskaia reforma* (Moscow, 1905), chs. 3–5.

[5] The divergence was principally between the landowners of the more fertile regions of the black-soil area, where land itself was the most valuable element of the estate economy, and the much less fertile nonblack-soil area, where the landowners to a large extent derived their income not from farming of their own, but from quit-rents paid by the serfs, who gained their livelihood partly from agriculture and partly from nonagricultural pursuits.

toyed with during the early preparatory stage of the emancipation reform but later abandoned.

The peasants did not obtain all the land they hoped for in accordance with the strongly implanted concept that land should belong to those who toil on it. Actually, the landowning nobility retained about 45 percent of the best land.[6] In the allotment of the remainder to the more than 20 million peasants, however, there were considerable regional variations, dictated by the divergent interests of the landowning gentry in different areas.

A large section of the liberated peasantry in the more fertile regions, where land was valuable, was allotted even a smaller area than it had tilled for its own needs under serfdom. The holdings allotted were also often of poor quality and location, and lacking such important components as meadows (hayland) and woodland, necessitating the leasing of these types of land from the former master. In these and other aspects of the land-allotment process was the genesis of the continued economic dependence of the liberated peasants on their former master which persisted long after the emancipation. Here was a source of irritation and conflict which poisoned the liberated peasant-landlord relations.

The situation was aggravated by the financial aspects of the emancipation reform. The peasants were saddled with a heavy redemption price for the allotted land that exceeded its market value before allotment. The fiscal burden of redemption payments and taxes, sometimes even exceeding the income from land, began early to figure as one of the chief causes of rural destitution in the findings of official investigating commissions and of private investigators and observers during the postemancipation era. Moreover, fiscal considerations involved in the task of extracting the burdensome redemption payments and taxes were, to a large extent, responsible for the fact that the peasant was not made an independent land proprietor or full-fledged citizen and that his mobility was restricted.

Thus, over a large part of the country, ownership of peasant land was vested in the whole village community or *mir* and not held as private property in fee simple by the individual peasant farmer.[7] The mir ap-

---

[6] Lyashchenko, 393. The reduction of the land area allotted to peasants after the emancipation amounted to 9.9 per cent in 15 nonblack-soil provinces and 26.2 per cent in 21 black-soil provinces, and 18.1 per cent for the combined 36 provinces. In some provinces the reduction exceeded 30 to 40 per cent (Lyashchenko, 384). It should be noted, however, that in addition to the more than 20 million private serfs there were also the so-called crown (state) peasants and those belonging to the imperial family, numbering altogether close to 20 million. These categories fared much better and suffered no reduction of their land area.

[7] For a discussion of the *mir,* see Lazar Volin, "The Peasant Household under the *Mir* and the *Kolkhoz* in Modern Russian history," in Caroline F. Ware, ed., *The Cultural Approach to History* (New York, 1940), 125–39.

portioned the land on some egalitarian basis to the peasant family or household (*krest'ianskii dvor*), which was the actual farm unit. The latter could not even refuse to accept an allotment, however unprofitable. For taxes had to be paid under a system of unlimited responsibility of the whole membership—whether the land was tilled or not. Incidentally, the legal registrictions with which the allotted land was hedged and segregated from other privately owned land were further tightened by the law of December 14, 1893.

The mir also assumed much of the police authority over the peasants which was formerly exercised by the landlords, including the power of deportation to Siberia. It shared with the heads of the households the important power to grant or withhold permission to obtain and renew the much-coveted passport, without which a peasant could not leave his native village for any length of time. It was, however, mainly the persistent and vexing tax arrears which led to intervention of the mir in the affairs of the individual household. To ensure payment, a member of the defaulting household could be hired out or the head of the household could be removed and a different member appointed in his place.

Thus the mir, usually under the leadership of its more prosperous or more aggressive elements, lorded it over the average peasant. In turn, the mir and the volost (a unit of rural self-government which comprised several village communities) were dominated by government officials, whose legal power of interference was increased during the latter part of the nineteenth century. The elected peasant aldermen were "elective in name only and depend to such an extent on the local government bureaucracy that they cannot even think about defending the interests of their community. As a result the better element of the village as a rule shuns service and the positions are occupied by the scum of the peasant population." [8] Such was the testimony gathered from various sources by an investigation at the beginning of the century.

The peasants also had separate lower courts, where minor criminal and civil cases were tried in accordance with custom law. This "very often proved to be no law at all," [9] so ill-defined and unfairly and arbitrarily administered was it. The quality of the village judges was no better than that of other elective officials, who were tools of the *chinovniki* (government officials). Corporal punishment was retained in these peasant courts long after it was abolished in the penal system of the general courts, which had undergone a thorough and highly progressive reform in the 1860s.

Still another set of limitations to which the peasants, but not other

[8] S. N. Prokopovich, *Mestnye liudi o nuzhdakh derevni* (St. Petersburg, 1904), 99.

[9] Paul Milyoukov, *Russia and Its Crisis* (Chicago, 1906), 343.

classes of the population, were subjected stemmed from the customary joint family ownership of the property of a peasant household, which was retained after the emancipation. While it protected individual members against the improvidence of the head of the household, it also had disadvantages for the individual. For instance, all his earnings from whatsoever source were supposed to go into the common pool—a serious matter, considering the prevalence of migratory work in the overpopulated Russian village. Even peasants who had long lived and worked away from the village were often forced to continue their contributions to the household of which they legally remained members. The weapon here was the famous Russian passport, which hung like the sword of Damocles over the head of any peasant who wanted to live away from his native village.

Despite the various restrictions the traditional Great Russian large peasant family began to feel the disintegrating impact of individualism following the emancipation. This was manifested in numerous family divisions, notwithstanding certain economic advantages possessed by a large peasant family. In the 1880s the government became so alarmed over the adverse effects of family divisions that it tried to restrain them by law. Such restraint, however, was unavailing and served only to provide an additional source of vexation to the peasant.

This all adds up to a picture of the liberated Russian peasantry remaining "a peasant nation consistently segregated from the general life of the community (state)," instead of being drawn closer to the rest of the citizenry.[10] Such a view has not been seriously challenged. Writing fifty years later, as moderate a political thinker as V. A. Maklakov likened the postemancipation status of the Russian peasant to a "kind of caste" [11] —an oppressed caste, we may add—lorded over by the chinovniki and their stooges.

The segregation or insulation of the peasant class was enhanced by the growing cultural lag between the town and the country. Culturally, urban Russia made great strides during the second half of the nineteenth century with a significant democratization and broadening of the predominantly upper-class culture. But this progress hardly touched the Russian village, which continued to live in ignorance. Precious little was done by the Tsarist government even to stamp out wholesale illiteracy until the revolution of 1905. On the contrary, it did its best to hamper the educational and cultural activities undertaken by the local self-government (zemstvo), private organizations, and public-spirited individuals. The government attitude was summed up by a well-known authority, N. N. Kovalevsky, as follows:

[10] I. M. Strakhovsky, in *Krest'ianskii stroi* (St. Petersburg, 1905), I, 388.
[11] V. A. Maklakov, "The Agrarian Problem in Russia before the Revolution," *Russian Review,* IX (January 1950), 3–15.

The principal objective of the government was not to spread popular education as widely and as rapidly as possible, but to ward off some kind of a danger to the nation because the people will acquire too much knowledge unnecessarily through schools and books, and will broaden their intellectual horizon. There are still not a few persons who are convinced that popular ignorance is the best guarantee of social order.[12]

"The access of peasants to books was hindered to the utmost by the authorities; lectures and talks in the village, even when dealing with strictly specialized subjects, met actually almost insurmountable obstacles," wrote the eminent Russian economist and educator, A. A. Manuilov.[13]

It was the consensus of experts and observers of Russian rural conditions at the turn of the century that the legal, social, and cultural isolation and ignorance of the liberated peasantry failed to develop its power of initiative, stifled the spirit of enterprise, and tended to reinforce the natural inertia. Thus it also contributed to the growing economic destitution caused by the inadequate land allotment in many areas and aggravated by a rapidly growing population and heavy fiscal burdens. This situation was complicated by a transition from a self-sufficient to a money economy and by inadequate outlets for the surplus manpower. These were lacking because of slow industrial development, failure to encourage agricultural resettlement, legal restrictions on mobility, and insufficient improvement and intensification of agricultural techniques. The latter process was, in turn, retarded by peasant poverty and the consequent shortage of capital, inadequate markets for farm products, lack of know-how, cultural backwardness of the farm population, and lack of agronomic assistance.

The idea that all was not well with emancipated rural Russia began to gain ground in the public mind soon after the emancipation reform. As a matter of fact, as we saw above, serious criticism of the reform began with its very proclamation. A decade later, in 1872, an official commission of inquiry into rural conditions was set up, the Valuev Commission, before which much pessimistic testimony was given. Twenty years later, following the catastrophic famine in 1891, an even gloomier view that the Russian village was in the throes of a serious crisis because of increasing impoverishment gained wide acceptance. The paradox of a chronic undernourishment of the farm population in a country which had become one of the leading exporters of grain and other foodstuffs was stressed by numerous observers and witnesses before the official investigating commissions, such as that established under the chairmanship of the Minister of Finance, Count Witte. The increase in the number of peasant households without work horses and the generally poor condition of peasant livestock lacking an adequate feed-supply base, the in-

---

[12] Prokopovich, 54.
[13] A. A. Manuilov, *Pozemel'nyi vopros v Rossii* (Moscow, 1905), 47.

creasing parceling of peasant holdings, the piling up of tax arrears—these were some of the symptoms of the growing deterioration of peasant agriculture.

If the peasant could still, with some difficulty, keep his head above water in years of good or average harvests, he was faced with disaster when crops failed, as they often did, especially in the large semiarid belt of Russia. Famine conditions, epidemics, increased mortality, decrease in the number of livestock (including work horses which, by striking at the sole source of farm power, did more than anything else to undermine the very foundation of peasant farming)—this is the spectacle of the growing destitution of a famine-stricken Russian village. The adverse effects of such conditions were felt long after the worst of the famine had passed. What Kipling wrote of the Indian peasant in the 1890s could be applied to his Russian counterpart as well: "His life is a long-drawn question between a crop and a crop."

The chronic rural distress should not obscure the fact that there always had been a small group which was economically better off than the great mass of the peasants. Leadership in the village and also a tendency to exploit the poorer peasants through usurious loans, and such, was often characteristic of this group. Such economic stratification in the village was noted, for instance, as early as the 1870s by the astute observer, A. N. Engel'gardt, in his celebrated *Letters from the Village* which, incidentally, can still be read with much interest and were recently republished by the Soviets.[14] But growing economic stratification in the village was particularly stressed by Marxist socialist writers, who appeared on the scene in the 1880s. At that time a split took place in the Russian socialist movement between the new orthodox Marxist wing and the older populist (*narodnik*) or agrarian-minded current which based its socialist ideology on the peasant mir and not on the industrial proletariat. A vigorous controversy developed between the Marxists and the populists concerning the trend of economic development of Russia and, more specifically, the inevitability of its passing through a capitalist stage. The populists took a dim view of this. The Marxists, on the contrary, found supporting evidence for their traditional analysis of economic development (which postulates class stratification and polarization concomitant with the growth of capitalism) in the stratification process taking place in the Russian village. They claimed that the mir system with its egalitarian tendency of land tenure retarded but did not eliminate this process. However, in their preoccupation with economics, the Marxists neglected other influences in rural stratification, notably the demographic factor —that is, the composition and the size of the family. These, as Kaufman,

[14] A. N. Engel'gardt, *Iz derevni. 12 pisem 1872–1877* (Moscow, 1937).

Chaianov, and others showed, played an important role in the process of village stratification. Larger and stronger peasant holdings were usually associated with larger families, and vice versa.[15]

The public discussion of the agrarian question and the toil of scholars and official investigating commissions produced copious and highly valuable material on rural conditions in Russia for which a student of Russian agrarian history must be eternally grateful. But they did not result in any serious corrective measures until the revolution of 1905. To be sure, the peasant had the active sympathy of the progressive Russian intelligentsia which considered it a sacred duty to help the poverty-stricken masses. As ill-paid doctors, teachers, nurses, and zemstvo workers, the intellectuals threw themselves unsparingly into this work, undeterred by the discouraging opposition and persecution of the government. Famine relief especially brought out strenuous efforts by the intelligentsia on behalf of the stricken population. But all this devotion was a drop in the ocean of peasant need. However, it greatly helped to keep the issue in the public spotlight. And so did the sympathetic interest in the peasant by the Russian literature of the pre-Soviet era, imbued with a strong humanitarian tradition.

The more radical populist section of the intelligentsia also tried, against great odds, to arouse the peasantry by spreading socialist propaganda in the villages. It considered the Russian peasant partly prepared to embrace socialism because it detected a socialist germ in the institution of peasant communal land tenure, the mir, to which even Karl Marx gave qualified approval.[16] But this socialist propaganda, even if it had not been quickly suppressed by the government, proved an abysmal failure. The peasants were not interested in socialism.

> "What will you do," one of the propagandists (Zheliabov) asked a peasant whom he thought entirely converted to the socialist doctrine, "if you should get some five hundred rubles?" "Well, I will open a saloon," said the peasant.[17]

And what about the peasant's attitude toward the crisis? What was his solution? It could be summed up in two words: "more land." He saw

---

[15] The larger the family, the greater as a rule the number of workers as well as of the mouths to be fed. This meant that more land could be and needed to be taken on from the mir or leased from the neighboring estate or fellow peasants. If a large peasant family, however, was short of work horses or farm equipment, some of its workhands could seek employment in the city and, with the money thus earned, purchase the needed draft animals and implements. See A. A. Kaufman, *Voprosy ekonomiki i statistiki krest'ianskogo khoziaistva* (Moscow, 1918), 19–20; A. A. Chaianov, *Organizatsiia krest'ianskogo khoziaistva* (Moscow, 1925), chs. 1–2.

[16] See David Mitrany, *Marx against the Peasant: A Study in Social Dogmatism* (Chapel Hill, 1951), 31–35.

[17] Milyoukov, 408.

the root of all his difficulties in a shortage of land and his only salvation in extension of the cultivated area. It was easier, of course, to continue the same type of farming in a larger area than to reorganize the system of farming on the old holdings, especially when capital and knowledge were lacking. Moreover, some holdings were too small for any practicable improvement of farming. There were also historical and psychological reasons for the peasants' attitude. There was the traditional view that only the tillers of the soil were entitled to land; hence the disappointment of the peasants when they did not obtain all the estate land after emancipation. What rankled most, however, was the loss of the land which they tilled as serfs on their own—the so-called *otrezki* (literally, cut-off land). Lenin sensed this feeling when he sought, as a means of enlisting the peasantry, the inclusion of a demand for restoration of *otrezki* in the platform of the Social Democratic Party.

While the peasants acquiesced in the new land arrangements more peacefully than the government expected, despite a number of local mutinies,[18] they never fully accepted them as a just solution. The peasants continued to dream, after emancipation, of a new partition of land to be ordered by the kind tsar, once he was able to overcome the resistance of the nobles and his ministers. Naturally, as the crisis deepened, they looked with increasingly covetous eyes on the broad acres of the "nobles' nests" which adjoined their narrow strips. How he could lay his hands on this land, of which he considered himself unjustly deprived, became the central preoccupation of the Russian peasant.

There was another influence which tended to reinforce this peasant outlook with respect to estate land. This was again the mir. I shall not deal here with the intense controversy, historical, economic, and ideological, which this institution provoked and which did not cease until the revolution of 1917. I only want to call attention to the central feature of the repartitional mir system: the peasant family held its strips of land not permanently (except for the homestead and the attached kitchen garden), but only until the next repartition. Then the holding could change both in size and location. Such repartitions took place at regular or irregular intervals. If the land was given up for one reason or another by a member, it reverted to the mir, which had the right to redistribute it. But the member still retained his right to an allotment. In other words, the peasant had a right to a holding but not to a particular holding; and he could not sell it. The actual farming unit, however, was the individual peasant household and not the mir, just as the kolkhoz is at present.

The repartitions of land and physical changes in holdings kept alive

[18] Kornilov, 175. It was, however, by no means a submission without a protest, inasmuch as there were more than 1,100 cases of disorders and uprisings in different villages during the two years 1861–1863. V. Gorn, *Krest'ianskiia dvizheniia za poltora veka* (Moscow, 1909), 29.

in the peasant mind the idea of the egalitarian distribution of land in accordance with the dictates of rough primitive justice. And why should such egalitarianism stop at the boundary line that divided the allotted from the estate lands? The peasant mind, unaccustomed to legalistic niceties, saw no reason for such a segregation. With his peculiar concept of the right to land and the continuing practice of flexible landholding, the peasant considered the property right of the landlords less than sacrosanct.

Until 1905 the peasants, while constantly dreaming of a new partition to relieve their distress, were nevertheless resorting to legal means of allaying their land hunger. They purchased some estate lands and leased a much larger proportion, often on difficult terms. But as we saw, abundant explosive material was accumulating for a revolutionary conflagration in the village. The spark was provided by the outbreak of revolutionary disturbances in the cities in 1905, following the unpopular and unsuccessful war with Japan. Unrest, punctuated by numerous *jacqueries,* spread through the countryside. In the new Russian parliament, the Duma, in 1906 and 1907 the peasant deputies clamored for distribution of estate lands. And again, as during the emancipation reform half a century earlier, they were generally supported by all the progressive elements of Russian society. Even the moderate liberals, the Kadets, strongly advocated distribution of a major part of the estate land, with fair compensation of the landowners, in order to increase holdings of the poorer peasants. Many liberals acknowledged that such a land reform was no panacea for Russia's agrarian ills, which stemmed fundamentally from agricultural underproduction. But, with the peasant temper being what it was, this was a first inevitable step in the solution of a difficult problem. The government itself, when the revolutionary disturbances were at their height, toyed with the idea of a land reform, proposed by the Minister of Agriculture, N. N. Kutler. But as soon as it felt that it was riding out the revolutionary squall, the government, reflecting the aspirations of the majority of the landowning class, adamantly turned its back on all such schemes.

However, as an alternative to the radical and liberal proposals, P. A. Stolypin as prime minister (1906–1911) enacted his own kind of agrarian reform, epitomized by his famous slogan, a "wager on the strong." Its essence was to split the peasantry by the development of a class of independent, economically viable peasant proprietors who would be attached to the principle of private property, and therefore better coexist with the estate system and act as a bulwark against any future revolution in the village.

With this end in view, legislation was passed aiming at the breakdown of the mir and individualization of the peasant land tenure and other property relations.[19] At the same time, much greater attention was paid by the government to technical progress in agriculture in its various aspects; much more was done in the way of technical and credit assistance to peasant farmers and encouragement of agricultural resettlement in Asiatic Russia. The redemption payments also ceased in 1907, while the gradual abolition of mutual collective responsibility for taxes began even earlier. The peasant could now sell his allotted land with some limitations. Some other legal disabilities were removed, and the Russian peasant doubtless became a freer individual than he was prior to 1905.

Central in this program, however, was the turnabout of the government with respect to mir tenure, which it had zealously guarded during the preceding half century. The new policy was not supported by many conservatives, who feared the sharp break with the paternalistic tradition, and it had a highly unfavorable reception among the liberal and radical opposition, including even those who were critical of the mir. It was felt that the government's antimir policy was too precipitate, too arbitrary, and, above all, sharply slanted in favor of a minority of the peasantry as against the great majority. Paul Miliukov sums up the opposition attitude thus:

> The Stolypin reform tried to divert peasants from the division of the land of the nobles by the division of their own land for the benefit of the most prosperous part of the peasantry.[20]

Lenin, by the way, did not share this sentiment, common to the liberal and radical opposition. He wrote in 1912:

> Most reactionary are those Kadets from the [newspapers] *Rech'* and *Russkie vedomosti,* who reproach Stolypin for the breakup [of the mir] instead of demonstrating the necessity of a more consistent and decisive breakup.[21]

The peasant reaction to the legislation may be gauged from the fact that out of more than nine million peasant households with communal land tenure in European Russia, about three million shifted voluntarily or involuntarily to hereditary tenure during the decade before the Revolution of

---

[19] For a discussion of the Stolypin legislation, see: Robinson, ch. 2; Pavlovsky; A. D. Bilimovich, "The Land Settlement," ch. 2, in A. N. Antsiferov and others, *Russian Agriculture during the War* (New Haven, 1930); N. P. Oganovsky, *Ocherki ekonomicheskoi geografii SSSR* (2nd ed., Moscow, 1924), 119–121. K. P. Kocharovsky, "Vykhody iz obshchiny," *Zapiski Instituta Izucheniia Rossii* (Prague), II (1925), 43–101.

[20] "Respublika ili monarkhiia," *Krest'ianskaia rossiia* (Prague, 1923), 54.

[21] V. I. Lenin, *Sochineniia* (2nd ed., Moscow, 1931), XVI, 14.

1917.[22] Thus, despite all blandishments and pressure, a majority of the peasants were still clinging to mir tenure on the eve of the revolution. Whether this phase of Stolypin's policy contributed materially to agricultural progress, of which there was some after the Revolution of 1905, is a debatable question. But this should not obscure the fact that other government measures, such as those leading to consolidation and segregation of fragmented peasant holdings, were clearly beneficial. Apart from any positive government action, however, the revolutionary storm and the freer climate after 1905, despite the reactionary character of the post-revolutionary political regime, doubtless had an energizing effect on the village. The vigorous growth during this period of the rural voluntary cooperative movement was a significant manifestation of the new spirit of grass-roots initiative.[23]

Even in the matter of land, though the revolutionary disturbances of 1905 were suppressed and peasant aspirations for a new partition thwarted, many landowners became insecure and anxious to liquidate their estate properties at a good price. Thus, the acquisition of estate land by peasants through purchasing from landlords, which began soon after the emancipation, gathered momentum after 1905. It was assisted by the much expanded financial aid of a special government institution— the Peasant Bank. To be sure, a smaller area was involved and a stiffer price was exacted than would have been the case under the proposed liberal land-reform schemes of 1906–1907. Furthermore, the land often did not pass into the hands of those who needed it most. Be this as it may, about 30 percent of the estate area was purchased by peasants between 1861 and the revolution of 1917. And on the eve of the revolution, small peasant farmers owned approximately two thirds of all land in European Russia outside of the public domain, which consisted mostly of nonagricultural land.[24]

Peasant agriculture also extended eastward as the growing railroad network opened new agricultural areas for large-scale settlement beyond the Volga and the Urals. This colonization process, resembling in some respects the westward expansion of agriculture in the United States, was aided by the peasant disappointment produced by the abortive 1905 Revolution as well as by the lifting of various legal obstacles to mobility

---

[22] Kocharovsky, 55. The number of households is based on the 1905 land census. See I. V. Chernyshev, *Sel'skoe khoziaistvo dovoennoi rossii i SSSR* (Moscow, Leningrad, 1926), 39.

[23] See E. M. Kayden and A. N. Antsiferov, *The Cooperative Movement in Russia during the War* (New Haven, 1929).

[24] N. P. Oganovsky, *Sel'skoe khoziaistvo Rossii v XX veke: Sbornik statistiko-ekonomicheskikh svedenii za 1901–1922 g.g.* (Moscow, 1923), 60–61; A. N. Chelintsev, "Pomeshchich'e khoziaistvo v Rossie pered revolutsiei," *Zapiski Instituta Izucheniia Rossii*, I (1925), 10.

and by positive measures of government assistance. While speaking of the railroads, their effect in a country of vast distances in reducing the cultural and especially the economic self-sufficiency of the village and bringing it within the orbit of the market and money economy cannot be overestimated. Another important factor of change was the industrial revolution, which began in earnest during the closing decade of the nineteenth century. It expanded the domestic market for farm products and created new employment outlets for the underemployed rural manpower. Also the growth of the industrial working class, subject to strong radical propaganda by the intelligentsia, was bound to have political repercussions in the countryside, the more so since ties between the young Russian city proletariat and the village were far from sundered.

It seems legitimate to speculate that if a prolonged and exhausting war, culminating in a revolution and civil war, had not intervened in 1914–1918, agricultural improvement would have continued. If, in conjunction with such progress, the Stolypin policy of the "wager on the strong" could have been further implemented for a period of several decades, it is possible, though by no means certain, that the projected bulwark against an agrarian revolution might have been created. Again, it is probable that if a land reform could have been speedily enacted after the overthrow of the monarchy in 1917 by the democratic Provisional Government—and the difficulties of such an undertaking cannot be exaggerated—a peasant revolution might have been obviated. But all this was not to be.

5. KINDER, KÜCHE, KIRCHE

Nothing is harder to define, or to enforce, than a standard of morality. Even in the most stable of circumstances, it is never easy to separate right from wrong or the proper from the improper—much less in a period of turmoil. We associate the Victorian age with a strict and indeed prudish code of morality but that has little to do with the way most common people actually conducted their private lives. How were most children raised and educated? What standard of behavior was set in the home? What role did religion continue to play in shaping public morality? These are the questions which the following selections attempt to answer.

K. H. Connell writes of Ireland which, for the most part, remained an anomalous backwater of British society. The Irish were conspicuously provincial by English standards, far less industrialized and far more Catholic. Their modern history could be divided into the periods before and after the potato famine of the mid-nineteenth century. The disastrous failure of a one-crop economy produced two significant results: a massive wave of emigrants to the New World and an alteration of family patterns among those who remained behind in Ireland. Those who went to America do not directly concern us here. The effects of the famine on the life style of those who stayed in Ireland can be gauged in terms of more arranged marriages, increased celibacy, and stricter social constraints against illegitimacy. Connell decides, not surprisingly, that a major agent of this retrenchment was the priest, to whom he ascribes a rather unflattering image. However that may be, it appears that the moral con-

170

duct of a late nineteenth-century Irish family was more firmly rooted in material considerations than in any formal code of ethics.

Robert Cecil investigates child-rearing at the turn of the century. It is difficult to read his account without wincing at some of the harsher practices of discipline which he describes. Beyond this, one sees some of the ways in which Victorian adults attempted to cope with the offsprings of an industrial society. Characteristic of these attempts were scouting and universal primary education. There is an unmistakable undertone of cynicism in Cecil's contention that both flourished when it became clear that skilled industry required workers with good health and a modicum of learning. English schools were ill adapted, Cecil holds, to help pupils cope with existing problems in their daily lives, still less to prepare them for an uncertain future.

Theodore Zeldin appraises the anticlerical attack on the Catholic Church in France and (if his sources were to be taken at face value) the Church's corrupting influence on family life and sexual morality. The chief victims, it was charged, were the woman and the child; the main instrument, the confessional. Zeldin's concern is not primarily with the truth or falsity of such accusations. He allows his protagonists to speak their mind, however biased, in the belief that the polemicist thereby reveals the moral preoccupations of his time. At least it is clear that old attitudes and prejudices die exceedingly hard, and perhaps especially hard when traditional mores are challenged by social transformation.

While the evidence here is less than conclusive, it suggests that conceptions of morality lagged far behind economic and social changes. The very fact that the religious authorities were so vigorously attacked confirms that their influence was not negligible, and the programmatic emphasis on secular education testifies to the persistence of ignorance and superstition. What Nietzsche called the transvaluation of values was to be, like industrialization itself, a long and painful process—one which remains, and is likely to remain, incomplete.

K. H. CONNELL

Catholicism and Marriage in Ireland

. . . The peasant's wariness of marriage, however moralized or accentuated by Catholicism, was economic in origin. By peasant experience
elsewhere, more extraordinary than restricted marriage was the haphazard,
happy-go-lucky marriage of the late eighteenth and early nineteenth centuries. In the two or three generations following the 1780s peasant
children, by and large, married whom they pleased when they pleased.
The opportunity to marry in their society was the occupation of land
that promised a family's subsistence. Dependence on the potato, ever
more extreme, on varieties ever more prolific, reduced the area needed
for food. At the same time, rising corn prices and the conversion of
pasture to tillage allowed a given rent to be earned on less land. There
appeared, in consequence, a margin of land needed neither to sustain
the customary population nor to pay the customary rent. An exigent
landlordism tended to annex it for rent. But, with the maximization of
rent resting now on the maximization of small tillage farms, landlords
allowed sons to settle on holdings carved from their parents'. More holdings meant more and earlier marriage, more and larger families: but in
the event they underlay not just the extra labor tillage needed, but so
sharp a growth of population that subsistence land tended to encroach
on rent land. Landlords were alarmed, the more so after 1815 as corn
prices slumped; as the small man's endless corn and potatoes exhausted
the soil; as there was talk of a poor-law financed by the landlords' rates.
"Consolidate and clear" became their cry. But they had lost the power
to do what they would with their own. Their short-lived encouragement of subdivision had shown the peasants how easily and (it seemed)
painlessly second sons might be established; and, as these sons married
young, soon there were yet more second, and third, sons. Only a minority
was drawn or pushed to the Irish towns, to Britain or America. For
most, the landlord notwithstanding, provision was made by continued di-

K. H. Connell, *Irish Peasant Society* (Oxford: Clarendon Press, 1968), pp. 114–
22, 125–32, 151–55. Copyright © 1968 by Oxford University Press by permission
of The Clarendon Press.

vision, facilitated by the potato's bolder trespassing on rent land, by its reaching higher up the mountain and farther into the bog.

Subdivision, earlier marriage, larger families, more subdivision; clearly there was a vicious circle: landlord, economist, and State emphasized its peril; but the peasantry, until disaster was imminent, knew more of its pleasure, the pleasure of unrestricted marriage and a large family; the pleasure, perhaps, of letting the landlord whistle for his rent.

By the decade or two before the Famine the price of this improvident pleasure was brought home to the peasant: many a holding was so reduced, the land so exhausted, that in the aggravating run of bad seasons, there was acute shortage of potatoes: many fathers no longer dared divide; their sons and daughters made up the gathering stream of emigration; their friends, risking life in Ireland, married more circumspectly.[1]

Much in the following decades underlined and helped to implement this new hesitancy to marry. Peasant society still, as before the Famine, made the occupation of land the preliminary of marriage: then, certainly in the heyday of division, there was land for all; but now, by and large, there was land only for the elect; and even they, for so rare a prize, must wait. The Famine, if it taught only the richer peasants the wisdom of eviction, made most of the rest chary of division. The western seaboard apart (where the old economy lived on), holdings usually passed from father to son intact, if not enlarged by neighboring land cleared by death or emigration. Boys, needing land to marry, could no longer marry as they wished on plots pared from their fathers' land or won from the bog; they must, instead, put off their marrying until, by gift or inheritance, they acquired intact their family farm. One boy, traditionally the eldest, was thus established; one sister married the heir to a neighboring farm. The rest of the family, chafing, as the Famine receded, at so inequitable an arrangement, might have pressed once more for a share of the land and a chance to settle at home; but family loyalty was stronger than brotherly jealousy—family loyalty supported, then overlain, by the pull of emigration, until today the peasant as likely as not envies his emigrant brother.

The Famine dramatized the risks of improvident marriage and halted the division that made it possible. Soon the land legislation made the peasant more ambitious and calculating—more ambitious because, as proprietor, tenant-at-will no longer, he yearned, peasant fashion, to establish his name at the land; more calculating because calculation, with no landlord to annex its fruits, became a rational proceeding. But his

[1] The argument to this point is elaborated in Connell, 1950, op. cit.; that of the next stage in K. H. Connell, 'Peasant Marriage in Ireland after the Great Famine,' *Past and Present*, 12 (1957), pp. 76–91; 'The Land Legislation and Irish Social Life,' *Economic History Review*, 2nd Ser., xi, 1958, pp. 1–7, and 'Peasant Marriage in Ireland: its Structure and Development since the Famine,' *Ec. Hist. Rev.*, 2nd Ser. xiv (1962), pp. 502–23.

children's reckless marrying might bedevil his calculation: they must be restrained by a disciplined marriage geared to his ambition. An appropriate form was ready-made in the "snug farmer's" family, its success proven by their retaining their land while neighboring holdings were divided and redivided. Much in this arranged marriage appealed to the new peasant. Disinheriting his other children, it preserved the land for his worthiest son. It saved land and son (if sober judgment could) from a lazy, thriftless wife, from the harder disgrace, a barren wife. With the father deciding not only whom, but when his son should marry, the land was not strained to support a second family before the first was dispersed; nor (for fathers put off their sons' marriage—and rivalry—and chose for them brides who were staid and mature) was the land burdened with families of maximum size, a material drain, but threatening also because the more numerous his brothers, the less secure the privileged heir.

By, perhaps, the end of the century, peasant marriage was usually "arranged"; and then, more markedly than before, peasant children married little and late. They married late because a "boy," not needing a wife until his mother could no more milk the cows, was not entitled to one until his father, at last, made over the land; and because the years had gone by before Lolita had the muscle and bone, the skill and dowry, sought in an old man's daughter-in-law. They married little because, though the normal family was large, only one of its boys and one of its girls married like their parents into peasant society: for the others (save in emigration) there was small chance of wife or husband.

This marriage, on the face of it, was gratifying less to its partners than to their fathers: well made, it reassured the old man, reanchoring his line to the land; but his son knew more of its cost—in brides forgone when wanted; in decades' chafing at parental dominance, ended, ironically, as he came to terms with dependence and celibacy, by a bride complementary to the land, complementing him fortuitously if at all.

And this was the cost to the elect, the boy chosen to follow his father. Similarly (though for ten not twenty years) one girl waited, single and dependent, for the dowry that bought her match. For the other children, unless they traveled, lifelong celibacy was the rule; staying on at home, they became professional aunt or odd-job uncle, despised, a little ridiculous, working away for food, clothing and shelter and a shilling on fair day, never to work, accidents apart, for husband or wife of their own.

Few comparable communities have acquiesced in celibacy as has the Irish peasantry—taking almost for granted that a quarter of their number never marry; the rest, on the average, not until they are 38 if men, 30 if women. We have seen why old people wanted so unnatural an order; but why did their children submit? Initially, no doubt, young as well as old were shocked by the Famine; they shook off some of the old, easy-going ways and married with discretion. The land legislation, too, grati-fied young as well as old: the favorite son, with his father's reverence for the land, felt the folly of marriage before it brought so rich a prize: younger sons, such was their family loyalty, effaced themselves in America or as bachelors at home to strengthen their brother's "hold of the land." Then emigration was a safety-valve: probably still, in the 1950s, there were nearly six children in the average farming family in the Republic;[2] tra-ditionally, fewer than two had followed their parents, and those, maybe, were the third most attracted by the life, least irked by the cost. No doubt, too, there was an element of compulsion: land qualified a boy for the customary marriage; fathers held the land, withheld it (if they wished), from a boy who balked at the match. But too much can be made of this: given the pressure, peasant marriage (as, say, in Poland)[3] might have allowed the heir to marry more normally: and many an Irish farm might have provided no less comfortably for a second, even a third, family: this, though no ultimate solution, would have allowed the heir of any generation to marry before his father's old age; and let a brother or two have families of their own, in their own country. Finally, young people in recent decades, though reared on Hollywood's ideas of marriage as well as their fathers', have complied with the match from a family loyalty different from their predecessors'. They have no vision of son and grand-son drawing manure and planting potatoes; they yearn themselves for the Birmingham garage, the London office-site. Against this, life like their fathers' is all but intolerable, tolerated at all from a dread of for-saking their parents: one child, whatever the sacrifice, must look after the old people, pretending, if need be, that they are not the last of their line, that their land, when they go, will stay safe in the family, reverting neither to sheep nor alien hands.

But all this, however true, begs not the least, or least interesting, ques-tion: did the limitation of marriage imply comparable limitation of sexual activity? and if so, what reconciled the Irish to so much restraint?

Continuously, it seems, the incidence of extramarital relations has been relatively low in Ireland—astonishingly low for a people marrying so little and late. Few observers question this conclusion, whether they find it matter for praise or jest; it is confirmed, for what they are worth, by the statistics of illegitimacy. In Sundbärg's table, showing for the late

---

[2] *Reports of the Commission on Emigration and Other Population Problems* (Dublin, 1954), p. 96.
[3] William I. Thomas and Florian Znaniecki, *The Polish Peasant in Europe and America* (New York, 1927), i, 90–126; Sula Benet, *Song, Dance and Customs of Peasant Poland* (1951), pp. 145–55.

1890s the percentage of illegitimate to total births in fifteen countries, the Irish figure is lowest. More recently, Ireland still is favorably placed [4] —and, were figures available for the peasantry, they would probably be lower than those for the whole population. They might, of course, be deceptive: Irish seasonal laborers, it has been said, fathered more children in Glasgow or Liverpool than in the Rosses or Achill: abortion and infanticide were sometimes practiced: priests, parents, and public opinion all did their bit to make legitimate births of illegitimate conceptions; and pregnant Irish girls, harshly regarded at home, sometimes have their babies in Britain. We know something of the number of Irish girls, pregnant before leaving home, whose babies are born in English Catholic institutions: their number, estimated in 1956 at some 20 percent of the number of illegitimate births in the Republic,[5] would by no means have raised its illegitimacy rate to the level of Britain's. We know, too, for Ireland and England in 1911, the number of children born to couples married for less than a year. Of the Irish wives marrying in 1910–11 while under twenty, fewer than 13 percent had babies within the year: the corresponding figures for England and Wales was 34 percent [6]—the discrepancy presumably reflecting the smaller proportion of Irish girls marrying "because they had to." But for all the treachery of the figures, the unmarried Irish are probably more, not less, chaste than is suggested by the international comparisons; for usually (certainly until recently), contraceptives are not available to the peasantry in the south, and unfamiliar, at least to the Catholic peasantry, in the north.

Granted, then, that there are few extramarital sexual outlets, the Irish tolerance of restricted marriage is the more puzzling. What compensations have been found? what barriers built around sexual indulgence? [7] Drink and dogs, cards, horses and gambling, religion, even the bombing and burning of Border posts, have been seen as the Irishman's way out. But the barriers to indulgence—his adaptation to continence—provide, I think, a more fruitful enquiry.

Migration and emigration make the problem more manageable. One child of every three born to peasant couples lives on in peasant society:

[4] G. Sundbärg, *Aperçus statistiques internationaux* (Stockholm, 1908); *Reports of the Commission on Emigration and other Population Problems* (Dublin, 1954), p. 295. Sundbärg's percentages (as shown above, 'Illegitimacy before the Famine,' pp. 82–3) range from 2.46 for Ireland to 12.10 for Portugal: that for England and Wales was 4.10 and that for Scotland 6.81.

[5] Ambrose Woods, 'Safeguards in England for the Irish Emigrant,' *Christus Rex, x* (1956), p. 367.

[6] Censuses of Ireland and England and Wales, 1911.

[7] To some degree, no doubt, the coincidence of little and late marriage and extra-marital 'chastity' implies neither 'sublimation' nor restraint, but the substitution of other sexual outlets for heterosexual intercourse: this is a matter I hope to consider elsewhere.

not the least inducement to break away is the wish to marry and marry young: those left behind may be those less interested in marriage. Some years ago a Cambridge zoologist suggested that this point might be pressed farther [8]—dubiously far, indeed. On the assumption that the children of people more or less interested in marrying tend, in this trait, to resemble their parents, the Irish (he suggested), drained of their "marriers" over three or four generations, are now genetically reluctant to marry—relieved, indeed, that their expectation of celibacy is so high. This hypothesis is not obviously compatible with the high fertility of the Irish when they do marry; but it is implausible also in its assumption that the degree of one's sexuality is determined by heredity, not environment.

Certainly, much in the peasant's environment made sexual gratification and marriage suspect. The volume of emigration is relevant yet again. In much of the country practically every peasant child has grown up to regard his own emigration as a real possibility: the worldly-wise, intending to travel light, uncluttered by wife and children, have been slow to marry while there was the chance of emigration.

A father's reluctance to name his heir tended, too, to keep his sons at home, uninclined as well as unable to marry: each, hoping for the land, waited for the match its succession would involve; each, reckoning to emigrate if his brother were chosen, was the less likely to marry. Commonly, fathers so dilatory, with sons so irresolute, were denied a grandson to inherit the land. Two or three sons waited on into their thirties for their father to make up his mind. Their mother, perhaps, died meantime. With no boy designated heir, none was entitled "to bring in a new woman." A sister might stay on to do the housework. Then, eventually, when the old man died or named his heir, his children were jogging along happily enough, each as loath to disturb the rest of the family as to face what now was the ordeal of marriage.

Many a mother, too, though happy enough to see her daughters settle down—even the sons who had left home—resisted the marriage of the heir. Perhaps with justification, she pictured herself the object of his affection over forty years and dreaded her relegation; she dreaded, too, the daughter-in-law, scheming not only for her son, but for the kitchen and yard she had ruled so long. By rousing a sense of sin, by ridicule, even by words unspoken, she kept her boy from girl-friends, leaving him awkward with women, perhaps incapable of courtship—a bridegroom, if at all, in a match made for him when her day was done.

But the peasant's Catholicism, it may be, was the most pervasive, the most persuasive, of the agencies reconciling the young to their curious marriage. This, looking at the Church's formal teaching, is an odd sugges-

[8] C. B. Goodhart, 'Natural Regulation of Numbers in Human Population,' *Eugenics Review*, xlvii (1955), pp. 173–8.

tion. The wildest critic can hardly maintain that the Catholic Church urges its lay members not to marry. "Paul is no enemy of marriage. If he favors virginity, it is not because marriage is not good; it is only because virginity, accepted for the love of Christ is better." [9] "To abstain from marriage for supernatural motives and to dedicate oneself to a life of religious celibacy is . . . not merely good but a greater good than marriage." But "to avoid marriage for purely selfish reasons is indeed blameworthy." [10] The argument hinges, not on the intent of the Church's teaching, but on its transmission, on whether the Catholic, coming from convent or Church school, from mission or confessional, was as convinced as the schoolmen wished of the propriety of marriage. Priests rarely (and briefly) challenged their Church's teaching: many, none the less, were ineffectual champions of marriage; their origin, training, and vows of celibacy had made it a perplexing matter, too perilous, temporally as well as spiritually, to earn their whole-hearted advocacy. . . .

It is hard to come by statistical evidence of the priests' social origins: since the middle of the nineteenth century, however, observers are virtually agreed (whether they are galled or gratified) that many a peasant's son has found his way to the priesthood: they are "the sons of persons in business and trade," a Catholic curate testified in 1853, "and the sons of comfortable, middle, and humble farmers": [11] a more critical contemporary believed "they are all taken from the humblest classes in society": [12] *The Economist* in 1881—and George Birmingham thirty years later—thought "they are drawn, for the most part, from the peasant class;" [13] Robert Lynd that they were usually the sons of farmers if not of publicans [14]—and the rare country publican was neither a peasant as well, nor the achievement and vindication of peasant virtue and prejudice. [15]

[9] Alan Keenan, O.F.M., and John Ryan, *Marriage, a Medical and Sacramental Study* (1955), p. 222.

[10] C. B. Daly, 'Family Life: the Principles,' *Christus Rex*, v (1951), p. 3.

[11] Rev. John Harold, before Maynooth Commission, P.P., 1854–5, XXII, *4*, 18. In the minutes of evidence heard by the Maynooth Commission each witness is given a number, and the questions put to him are numbered in a separate series: in references here the witness's number is italicized and precedes the number of the question.

[12] *Ireland and its Rulers*, i, 1844, op. cit., p. 252.

[13] *The Economist*, 11 June 1881; 'George A. Birmingham' (J. O. Hannay), *Irishmen all* (1913), p. 178.

[14] Robert Lynd, *Home Life in Ireland* (1909), p. 124.

[15] One of the few dissentient voices was that of the Rev. P. J. Nowlan, a Catholic curate in Dublin. 'The Catholic clergy,' he said, 'is recruited almost altogether from the great middle class of the town and country, principally from the towns: it is not a peasant clergy.' Nowlan, it may be, was generalizing from his own diocese: certainly in 1808 (the only year for which figures seem to be available) Maynooth students drawn from and destined for the archdiocese of Dublin came, more generally than their fellows, from urban and seemingly-comfortable homes (P. J. Nowlan, *An Irish Primer for English Statesmen* (Dublin, 1867), p. 12); *Papers*

Now many a priest's attitude to marriage, whatever its veneer of learning, was that of the peasant society from which he sprang: that same society explains much of the quaintness and boisterousness of his teaching; and the obedience curiously accorded to teaching so unnatural. "A young giant, whom nature had evidently cut out, mind and body, for a farmer; but who was doomed for the priesthood by family decree:" [16] an anachronism so extreme might become a "spoiled," [17] not a practicing, priest: "the clergy," none the less, "share all the passions of their class:" [18] "the Irish priest looks at the economic problems of his parishoner from the point of view of the prejudiced peasant." [19] To the priest's parents, in all probability, marriage was incidentally a source of its partners' happiness: lightly entered, indeed, it threatened acute unhappiness: essentially, marriage ensured labor for the land and an heir for the family: barring a parent's premature death or incapacity, every child was wise to postpone it, not a few to forgo it altogether.

This wisdom not only guided the teaching (or the silence) of the priest's parents on relations between the sexes: it was reiterated (as we shall see) by his teachers and spiritual advisers and exemplified by the marriages (or the celibacy) of his brothers and sisters—indeed of his responsible fellow-countrymen. So stern a view of marriage might, it is

---

relating to the Royal College of St. Patrick at Maynooth, P.P., 1808, reprinted 1812–13, VI, pp. 6–27). More recently M. Blanchard has published the following table showing the proportion of student-priests drawn from various social classes:

Classe paysanne	30%
Classe ouvrière	20%
Classes moyennes (fonctionnaires, commerçants)	30%
Professions libérales	20%

These figures, if they can be accepted, suggest that in recent years the field from which the clergy are recruited has broadened markedly: M. Blanchard, however, stresses that they are based on no precise inquiry; and he contrasts them with the following (presumably accurate) figures relating to the student-priests from a rural diocese in the west:

Classe rurale	45%
Commerçants	27%
Instituteurs-professeurs	15%
Fonctionnaires	8%
Professions libérales	2.3%
Classes ouvrières	1.7%

(Jean Blanchard, *Le droit ecclésiastique contemporain d'Irlande* (Paris, 1958), p. 87).

[16] Patrick Kennedy, *The Banks of the Boro* (1867), p. 3.

[17] In Irish usage, a 'spoiled' priest is a former clerical student who left the seminary without taking his final vows. An ordained priest 'suspended from his priestly functions by his ecclesiastical superiors: "unfrocked",' is a 'silenced' priest (P. W. Joyce, *English as we speak it in Ireland* (1910), p. 323).

[18] 'Philippe Daryl' [Paschal Grousset], *Ireland's Disease* (1888), p. 229.

[19] E. B. Iwan-Müller, *Ireland: Today and Tomorrow* (1907), pp. 100–1.

true, be challenged by his own emotions, or by a liking for the looser ways of the outside world: the man, however, taking vows of celibacy, was not powerless against the relevant emotion: his insular training instilled a scorn for laxity, un-Irish and un-Catholic; and the student, persistently perverse, might find his vocation in doubt.[20] Certainly his background and training left him ill-equipped for rational exposure, for logical approach to a less calculating marriage. Almanacks, newspapers, "speeches from the dock:" farmhouse reading, whatever it was, hardly spurred a boy to broaden or oppose his father's analysis of peasant society. At the age of twelve or fourteen the intending priest probably left the farmhouse for the diocesan seminary, and from there, when he was eighteen or more, he began his seven- or eight-year course at Maynooth.[21] The seminaries were "manned by ill-educated young priests, fresh from Maynooth . . . whose main anxiety is to get promoted as quickly as possible to parish work." [22] Here, no doubt, is Protestant prejudice: continuously, nevertheless, from early adolescence into his twenties, the trainee-priest was impressed with Maynooth's view of social and economic problems, a view, implicit or formulated, which he questioned on pain of spiritual penalties, and questioned the more rarely because it coincided with the convictions of the class which reared teachers and students alike.

"You were the typical priest," one of George Moore's characters says, "who looks upon women as the deadly peril and the difficulty of temporal life." "I remember," the priest replies, "how at Maynooth the tradition was always to despise women." [23] In the 1850s, according to the professors of theology, teaching on the sins against chastity was reserved until the students' last year: "it is always treated of in a learned language, and every security taken, which piety and prudence can suggest, that it shall be handled with reverence and reserve, and in no spirit of licentious curiosity." [24] Our students are taught to strengthen and fortify, by prayer and other pious exercises, their natural infirmity, and to regard and abhor as a soul-destroying sin, any wilful or deliberate complacency in an impure thought.[25] They were instructed, as confessors, "never to omit pointing out . . . the means of overcoming temptation; such as, avoiding the external occasions of sin, averting the mind instantly from the object of temptation and fixing it on some other object." The young should be "special objects of a most paternal solicitude:" "if, in

[20] *Report, Maynooth Commission,* P.P., 1854–5, XXII, p. 39.
[21] Brooks, 1912, op. cit., p. 183.
[22] Ib.
[23] George Moore, *The Lake* (1905), pp. 105, 250.
[24] *Report Maynooth Commission,* P.P., 1854–5, XXII, p. 65.
[25] Rev. J. O'Hanlon, D.D., Prefect of the Dunboyne Establishment and Librarian, ib., Answers to Paper K, p. 362.

early youth, the heart be preserved from the taint of corruption; if the virtue of chastity be firmly planted therein, resistance to temptation grows into a habit and becomes easy, and virtue strengthens with advancing years." Priests, accordingly, must impress on parents the importance of watching over their children, "of seeing the sorts of books they read; the sports they engage in; the places they frequent; and, above all, the companions with whom they associate." [26] A former student of *De Matrimonio,* asked if his class had treated the subject lightly or with ribaldry, said that, on the contrary, "it was a dirty or a dreadful matter—a horrible matter. They . . . seriously thought it was filthy stuff altogether." [27] Another looked back on it with much pain: "I have known many of the young men, when studying certain parts of it, to have gone into the chapel, and to have read it on bended knees; I saw many young men that I conceived to be not of very strong passion, they thought it necessary to go in before what they believed to be the body and blood of Christ Jesus, on bended knees." [28]

Teaching accepted with such sincerity and such turbulent emotion was transmitted with little less effect. It yielded, a Maynooth theologian believed, "wonderful fruits of chastity and purity of heart . . . in every condition, and in every age of life": he had witnessed "hundreds upon hundreds coming to confession under the weight of terrible passion . . . thenceforth, week after week, month after month, leading pure lives; struggling, as St. Paul had to struggle against the angel of Satan that buffeted him, and, like him, still victorious." [29]

But a shadowy line divided godly chastity from sinful renunciation of marriage: the very success of this teaching—the stifling of "impure thoughts," wresting the mind from "objects of temptation," the avoidance of much social life, the wariness of mixed company—all this raised psychological (indeed, practical) barriers to marriage: all too readily the overzealous confessor instilled in simple penitents not only a caution of marriage, but their reputed "complete and awful chastity;" [30] a perversion, of course, of the theologians' chastity, but sinless, even glorious, to the priest who slightly, perhaps unwittingly, twisted their teaching. Not surprisingly, to a liberal Catholic, it is "partly through Maynooth, and the ideas it has spread, [that] the Irish popular mind has become poisoned and ashamed on the subject of love and marriage." [31]

[26] Rev. P. Murray, D.D., Professor of the First Class of Theology, ib., p. 377.
[27] Rev. D. L. Brasbie, in evidence before Maynooth Commission, P.P., 1854–5, XXII, *35,* 94. The former students quoted in this and the following sentences had both left the Catholic Church when they gave the evidence quoted here.
[28] Rev. W. J. Burke, ib. *36,* 10.
[29] Murray, Answers to Paper K, ib., p. 377.
[30] See below, pp. 137–8.
[31] William Patrick O'Ryan, *The Plough and the Cross* (Dublin, 1910), pp. 156–7.

Marriage, to many a priest, was suspect on social and economic as well as on moral grounds. After the Famine, if the surviving population were to remain at home, marrying as men did in the outside world, the overriding problem was to increase agricultural productivity—and provide for more families. Traditionally, landlord and tenant had been laggardly improvers; landlords because they were preoccupied instead with immediate receipts and mounting debts; tenants, because they were deprived, in consequence, of the incentive, the knowledge, and the capital to improve. The old, ramshackle society, its population multiplying fast on a slovenly potato-culture, had been shaken by the Famine. By the fifties death and emigration had released the pressure on the land, but insufficiently to curb emigration. The treachery of the potato could never be forgotten; some other food must eke it out, if not take its place; but, whatever food replaced the potato, more land (or land more efficiently farmed) was needed to grow or buy it. And presently this insistence on a costlier standard of living was fostered by schools and newspapers, shops and advertisers, by emigrants' letters and visits and the seasonal laborer's dreams. To stay contentedly in Ireland, the peasant family must live more comfortably—its land be made more productive. In the generation after the Famine the peasant, suffering still a mercenary landlordism, still lacked incentive, knowledge, and capital. By the seventies, however, the landlord's exactions were being restrained, extralegally and then legally. Increasingly, the means to improve lay within the peasant's grasp; and the incentive was more compelling as the land, in essentials, became his own. But convention, ignorance, laziness, a drive insufficient against the easier attractions of emigration—these all encouraged extensive rather than intensive improvement; they encouraged the peasant to add to the area, rather than the productivity, of his soil: and here, of course, there might be no lasting solution, for (certainly in the remoter parts of the country) their neighbors' progressive emigration might simply allow the remaining families to live more comfortably until, at last, loneliness drove them out.

In the peasant's religion, as in his tenure, discouragement to improvement was detected. "Excessive and extravagant church-building in the heart and at the expense of poor communities:" [32] the point has been made, too often and too carpingly: [33] plainer churches, nevertheless—an affront to priestly or parochial pride more than to religious or aesthetic sensibility —, plainer churches might have spared Irish shillings and American dollars for richer grass and cleaner dairies—even for more welcoming schools,

---

[32] Horace Plunkett, *Ireland in the New Century* (popular edn. 1905), p. 107.
[33] See, for instance, Michael J. F. McCarthy, *Priests and People in Ireland* (Dublin, 1902).

for "we, the clergy . . . are very apt to forget that God has not one, but two houses in the parish, and that His interest in the second one is certainly greater than a comparison between the school and the church commonly suggests." [34] More important, it was said also that the Catholic peasant's indifference or antipathy to improvement was heightened by "the reliance of [his] religion on authority, its repression of individuality:" [35] looking to the priest for guidance in business as in theology, the laity "largely lost their capacity and their judgment in their own affairs." [36] Authoritarianism in religion "and its complete shifting of . . . the moral center of gravity to a future existence . . . [these] appear to me calculated, unless supplemented by other influences, to check the growth of the qualities of initiative and self-reliance, especially among a people whose lack of education unfits them for resisting the influence of what may present itself to such minds as a kind of fatalism with resignation as its paramount virtue." [37]

Improvement, then, there had to be, unless part of the population emigrated and much of the rest postponed or avoided marriage. But the peasant, having lived long under an unjust tenure, was slow to improve, and slower still for being sustained by a religion little concerned with material reform, the more inimical to it because of the solace it brought in hardship. Clearly, if the peasant were to resist emigration and marry young, he needed outside encouragement and guidance—advice based on knowledge beyond his reach of the technique and economics of farming efficiency. Now, however other-worldly their religion, there was some obligation on the priests to acquire such knowledge and offer such advice: souls were being lost in emigration and in marriage too long deferred: deprivation, moreover, was not simply of inessentials; priestly, even plain human, compassion—for hungry children and needless illness—must have made many a priest anxious to explain a better farming—the more eager, in much of the country, because nobody would do it if he did not.

But the priest, by and large, was poorly equipped to show the way to more productive farming. If he came from a country home (indeed, if he came from the town) he was probably disdainful already of peasant life; almost certainly he knew less than his brothers and sisters of its realities and potentialities. His training, far from giving him the knowledge, the capacity, the values to regenerate country life, sheltered him from it the more. . . .

[34] Neil Kevin ('Don Boyne'), *I remember Karrigeen* (1944), pp. 60–1.
[35] Plunkett, 1905, op. cit., p. 102.
[36] 'Pat' [P. D. Kenny], *Economics for Irishmen* (Dublin, 1906), p. 147.
[37] Plunkett, 1905, op. cit., p. 102.

By and large, however, people yielded to the priest gladly; not grudg-
ingly, for want of a better leader. They did so partly because of the
quality of their faith. Observers, Irish and foreign, clerical and anti-
clerical, are all but agreed on the firmness of religious conviction in Catholic
Ireland: "in no other country in the world, probably, is religion so dominant an element in the daily life of the people:" [38] "the faith of the Irish
peasant is entire, unquestioning, absolute as that of a thirteenth century's
serf:" [39] not even in Spain were "devotion to the church" and "earnest
piety" "so deeply rooted in the hearts of the people:" [40] well into the
present century "a maid seeking a situation will inquire how far the
house of her employer is from the nearest church . . . a gardener or groom
will accept lower wages for the sake of getting near a church which his
children can attend and a school where he can be sure that they will be
taught their catechism." [41]

There is, no doubt, an intricate explanation of faith so firm. Living
wretchedly, the Irishman certainly needed all the comfort religion might
bring: irrelegion was horrifying alike to parents, teachers, and priests;
and the skeptic, shunned by his neighbors, [42] his livelihood endangered,
more probably emigrated than spread his doubts at home. Under the
Penal Laws the peasantry had cherished their Church for sharing their
suffering; [43] and they respected afterwards its remarkable resilience. "From
the bosom of the darkness of the Penal days the Church seemed to have
stepped into the dazzle of medieval Italy. . . . Religion was now coming
out of the catacombs and marching on the seat of Empire. After the
Fathers of the Desert, the founders of the Basilicas." [44] Long deprived
of its ancient edifices and permitted at last to replace them, the Catholic
Church was the most grandiose builder in nineteenth-century Ireland:
many a peasant member was impressed by the number, [45] the architecture,
and the fitments of its buildings—by the realization that he and his emi-

[38] Plunkett, 1905, op. cit., p. 94.
[39] Daryl, 1888, op. cit., p. 227.
[40] Richard F. Clarke, S.J., *A Personal Visit to Distressed Ireland* (1883).
[41] Birmingham, 1919, op. cit., p. 88. But, on the other hand, 'we have only to
look at the extent of the "leakage" from Roman Catholicism amongst the Irish
emigrants in the United States and in Great Britain, to realise how largely emotional and formal must be the religion of those who lapse so quickly in a non-
Catholic atmosphere' (Plunkett, 1905, op. cit., p. 111).
[42] Brooks, 1912, op. cit., p. 189.
[43] John O'Driscol, *Views of Ireland* (1823), i, 139 ff.
[44] William O'Brien, 1920, op. cit., pp. 168–70.
[45] The following table, showing, for various dates, the number of Catholic
churches and houses of religious orders, may much underestimate the rate of new
building; for it gives no indication of additions to existing churches or religious
houses, of the proportion—presumably increasing—of new to old buildings, or
of any tendency for new edifices to be larger either than those they replaced or than
comparable buildings, newly completed.

grant children (with the dealers their custom enriched) had largely financed them.[46] With a troubled parishioner, Gerald O'Donovan's saintly
Fr. Ralph climbed the cliff looking down on the little town where he was
curate. "Would you tell me now," the cobbler asked, "what buildings
you can make out from here?" "The cathedral," Father Ralph replied,
"the two convents, the monastery, the asylum, the workhouse, the bishop's
palace, the parochial house, and, I think, the Emporium." Spreading
buildings, "the garish brasses surrounding the altar, the vulgar lamps,
the gorgeous vestments of the priest . . ., the purple robes of the bishop:"
to the peasant, these were the marks, proper and unforgettable, of the
Church's pomp and power, seldom prompting him to ask, with Fr. Ralph,
"Was his God the God of all this tinsel magnificence, who bedecked himself at the expense of hungry children and toiling underfed men and
women?" [47]

The people's piety, the Church's grandeur: these were no bad base
for priestly power. But the Irish priest was esteemed for more than his
office. "He was zealous and untiring in the discharge of religious duties." [48]
Sometimes a gormandizer,[49] rarely a drunkard (more rarely, if he were,
retaining his cure), what popular criticism there was bore mostly on his
arrogance [50] and eagerness for fees: there was talk of his "almost insane
craving for money;" * of his "hysterical fits of rage over paltry little
coins;" * of his bargaining so hard for marriage fees that matches were
postponed or abandoned.[51] Catholic peasants, it is said, showed a "uni-

---

Catholic churches and religious houses, Ireland, 1849, 1901, and 1958

	Catholic churches	Houses of religious orders and communities
1849	2152	207
1901	2418	587
1958	2508	980

(*Irish Catholic Directory*, 1851, p. 210; 1903, p. 414; 1960, p. 640. Note (a) to
the table in the Appendix (p. 160) applies also to this table. The *Directory* for
1851 gives the number of churches in 24 dioceses, but not in the remaining three—
Dublin, Tuam and Kilmacduagh, and Kilfenora: the figure given here for 1849 is
the total for the 24 dioceses, increased by one-eighth.)

[46] Jean Blanchard, *Le droit ecclésiastique contemporain d'Irlande* (Paris, 1958),
pp. 101–2; Arnold Schrier, *Ireland and the American Emigration* (Minneapolis,
1958), p. 120; Gerald O'Donovan, *Father Ralph* (1913), pp. 110, 314, and *passim*.

[47] O'Donovan, 1913, op. cit., pp. 313, 317.

[48] Daryl, 1888, op. cit., pp. 221–2.

[49] Ib.

[50] K. H. Connell, *Irish Peasant Society* (1968) p. 147–50.

[51] In the diocese of Elphin, early in the present century, "a bargain was always
struck [with the priest] in the 'fortune' matches and the holy sacrament was often
prefaced by such a conversation as 'Do it for £ 13, father'—'No; I won't marry
you under £ 16'—'Split the difference, father,' etc. etc." (*Irish Nation*, 19 June

versal preference" for banks with Protestant managers; they looked and lived below their means because of the priest's as well as the landlord's exactions.[52] No doubt the seeming greed of many a priest was the mark of peasant stock,[53] hardened by his, and his Church's, dependence on the people's offerings; no doubt, either, that it indulged his relations or Church more often than unpriestly leaning to luxury or avarice:[54] it sustained, nevertheless, the very real comforts of Irish clerical life—comforts enjoyed by few of the laity, by few, indeed, of the clergy abroad. Paschal Grousset, touring Ireland in the 1880s, shared a car for a few days with a party of "village and parish priests:" "their black coat has all the softness of first quality cloth; their travelling bag is of good bright leather; their very umbrella has a look of smartness;" "they . . . would on no account stop at second-rate inns;" "the appetite of the reverend fathers is excellent, and . . . the *carte* of the wines is a familiar object with them. They each have their favorite claret: one likes Léoville, another Château Margaux, while the third prefers Chambertin. . . . After dessert they remain last in the dining room, in company with a bottle of port. At ten o'clock that night, entering it to get a cup of tea, I find the three seated round glasses of smoking toddy."[55] More recently, another French observer has stressed that the Catholic Church in Ireland, poorer in property than elsewhere, is freer of financial worry, *"et son clergé a le niveau de vie le plus élevé parmi ceux observés en Europe."* In general, M. Blanchard concludes, "la condition des prêtres est aisée, comparée du moins à celle des ecclésiastiques de France. Les fidèles sont généreux et les pourvoient largement de moyens d'existence. Curés et vicaires ont une garde-robe correcte, voire soignée, des maisons biens entretenues. *Ils portent sur leur visage et leur personne un air de prospérité. Ils n'ont pas de soucis matériels."*[56] But, for all the muttering against clerical

---

1909, p. 7). "In his calm, pleasing way, he argues that he has two curates who immediately take half of the fee and that times have been improving recently. Then he gives them a goodly measure from the bottle." How do the very poor "find the bright coin? The Church will refuse to tie the knot until it is forthcoming" (*Irish Nation,* 19 June 1909, p. 7). "Long ago," in co. Cork, "poor people went from house to house to make up a little for the priest's money to get a girl married" (I.F.C., MS. 939, p. 214).

[52] Brooks, 1912, op. cit., pp. 196–7.

[53] Lynd, 1909, op. cit., pp. 125–6.

[54] But when the will of a Munster priest who 'craved for money, money, all the time . . . was published he had nearly four thousand pounds . . . [Christ struggled] to prevent His disciples from falling victims to avarice and it is a sad reflection that after almost two thousand years continual teaching of the opposite virtue the clergy themselves have not yet learned it.'

[55] 'Philippe Daryl' [Paschal Grousset], *Ireland's Disease* (1888), pp. 217–20.

[56] Blanchard, 1958, op. cit., pp. 159, 140–1. The passages I have italicized are ignored in the unattributed translation of M. Blanchard's study published *'Permissu Ordinarii Dioec. Dublinen. die 16 Aug. 1962'* by Clonmore and Reynolds in Dublin and Burns and Oates in London (Jean Blanchard, *The Church in Contemporary Ireland* (Dublin, 1963), pp. 90, 79, iv).

greed, ordinary clerical indulgence bred respect rather than bitterness. The Irish priest, too, was exculpated from "the vices of the Italian and Spanish priests" and commended for his "exemplary purity." [57] He was, moreover, one of the peasantry: they paid him: he was "laden with the prejudices" of his class: [58] "the most brilliant thing ever done by the Irish priests was the invention of the legend that they had always been on the side of the people:" [59] rightly or wrongly, they wore much of the patriot's glory. . . .

ROBERT CECIL

Childhood, Youth and Education

The attitude of parents towards their children born towards the end of the nineteenth century was not, on the whole, a healthy one: it tended to vacillate between an undiscerning faith in childish innocence and an equally misguided determination to treat disobedient children as sons of Belial. Both extremes were based on ignorance of the child's nature; it is as if the great majority of Victorian parents forgot what it was like to be a child. Nor were opportunities of observing the behavior of their young as frequent as a modern parent would suppose. Among the poor, long hours of work abbreviated family life, especially in the towns, and childhood itself was cut short by the early beginning of wage-earning, even after the worst abuses of juvenile employment had been remedied. In the middle and upper classes a nurse and later a governess took charge of the young and in many households even the mother only saw her children at certain hours. There were fathers who, when they wished, like the Creator, to walk in the garden in the cool of the evening, caused a handbell to be rung as a warning to the children to make themselves scarce.

It was easy to be sentimental or stern towards children whom the

[57] Daryl, 1888, op. cit., p. 221; Ryan, 1912, op. cit., p. 90.
[58] John O'Driscol, *Views of Ireland* (1823), ii, 115.
[59] W. P. Ryan, *The Pope's Green Island* (1912), p. 41.

parent seldom saw; to enter with understanding into their lives and problems was more difficult. Kenneth Grahame dubbed the grown-ups the Olympians, because of their remoteness from the young. "The estrangement was fortified by an abiding sense of injustice, arising from the refusal of the Olympians ever to defend, to retract, to admit themselves in the wrong, or to accept similar concessions on our part." Rosamund Lehmann, recalling a rather later period, strikes a similar note.

> No grown-up, in my personal experience, ever said sorry to a child in those days. None, in the event of inability to answer a question, ever confessed to simple ignorance. As for such subjects as birth, death, physical and sexual functions, these were taboo, and invested with an aura of murk, shame, guilt, suggestiveness and secrecy.

Much of the blame for this state of affairs must be laid at the door of the paterfamilias; in all ranks of society his word was law. In middle-class families, in which Puritanism was especially strong, religion took a heavy toll of the exuberance of youth. Much of what a later generation has been willing to write off as animal spirits was somberly ascribed to original sin, which required to be pitilessly reproved. Sons were consigned at an early age to schools at which the birch was known to be an inescapable part of the curriculum. "The word had gone forth, the school had been selected; the necessary sheets were hemming and Edward was the designated and appointed victim." It was the beginning of the process that would transform the carefree child of Kenneth Grahame's story into a staid young man who might, like Grahame himself, marry an unsatisfactory wife and become Secretary to the Governor of the Bank of England.

If gentlemen's sons were exposed to the rigors of school life and subjected there to the customary floggings, a poor and orphaned child could not hope to fare better. In 1896 Charlie Chaplin was consigned to the Hanwell School for Orphans and Destitute Children. He gives the following description of the punishment meted out to the young offender:

> For minor offences a boy was laid across the long desk, face downwards, feet strapped and held by a sergeant, then another sergeant pulled the boy's shirt out of this trouser and over his head, then pulled his trousers tight. Captain Hindrum, a retired Navy man weighing about two hundred pounds, with one hand behind him, the other holding a cane as thick as a man's thumb and about four feet long, stood poised, measuring it across the boy's buttocks. Then slowly and dramatically he would lift it high and with a swish bring it down across the boy's bottom. The spectacle was terrifying, and invariably a boy would fall out of rank in a faint.

It was not to be expected that the new century would at once lead to a new approach to the problems of childhood; but if the process was slow the measures introduced by the Edwardians were practical ones and operated from birth. Infant mortality had reached its peak in 1899 and many of the deaths were known to be preventable. A beginning was made in 1902 with the registration of midwives; they were not required to be qualified as nurses, but at least the machinery of control now existed. In 1907 the first Notification of Births Act was passed, although notification did not become general and compulsory until 1915. In the period 1906–1910 infant mortality per 1,000 births fell to 117, as compared with 138 for the preceding five years. The first Nursery School started at Deptford in January 1900 and its inauguration was greeted as the dawn of "the children's century." Legislation providing for school meals was adopted in 1906 and in the following year the Board of Education established its own Medical Department and enjoined upon Local Education Authorities the medical inspection of schoolchildren. Special schools for incapacitated children began in 1908. Between 1907 and 1908 Parliament gave some attention to the problems of delinquent children; it was belatedly recognized that it was neither rational nor socially expedient to treat young offenders in the same way as hardened criminals. Herbert Samuel, as Under Secretary of State at the Home Office, was mainly responsible for legislation collectively known as "The Children's Charter." Probation Officers and Juvenile Courts were instituted and Borstals were set up to inculcate better habits.

Even this more humane approach to delinquency, however, had primarily a negative character. Just as in the field of medicine doctors were recognizing that prevention was better than cure, so in the juvenile field there were farsighted men who came to the conclusion that the interest of the individual child and of the State lay in channelling the activity of young people in a healthy direction before antisocial habits were formed. The Church Lads' Brigade and the Boys' Brigade had already made progress along this road and by 1904 the latter claimed a membership of 54,000 in the British Isles.

The movement that captured the imagination of young people all over the world had its genesis not in the slums of Glasgow, like the Boys' Brigade, but within the beleaguered town of Mafeking, where Colonel Baden-Powell and his Chief of Staff, Major Lord Edward Cecil, had organized the boys to make themselves useful during the siege. The germinal idea lay dormant until April 1904, when Baden-Powell, now Inspector-General of Cavalry, inspected the twenty-first anniversary parade of the Boys' Brigade. He approved of what he saw; but it struck him that the reproduction in miniature of the drill of soldiers could scarcely exercise as strong an appeal to a boy's mind as would an adaption of some of the activities that he had already outlined in his manual *Aids to Scouting*. His aim was to lead the young people out of the towns, with their squalor and temptations, towards the healthy countryside and coast; to make them active and train them to use their powers of observation and acquire simple skills. The age of "spectator sport" had begun and he had seen, as he put it, "thousands of boys and young men, pale, narrow-chested, hunched-up miserable specimens, smoking endless cigarettes, numbers of them betting."

Powerful backing was provided by the newspaper magnate, C. Arthur Pearson, and the next step led to Brownsea Island in Poole Harbor, which had been acquired a few years earlier by a wealthy stockbroker, Charles van Raalte, who was sympathetic to Baden-Powell's aims. There on the sun-baked clay at the end of July 1907 the first Scout camp was pitched and for the next ten days the first patrols of Curlews, Ravens, Wolves and Bulls crawled through the gorse and bracken, raced through the pine trees and gathered in the evening round the campfire to listen to the wise words and exciting tales of the "Hero of Mafeking." The Union Jack flew from the flagpole; the boys stood for a prayer before turning in for a night under canvas. Scouting was born.

The new movement answered a need; it was an immediate success. In January 1908, Part I of *Scouting for Boys* was on sale for 4d. In May, all six were published in book form at 2s. a copy. Soon the weekly, *The Scout*, was also in circulation and by the end of 1908, 110,000 copies were being sold each week. C. B. Fry, the Edwardian ideal of the scholar-athlete, who was preparing boys for a life at sea in the training ship *Mercury*, cooperated with Baden-Powell in organizing an amphibious camp and the Sea Scouts were launched. In the same year, 1909, at the great Scout rally at the Crystal Palace Baden-Powell came upon a small group of girls in white blouses, with floppy sleeves, blue skirts below the knees and black stockings. They had organized themselves; they were the first Girl Guides. The appeal was irresistible and Baden-Powell's sister, Agnes, accepted responsibility for them. The movements spread: broom-sticks were hastily improvised to serve as Scout staves and strange symbols began to appear on woodland paths, signifying "Turn left" or "I have gone home." By the end of 1910 there were nearly 108,000 Scouts in Britain and Scouting was starting up in the Empire and in Europe. It had all sprung from B.-P.'s original objective: "To help existing organisations in making the rising generation, of whatever class or creed, into good citizens or useful colonists."

The middle-class child might join a Scout or Guide camp in the summer, but not at the expense of the annual family holiday by the sea. For privileged children this was indeed a Golden Age. One can still conjure up those halcyon days; stretches of sand uncontaminated by oil slick or the litter of the urban masses; no speedboats to terrorize swimmers, but a peaceful seascape with cliffs of gorse and heather or sandy turf, where a few bungalows were beginning to show but had not yet destroyed the skyline. Friendships would grow up between families in neighboring tents, or housed in the same boardinghouse. Rosamund Lehmann has evoked it in a story recalling her own Edwardian childhood.

> There, as usual, comes the sailing dinghy *Seamew;* the dark boy in a white public school sweater at the tiller; with him the fair pig-tailed girl in a green blazer; brother or sister, or maybe cousins, fortunate pair; and they are hero and heroine of a voluminous Book for Girls about a jolly pair of boy and girl chums, Jack and Peggy (Pegs), who charter a boat for the hols and have all sorts of adventures. They wave to us; we wave back; romantic moment. Receding, they stay fixed, an illustration, between blue water and blue sky, their crimson sail behind them. Till next summer, next summer. . . .

A few philanthropic bodies gave a thought to the vast majority of children, whose parents could not afford a seaside holiday. The Children's Country Holiday Fund was one, and the Pearson Fresh Air Fund also organized outings for poor children. As there were no motor charabancs, the trip, unless short enough to be made in a horse-drawn vehicle, would be made by train and the children would debouch on to the sands of one of the large and rapidly expanding resorts, such as Blackpool, Brighton, Margate, or Clacton; *Punch* had already described the last mentioned as the "Mentone of the East." On these more densely populated beaches there would be Pierrots and Punch and Judy shows and donkey-rides and, if charity extended to a penny for the turnstile, there would be a helter-skelter down the pier, and perhaps whelks from a barrow to satisfy young appetites before the return journey to the slums of some industrial town.

The main hope of the poor child, wishing to escape from the insanitary and dispiriting surroundings in which he had been born, lay in education. The foundation of our modern State educational system was laid in 1902, when Balfour's Education Act was passed. It was probably the most momentous piece of legislation enacted by his Government, but the Liberals, mindful of the Nonconformist vote, attacked the measure on the ground that it allowed financial support for denominational private schools. Lloyd George even proposed that his fellow Welsh-Nonconformists should refuse to pay rates in support of the new system. In fact, the Act was timely and farsighted. From an industrial point of view, Britain could no longer prosper on unskilled labor; from a political point of view, democracy required that the majority of the population should receive enough education to become responsible citizens.

The new Act, for which the Permanent Secretary of the Board of Education, Sir Robert Morant, has been given much of the credit, created a national system of primary and secondary education. Whilst abolishing the old School Boards, however, it wisely kept the principle of local responsibility; Local Education Authorities, based on the Counties, were accordingly set up throughout England and Wales. Common standards were assured by the continued existence of a corps of Inspectors; but the highly centralized French system, with all control vested in the Ministry, was sedulously avoided. It was a decision that nobody has regretted.

The reorganization of education on sound lines did not, of course, solve all problems; the quality of teaching in State Elementary Schools left much to be desired. Half a degree up the social scale from the Elementary School was the Free Church School; it did not follow that the education was better. Here is young Harold Owen, no doubt wearing the Norfolk knickerbocker suit, with stockings and boots and a narrow white collar which, he tells us in *Journey from Obscurity,* was

> much in vogue among schoolboys of that period. . . . The other pupils, coming as they did from some of the poorest homes in Birkenhead, were ragged and dirty, always with running noses and often with running sores. . . . We were marshalled into the schoolroom for regulation hours, piped some miserable hymn or the Lord's Prayer and after chanting a multiplication table (I cannot recall any other instruction we were given) we children would sit at our desks in apathetic trances of varying degree. The master in charge sat at his desk, scanning a piece of newspaper in an even more dejected and dispirited manner. . . . We were all cold and hungry. . . .

Even the older Grammar Schools left much to be desired. Sir Reader Bullard describes one in Walthamstow, which was

> taken over later by the Education Authority under the Act of 1902, and transferred to a fine new building with playing fields. . . . In 1899, however, the school consisted of a small one-storeyed building with a gravel yard, across the road from an active pickle-factory. The backbone of the school consisted of two masters: neither had a degree, but both were hard workers and good teachers. At the bottom of the school was a large, noisy form. . . . The two top forms (maximum age perhaps just 16) worked in the same room and often together, under an unqualified master who left soon after to become secretary to a firm of dairymen. . . . Because of the openings for office-workers in London, all the top forms studied Pitman's shorthand.

It was not surprising that the teaching profession offered few attractions to the bright student on the threshold of a career. A pupil-teacher in an elementary school had four years' training from the age of fourteen. He would begin by working five and a half days a week for a wage of 6s., attending secondary school courses on half-days. It was arduous and not very rewarding, but at 18, if he passed matriculation, he would qualify as an assistant master, earning £70 a year. This is how Sir Reader Bullard describes the first step in a teaching career that was later diverted to the Consular Service and ended in the British Embassy in Teheran.

> I was posted to a school in the poorest corner of Walthamstow. There were no official school meals then, but a benevolent society ran a soup kitchen to provide a midday meal for the most needy children. Six meal tickets were allotted to my class, but I had twelve boys who were acknowledged to be in need of them. Every day six of the boys had a soup-kitchen meal, the other boys consumed several slabs each of bread thickly spread with butter which I brought to school with me, my mother and sister helping with the cost.

The children from well-to-do homes had very much less to contend with in their search for knowledge and advancement in their careers. They need never go to school too cold and hungry to concentrate on their lessons; their classrooms were less draughty and less congested and their teachers were likely to have shared the same educational advantages as themselves. Moreover they came from homes well furnished with books. They might well have learned to read with the help of *Benjamin Bunny* by Beatrix Potter, which in October 1904 *Punch* described—rather inadequately, as generations of children must think— as "a pretty booklet. Suitable as a present." Older children would read E. Nesbit's *The Railway Children* and would spend long hours browsing in *The Children's Encyclopaedia,* which was brought out by the enterprising Harmsworth Press. *Kim* had recently appeared, and, after 1906, they might be taken by their parents at Christmas to see the fantasy that J. M. Barrie in *Peter Pan* constructed round Kensington Gardens, which had seemed such a prosaic place when Nanny had taken them for a walk there. For a halfpenny the schoolboy could subscribe each week to *Pluck* or *Marvel,* graduating later to *Chums* or *The Boys' Own Paper.*

Books about school life, which in the days of F. Anstey's *Vice Versa* or Dean Farrar's *Eric, or Little by Little* seemed to have been written primarily to amuse or edify grown-ups, had taken a turn for the better with Kipling's famous *Stalky and Co.* (1899) and the novels of E. F. Benson and Hugh Walpole. The Public Schoolboy even found a Laureate in Henry Newbolt, an Old Cliftonian, who declaimed that:

> *For, working days or holidays,*
> *And glad or melancholy days,*
> *They were great days and jolly days*
> *At the best school of all.*

Anyone who believes that the boisterous life of Westward Ho, as depicted by Kipling, is exaggerated would do well to study the Haileybury mutiny of the year 1900. It was touched off by the refusal of the headmaster, Canon Edward Lyttelton, to grant a half-holiday in celebration of the relief of Ladysmith. After taking the wise precaution of first eating their lunch, some five hundred boys marched to Hertford, singing "Rule Britannia" and other patriotic songs. They then marched on to Ware, where the headmaster was said to be playing golf, but failed to make contact with him. Contact was made all right after Chapel that evening, when Lyttelton, who came of a family famous for athletic prowess, proceeded to beat ten selected boys in each house, thus dealing with over 100 before close of play. One boy had padded himself with the Union Jack, but even this example of interested patriotism brought no reprieve.

In a more serious spirit, however, it must be said that in the new century the legacy of Arnold, which has been well summed-up as classics, cricket and Christianity, was proving less and less adequate. For one thing, to teach Greek and Latin intelligibly makes exceptional demands upon the teacher and few could meet them. Sir Llewellyn Woodward records,

> I was introduced to the grammar of the classical languages. Hic haec hoc hunc hanc hoc hujus hujus hujus huic huic huic hoc hac hoc. This was how I learned Latin grammar. No wonder that I disliked it. . . . I had no idea why I was learning Greek and Latin. It rarely occurred to me that, once upon a time, Greek and Latin were spoken languages. . . . From the first to the last hour of my schooldays I was not given any ininstruction in the physical or biological sciences. . . .

The Public Schools, by and large, were strongholds of educational complacency and conservatism because Oxford and Cambridge were likewise. At Cambridge remarkable scientific work was being done; but until 1907 the demand for physics and chemistry for the whole University was being catered for by five lecture-rooms and a teaching staff of forty-six. There were, of course, enlightened dons and schoolmasters who recognized the need to rethink the nineteenth-century concept of the aim of education. Then, as now, the root question was whether education should seek to produce a man who could use in his career the knowledge he had acquired, or whether the object was to train a mind and character which would respond afterwards to the stresses of life. If we criticize the Edwardians for allowing this important debate to degenerate, as it tended to do, into a stereotyped argument about the benefits of a classical, as against a scientific and more modern education, we must remember how difficult it was for them to envisage the environment for which young

her spiritual director, he visited her at her home whenever he pleased. He asked her questions on matters about which she would never dare talk to her husband. As spiritual director he demanded to know not just her sins, but everything about her, and in this role, he was not obliged to keep her secrets. He might postpone absolution to wring information out of her, facts about her husband, the name of her lover. Husbands no longer used fear as an instrument for keeping the love of their wives, but priests did: the priest "always has the stick of authority in his dealings with the wife, he beats her, submissive and docile, with spiritual rods. There is no seduction comparable to this." The wife is isolated; her will and personality are destroyed. Families are divided. "The home [becomes] uninhabitable." A man cannot express an opinion without the certainty that his wife (and daughters) will contradict him, and report him to the curé.

Michelet protested on two grounds, in the name of the family and in the name of morality. The family needed to be transformed and the Church stood in the way of this. The husband must be master in his own house, but he must not repress his wife to such an abject role that she sought protection and consolation from the priest. Women should be the associates of their husbands, a condition so far seen only among small shopkeepers. This was Michelet's ideal. Men must learn to explain their work to their wives, instead of priding themselves on their specialized knowledge and taking refuge in technical language. Women should rear their familes with the advice of their husbands and family unity—destroyed by disagreement on religion—would be restored. "May the religion of the home replace religion." Seen from this point of view the emancipation of women, as a liberal ideal, involved strengthening the rights of men as well as those of women. Likewise, it was not a relaxation of stringent moral laws that Michelet demanded in his protests against priestly rule but, on the contrary, greater puritanism. He wished to protect women from new temptations. Priests had confessors' manuals filled with lists of sins which no honest woman would think up on her own, and in their questioning they "put terrible ideas into innocent minds." There was a strange contrast between the education the laity received, which carefully omitted all reference to sex, and that of the priesthood, which involved a full diagnosis and classification of every known sexual practice and perversion. These might have been a problem in previous centuries, "horribly corrupt and barbarous," but from which "thanks to God, we are now far." Worst of all, the casuistry of the Jesuits—for whom Michelet had a special antipathy—had modified the teaching of the Church on the subject of sin, to find increasing excuses for immoral conduct. By their laxity they had increased their influence and popularity. But this was part of a great conspiracy to "weaken the will."

The Church indeed needed to be protected against itself—it was polluting the minds of the innocent young men it trained. Michelet was thus on the side of puritanism. He laments the victory of the Jesuits over the rigorist Jansenists, who, whatever their theological views, were "the party of virtue."

There were many attacks on the confession in the name of morality. Comte C. P. de Lasteyrie, in a social history of the sacrament, accused it of inspiring either terror or alternatively a relaxation of morals, because of the assurance of pardon. Its questions enabled priests to excite and seduce oversexed women. It was an obstacle to true religion, to intellectual liberty and the progress of civilization; it had been invented to give power and riches to the Church.[2] Confession, wrote Edgar Monteil, later to be one of Gambetta's prefects, involves the delation of the most intimate secrets of families and the loss of all chastity and all honor. His novel, *Sous le Confessional,* attacked priests on puritan grounds, "for their worldly existence, their love of luxury, good living, idleness and all evil passions." [3] "Many women and most girls are in love with their confessors," wrote two other authors, who declared themselves to be in favor of Christianity but against the clergy who have spoilt it. The confession "by the habit of avowal falsifies the moral sense of women, spoils their innate sentiments of modesty and places them, through fear, under the dependence of the priests." [4] The anticlericals seized on the dubious but vivid polemic of a temperance-preaching Canadian priest defrocked for immorality, Père Chiniquy, who denounced confession as "the cornerstone of [priests'] stupendous power: it is the secret of their almost irresistible influence. . . ." A woman's most happy hours, he admitted, "are when she is at the feet of that spiritual physician showing him all the newly made wounds of her soul, explaining all her constant temptations, her bad thoughts, her most intimate secret desires and sins." But the Church was thus making her speak "on questions which even pagan savages would blush to mention among themselves. . . . Whole hours are thus passed by the fair penitent in speaking to her Father Confessor with the utmost freedom on matters which would rank her among the most profligate and lost women, if it were only suspected by her friends and relatives." [5]

What confessors said to their penitents could be guessed from the

[2] C. P. de Lasteyrie, *Histoire de la Confession sous ses rapports religieux, moraux et politiques chez les peuples anciens et modernes* (1846).

[3] Edgar Monteil, *Sous le Confessional* (1873), 62, 67.

[4] Emile Faure and Thomas Puech, *Le Confessional* (1869), 41. See also, for example, Francisque Bouvet, *De la Confession et du célibat des prêtres* (1845), 275–82.

[5] Père Chiniquy, *The Priest, the Woman and the Confessional* (London, 1874), 7, 103–4, 122. (French translation 1880).

manuals published by the Church for the guidance of curés and for the education of seminarists. These were avidly studied by the anticlericals and denounced as immoral. Ecclesiastical treatises on sins against the sixth commandment were particularly condemned as obscene, polluting not only the minds of the clergy and those of penitents but of a large number of salacious readers: it was claimed that the best known of these, by the Bishop of Mans, sold two hundred thousand copies, even though it was in Latin. Dog-Latin was what all the manuals slipped into when they discussed sex, but it is significant that all but one of the anti-clerical critics prudishly kept to this language for at least the more intimate details of intercourse and perversions.

It is instructive to see exactly what the critics objected to. Paul Bert, Professor of Physiology at the Sorbonne, and another of Gambetta's lieutenants, minister in 1881–82, published a study of a leading manual of moral theology by the Jesuit Gury. He complained that the book lacked general principles, inclined towards the most lenient solutions, found excuses for many crimes and always took the side of the sinner. It showed a profound contempt for women; it did not know what love was, only fornication. "It is not only the mysteries of the bed of young couples that he scrutinizes with an insatiable lubricity, at the bottom of which jealousy quivers; it is the chaste conversations of fiancés that he surveys obliquely, the kisses of sister and brother, of father and daughter, of mother and child, that he condemns with his impure suspicions. . . ." It was a treatise on morals, but it said nothing about virtue—Gury "does not know what love is, nor even decency; he does not know what delicacy, generosity, devotion, friendship, personal dignity, civic duty or patriotism are. He is so ignorant of these noble things that he does not even know their name. You will not find a single one of these words in the *Morale* of Gury. All that makes the heart of humanity beat leaves him cold. Do not speak to him of progress, fraternity, science, liberty, hope; he does not understand; in his obscure corner he chops away minutely at erroneous consciences, secret compensations, mental reservations, shameful sins and out of this he tries to compose I know not what kind of concoction to brutify and enslave mankind. For he lowers everything he touches—abolishing conscience, delivering free will into the hands of a director, making delation into a means of governing souls. . . . Beware husbands . . . beware fathers. . . ."

Paul Bert also published an analysis, partly in Latin and partly in translation, of Soettler's commentary on the sixth commandment, revised by Rousselot, Professor of Theology at the seminary of Grenoble (1844). He insisted that he was not just concerning himself with the education of priests: the enumeration and explanation of different forms of sexual activity were rapidly communicated by them to children. He claimed to have before him an exercise by a schoolgirl aged fifteen called "The Empire of Vice." This was divided into seven provinces, the largest of which was Lust. It had a river running through it, The Filth, its capital was Lewdness, it had nine major towns: Debauchery, Voluptuousness, Immorality, Adultery, Incest, Prostitution, Cynicism, Violation, Impurity; and eleven communes: Seduction, Evil Desires, Laxity, Turpitude, Fornication, Depravation, False Pleasures, Orgy, Sensuality, Immodesty and Rape.[6]

An anonymous criticism of Moullet's *Compendium Theologiae Moralis* (1834), used in the seminary of Strasbourg, likewise complained of its relaxed moral standards. If a girl, for example, was pursued by a man having evil intentions, she commits a sin unless she tries to flee or cry for help. But, says Moullet, if by her flight or by her cries she is exposed to having her life endangered, or to losing her reputation, she is not required either to flee or to cry out. If an innkeeper sells wine to men who are half drunk, with the probability that they will be made completely drunk, he commits a grave sin, "except however if by refusing to give wine, he exposes himself to injury or to notable unpleasantness." If a man commits improper acts with a married woman, not because she is married but because she is beautiful and putting completely aside the fact that she is married, these relations "according to certain authors do not constitute the sin of adultery, but simple impurity." If a man swears an oath, but without the intention of swearing, and only using the formula of an oath, he is not fully bound by his word. If a man kills a thief in order to preserve property necessary to his life, he is in effect saving his life as well as his property, and the killing is not sinful. But what if the goods threatened are not necessary to life? The probable answer is that it would be lawful to kill the thief in such a case, "because charity does not require that one should undergo a notable loss of temporal goods to save the life of another." Moullet's book is denounced as a justification of vice.[7]

Though these anticlericals are prudes, they are not opposed to sex in marriage; indeed, they object to the Church's hostility to it. Another anonymous author, "Le Curé X," attacking Bishop Bouvier's treatise on the sixth commandment, complains of the interference in the rights of husbands. The message of the bishop's book, he claims, is that "to be agreeable to God the conjugal duty must be performed weeping and praying; a truly chaste husband must neither put his hand into his wife's blouse in the daytime, nor lift her nightgown in bed." They must resign themselves to living like brother and sister if one or the other is impotent.

[6] Paul Bert, *La Morale des Jésuites* (1880), preface xxxiv, and 523n.
[7] [F. Busch?], *Découvertes d'un bibliophile ou lettres sur différents points de morale enseignés dans quelques séminaires de France* (Strasbourg, 2nd ed., 1843).

A woman must, even at the price of her life, refuse the conjugal act if her husband does not carry it out according to the rules. But she is herself threatened, because Bouvier's book concludes with a treatise on Caesarian operations, to enable priests to cut her open, so as to baptize her child.[8]

The accusation that these divines were hypocritically peddling pornography is immediately shown to be false if one examines their works. Bouvier, Bishop of Mans, has not the slightest trace of salaciousness. His book, given its premises against carnal pleasure, is a very logical, straightforward work, which reads like a legal or medical textbook, with precise and careful definitions. He makes sex sound very grim. Moreover, he warns confessors to be extremely careful in the questions they pose, lest they put bad ideas into innocent heads. If a child has not reached puberty, he warns the confessor, he is unlikely to masturbate: so do not ask about this. When you do ask, enquire in a roundabout way, to avoid making suggestions, for example, "Have you felt movements in the body, agreeable delights in the private parts, followed by calm?" It is true there were cases of priests who were prosecuted for pointing out to children those parts of the body which they must not touch, and for posing questions, as one court ruled, of "an undoubtedly licentious character . . . likely to overexcite the imagination of very young children and of developing unhealthy ideas in their minds." [9] But they were defying the warnings frequently given to priests by their teachers. Abbé Gaume's popular manual for confessors urged them to take special precautions with women: not to call them "My dear daughter;" to be modest with married women, asking them only whether they have obeyed their husbands, and remaining silent about the details, unless questioned. They should take care not to teach them sins they did not know; they should be brief about "impure matters," to show the horror they felt for these and also to protect themselves against temptation.[10] But that there was some justification in the complaints about the use to which confession, and these guides to it, could be put, is seen in Bishop Pusey's preface to his translation of Gaume's *Manual*. His translation was purposely incomplete, leaving out Gaume's sample questions to be posed to penitents, which he considered improper. "The English clergy," wrote Pusey, "are gentlemen and I do not believe that they could ask such questions." He urged even greater care than his French colleagues, especially in dealing with women who confessed details of domestic life "which have not a right or a wrong;"

---

[8] Le Curé X, *Les Mystères du confessional par Mgr. Bouvier* (n.d., Brussels).
[9] Cases of 1879, quoted by Bert, 523n.
[10] J. J. Gaume, *Manuel des Confesseurs* (1st edition 1837, 9th edition 1865) 157, 191.

the clergyman's aim, he said, should be to strengthen the sense of personal responsibility in those who consult him.[11]

It is clear that different methods were employed by confessors. It is possible that in England, and in Italy, for example, questioning was far less severe than it was in certain regions of France. In Spain there is a tradition in some areas for people to confess not to their own parish priest but to go to the neighboring town—which must reduce tensions and clerical power considerably. In Colombia, many priests in this century have been trained in France and have brought back a severity in their methods which contrasts notably with that country's laxer Spanish traditions, and this has inevitably had repercussions in the form of increased anticlericalism. A comparative study of the intimate relations of priest and penitent has never been undertaken. These generalizations are very tentatively offered as possible hypotheses. If there is truth in them, some explanation of the different amount of anticlericalism found in various countries might be sought in this personal, rather than the traditional, political context.

In France there were two attitudes to confession which at their extremes were pretty different. One school of theologians urged laxity and gentleness towards sinners. They drew their inspiration from Italy, and particularly from St. Alphonse of Liguori. Gaume's *Manual*, which based itself on him,[12] urged confessors to avoid imposing excessive penances, particularly on new converts, and penances should not be public. Excessive penances, he insists, are not carried out and the penitent simply reverts to sin. The best one is therefore the frequentation of the sacraments. If in doubt, incline towards leniency. Do not forbid a drunkard to drink altogether, but only limit the amount he must not exceed. Do not show anger or astonishment at sin. Do not refuse absolution except in very exceptional circumstances: if you defer it because you doubt the penitent's contrition, defer it say for fifteen or thirty minutes, at most for a week.[13]

The extent to which laxity could go is seen in a guide written by an appropriately named Abbé Léger, director of the seminary of Nimes (1864). It carried the approval of his bishop and it shows what some provincial priests were being taught. Léger was opposed to severity. "It is better to allow the penance for a sin to be completed in purgatory than to expose the sinner to damnation by setting a penance he will not

[11] E. B. Pusey, *Advice for Those who Exercise the Ministry of Reconciliation through Confession and Absolution* (London, 1878), preface.

[12] As well as on various other authors, for example St. Francis of Sales, St. Francis Xavier, and St. Charles (Archbishop of Milan): with the last named, Gaume says his reputation for severity is due to faulty translation, which he remedies.

[13] Gaume, 348–50, 421–33.

carry out." He firmly says that serious sins deserve heavy penances, but the worst he can think of are the recitation of a few prayers, psalms or the rosary, the reading of one or two chapters of the *Imitation,* or a long period of kneeling.[14] Fasting should not be required of those who are delicate or working. No long penances, for six months or a year, should be set; they were rarely fulfilled. Abbé Léger believed in the most discreet questioning at confession. Ask only, he says, if peace reigns in the home, if there are children and if they are being raised in the Christian way. "Has the penitent anything to reproach himself for on the subject of conjugal duty or the sanctity of marriage? It is better in this matter to ask less than too much. . . . It is best to leave them in good faith than to instruct them, with the danger that they might sin formally, be scandalized and that their idea of the priest's holiness should be weakened. In fact, many people do not reveal certain acts, because they fear they would scandalize the priest. The confessor must therefore demand only what is strictly necessary and forbid every explanation which would be improper."

The abbé took a very practical view of sin. Do not refuse absolution to all who dance, he says. Discover first what kind of dance was involved, the reason for participating in it, and if the dance actually caused a sin. "If you do otherwise, you will force people to abandon the sacraments which were their only chance of salvation and they will fall into all sorts of trouble." Dishonorable dances, like the waltz, must not be tolerated, because even if the penitent commits no sin, he may have caused another to sin. But people who have to dance because of their social position, or to please a husband, may be absolved, provided no sin was committed and that the woman was not too indecently clothed. The theatre, as all authorities acknowledged, was morally dangerous, and "you should as far as possible turn everybody away from it, but not under pain of total refusal of absolution." Bullfighting, again, was a popular sport in Nimes. Pius V had forbidden it on pain of excommunication. Clement VIII had suspended this prohibition in Spain only. What were the people of Nimes to do? "In France, this excommunication is generally unknown, and as people often do not think they are doing wrong by watching bullfights, the confessor must not bother those who say nothing to him about it; but if they express doubts to him, he must tell them to keep away from this sport, when there is danger of death or scandal, and this on pain of refusal of absolution." If the toreadors were good, and there is no danger of their being killed, people may watch; "if someone was killed or wounded, it would be an accident and one is not required to foresee

---

[14] See J. B. Bouvier, *Traité dogmatique et pratique des indulgences des confreries et du jubilé, à l'usage des ecclesiastiques* (1826, 10th edition 1855), 10, on the stern penances imposed in the Middle Ages: 'but, so as not to discourage sinners, the church allows them to be treated nowadays with greater leniency.'

an accident. But fights held in the country, where everybody goes into the arena and where it is rare for someone not to be wounded or killed, one may not attend, because one may not contribute without reason to the death or injury of anyone, even if this contribution is distant." . . .

In the Second Empire there was still a party among the clergy—its size can only be guessed—in favor of using confession as a severe instrument of repression.[15] Mgr de Ségur—a best selling popularizer, some of whose works ran into seventy-five editions—used a telling phrase in defending it: "Let yourself be taken by the good God's police; they will take you not to prison but to paradise." To those who complained that they did not like priests to meddle in their affairs, he stated that "the priest has not only the right but the rigorous duty to teach you in general and in detail what you ought to do and what you ought to avoid." [16] A work recommended by Bishop Pie of Poitiers insisted on the importance of confession as "the most powerful dyke opposed to the overflow of human passions" and pointed to the "terrible moral degradation" of England and Germany, where it had been largely abandoned.[17]

The questions which confessors implementing this policy asked might relate to business activities. Merchants would be questioned about excessive profits, innkeepers about whether they had adulterated their wine, tailors whether they had returned the extra cloth and ribbons left over from each garment, barbers whether they did ladies' hair "following the cursed custom recently introduced in our time by the devil." [18] A Christian should never seek pleasure for its own sake, but always relate it to some useful and legitimate end." He should take pleasure only by necessity, like sleep, to enable him to work better. So it was the duty of the confessor to discourage many normal recreations. Travel simply for pleasure, said a guide on *Relaxations Permitted to Pious Persons,* was undesirable; and if it had to be undertaken for business or other reasons, conversation with fellow-travelers should be avoided and limited to the needs of politeness: the best course was to read or pretend to be asleep. But great care should be taken in what was read. Novels "exalt the imagination, trouble the heart, spoil the judgment . . . and produce boredom and distaste for the real world. . . . The number of young people who have been ruined by the reading of novels is incalculable." [19] The aim of the confessor should be to keep his penitents in ignorance of sin as long as possible.

[15] Cf. Anon.; *Quelle est la bonne confession et quelle est la véritable absolution* (Valence, 2nd edition 1848), 2.
[16] Mgr de Ségur, *La Confession* (1862), 21.
[17] Abbé Jarlit, *De l'institution divine de la confession* (Poitiers, 1858), 371, 383.
[18] J. J. Gaume, *Manuel des Confesseurs* (9th edition 1865), 205–6.
[19] R. P. Huguet, *Des Délaissements permis aux personnes pieuses appelées à vivre dans le monde* (Lyon, new edition, 1857), 21, 60–3, 108.

A treatise on the confession of children and young people, by the director of a church working-class youth organization in Marseille, published in 1865 with recommendations from five bishops (and still being used in 1924, when it was reprinted for the fourteenth time) warns sternly against sex education. A child often asks, it says, why there are two sexes. "If you cannot elude the question, which is always the best thing to do, if he is certainly likely to ask the same question of others, reply that God has arranged it so because it seemed right to His wisdom. Let him think you have told him everything. . . . So many children naïvely ask questions on which any answer satisfies them: therefore it is unnecessary to say more. . . . A prudent mother used invariably to reply to the embarrassing questions of an extremely inquisitive child: You will know when you get to the upper sixth form (the philosophy class); and this child, satisfied, patiently awaited this happy hour." The author somewhat contradicts himself when he goes on to describe, on the basis of his experiences in the slums of Marseille, the sexual license of children he knows, the mistresses they have at fourteen, their experimental visits even earlier to brothels, full of secondary schoolboys on the *jours de sortie* (holidays), the widespread homosexuality, which he regards as a major problem and to which he devotes over twenty pages.[20] Not just obscene books should be avoided, but also "indecent pictures and sculptures" and "evil newspapers, that is to say, newspapers hostile to the Church, to the Pope, to priests, to monks and those which do not hesitate to publish serial stories contrary to good morals." Greed, the desire for riches, for the goods of this world, for honor and esteem were all of the same kind.[21] Women's clothes were a constant source of danger. Married ones who dressed to please their husbands, or girls who dressed in order to win husbands should be given some concessions, but not if they sought to please others apart from their husband, or if their aim was not to get married. Those who leave their arms or shoulders naked or only lightly covered were, if they were following the fashion, not guilty, but those who invented these fashions were guilty of mortal sin. . . .

The Church told people what to do when they were married. The republican state, even when it took over the teaching of morality, was too prudish to do so. The hints it gave suggested that it was legitimate to enjoy sex in moderation but that it was best not to talk about it. Janet wrote: "The honorable man enjoys his pleasures with simplicity and without thinking about them." [22] A best-selling guide to the *Hygiene and*

[20] Abbé Timon-David, *Traité de la confession des enfants et des jeunes gens* (1865, 14th edition 1924) 2. 180–262.

[21] See Mgr de Ségur, *Aux Enfants: Conseils pratiques sur les tentations et le pêché* (1865), 25.

[22] Janet, 250n.

Physiology of Marriage, by a retired army medical officer, which between 1848 and 1883 went through 172 editions, is as near as one can get to enlightened lay opinion on this matter. The author dispels the myth that women do not enjoy intercourse, and his book is designed to show how both sexes can derive pleasure from it and maintain their enjoyment into old age. He urges women to satisfy their husbands, if they want to keep them; but he advises husbands to win their wives by affection and caresses, rather than by force or command. But he too counsels moderation. (Copulation more frequent than two to four times a week for those under thirty, twice a week between thirty and forty, once a week till fifty, will destroy the freshness of women's charm and possibly give them cancer of the ovaries; it will make men impotent.) He is not willing to discuss the details of "permitted postures," as the Catholic casuists do: "Where the devil were they sticking their noses?" he asks angrily. And he says not a word about contraception.[23]

Another doctor, a member of the inspectorate of public health, said it "would dirty his pen" to describe contraceptive methods. However, his book on *Marriage Relations,* which went through six editions, was an attack on conjugal onanism, which he declares, was "an almost universal usage" in every social class. He condemns it as the scourge of the times, in language which is just as vigorous as Bishop Bouvier's. He reaches the same conclusions as the Church, though by a different route. He quotes the latest scientific publications to argue that conjugal onanism produced appalling nervous disorders (though he does not say these were universal: he cites only a few cautionary examples). He recommends the rhythm method as a substitute—"chastity within certain limits," moderation once again. It is interesting that in theory this doctor was liberal, indeed advanced. He sings the praises of Fourier, who had believed in free love and trial marriages; he thinks that sexual instincts should be satisfied from the outset of puberty and he condemns the law against marriage before eighteen. However, like the radical party in politics, which had the most advanced ideals in theory but practised the most prudent moderation, he is in no hurry to put Fourier's ideas into effect. Contradicting himself he insists, like the Church, that the purpose of sexual relations should be reproduction.[24]

The ordinary man was thus not presented with alternatives which were wholly clear cut. Proudhon might say that the masses looked on the Church as an institution that stopped them from being happy, but his

---

[23] A. Debay, *Hygiene et physiologie du mariage* (n.d., 54th edition), 94, 103, 135–9.

[24] Dr Alex. Mayer, *Des Rapports conjugaux considérés sous le triple point de vue de la population, de la santé et de la morale publique* (1874, 6th edition), viii, 76, 221, 254.

own moral code was asceticism itself. Comte likewise did not attack Catholicism in order to foster moral license: he invented frightening totalitarian schemes to instill altruism into everybody. The republican attitude was well put by Louis Havet, professor at the Collège de France and later a leading Dreyfusard, who thus defined how France should be saved "by the republic and by free thought, by morals and by *discipline.* . . . We must free ourselves from all authority and all tradition that is not based on reason; we must at the same time govern ourselves severely, repress every weakness and every petty interest, practice respect and obedience to every proper command." The function of philosophy was to establish the rule of truth and duty. "The best religion is that which keeps moral character in its greatest purity and which prescribes to people the most *severe* rule of morals." [25]

Did the masses know what they were doing when they gave their support to the anticlerical leaders? Did they believe that liberation from the Church would give them freer lives? Were the bourgeois morals which the intellectual anticlericals dispensed to them a disappointment, so that they were cheated by the Third Republic, as they had been cheated in 1789? Or were the masses so indoctrinated by traditional values that they did not want a moral revolution? Louis Veuillot, one of the most influential Catholic journalists of the century, said that he was opposed to anticlericalism not least because he was "a son of the *petit peuple*" and anticlericalism was a bourgeois doctrine.[26] Many socialists said the same thing. It is certainly impossible to isolate anticlericalism from the social and moral conflicts of the nineteenth century.

[25] L. Havet, *Le Christianisme et ses origines* (3rd edition 1880), 1. xi. (My italics.)
[26] Louis Veuillot, *Les Libres penseurs* (1850, 2nd edition), 1.

6. PRIMITIVE AND CIVILIZED REBELS

If the most difficult days of early industrialization had been overcome by the mid-nineteenth century, at least in the West, it was by no means certain that Europe could thereafter expect a bright and glorious tomorrow. In terms of economic development, there was a striking surge of growth from 1850 to the early 1870s. It was followed by two decades of fitful depression, and then a remarkable upturn once again in the years prior to the Great War. A social pattern is more difficult to discern. One might perhaps speak of a gradual improvement of living conditions and a general simmering down of lower class dissatisfaction but this would ignore such violent episodes as the Paris Commune and overlook the rising wave of industrial strikes at the century's end. The only safe assumption is that social protest was beginning to erupt in new forms.

Lewis H. Gann explains the error made by nineteenth-century radical thinkers in placing their hopes primarily in the revolutionary potential of the urban working class. In so doing, they almost completely overlooked the peasants and those living in the colonies. Both were considered too widely dispersed, too backward or conservative, and too difficult to organize for revolutionary action. Karl Marx himself not only underestimated the strength of the peasants and the colonial peoples but expected them to be grateful for the progress brought to them by the industrial revolution. In reality, military technological development, city planning, wider streets and more efficient police methods made urban insurrection a hopeless undertaking. On the other hand, the guerilla warfare of colonial peoples proved to be a major threat which the colonists could subdue only with difficulty.

E. J. Hobsbawm views this problem from the other end of the telescope. He analyzes the various meanings of the term Mafia, defining it as a code of extralegal behavior, a set of personal relationships, and a loose network of "families." Ties of blood, ritual, and common danger made the Sicilian Mafia a kind of shadow government which, in the absence of close state control or concern, assumed the function of social care for its own. The Mafia was, as Hobsbawm shows, not a feudal but a modern creation, based on an older social order but deriving its leadership mostly from business and professional ranks. He offers a fascinating insight into this "incident in the rise of rural capitalism," and he briefly explains how it made the leap to the urban scene of the twentieth century.

Charles Tilly summarizes the leading conclusions drawn from a team-study of collective violence in western Europe, especially France, following the onset of industrialization and urbanization. He asserts that violent means are a "normal" function of the political process of modern society, but he advances the surprising hypothesis that a greater concentration of population initially mitigated against the tendency to group violence. His view of the longer-run potentialities is more cautious, however, and it is also less comforting for those whose preoccupation is the maintenance of law and order.

In no way can we accurately measure the level of tension in a society. The appearance of things is often deceptive. Strikes and local insurrections may be only adjustments to a given situation rather than preludes to a paroxysm of widespread violence. Acts of destruction or incidents of criminality may be a justifiable corrective to social injustice rather than the wanton aggression of misfits. We have learned to be cautious in making categorical judgments. The surface does not always betray the profound sources of social unrest, and we know in retrospect that the relative equilibrium which had been ostensibly attained by 1914 was not to endure.

LEWIS H. GANN

Partisan Warfare in the Heyday of Imperialism

The late eighteenth century witnessed a rapid acceleration of technological development especially in England, where the steam engine was
first applied to industrial use. The use of more advanced machinery also
spread to parts of France, Belgium, Rhenish Prussia, and other parts of
Western Europe. Older cities expanded their population. New manufacturing towns grew apace, as factories provided landless men with new
means of employment. Urban unrest acquired increasing political importance as a larger portion of Western Europeans migrated to the towns,
as the new industrial working class acquired a greater measure of literacy
and of discipline than had been customary among the urban poor in the
preindustrial era.

Revolutionary theorists in Western Europe thus began to look on
popular warfare in a different way. They no longer thought in terms
of national wars alone. They began to emphasize the divergent interests
of different social classes. They increasingly placed their trust in the
towns, where they looked to the urban middle and working classes, and
thought in terms of urban insurrections. Their model was the French
Revolution; their heroes the Jacobins, a predominantly middle-class group
that drew much of its strength from Paris.

Most revolutionary thinkers now took inadequate account of the peasants, despite the fact that rural unrest had played an important part in
shattering the Bourbon monarchy. Urban intellectuals, a class of increasing political and numerical importance, tended to be insufficiently
acquainted with the practical problems of the countryside. They commonly considered the peasants at best as auxiliaries in the coming struggle
for power. The peasants were geographically dispersed and often remained wedded to what Marx considered religious superstition. They
were harder to assemble and discipline than workmen used to the imper-

Reprinted from *Guerrillas in History* by Lewis Gann with the permission of the
publishers, Hoover Institution Press. Copyright © 1971 by the Board of Trustees
of the Leland Stanford Junior University.

sonal routine of a large factory. The peasants' revolutionary aims were generally limited in kind. Servile farmers wished only to be rid of seignorial dues and services and to become small landowners. Once this aim had been achieved, the peasants became a conservative rather than a revolutionary force. When the Parisian workers rose against the newly established Republic in June 1848, French countrymen looked down on the rebellious proletarians as bloodstained anarchists. In the Austro-Hungarian empire, concessions were made to the peasants. Hence the villagers for the most part remained aloof from the revolutionary struggles of 1848. Marx thus bitterly concluded that the smaller Slavonic nationalities of the Austrian Empire were religious-minded reactionaries, backward rural people who had betrayed the revolution. The Slavs of Germany—Marx argued—had long since lost their political vitality; they must perforce follow in the footsteps of their more powerful neighbors. The Welsh in Britain, the Basques in Spain, the French Canadians in North America, the Carinthians, and the Dalmatians were on the way out.[1] The future lay with large nations bent on industrialization.

Marx took a similar attitude toward the colonial peoples. He felt quite convinced that the British in India, for instance, were carrying out a "progressive" function in smashing the precapitalist institutions of the subcontinent; he similarly sympathized with the white settlers in New Zealand, and never worried about the indigenous Maori. The revolutionary future, Marx believed, lay with the industrial workers in the Western cities.

Marx's revolutionary theories, however, were worked out at a time when the conditions for insurrection began to undergo a rapid change. From the purely military point of view the barricade was never a very effective device. Reliance on it entailed tactics of passive defense. Insurgencies up to 1848 were effective when working-class rebels received active or passive support from middle-class national guards, and when the leadership of the government forces had lost its grip and its confidence. From 1849, however, the political conditions became more unfavorable. The bourgeoisie usually rallied in support of existing institutions; soldiers no longer saw their opponents as the people, but rather as a gang of looters.

In addition, there were important changes in the structure of the city. Revolutionary tacticians in preindustrial cities used to place their trust on barricades that could quickly be thrown up in narrow lanes, and whose construction required no technical skill. These tactics made good sense in preindustrial cities with their winding lanes and dark back-alleys, where the populace could fire muskets from rooftops, hurl stones from windows,

---

[1] Karl Marx, *Revolution und Kontre-Revolution in Deutschland* (Stuttgart, T. H. W. Dietz, Nachf., 1920), pp. 97–100. Karl Kautsky's preface tries to explain away these sentiments in the light of conditions of 1896.

and where meandering streets could not easily be swept by artillery. In the older cities of Europe, moreover, the mean hovels of the poor often adjoined the magnificent palaces of the nobility. The various strata of society mingled on the streets, and urban mobs were an ever-present threat. Urban expansion and the development of industries, however, tended to emphasize residential segregation between the various social classes. The factory owners moved away from the vicinity of the factory; the workers became concentrated in huge urban aggregations. Merchants and proletarians no longer lived cheek by jowl. Mob action, whether spontaneous or organized, ceased to be as effective a threat as in the olden days.

Technological development likewise favored established governments. Troops could move much more rapidly by railway than on ill-kept roads. Breech-loading, and later magazine-loading, rifles greatly added to the rapidity and accuracy of an army's firepower. The gunmaker's craft made rapid advances, and engineers perfected their methods of destruction.[2] Changes in city planning greatly favored government forces equipped with the new armaments. Baron Haussman's work in driving straight boulevards through the ancient quarters of Paris is well known. But similar changes were made in scores and scores of minor cities. A street-map of Mainz, a medium-sized city on the middle Rhine, will serve as a perfect case study. The old center was a maze of narrow, little streets. In 1822 the city architect effected a breakthrough from the cathedral in the center to the so-called Schillerplatz,[3] thereby completely changing the city's internal strategic situation. The new quarters built east of the *Grosse Bleiche* were planned on a rectangular pattern and follow Haussman's idea. They dominated the main railway station and the new industries; successful insurrectionary fighting in a fine boulevard like the Kaiserstrasse would be extremely difficult.

The nineteenth century also witnessed major changes in police techniques. Perhaps the most far-reaching reforms took place in Great Britain, which may therefore serve as a convenient model. In the eighteenth century the United Kingdom relied for its security on a system of parish constables. This arrangement worked well enough in small villages but broke down completely in great urban centers like London. Two hundred years ago the British capital was virtually unpoliced; vice and violence flourished to an extent that make modern "crime waves" seem like Sunday School outings. British mobs were fearsome aggregations that could be controlled, in the last instance, only by calling out troops and firing

[2] Friedrich Engels, "Neue Bedingungen des bewaffneten Aufstandes," in F. Engels-V. I. Lenin, *Militärpolitische Schriften,* K. Schmidt, ed. (Berlin, Internationaler Arbeiterverlag, 1930), pp. 131–35.
[3] W. F. Volbach, *Mainz* (Berlin, Deutscher Kunstverlag, 1928), pp. 28–29.

into the crowds after great devastation had already taken place. Rich merchants or great noblemen did not fare too badly under this system, since the wealthy hired armed footmen for their defense. Eighteenth-century politicians were not above using mobs for political purposes; the richer rate-payers disliked the idea of spending more money on police-men.

The demand for improved protection came from the ranks of the petty bourgeoisie and from "respectable" working men, who could not afford to pay for their own protection. The campaign for a better police force was supported by men like Francis Place, a Radical, and a tailor by profession, who battled for the rights of labor unions, for Parliamentary reform, and who also invented the technique of massed police baton charges. Police reorganization began in 1829. British reformers intro-duced ideas adapted from light infantry training in the Peninsula War, and thereby brought about remarkable changes. Within about two de-cades the British had built up one of the most efficient and humane police systems the world had ever known. Their system relied on decentraliza-tion and civilian control, and it laid special stress on the preventive role of the police. The new forces were highly visible and yet civilian in status and ethos. They instituted continuous patrols in place of the old system of penal repression.[4] They recruited an excellent body of men from the élite of the lower middle and upper levels of the British working class, who in turn policed the other orders of society, including the *Lumpen-proletariat*. The various British police forces generally contained people with a reasonably good education and good moral character, who earned the respect of their fellow countrymen. The police learned the art of coping with mobs by nonlethal means. Rising police standards thus played their part, together with rising living standards and administrative and political reforms, in slaying the specter of a British revolution.

In France, urban insurrections likewise yielded diminishing military returns. The armed city folk of Paris played a vital part in the French Revolution. The revolution of 1830 which, for the second time, defeated a Bourbon regime, likewise had its origins in Paris, though the provinces subsequently assumed control. Gradually, however, Paris began to lose some of its former importance. The extension of the telegraph made the provinces more aware of what was going on in the capital. The con-struction of railways facilitated the rapid movement of troops and supplies to the capital. When, in June 1848, the urban proletariat of Paris rose against a newly established Republican regime, the provinces unexpectedly

---

[4] See Patrick Pringle, *Hue and Cry: The Birth of the British Police Force* (London, Museum Press, 1955); and Sir Charles Reith, *A New Study of Police History* (Edinburgh, Oliver and Boyd, 1956).

came into their own. The French peasants were incensed against what they regarded as a threat against property. The Paris workers constituted but a small minority within the nation at large, and the workers' revolt was overthrown after savage slaughter.

Despite the lessons of the June battle, and despite the warnings issued by Engels and others, many revolutionaries continued to put their trust in urban insurrections. But city-based risings deriving from a few social strata, without support from the country as a whole, were always doomed to military failure—whatever intended or unintended political advantages might accrue to the rebels. City-born risings nevertheless retained some political importance, especially when the rebels were able to add luster to their cause by fighting a grim street-battle. After the French were defeated by the forces of a united Germany, Paris in 1871 was shaken by the rising of the Paris Commune. This was a patriotic insurrection directed against an Establishment accused of having betrayed the country to the hated Prussians. The rebels were determined to wage an all-out war, but they had no backing in the provinces, and could not make any headway among the remnants of the defeated French army. The government forces reoccupied Paris, slaughtered their opponents, and inflicted terrible losses on the Parisian proletariat. The Communards did, however, make a profound ideological impact on their age. The French proletarians once again proved that they could wield arms when in desperate circumstances. Equally important was the fact that Marxists who had disapproved of the outbreak when it started won vicarious glory by their subsequent support of the movement. They suddenly acquired a reputation for being red-blooded revolutionaries—a label that has stuck ever since. (Ironically enough, Maoists today still gain inspiration from the Paris Commune, even though the Communards were in no sense Communists, and their program of social reconstruction was sketchy.)

The military, technological, and social revolution that rendered old-fashioned urban insurrections obsolete also helped established governments to enforce order in the most remote rural regions of the European hinterland. "Social bandits" of the Robin Hood and the *Schinderhannes* variety could only prey on the rich in backward areas where communications were poor, and where robbers could rely on support from the poverty-stricken and ignorant peasantry. The railroad engineer, the road builder, and the village schoolmaster in the long run turned out to be even more dangerous to the highwayman than the most enterprising *gendarmes*. By the end of the nineteenth century, "social bandits" of the old-fashioned kind were found only in a few backwaters of Europe such as Sicily and Macedonia. In the end the robber was driven into the city. Western gangsterism today is an urban problem. Today's gangsters depend on city-skills like driving an automobile, opening a safe, manipulating the currency, or practicing graft connected with welfare projects.

The Europeans not only managed to subdue their own backward rural areas; they were equally successful in crushing country-bred warriors in many parts of Africa and Asia. The nineteenth century is indeed the century of the classical "small wars" in the colonies. European troops and their colonial auxiliaries waged "subalterns' wars" against indigenous fighting men on the rough *kopjes* of Matabeleland, on the South African veld, in roadless hill-country on the North-Western Frontier of India, in Burmese jungles, and on drought-ridden Mexican plains.

British theoreticians of war, including a distinguished military historian like Cyril Falls, tend to group all kinds of operations against primitive peoples under the general heading of "small wars." In actual fact, these categories should be sharply distinguished. Many colonial campaigns entailed regular wars against regular armies. For instance, the Matabele, a warlike cattle-keeping warrior people who had established a powerful kingdom in what is now Rhodesia, had regular armies whose training and mobilization depended on a peculiar "age set" system. The Matabele perfected infantry tactics that depended on tight discipline, rapid movement, and the shock effect of masses of spearmen charging in close formation. The Matabele won many victories over their neighbors, but their tactics became ossified. The Matabele made insufficient use of firearms. Their generals were in some ways oddly like their opposite numbers in British Guards Regiments. They placed too much emphasis on the cult of cold steel, on the pomp and circumstance of military might, on the elaborate splendor of the "Great Dance" (in some ways like a great troop review), on the magnificence of gorgeous plumed headdresses, and on other unessential appurtenances of war.

In 1893 the Matabele armies were overthrown by British settlers, who pitted mounted riflemen and automatic weapons against great masses of infantry armed primarily with assegais, knobkerries, and ox-hide shields. It was only when the Matabele had suffered defeat that they turned to partisan warfare against the whites and began to make more effective use of firearms. So did the supposedly unwarlike Mashona, the erstwhile foes and victims of the Matabele, who proved even more adept at guerrilla operations than their Matabele neighbors.

Between 1896 and 1897, the British nevertheless effectively subjugated Rhodesia. In other parts of the world, white troops and their indigenous auxiliaries were equally successful against tribal warriors. Throughout the nineteenth century, Europeans and Americans had indeed to contend with partisan warfare of the most variegated kind. American cavalrymen, for instance, battled against such opponents as the Apache, perhaps the most skillful guerrillas of world history. They were a people completely specialized in the art of warfare. Their warriors were brilliant horsemen and deadly shots, who could live off the land, make a quick get-away on captured horses, and who knew how to use to perfection every ruse of warfare and every artifice of camouflage. British soldiers battled against Somali desert warriors mounted on camels, aganst Ashanti soldiers seeking cover in the tropical forests of the Gold Coast, and against Pathani partisans operating in roadless hills.

By and large, white or white-led troops won in such encounters. It was only on such rare occasions as when they had to seek out the foe in remote mountain country where the terrain placed impossible obstacles in the invaders' way that they suffered defeat. Much of the Europeans' initial advantage depended on superior organization, on better-organized supply services, on tighter discipline, and on superior leadership. Of course the white soldiers had better weapons too. They had factory-made guns and rifles. But the technological factor should not be overestimated. In many colonial campaigns, distance and difficult terrain precluded the effective use of artillery. The development of rifles was relatively slow. The first efficient breechloader was the Prussian needle gun, adopted in 1848. In 1867 a British officer devised a rolled metal cartridge, and in 1871 the British adopted the single-loading Henry-Martini rifle. Smokeless powder and repeating rifles only came into use in the latter part of the nineteenth century, a major step forward being the construction of the Mauser rifle with bolt action and a charger-loaded magazine. Many colonial insurgents moreover managed to acquire modern European rifles. Others bought weapons discarded by European armies. The more modern and expensive arms went to wealthier people like some of the Arab slave traders on the East African coast. The most out-of-date weapons went to the most backward tribes, people like the Bemba of northeastern Rhodesia, who, by the end of the nineteenth century, were found to be well-armed with the British "Tower Musket," which had once done duty for Wellington's veterans.

The most decisive technical innovations affecting "small wars," however, only came toward the end of the nineteenth century. Especially important was the fully automatic gun, a weapon similar to the Maxim which African tribesmen could neither buy nor service. The automatic gun did not, however, come into use until the early 1890s, when British settlers first employed Maxims against the Matabele of Southern Rhodesia. This meant that throughout most of the nineteenth century Europeans usually had only a limited superiority in firepower. The same holds true in the field of transport. In many cases European troops gained considerable assistance from steam power applied to railways and ships. Steam power might greatly affect the strategy of a colonial war, but it rarely influenced its tactics.[5] Throughout the nineteenth century, colonial forces lacking motorized transport generally depended on their ability to out-march their opponents in battle. Nevertheless, the colonial powers generally managed to cope with indigenous resistance movements; anticolonial guerrillas were successfully crushed. . . .

E. J. HOBSBAWM

The Mafia as a Social Phenomenon

Mafias . . . have a number of special characteristics. *First,* they are never pure social movements, with specific aims and programs. They are, as it were, the meeting-places of all sorts of tendencies existing within their societies: the defense of the entire society against threats to its traditional way of life, the aspirations of the various classes within it, the personal ambitions and aspirations of individual energetic members. Hence they are to some extent, like national movements, of which perhaps they are a sort of embryo, fluid. Whether the tinge of social protest by the poor determines their general color, as in Calabria, or that of the ambitions of the local middle classes, as in Sicily, or pure crime, as in the American *Mafia,* depends on circumstances. *Second,* they are to some extent unorganized. It is true that some *Mafias* are, at least on paper, centralized and with proper "chains of command" and promotion, perhaps on the model of masonic orders. But the most interesting situation is that in which, as in the classical Sicilian *Mafia,* there is—or at one stage was—no proper organization above local level and only very primitive organization even there.

Under what conditions do *Mafias* arise? The question simply cannot be answered, because we do not even know how many of them there are

E. J. Hobsbawm, *Primitive Rebels: Studies in Archaic Forms of Social Movement in the 19th and 20th Centuries* . © 1959 by E. J. Hobsbawm. Reprinted by permission of Manchester University Press, Manchester, England, pp. 30–44.

[5] There were a few exceptions. In the Boer war the British used armored trains against Boer commandos operating in Bechuanaland.

or have been. Sicilian *Mafia* is the only body of its kind in modern Europe which has provoked description and analysis in any quantity. Apart from casual references to "delinquent associations," "secret associations of robbers" and protectors of robbers, and the like, we know hardly anything about the situation in other places, and what we know allows us at best to say that a situation out of which *Mafia could* have arisen, existed, not whether it actually did.[1] We cannot conclude that absence of information means that no such phenomenon existed. Thus, as we shall see, there is absolutely no doubt of the existence of a body of *mafia*-type in Southern Calabria. But apart from a passing reference to such secret societies in Calabria and the Cilento (the region south of the gulf of Salerno) it seems to have been wholly unrecorded in the past.[2] This is less surprising than it might seem. Secret bodies composed largely of illiterate countrymen work in obscurity. Middle-class townsmen are profoundly ignorant, and were normally profoundly contemptuous, of the low life under their feet. The only thing we can therefore do at present is to concentrate on one or two examples of known *Mafias* and hope that these may eventually throw light on the situation in hitherto uninvestigated areas.

Mafia is less well known than one might suppose. Though there is no dispute about the facts and a good deal of useful descriptive and analytical literature,[3] public discussion has been confused, partly by all manner of journalistic romancing, partly by the simple failure to recognize that "what

[1] See Zugasti *op. cit.*, Introduction, vol. I for the *alcaldes'* reports on the state of crime in their areas of Cordoba province, *c.* 1870; e.g. a "secret association of robbers" in Baena, a "sociedad de ladrones" in Montilla, some thing that looks rather like *mafia* in the famous smugglers' pueblo of Benameji, and the dumb opposition of Iznajar where 'according to the inveterate custom of this town, all these crimes have remained unpunished' (i.e. unsolved). I am inclined to accept Brenan's view that this was a proto-*mafia* rather than a *Mafia* situation. Cf. also Chapter V on Andalusian anarchism, below.

[2] G. Alongi, *La Camorra* (Turin 1890), 30. The note on La Camorra in Calabria (*Archivio di Psichiatria*, IV, 1883, 295) appears to deal exclusively with an organization of city crooks in Reggio Calabria, and appears to be quite unaware of the rural body. It may be noted that nobody was more passionately interested in this type of phenomenon than the Italian positivist (Lombroso) school of criminology, whose organ the Archivio was.

[3] The main sources used in this article, besides some personal conversations in Sicily, are N. Colajanni, *La Delinquenza in Sicilia* (1885), *La Sicilia dai Borboni ai Sabaudi* (1900), A. Cutrera, *La Mafia ed i Mafiosi* (1900), G. Alongi, *La Maffia* (1887), G. Montalbane, 'La Mafia' (*Nuovi Argomenti*, Nov.–Dec. 1953), various official enquiries and standard works on Sicilian economic and social conditions, of which L. Franchetti, *Condizioni Politiche e Amministrative della Sicilia* (1877), is a favorable specimen, and G. Mosca's articles in the *Giornale degli Economisti*, 1900 and the *Encyclopedia of Social Sciences*. The vast bulk of scholarly and sensible literature about *Mafia* appeared between 1880 and 1910, and the comparative dearth of more modern analyses is much to be deplored.

appeared to the Piedmontese or the Lombard as 'Sicilian delinquency' was in reality the law of a different society . . . a semi-feudal society." [4] It may, therefore, be as well to summarize what we know about it.

The word *Mafia* stands here for several distinct things. First, it represents a general attitude towards the State and the State's law which is not necessarily any more criminal than the very similar attitude of, let us say, public schoolboys towards their masters. A *mafioso* did not invoke State or law in his private quarrels, but made himself respected and safe by winning a reputation for toughness and courage, and settled his differences by fighting. He recognized no obligation except those of the code of honor or *omertà* (manliness), whose chief article forbade giving information to the public authorities. In other words *mafia* (which will be spelled with a small *m* when used in this sense) was the sort of code of behavior which always tends to develop in societies without effective public order, or in societies in which citizens regard the authorities as wholly or partly hostile (for instance in jails or in the underworld outside them), or as unappreciative of the things which really matter (for instance in schools), or as a combination of both. One should resist the temptation to link this code with feudalism, aristocratic virtues or the like. Its most complete and binding rule was among the *souteneurs* and minor hoodlums of the Palermo slums, whose conditions approximated most closely to "lawlessness," or rather to a Hobbesian state in which the relations between individuals or small groups are like those between sovereign powers. It has been rightly pointed out that in the really feudal parts of the island *omertà* tended to mean merely that only denunciation of the weak or defeated was permissible.[5] Where there is an established structure of power, "honor" tends to belong to the mighty.

In lawless communities power is rarely scattered among an anarchy of competing units, but clusters round local strong-points. Its typical form is patronage, its typical holder the private magnate or boss with his body of retainers and dependants and the network of "influence" which surrounds him and causes men to put themselves under his protection. *Mafia,* in the second sense of the word, is almost a synonym for this, though it tended to be applied to the retainers (the "low *Mafia*") rather than to the patrons. Some of the forms of this system were certainly feudal, especially in the inland *latifundia;* and it is very probable that in Sicily (where legally feudal relations were not officially abolished until the 19th century, and their symbolism lives on even today in the painted battles between knights and Saracens on the sides of peasant carts) feudal forms of loyalty helped to shape it. However, this is a minor point, for retainership and patronage can come into existence without any feudal

[4] E. Sereni, *Il Capitalismo nelle Campagne, 1860–1900* (Turin 1948), 187.
[5] Franchetti, 219–21.

tradition. What characterized Sicily was the universal prevalence of such patronage and the virtual absence of any other form of constant power. *Mafia* in the third, and most usual sense of the word, is not easy to distinguish from the second: it is the control of the community's life by a secret—or rather an officially unrecognized—system of gangs. So far as we know, this type of *Mafia* was never a single secret society, centrally organized, like the Neapolitan Camorra, though opinions about its degree of centralization have always differed.[6] The Palermo Procurator's report of 1931 probably expressed the situation best:

> The associations of the small localities normally exercise jurisdiction within these and the neighboring Communes. Those of the important centers are in relations with one another even to the most remote provinces, lending each other mutual aid and assistance.[7]

Indeed, being essentially a rural phenomenon to begin with, it is difficult to see how *Mafia* could have been hierarchically centralized, communications being what they were in the nineteenth century. It was rather a network of local gangs (*cosche*—today they seem to be called "families") sometimes two or three strong, sometimes much larger, each controlling a certain territory, normally a Commune or a *latifundium,* and linked with one another in various ways. Each *cosca* milked its territory; though sometimes, as during transhumance of cattle, the gangs of the territories through which the beasts travelled would cooperate. The migrations of harvest laborers, and especially the links between *latifundia* and the urban lawyers and the mass of cattle-markets and fairs all over the country, would provide other contacts between local groups.[8]

Their members recognized one another less by accepted secret signs and passwords than by bearing, dress, talk and behavior. Professional toughness and virility, professional parasitism and outlawry, breed their specialized behavior, designed in a lawless society to impress the sheep—and perhaps also the lions—with the power of the wolves, as well as to set them apart from the herd. The *bravi* in Manzoni's *Betrothed* dress and behave very like the "lads" (*picciotti*) in Sicily two and a half centuries later. On the other hand each gang did have strikingly standardized initiation rituals and passwords in the 1870s, though these seem to have

[6] *Mafia* by Ed. Reid, an American newspaperman (New York 1952), which holds the centralized view, is to be neglected, for the book—probably produced quickly to catch a market alerted by Sen. Kefauver's Crime Enquiry (which made vast accusations against *Mafia*)—shows a remarkable lack of appreciation of Sicilian problems. The strongest evidence for centralization comes from the post-1943 period, but even this is ambiguous.

[7] Quoted in Montalbane, *loc. cit.,* 179.

[8] Alongi, *op. cit.,* 70 ff.

been allowed to lapse subsequently.[9] Whether or not, as Cutrera holds, they had been evolved long since in Milazzo jail, and popularized through songs and such pieces of literature as the *Life and Brave Deeds of the Bandit Pasquale Bruno,* I do not know. But they were clearly the rituals of an old-fashioned Mediterranean blood-brotherhood. The crucial ritual —normally (except where this was impossible as in jails) carried out in front of a saint's image—was that of piercing the candidate's thumb and extracting blood, which was daubed on the saint's image, which was then burnt. This last act may have been designed to bind the novice to the brotherhood by the ceremonial breaking of a taboo: a ritual involving the firing of a pistol at a statue of Jesus Christ is also reported.[10] Once initiated the *Mafioso* was a *compadre,* co-godparenthood being in Sicily, as elsewhere in the Mediterranean, the form of artificial kinship which implied the greatest and most solemn obligations of mutual help on the contracting parties. The passwords also seem to have been standardized. However, this does not prove that the association was centralized, for the Camorra—a purely Neapolitan organization without Sicilian links—also had a blood-brotherhood initiation of a similar type.[11]

So far as we can see, though standardized, each group seems to have regarded these rituals as its private bonds, rather as children adopt standardized forms of twisting words as strictly private languages. It is indeed probable that *Mafia* evolved some sort of quasi-national coordination; its central direction, if this term is not too precise, settling in Palermo. However, as we shall see this reflected the economic and political structure and evolution of Sicily rather than any criminal master-plan.[12]

Beneath the rule of the Bourbon or Piedmontese state, though sometimes living in strange symbiosis with it, *Mafia* (in all the three senses of the word) provided a parallel machine of law and organized power; indeed, so far as the citizen in the areas under its influence was concerned, the only effective law and power. In a society such as Sicily, in which the official government could not or would not exercise effective sway, the appearance of such a system was as inevitable as the appearance of gang-rule, or its alternative, private posses and vigilantes in certain parts of *laissez-faire* America. What distinguishes Sicily is the territorial extent and cohesion of this private and parallel system of power.

---

[9] Montalbane, *loc. cit.* The fullest description of these is for the *Stoppaglieri* of Monreale and the neighborhood, and the *Fratellanza* of Favara (prov. Agrigento) and the neighborhood. These are printed in various places, e.g. Montalbane. See also F. Lestingi, 'L'Associazione della Fratellanza,' in *Archivio di Psichiatria,* V (1884), 452 ff.

[10] Montalbane, 191.

[11] Ed. Reid, *op. cit.,* for an initiation in New York 1917, 143–4; Alongi, 41.

[12] It is also probable that *Mafia* among the immigrants in America was more centralized than at home, because these were transferred to the new world along relatively few lanes, and settled in a handful of big cities. However, this need not concern us.

It was not, however, universal, for not all sections of Sicilian society were equally in need of it. Fishermen and sailors, for instance, never developed the code of *omertà* and—apart from the underworld—it was weakly developed in the towns, that is to say the real towns, not the great agglomerations in which Sicilian peasants lived in the midst of an empty, bandit-ridden or perhaps malarial countryside. Indeed, the urban artisans tended, especially during revolutions—as in Palermo in 1773 and 1820–21—to organize their own "train bands" or *ronde,* until the alliance of the ruling-classes, afraid of their revolutionary implications, imposed the socially more reliable National Guard and eventually the combination of policemen and *Mafiosi* on them after 1848.[13] On the other hand certain groups were in special need of private defenses. Peasants on the large inland *latifundia,* and sulphur-miners, needed some means of mitigating their misery besides periodic jaqueries. For the owners of certain types of property—cattle, which was as easily rustled on the empty Sicilian ranges as in Arizona, and oranges and lemons, which invited thieves in the untended orchards of the coast—protection was vital. In fact, *Mafia* developed precisely in the three areas of this kind. It dominated the irrigated fruit-growing plain round Palermo, with its fertile, fragmented peasant tenancies, the sulphur-mining areas of the southern center, and the open inland *latifundia.* Outside these areas it was weaker, and tended to disappear in the eastern half of the island.

It is a mistake to believe that institutions which look archaic are of great antiquity. They may, like public schools or the fancy dress part of English political life, have come into existence recently (though built of old or pseudo-ancient material) for modern purposes. *Mafia* is not a medieval, but a nineteenth- and twentieth-century institution. Its period of greatest glory falls after 1890. No doubt Sicilian peasants have throughout history lived under the double régime of a remote and generally foreign central government and a local régime of slave or feudal lords; since theirs was *par excellence* the country of the *latifundium.* No doubt they were never, and could never be, in the habit of regarding the central government as a real State, but merely as a special form of brigand, whose soldiers, tax-gatherers, policemen and courts fell upon them from time to time. Their illiterate and isolated life was lived between the lord with his strong-arm mien and parasites and their own defensive customs and institutions. In a sense, therefore, something like the "parallel system" must always have existed, as it exists in all backward peasant societies.

Yet this was not *Mafia,* though it contained most of the raw material out of which *Mafia* grew. In fact it seems that *Mafia* in its full sense developed only after 1860. The word itself, in its modern connota-

[13] Montalbane, 194–7, for a valuable discussion of the problem.

tion, does not occur before the early 1860s,[14] and had in any case previously been confined to the argot of one district in Palermo. A local historian from western Sicily—a hotbed of *Mafia*—finds no trace of it in his town before 1860.[15] On the other hand by 1866 the word is already used as a matter of course by Maggiorani, and by the 1870s it is common currency in political discussion. It is fairly clear that in some regions—perhaps mainly in Palermo province—a developed *Mafia* must have existed earlier. Nothing could be more typically *mafioso* than the career of Salvatore Miceli, the boss of Monreale, who brought his armed *squadre* to fight the Bourbons in Palermo in 1848, was pardoned and made a captain of arms by them in the 1850s (a characteristic touch), took his men to Garibaldi in 1860 and was killed fighting the Piedmontese in the Palermitan rising of 1866.[16] And by 1872 the Monreale *Mafia* was developed to the point where the first of the subsequently endemic revolts of the "young *Mafia*" against the "old *Mafia*" took place,—aided by the police which sought to weaken the society—and produced the "sect" of the Stoppaglieri.[17] Nevertheless, something pretty fundamental obviously happened to the "parallel system" after the official abolition of feudalism in Sicily (1812–38), and especially after its conquest by the northern middle class; and this is, after all, no more than we should expect. The question is what? To answer it, we must summarize what is known of the composition and structure of the developed *Mafia*.

Its first, and by far its most important characteristic is, that *all* the heads of local *Mafias* were (and are) men of wealth, some ex-feudalists in the inland areas, but overwhelmingly men of the middle class, capitalist farmers and contractors, lawyers and the like. The evidence on this point seems conclusive.[18] Since *Mafia* was primarily a rural phenomenon, this in itself marks the beginnings of a revolution, for in mid-nineteenth century Sicily bourgeois owned land still amounted to only about 10 percent of the cultivated area. The backbone of *Mafia* were the *gabellotti*—wealthy middle-class persons who paid the absentee feudal owners a lump rent for their whole estate and sublet at a profit to the peasantry, and who virtually replaced them as the real ruling class. Virtually all of them, in the *Mafia* areas, seem to have been *mafiosi*. The rise of *Mafia* thus marks a transfer of power in the "parallel system" from feudal to rural middle class, an incident in the rise of rural capitalism. At the same time *Mafia* was one of the main engines of this transfer. For if

[14] G. Pitré, *Usi e costume* . . . *del popolo siciliano*, III, 287ff (1889); art. "Mafia," in *Enc. Soc. Sciences*.

[15] S. Nicastro, *Dal Quarantotto a la Sessanta in Mazzara* (1913), 80–1.

[16] Cutrera, 170–4.

[17] *Giornale di Sicilia* 21.8.1877, quoted by Montalbane, 167–74.

[18] Cutrera, 73, 88–9, 96. Franchetti, 170–2. The spectacle of gangsterism as a typically middle-class phenomenon amazed and troubled Franchetti.

the *gabellotto* used it to force terms on tenant and share-cropper, he also used it to force them on the absentee lord.

Because *Mafia* was in the hands of something like a local "business-men's" class, it also developed a range of influence which it could never have done had it merely been an affair of "tough guys," whose horizon was bounded by the frontiers of their township. Most *gabellotti* were linked with Palermo, where the absentee barons and princes received their rents, as all Irish townlands in the eighteenth century were linked with Dublin. In Palermo lived the lawyers who settled major property transfers (and were as like as not educated sons and nephews of the rural bour-geoisie); the officials and courts which had to be "fixed"; the merchants who disposed of the ancient corn and cattle and the new cash crops of orange and lemon. Palermo was the capital in which Sicilian revolu-tions—i.e. the fundamental decisions about Sicilian politics—were tra-ditionally made. Hence it is only natural that the local threads of *Mafia* should be tied into a single knot there, though—for obvious reasons—the existence of a Palermitan "high *Mafia*" has always been suspected rather than demonstrated.

The apparatus of coercion of the "parallel system" was as shapeless and decentralized as its political and legal structure; but it fulfilled its purpose of securing internal quiet and external power—i.e. of controlling the local inhabitants and harassing a foreign government. It is not easy to give a lucid and brief account of its structure. In any society as miser-ably poor and oppressed as that of the Sicilians there is a vast potential reserve of strong-arm men, as there is of prostitutes. The "bad man" is, in the expressive phrase of French criminal slang, *affranchi;* and there are no other individual methods of escaping the bondage of virtual serfdom but bullying and outlawry. In Sicily this great class consisted in the main of three groups: the retainers and private police-forces (such as the *guardiani* and *campieri* who guarded the orchards and ranges); the bandits and professional outlaws; and the strong and self-reliant among the legitimate laborers. We must bear in mind that the best chance the peasant or miner had of mitigating his oppression was to gain a reputation for being tough or a friend of toughs. The normal meeting-place of all these was in the entourage of the local great man, who provided employment for men of daring and swagger and protected the outlaws—if only be-cause his prestige required him to demonstrate his power to do so. Thus a local network, which enmeshed estate guards, goatherds, bandits, bullies, and strong men, with the local property-owners, already existed.

Two things were almost certainly responsible for turning this into *Mafia*. First, there was the attempt of the feeble Bourbons to set up the "Armed Companies." Like most other attempts by feeble governments to hand over the maintenance of public security to private enterprise, spurred on by the fear of financial loss, this failed. The "Armed Companies," which were set up independently in different areas, were responsible for making good what the thieves and robbers took. It follows, that under Sicilian conditions, each company had an overwhelming incentive to encourage its local bad men to rob elsewhere against the promise of local sanctuary, or to negotiate privately with them for the return of stolen goods. A small step separated this from the actual participation of the Armed Companies in crime, for they were naturally composed of the same kind of toughs as the brigands. Secondly, there was the increasing danger of urban and peasant discontent, especially after the abolition of feudalism. This, as usual, bore heavily on the peasants, and moreover involved them in the henceforth perennial tussle with the rural middle class about the ownership of the common and ecclesiastical lands, which the middle class tended to appropriate. At a period when revolutions occurred with terrifying frequency—four or five in forty-six years—it was only natural that the rich tended to recruit retainers for the defense of their own interests—the so-called *contro-squadre*—as well as taking other measures to prevent the revolutions getting out of hand, and nothing lent itself to *mafioso* practices as well as such a combination of the (rural) rich and the toughs.

The relationship between the *Mafia,* the "lads" or retainers and the brigands was therefore somewhat complex. As property-owners the *capi-mafia* had no interest in crime, though they had an interest in maintaining a body of armed followers for coercive purposes. The retainers, on the other hand, had to be allowed pickings, and a certain scope for private enterprise. The bandits, lastly, were an almost total nuisance, though they could occasionally be made use of to reinforce the power of the boss: the bandit Giuliano was called upon in 1947 to shoot up a May Day procession of peasants, the name of the influential Palermitan who arranged the transaction being known. However, in the absence of *central* state machinery, banditry itself could not be eliminated. Hence the peculiar compromise solution which is so typical of *Mafia*: a local monopoly of controlled extortion (often institutionalized so as to lose its character of naked force), and the elimination of interlopers. The orange-grower in the Palermo region would have to hire an orchard guard. If wealthy, he might from time to time have to contribute to the maintenance of the "lads"; if he had property stolen, he would have it returned minus a percentage, unless he stood specially well with *Mafia*. The private thief was excluded.[19]

[19] One of the commonest misconceptions about *Mafia*—perpetuated in such works as the ineffable Prefect Mori's *Last Battle of the Mafia* and in the first edition of Guercio's *Sicily*—is the confusion between it and banditry. *Mafia* maintained public order by private means. Bandits were, broadly speaking, what it protected the public from.

The military formations of *Mafia* show the same mixture of retainers' loyalty and dependence, and private profit-making by the fighting men. When war broke out, the local boss would raise his *squadre*—mainly, but perhaps not exclusively, composed of the members of the local *cosche.* The "lads" would join the *squadra,* partly to follow their patron (the more influential the *capo-mafia,* the larger his troop), partly to raise their personal prestige by the only way open to them, acts of bravery and violence, but also because war meant profit. In the major revolutions the *capi-mafia* would arrange with the Palermo liberals for a daily stipend of four *tari* per man, as well as arms and munitions, and the promise of this wage (not to mention other pickings of war) swelled the numbers of the *squadre.*

Such, then, was the "parallel system" of the *Mafia.* One cannot say that it was imposed on the Sicilians by anyone. In a sense, it grew out of the needs of all rural classes, and served the purpose of all in varying degrees. For the weak—the peasants and the miners—it provided at least some guarantee that obligations between them would be kept,[20] some guarantee that the usual degree of oppression would not be habitually exceeded; it was the terror which mitigated traditional tyrannies. And perhaps, also, it satisfied a desire for revenge by providing that the rich were sometimes fleeced, and that the poor, if only as outlaws, could sometimes fight back. It may even, on occasions, have provided the framework of revolutionary or defensive organization. (At any rate in the 1870s there seems to have been some tendency for Friendly Societies and quasi-*mafious* bodies like the *Fratellanza* of the sulphur-town of Favara, the *Fratuzzi* of Bagheria or the *Stoppaglieri* of Monreale to fuse.[21]) For the feudal lords it was a means of safeguarding property and authority: for the rural middle class a means of gaining it. For all, it provided a means of defense against the foreign exploiter—the Bourbon or Piedmontese government—and a method of national or local self-assertion. So long as Sicily was no more than a static feudal society subject to outside rule, *Mafia's* character as a national conspiracy of noncooperation gave it a genuinely popular basis. The *squadre* fought with the Palermo liberals (who included the anti-Bourbon Sicilian aristocracy) in 1820, 1848 and 1860. They headed the first great rising against the domination of northern capitalism in 1866. Its national, and to some extent popular character, increased the prestige of *Mafia,* and ensured it public sympathy and silence.

[20] See N. Colajanni, *Gli Avvenimenti di Sicilia* (1894), cap 5, on the function of *mafia* as a code governing the relations between different classes of sulphurminers, esp. pp. 47–8.
[21] I am not convinced that the rise of these bodies in the 1870s can be interpreted purely in terms of the revolt of young against old *Mafia* elements, as Montalbane suggests; though this may have been the case in Monreale.

Obviously it was a complex movement, including mutually contradictory elements. Nevertheless, however tiresome to the historian, he must resist the temptation to pigeon-hole *Mafia* more precisely at this stage of its development. Thus one cannot agree with Montalbane that the *picciotti* who then formed the revolutionary *squadre* were not really *Mafiosi* with a capital M but only *mafiosi* with a small m, while only the *controsquadre*, already specialized strong-arm squads for the rich, were the "real" *Mafia*. That is to read the *Mafia* of the 20th century into a period where it does not belong.[22]

Indeed, we may suspect that *Mafia* began its real rise to major power (and abuse) as a Sicilian regional movement of revolt against the disappointments of Italian unity in the 1860s, and as a more effective movement than the parallel and contemporary guerilla warfare of the brigands in continental southern Italy. Its political links as we have seen were with the extreme Left, for the Garibaldian Radicals were the main Italian opposition party. Yet three things caused *Mafia* to change its character.

First, there was the rise of capitalist relationships in island society. The emergence of modern forms of peasant and labor movement in place of the old alternation of silent conspiratorial hatred and occasional massacre faced the *Mafia* with an unprecedented change. 1866 was the last time it fought against the authorities with arms. The great rising of 1894 —the *Fasci Siciliani*—saw it on the side of reaction, or at best neutral. Conversely, these risings were organized by new types of leaders—local socialists—connected with new types of organization, the *Fasci* or mutual defense societies, and independent of the "lads." The modern inverse proportion between the strength of *Mafia* and revolutionary activity began to appear. Even then it was observed that the rise of the Fasci had diminished the hold of *Mafia* on the peasants.[23] By 1900 *Piana dei Greci,* the socialist stronghold, though surrounded by *Mafia* strongholds, was markedly less riddled with it.[24] It is only in politically backward and power-

[22] Montalbane, 197.

[23] E. C. Calon, *La Mafia* (Madrid 1906), 11.

[24] See the invaluable *Mafia* distribution map in Cutrera. Piana, though apparently slow to adopt peasant organization, became the great stronghold of the 1893 Fasci, and has remained a fortress of socialism (and later communism) ever since. That it was previously impregnated by *Mafia* is suggested by the history of *Mafia* in New Orleans, whose Sicilian colony which arrived in the 1880s had, to judge by the occurrence of the characteristic Albanian family names—Schirò, Loyacano, Matranga—a strong contingent of Pianesi. The Matrangas—members of the Stoppaglieri—controlled the dockside rackets, and were prominent in the *Mafia* incidents of 1889 in New Orleans. (Ed. Reid, *op. cit.,* 100 ff.) The family apparently continued its *mafioso* activities, for in 1909 Lt. Petrosino of the New York police, later killed in Palermo—presumably by *Mafia*—was enquiring into the life of one of them (Reid, 122). I recall seeing the elaborate tomb of a Matranga in Piana in 1953, a man who had recently returned from emigration to the U.S.A. and had

less communities that brigands and *mafiosi* take the place of social movements. However, in spite of such local setbacks, there can be no doubt that *Mafia* as a whole was still expanding in the western part of Sicily throughout this period. At least a comparison of the Parliamentary Enquiries of 1884 and 1910 leaves one with a strong impression that it was.[25] Second, the new ruling class of rural Sicily, the *gabellotti* and their urban partners, discovered a *modus vivendi* with northern capitalism. They did not compete with it, for they were not interested in manufacture, and some of their most important products, such as oranges, were hardly produced in the north; hence the transformation of the south into an agrarian colony of the trading and manufacturing north did not greatly trouble them. On the other hand the evolution of northern politics provided them with an unprecedented and invaluable means of gaining power: the vote. The great days of *Mafia's* power, but days which portended its decline, begin with the triumph of "Liberalism" in Italian politics and develop with the extension of the franchise.

From the point of view of the northern politicians, after the end of the conservative period which succeeded unification, the problem of the south was simple. It could provide safe majorities for whatever government gave sufficient bribes or concessions to the local bosses who could guarantee electoral victory. This was child's play for *Mafia*. Its candidates were always elected, in real strongholds almost unanimously. But the concessions and bribes which were small, from the point of view of northerners (for the south was poor) made all the difference to local power in a region as small as half Sicily. Politics made the power of the local boss; politics increased it, and turned it into big business.

Mafia won its new power, not merely because it could promise and intimidate, but because, in spite of the new competitors, it was still regarded as part of the national or popular movement; just as big city bosses in the United States won their original power not simply by corruption and force, but by being "our men" for thousands of immigrant voters: Irish men for the Irish, Catholics for the Catholic, Democrats (i.e. opponents of big business) in a predominantly Republican country. It is no accident that most American big city machines, however corrupt, belonged to the traditional party of minority opposition, as most Sicilians supported opposition to Rome, which, in the years after 1860, meant the Garibaldians. Thus the crucial turn in *Mafia's* fortunes could not come until the "Left" (or men who sported its slogans) became the government party after 1876. The "Left," as Colajanni put it, thus

---

been found, in circumstances into which nobody was anxious to enquire, killed on a road a few years before.

25 A. Damiani, *Inchiesta Agraria* (1884), Sicily, vol. III; G. Lorenzoni, *Inchiesta Parlamentare* (1910), Sicily, vol. VI, i–ii, esp. pp. 649–51.

achieved "a transformation in Sicily and the south which could not otherwise have been brought about: the complete subjection of the mass to
the government." [26] Sicilian political organization, i.e. *Mafia,* thus became part of the government system of patronage, and bargained all the
more effectively because its illiterate and remote followers took time to
realize that they were no longer voting for the cause of revolt. When they
did (as for instance in the risings of the 1890s) it was too late. The
tacit partnership between Rome with its troops and martial law and *Mafia*
was too much for them. The true "kingdom of *Mafia*" had been established. It was now a great power. Its members sat as deputies in Rome
and their spoons reached into the thickest part of the gravy of government: large banks, national scandals. Its influence and patronage was
now beyond the dream of old-fashioned local captains like Miceli of
Monreale. It was not to be opposed; but it was no longer a Sicilian
popular movement as in the days of the *squadre* of 1848, 1860 and
1866. . . .

CHARLES TILLY

Collective Violence in
European Perspective

As comforting as it is for civilized people to think of barbarians as
violent and of violence as barbarian, Western civilization and various
forms of collective violence have always been close partners. We do not
need a stifled universal instinct of aggression to account for outbreaks of
violent conflicts in our past, or in our present. Nor need we go to the
opposite extreme and search for pathological moments and sick men in
order to explain collective acts of protest and destruction. Historically,

Charles Tilly, "Collective Violence in European Perspective," in *Violence in
America: Historical and Comparative Perspectives,* Hugh Davis Graham and Ted
Robert Gurr, eds. (New York: Frederick A. Praeger Publishers, 1969), pp. 4–5,
10–13, 31–37.

[26] *La Sicilia dai Borboni ai Sabaudi* (1951 ed.), 78.

collective violence has flowed regularly out of the central political processes of Western countries. Men seeking to seize, hold, or realign the levers of power have continually engaged in collective violence as part of their struggles. The oppressed have struck in the name of justice, the privileged in the name of order, those in between in the name of fear. Great shifts in the arrangements of power have ordinarily produced—and have often depended on—exceptional movements of collective violence.

Yet the basic forms of collective violence vary according to who is involved and what is at issue. They have changed profoundly in Western countries over the last few centuries, and those countries have built big cities and modern industries. For these reasons, the character of collective violence at a given time is one of the best signs we have of what is going on in a country's political life. The nature of violence and the nature of the society are intimately related.

Collective violence is normal. That does not mean it is intrinsically desirable, or inevitable. For century after century, the inhabitants of southern Italy endured malaria as a normal fact of life; today, American city dwellers endure smog and nerve-rending traffic as normal facts of life; few people hail malaria, smog, or traffic jams. Europeans of other centuries often destroyed children they could not provide for. Now infanticide has become rare. Few of us mourn its passing. But the fact that infanticide persisted so long in the face of persuasive teachings and fearsome penalties tells us something about the poverty and population pressure under which people once lived in Western countries. It also may help us understand some apparently barbaric practices of people outside the West today. In a similar way, both the persistence of the phenomenon of collective violence and the changes in its form within European countries over the last few centuries have something to teach us about their political life, and even about contemporary forms of protest. . . .

POLITICS AND VIOLENCE

My own explorations of Western Europe, especially France, over the last few centuries suggest a more political interpretation of collective violence. Far from being mere side effects of urbanization, industrialization, and other large structural changes, violent protests seem to grow most directly from the struggle for established places in the structure of power. Even presumably nonpolitical forms of collective violence like the antitax revolt are normally directed against the authorities, accompanied by a critique of the authorities' failure to meet their responsibilities, and informed by a sense of justice denied to the participants in the protest. Furthermore, instead of constituting a sharp break from "normal" political life, violent protests tend to accompany, complement, and extend organized, peaceful attempts by the same people to accomplish their objectives.

Over the long run, the processes most regularly producing collective violence are those by which groups acquire or lose membership in the political community. The form and locus of collective violence therefore vary greatly depending on whether the major ongoing political change is a group's acquisition of the prerequisites of membership, its loss of those prerequisites, or a shift in the organization of the entire political system.

The impact of large structural changes such as urbanization, industrialization, and population growth, it seems to me, comes through their creation or destruction of groups contending for power and through their shaping of the available means of coercion. In the short run, the growth of large cities and rapid migration from rural to urban areas in Western Europe probably acted as a damper on violent protest, rather than a spur to it. That is so for two reasons:

(1) The process withdrew discontented men from communities in which they already had the means for collective action and placed them in communities where they had neither the collective identity nor the means necessary to strike together.

(2) It took considerable time and effort both for the individual migrant to assimilate to the large city, and thus to join the political strivings of his fellows, and for new forms of organization for collective action to grow up in the cities.

If so, the European experience resembles the American experience. In the United States, despite enduring myths to the contrary, poor, uprooted newcomers to big cities generally take a long time to get involved in anything—crime, delinquency, politics, associations, protest, rioting—requiring contacts and experiences outside a small world of friends and relatives. These things are at least as true of European cities.

In the long run, however, urbanization deeply shaped the conditions under which new groups fought for political membership, and urbanization's secondary effects in the countryside stirred a variety of protests. The move to the city helped transform the character of collective violence in at least three ways:

(1) It grouped men in larger homogenous blocs (especially via the factory and the working-class neighborhood) than ever before.

(2) It facilitated the formation of special-interest associations (notably the union and the party) incorporating many people and capable of informing, mobilizing, and deploying them relatively fast and efficiently.

(3) It massed the people posing the greatest threat to the authorities near the urban seats of power, and thus encouraged the authorities to adopt new strategies and tactics for controlling dissidence.

For the people who remained in the country, the rise of the cities meant increasingly insistent demands for crops and taxes to support the urban establishment, increasingly visible impact on individual farmers of tariff and pricing policies set in the cities, and increasingly efficient means of exacting obedience from the countryman. All of these, in their time, incited violent protests throughout Europe.

Of course, definitive evidence on such large and tangled questions is terribly hard to come by. Until very recent times few historians have taken the study of collective violence as such very seriously. As Antonio Gramsci, the Italian socialist philosopher-historian, put it:

> This is the custom of our time: instead of studying the origins of a collective event, and the reasons for its spread . . . they isolate the protagonist and limit themselves to doing a biography of pathology, too often concerning themselves with unascertained motives, or interpreting them in the wrong way; for a social elite the features of subordinate groups always display something barbaric and pathological.

Since World War II, however, a considerable number of French and English historians, and a much smaller number of Americans, have begun to study and write history "from below"—actually trying to trace the experiences and actions of large numbers of ordinary men from their own point of view. This approach has had a special impact on the study of protests and rebellions. As a result, we are beginning to get a richer, rearranged picture of the political life of plain people in France and England (and, to a lesser extent, other European countries) over the last few centuries.

The new variety of evidence makes it possible to identify some major shifts in the predominant forms of collective violence in those countries over the modern period. Without too much difficulty we can place the forms of collective violence which have prevailed during that long period in three broad categories: primitive, reactionary, and modern. The primitive varieties once predominated, until centralized states began dragging Europeans into political life on a larger than local scale. As Thorstein Veblen put it in his sardonic *Imperial Germany and the Industrial Revolution,*

> . . . so soon as the king's dominions increased to such a size as to take him personally out of range of an effectual surveillance by neighborly sentiment . . . the crown would be able to use the loyalty of one neighborhood in enforcing exactions from another, and the royal power would then presently find no other obstacle to its continued growth than the limit placed upon it by the state of the industrial arts.

In the process, the king's retinue produced the apparatus of the state, which then acquired momentum of its own. That transformation accelerated through much of Western Europe after 1600. Since then, the primitive forms of collective violence have dwindled very slowly, but very steadily. Now they occur only rarely, only at the margins of organized politics.

The reactionary forms, by contrast, burgeoned as the national state began to grow. That was far from coincidence; they most often developed as part of the resistance of various communal groups to incorporation into the national state and the national economy. But the state won the contest; in most countries of Western Europe the reactionary forms of collective violence peaked and then faded away in their turn during the nineteenth century. They gave way to modern forms of collective violence, characterized by larger scale, more complex organization, and bids for changes in the operation or control of the state apparatus, rather than resistance to its demands. Although during very recent years we have seen what might be signs of another large shift in the form and locus of collective violence, for in the last century the modern forms have pushed all others aside. . . .

The twentieth-century figures from France include almost no primitive violence. By the beginning of the century the primitive forms had been fading slowly through most of Western Europe for three centuries or more. In some countries, however, the transition from predominantly reactionary to predominantly modern forms of collective violence occurred with striking rapidity. In England, the reactionary forms were already well on their way to oblivion by the time of the last agrarian rising, in 1830, although they had prevailed thirty years before. In Germany, demonstrations and strikes seem to have established themselves as the usual settings for collective violence during the two decades after the Revolution of 1848.

The situation was a bit more complicated in Italy, because of the deep division between north and south. The transition to modern forms of collective violence appears to have been close to completion in the north at unification. By the time of Milan's infamous *fatti di Maggio* of 1898, in which at least two policemen and eighty demonstrators died, the newer organizational forms unquestionably dominated the scene. In the south, mixed forms of the food riot and tax rebellion still occurred at the end of the century. Within ten years, however, even in rural areas the agricultural strike and the organized partisan meeting or demonstration had become the most regular sources of violence on the larger scale.

Spain, as usual, is the significant exception: while the country as a whole displays the long-run drift from primitive to reactionary to modern forms of collective violence, it also displays a marvelous array of regressions, mixtures, and hesitations. Surely, the country's erratic industrialization, uncertain, fluctuating unification, and exceptional military involvement in politics lie behind its differentiation from the rest of Western Europe in this respect. Spain, as Gerald Brenan says,

> . . . is the land of the *patria chica*. Every village, every town is the center of an intense social and political life. As in classical times, a man's allegiance is first of all to his native place, or to his family or social group in it, and only secondly to his country and government. In what one may call its normal condition Spain is a collection of small, mutually hostile, or indifferent republics held together in a loose federation. . . . Instead of a slow building-up of forces such as one sees in other European nations, there has been an alternation between the petty quarrels of tribal life and great upsurges of energy that come, economically speaking, from nowhere.

Thus Spain becomes the exception that tests the rule. For the rule says the shift from predominantly reactionary to predominantly modern forms of collective violence accompanies the more-or-less durable victory of the national state and the national economy over the particularisms of the past. In Spain, that victory was not durable, and the forms of violence wavered.

The precise timing and extent of the shift from reactionary to modern forms of collective violence in these countries remains to be established. For France, it is fairly clear that the shift was barely started by 1840, but close to complete by 1860. Furthermore, France experienced great, and nearly simultaneous, outbreaks of both forms of collective violence in the years from 1846 through 1851. The well-known events we customarily lump together as the Revolution of 1848 and the less-known but enormous insurrection of 1851 stand out both for their magnitude and for their mixture of reactionary and modern disturbances, but they came in the company of such notable outbreaks as the widespread food riots of 1846–47, the Forty-Five Centime Revolt of 1848–49, and the unsuccessful coup of 1849.

If this account of the transition from reactionary to modern collective violence in Western Europe is correct, it has some intriguing features. First, the timing of the transition corresponds roughly to the timing of industrialization and urbanization—England early, Italy late, and so on. Furthermore, the most rapid phase of the transition seems to occur together with a great acceleration of industrial and urban growth, early in the process: England at the beginning of the century, France of the 1850s, Germany of the 1850s and 1870s, Italy of the 1890s.

Second, there is some connection between the timing of the transition and the overall level of collective violence in a country. Over the last one hundred fifty years, if we think in terms of the frequency and scale of disturbances rather than the turnover of regimes, we can probably place Spain ahead of France, France ahead of Italy, Italy ahead of Germany, and Germany ahead of England. France is in the wrong position, and the contrast much less than the differences in the countries' reputations for stability or instability, but there is some tendency for the latecomers (or noncomers) to experience greater violence. If we took into account challenges to national integration posed by such peoples as the Catalans, and differences in the apparatus of repression, the connection would very likely appear even closer.

The information we have on hand, then, suggests that the processes of urbanization and industrialization themselves transform the character of collective violence. But how? We have a conventional notion concerning the life cycle of protest during the course of industrialization and urbanization: an early stage consisting of chaotic responses to the displacements and disruptions caused by the initial development of urban industry, a middle stage consisting of the growth of a militant and often violent working class, a late stage consisting of the peaceful integration of that working class into economic and political life. This scheme has many faults, as we have seen. Certainly we must correct and expand it to take account both of other groups than industrial workers and of the connections between industrialization and urbanization concerning the character of collective violence we have already reviewed raises grave doubts whether the underlying process producing and transforming protest was one of disintegration followed by reintegration, and whether the earlier forms of protest were so chaotic as the scheme implies.

The experience of France challenges the plausible presumption that rapid urbanization produces disruptions of social life that in turn generate protest. There is, if anything, a negative correlation over time and space between the pace of urban growth and the intensity of collective violence. The extreme example is the contrast between the 1840s, with slow urban growth plus enormous violence, and the decade after 1851, with very fast growth and extensive peace. Cities like St. Etienne of Roubaix that received and formed large numbers of new industrial workers tended to remain quiet while centers of the old traditional crafts, like Lyon and Rouen, raged with rebellion. When we can identify the participants in political disturbances, they tend to grossly underrepresent newcomers to the city and draw especially from the "little people" most firmly integrated into the local political life of the city's working-class neighborhoods. The geography of the disturbances itself suggests as much. It was not the urban neighborhoods of extreme deprivation, crime, or vice, George Rudé reports, "not the newly settled towns or quarters that proved the most fertile breeding-ground for social and political protest, but the old areas of settlement with established customs, such as Westminster, the City of London, Old Paris, Rouen, or Lyon." The information available points to a slow, collective process of organization and political education—what we may loosely call a development of class consciousness—within the city rather than a process of disruption leading directly to personal malaise and protest.

As a consequence of this process, the great new cities eventually became the principal settings of collective violence in France. Furthermore, collective violence moved to the city faster than the population did. Even at the beginning of the nineteenth century, the towns and cities of France produced a disproportionate share of the nation's collective violence. Yet tax rebellions, food riots, and movements against conscription did occur with fair regularity in France's small towns and villages. After these forms of disturbance disappeared, the countryside remained virtually silent for decades. When rural collective violence renewed, it was in the highly organized form of farmers' strikes and marches on Government buildings. This sequence of events was, to some extent, a result of urbanization.

Early in the nineteenth century, the expansion of cities incited frequent rural protests—obviously in the case of the food riot, more subtly in the case of other forms of collective violence. We have some reason to believe that groups of people who were still solidly established within rural communities, but were losing their livelihoods through the concentration of property and the urbanization of industry, regularly spearheaded such protests. The most important group was probably the workers in cottage industry. Their numbers declined catastrophically as various industries —especially textiles—moved to the city during the first half of the century. Large numbers of them hung on in the countryside, doing what weaving, spinning, or forging they could, seeking out livings as handymen, day laborers, and farmhands, and railing against their fate. Within their communities they were able to act collectively against power looms, farm machines, tax collectors, and presumed profiteers.

Slowly before midcentury, rapidly thereafter, the increasing desperation of the French countryside and the expanding opportunities for work in the new industrial cities drew such men away from their rural communities into town. That move cut them off from the personal, day-to-day contacts that had given them the incentive and the means for collective action against their enemies. It rearranged their immediate interests, placed them in vast, unfamiliar communities, and gave them relatively weak and unreliable relations with those who shared common interests with them.

The initial fragmentation of the work force into small groups of diverse origins, the slow development of mutual awareness and confidence, the lack of organizational experience among the new workers, and the obstacles thrown up by employers and governments all combined to make the development of the means and the will for collective action a faltering, time-consuming process. Collective violence did not begin in earnest until the new industrial workers began forming or joining associations—trade unions, mutual-aid societies, political clubs, conspiratorial groups—devoted to the collective pursuit of their interests. In this sense, the short-run effect of the urbanization of the French labor force was actually to damp collective violence. Its long-run effect, however, was to promote new forms of collective action that frequently led to violent conflicts, and thus to change the form of collective violence itself.

This happened in part through the grouping together of large numbers of men sharing a common fate in factories, urban working-class neighborhoods, and construction gangs. Something like the class-conscious proletariat of which Marx wrote began to form in the industrial cities. This new scale of congregation combined with new, pressing grievances, improving communication, the diffusion of new organizational models from Government and industry, and grudging concessions by the authorities to the right of association. The combination facilitated the formation of special-interest associations. At first workers experimented with cramped, antique, exclusive associations resembling (or even continuing) the old guilds; gradually they formed mutual-aid societies, labor exchanges, unions, and national and international federations.

The new associations further extended the scale and flexibility of communication among workers; they made it possible to inform, mobilize, and deploy large numbers of men fast and efficiently in strikes, demonstrations, and other common action. These potentially rebellious populations and their demanding associations proliferated in the big cities, in the shadows of regional and national capitals. They therefore posed a greater (or at least more visible) threat to the authorities than had their smalltown predecessors. The authorities responded to the threat by organizing police forces, crowd-control tactics, and commissions of inquiry. The associations, in their turn, achieved greater sophistication and control in their show of strength. The process took time—perhaps a generation for any particular group of workers. In that longer run the urbanization of the labor force produced a whole new style of collective violence.

The experience of the industrial workers has one more important lesson for us. In both reactionary and modern forms of collective violence, men commonly express their feeling that they have been unjustly denied their rights. Reactionary disturbances, however, center on rights once enjoyed but now threatened, while modern disturbances center on rights not yet enjoyed but now within reach. The reactionary forms are especially the work of groups of men who are losing their collective positions within the system of power, while the modern forms attract groups of men who are striving to acquire or enhance such positions. The reactionary forms, finally, challenge the basic claims of a national state and a national economy, while the modern forms rest on the assumption that the state and the economy have a durable existence—if not necessarily under present management. In modern disturbances, men contend over the control and organization of the State and the economy.

What links these features together historically? The coordinate construction of the nation-state and the national economy simultaneously weakened local systems of power, with the rights and positions which depended on them, and established new, much larger arenas in which to contend for power. In Western European countries, as locally based groups of men definitively lost their struggle against the claims of the central power, reactionary disturbances dwindled and modern disturbances swelled. The rapid transition from one to the other occurred where and when the central power was able to improve rapidly or expand its enforcement of its claims. Accelerating urbanization and industrialization facilitated such an expansion by providing superior means of communication and control to the agents of the central power, by drawing men more fully into national markets, and by spreading awareness of, and involvement in, national politics. In the process, special-purpose associations like parties and labor unions grew more and more important as the vehicles in the struggle for power, whether violent or nonviolent. Thus urbanization and industrialization affected the character and the incidence of collective violence profoundly, but indirectly.

BRAVE NEW EUROPE: 1914 TO THE PRESENT

part **III**

7. MECHANIZATION AND COLLECTIVIZATION

The sturdiest of Europeans has been the peasant. He has endured through it all. Yet the daily round of his existence has obviously changed since the days of slavery and serfdom; today he is more likely to be found sitting on a tractor than bending in the field. Change and progress, certainly. From the standpoint of efficiency there has undoubtedly been a remarkable advance in rural labor since the eighteenth century. But what of the quality of country life? Intangibles cannot be measured in average yield per acre, nor in the number of motorcycles owned by peasants. It is unnecessary to romanticize times past in order to grasp that the peasant has entered the modern era with some reluctance and a certain nostalgia.

John Ardagh illustrates the transformation of rural life in Western Europe since the beginning of this century. His focus is France, now the major agricultural area of the Common Market and, as such, one of the main breadbaskets of the West. There one still finds many small independent farms and the persistence of tenant farming. But the French government has made strenuous efforts to encourage the rationalization of production and to promote the regrouping and consolidation of scattered landholdings. A striking innovation has been group-farming, rendered necessary because of expensive mechanization. Such measures, because of bureaucratic sluggishness or peasant resistance to a loss of personal autonomy, have not always succeeded. The urge to own and to work one's separate plot of land is still very strong among those who are ostensibly to be helped by modernization. Many have preferred to abandon their place in the countryside altogether. While this rural exodus is not necessarily disadvantageous from the standpoint of productivity, it has created new social problems for the peasants who remain.

Hugh Seton-Watson examines Eastern Europe, an area which responded more slowly than did the West to the possibilities for technological and social change. He tries to separate the tourist office image of peasant life from the real one. He traces the development of the nations of east central Europe between the two world wars, showing how they remained economically depressed, having neither the strong industrial base of the West nor the authoritarian impetus for reorganization characteristic of the Soviet Union. As we know now, this time of relative stagnation proved to be only the prelude to a period of drastic change which occurred after 1945 when, under Soviet aegis, the entire area submitted to a policy of collectivization.

Merle Fainsod's classic account of the sovietization of Russia treats the difficulties which the Stalinist and post-Stalinist regimes inherited from tsardom. The establishment of thorough political control has not yet guaranteed adequate agricultural production, nor has it overcome the reluctance of Russian peasants to be absorbed into the regimentation of collective farming. Fainsod argues that agricultural interests have, to a great extent, been sacrificed to those of industrialization, and that the Soviet government has displayed toward the peasantry an attitude of dependence and hostility. He traces first the successive stages of official policy and peasant reaction before the Second World War, the impact of Nazi occupation and postwar upset, and finally the enforced merger of collective farms under Khrushchev in the 1950s. An unfavorable result has been a marked tension between different generations and various strata of the rural population. Still, an enduring basis for Russia's agricultural development has apparently been laid and, so far as one can see, the lot of the peasants has been irretrievably determined.

The peasant population of Europe is today embattled. As industrialization has proceeded, the peasantry's numerical and political importance has visibly declined. Yet the farm is an essential economic and social factor which must remain, since the urban population is forever dependent on rural labor to provide its food. It is evident that the decline of the agricultural sector would strike down the entire economy of Europe. The implications are already apparent: the increasing subsidization of agriculture by industry and the unrelenting application of technology to farm production. A civilization which has treated the rural worker so shabbily for so many centuries now finds that he is an indispensable member of modern society.

JOHN ARDAGH

The Slow Death of the Peasant

The campaign for agriculture is being fought on two separate fronts: to modernize the farms, and to modernize the marketing system. It is no use doing the one without the other. That is why progress in one sector is often frustrated by the problems of the other. It is no good increasing productivity if the markets cannot cope with it and prices collapse; it is no good providing modern markets if the farms are too inefficient to supply them adequately.

So far, it is down on the farms themselves, rather than in the markets, that progress has been the more effective. Everywhere the old order is steadily being swept aside by new men and ideas. And some of the outward contrasts in this age of transition are striking enough to the casual visitor. In a Brittany farm kitchen a huge TV set stands by the ancient open fireplace, but there is no running water; near Avignon, one son in a farmer's family hoes potatoes while his brother goes to work at the near-by plutonium factory; in the chalky uplands of the Aveyron, an old man vacantly minds the cows while his son brings home fertilizer in a smart new Simca. Techniques and home comforts are slowly improving, from a very low level; and for good or ill the peasant's life is becoming "urbanized," as it already is more or less completely in Britain. But the deeper changes, and the obstacles to change, are psychological. What is at stake is the peasant's rooted individualism, and his emotional attachment to his own piece of land.

Believing this to be the greatest barrier to progress, the new farm leaders have made land ownership reform the center of their policy. They want the land to be a common tool or resource, not a property. This, in France, is a highly complex problem. Until the end of the last war the feudal tradition of land property was strong. Some small farmers clung proudly to their own ancestral acres, but many others worked on a system of *métayage*, paying their landlords a tithe, usually half their produce. Often the landlord was the all-powerful local *châtelain*, and his *métayers*

From pp. 75–84 ("The campaign . . . of nature."), from *The New French Revolution* by John Ardagh. Copyright © 1968, 1969 by John Ardagh. By permission of Harper & Row, Publishers, Inc. and Martin Secker & Warburg Ltd., London.

were little more than serfs. If one of them gave offense, maybe by not going to Mass enough or hinting Left-wing views, he risked eviction. One of the keenest of the new ex-Jacist leaders, Bernard Lambert, who has a small farm in a very feudal area near Nantes, spoke to me with bitterness of the prewar days: "My father was *métayer,* and would always lift his cap to the *châtelain* and call him *Monsieur notre maître.* Once when my father won a radio in a raffle, the landlord confiscated it because we were in debt. No wonder there are so many Communists among farmers!"

A Socialist law in 1946 replaced the *métayage* system with a tenancy statute (*statut de fermage*) which gave much greater security from eviction and put a normal annual rent in place of the tithe. This is in force today: *métayage* has almost disappeared except in parts of the southwest. But the *statut de fermage* has created new problems. In some areas it is not applied fairly, because the tribunals are on the side of the landlords and the tenant gets victimized. In many other cases it works to the tenant's disadvantage in a quite different way. Because rents are fixed very low (they vary according to produce but average, say, forty to sixty francs per acre a year), the landlord has little incentive to keep the farms in repair or make improvements. Many farm houses are half in ruins, which harms efficiency and helps to drive the young into the towns. Lambert told me: "I've spent 110,000 francs on new cowsheds and other improvements here, which I vitally needed but my landlord wouldn't pay for. Yet, if he chucks me out, they belong to him." Others are luckier. In the Aveyron, I met a young man who had rented his farm from a friend, but had first made it a condition that the friend should provide new buildings.

Despite the drawbacks of the statute, most young farmers prefer to be tenants, not owners: land prices have been rising fast, and they would rather sink their limited capital into livestock and modern machinery. Probably more than half of all French farm land is rented. But many of the older farmers cling tenaciously to the idea of property. And despite the low rents, land is still considered a good investment by many nonfarmers too, city speculators and others, who will snap up any good estate that comes on the market. For a variety of reasons an ambitious young farmer usually finds it extremely hard to acquire new land, whether for rent or sale, if he wants to enlarge his farm to an economic size.

So the central innovation of the Pisani Law, directly prompted by the Young Farmers, was to set up *Sociétés d'Aménagement Foncier et d'Etablissement Rural* (SAFERs): regional agencies with powers to buy up land as it comes on the market, make improvements on it, and then resell it to the most deserving, who are usually young farmers wanting to make good use of modern techniques. The SAFERs also have some rights of preemption, at fixed prices, thus acting as a curb on speculation. If a farmer wants to sell a plot of land, say, for 10,000 francs to a speculator, the local SAFER can step in, offer maybe 8,000 francs, and have the matter settled by an independent court.

This was hailed as the biggest blow ever struck in France against the sacred rights of property. In practice it has worked slowly so far. The SAFERs' funds are small, probably less than a seventh of what is needed.(Pisani wanted more, but the Ministry of Finance said no—a typical example of a bold Gaullist structural reform spoiled by official cheeseparing. The SAFERs have also been impeded by the usual French legal delays, sometimes of up to five years for each transaction. And their powers of preemption are so hedged with limitations (due to concessions negotiated by the old guard of the FNSEA) that much of the most-needed land eludes their grasp. But the principle is clearly a good one, and it will probably work well in time, as the SAFERs funds increase. Success varies by region: it is poor in Brittany, but better in the Massif Central, where I was shown several useful SAFER operations.

Another grave land problem is the parcellization of the soil, and French Governments have been trying to solve this since 1940. Fly over many parts of France, and you will see a crazy quilt of thin strips; quite a modest farmer may often have ten or twenty different little fields, not next to each other but scattered over miles. This is partly a result of the equal inheritance laws, as farms were split up between sons and then the parcels changed hands. And it often makes modern mechanized farming extremely difficult.

The policy of *remembrement*—literally, the piecing together of limbs— was initiated by Vichy and has continued ever since. By subsidizing up to 80 percent of the legal, surveying, and field costs, the Government tries to entice farmers to make rational swaps of their fields. The results have been variable: far better among the big, go-ahead farms of the north than in the sluggish south. After a long resistance to *remembrement,* farmers in some areas are now coming to accept it more easily; in fact, in some places, the policy is now held up by shortage of official funds rather than by lack of local cooperation. Even so, in the small-farm districts the process of educating the peasants to make this kind of change can still be a long and arduous one. Nowhere else does the conservatism of the older peasants show itself more keenly, or their emotional attachment to the soil show a worse side. A farmer may eventually accept the idea in theory; but when the work actually starts, he will be struck with sentimental horror, and refuse to give up the field where his father taught him to plough, or the apple tree his grandmother planted—even if he is offered as good in return, and his costs are covered!

In the Aveyron, a poorish, upland department of small livestock and potato farms, *remembrement* was the main issue in the 1965 local elections. Several village councils that had earlier decided to go ahead with it were thrown out by the older voters. The commune of Privezac provided a *cause célèbre*. In 1963, it had voted 90 percent for *remembrement*. So surveyors arrived and drew up a plan. Then there were protests. The village split into two clans, but *across* the traditional rural lines of Reds against Whites, teachers against priests. In the pro-*remembrement* camp, the young Catholic Jacists were led by the Socialist mayor, an ex-teacher. Against them were the older farmers led by the deputy mayor, a Catholic ex-officer. When Government officials came to inspect the crisis, the police had to protect them. And when bulldozers arrived to tear down hedges and start the regrouping, the old guard charged them on tractors and tore up the surveyors' markers. Several people were arrested, and the *remembrement* finally went ahead. Later the old guard got their revenge and toppled the mayor in the 1965 elections. Even so, the *remembrement* was not undone. Some million francs had been invested in it; and, as in other such cases, the Government swiftly applied some effective blackmail, threatening to cut off all sorts of State aid from Privezac if there was any backsliding!

One young, local farmer told me: "I'm sure that in three years everyone in Privezac will be delighted with the results—it will be a test case round here, a show piece. It's simply a question of breaking down old habits. Often, too, the conflicts are the fault of the officials, who reshuffle the land without tact. The job needs psychologists, as much as surveyors." And not all the young guard are so in favor of the policy. "Is it worth raising fire and blood in a commune just for this?" said one. "Better, surely, to get rid of the surplus farmers first, and then regroup. After all, *remembrement* doesn't in itself make farms any bigger."

Yet, in many areas, it has been helping to make farms more efficient and to create a more flexible rural society, less obsessively attached to its *petits coins*. And the farms *are* getting bigger, too, which is more important. In one typical Aveyron commune, their number has halved since 1911, as people sell out to their neighbors, or drift away. But the Young Farmers reckon that only one farm in twenty is large enough to be viable today. It is partly a question of waiting for the old generation to die: half of all French farmers are over fifty-five. They block not only land redistribution, but also the kind of interfarm sharing of work and equipment that alone, as the young realize, can enable the small farm to survive. The conflict of generations within families is often bitter, and in many cases is made worse when cohabitation with in-laws is enforced by sheer lack of housing, or by the pressures of tradition. Realizing this, the Pisani Law set up a fund to help old farmers retire. But its scope is modest. The pension it allows is rarely more than £150 a year, and often there is nowhere to retire to.

In the Aveyron, a hardy region that furnished the JAC with many of its best leaders, several of the most dynamic ones now seem to have persuaded their fathers to retire. Down a muddy track near the department's main town of Rodez, I went to call on a former president of the JAC, Raymond Lacombe: the man who had once kept his beret on at meetings so as to be forced to make speeches! He is a tough little man of thirty-six with coarse peasant features but a mind sharp as flint; his wife is better spoken than he and comes from the Ardennes, finds the Massif Central a bit lonely; three kids are playing on the floor; the modern farm kitchen is spotless but there are no luxuries. Lacombe said: "I was my father's tenant till last year; now he's retired and just looks after the animals a bit. We built this house for ourselves, so we don't have to share. We're luckier than most. I've got forty acres, with cows, pigs, corn, and barley. I've raised money to buy a tractor and I share other equipment with friends; father wouldn't have done that. Recently I've bought a piggery and our net income's doubled. But costs rise so fast that forty acres isn't viable the way it used to be. If I could, I might get out, though I love this place. On twelve farms round here, there are only four young people left."

It is the same story nearly everywhere in France. In Lacombe's commune the population has dropped since 1911 from 717 to 426; it could safely lose another 200 without economic stress if the farms were fully modernized. In many places the exodus is even more striking: in the center of Brittany I met a couple *all ten* of whose children had left. Less than 18 percent of the French now work on the land, against 35 percent before the war.

It is usually the girls who leave first. More than the actual discomfort, they hate the isolation, the drudgery and sense of inferiority, and they rarely want to marry a farmer, even a prosperous one. Then the boys go too, in search of wives and a decent living, or because they are deprived of all responsibility on the farm so long as father is in charge. In one recent national survey of fifteen-to-twenty-nine-year-olds still on the land, half the boys and three-quarters of the girls intended to leave. In the old days they stayed out of duty or tradition; today, if they stay it is by choice. Some men remain on alone through apathy, habit, or a kind of vocation: in many isolated country districts the proportion of bachelor farmers is frighteningly high, and their life must be lonely and narrow beyond belief.

The nearest industrial town is the usual venue for the émigrés; or, in many cases, Paris. There are more Aveyronnais in Paris than in the Aveyron. Until recently parents often tried to stop their children from going, and regarded the towns as wicked and corrupting. But this has changed. Too many children have come home on visits obviously uncorrupted and happier. And TV and other modern changes have broken down much of the old suspicion between farm and town. One Breton farmer with three sons told me: "It would be nice if one of them felt he'd like to stay, but I certainly shan't stop them going. It's really up to me, isn't it, to make my farm attractive and viable for them to want to take it over."

At the same time, the older political demagogues have dropped their Mélinian hatred of the exodus as some sinister trick of enforced deportation, and have come to see its necessity. If all farms were large and modern enough, the farming population could well drop to 10 percent or less (in Britain it is 4 percent; in the U.S., 8) without any fall in output, and this is precisely what the Plan is working towards. It is a question of controlling the exodus. In very few areas has it yet reached its reasonable limits; in the Aveyron many farms are without successors, but when they fall vacant they always find ready buyers among other farmers.

The real problem is to ensure that it is not simply the dullards who stay behind, and that enough young people of caliber remain as active farmers to carry through the modernizing process efficiently. Debatisse and his friends see clearly that it is therefore essential to make rural life more attractive and varied, with more comfort, culture, education, and social stimulus.

At this point in time the French rural world, as in many Western countries, is in a bleak period of mutation between two cultures—the old folk culture, passing away, and a new modern one not yet properly installed. In the old days there was great poverty, but also a certain warmth and tradition that helped make it bearable. Many of the older people today speak of those times with feeling. In Breton moorland farmsteads young people drew round the fire on winter evenings to hear wise old women reciting Celtic legends. Auvergne had a whole world of traditional dances and music. In the Aveyron, and many other parts, there were *veillées,* where neighbors would gather in one farm to weave baskets or shred maize, and make it the excuse for a good party. And then, the harvests! In Auvergne, a farmer told me: "When I was a boy, at harvest-time, the seasonal laborers would come up by hundreds from Clermont-Ferrand and every night in the village hall there'd be gay parties and dances. Today the work's done by two men with a combine-harvester, and the laborers work in the new Clermont factories and go to the movies."

Today, folk culture rarely means more than putting on costumes for an annual fête to please the tourists. Even the JAC's music and drama activities of the post-1944 period have declined: the young have left the farms, or prefer to go off to the towns on their motor-scooters in the evenings. And the modern world is taking the place of the old culture, as the TV aerials sprout above the cow-byres. Some farms, where electricity is just arriving, have moved in one step from oil-lamps to the electronic age, as a TV set may be the first gadget they buy. Certainly, modern comforts and amenities are spreading: it is quite usual to see a huge new electric cooker in the kitchen of a shabby and crumbling farmhouse. Over 40 percent of farmers have cars; often they are those charmingly ugly two-horse Citroëns that bounce so readily down any rutty track. And even health insurance and welfare allowances now embrace peasants almost as completely as industrial workers.

But the lag behind living standards in the cities, or on farms in a country like Britain, is still great. Few small farmers yet feel they can go away for an annual holiday (maybe there is no-one else to milk the cows) and many older farmhouses are in a terrible state of repair. In isolated areas there is often a serious lack of public services, too. Though the percentage of farms with running water has doubled since Debatisse's childhood, Lacombe told me: "We're not on the mains and our well is too small. When it froze last winter, I had to fetch water with my tractor every day from a spring four hundred yards away. It was tough. Many farmers round here can't build modern piggeries simply because they've got no water. Most of them do have electricity now, but it's hard to get a telephone laid on if you want one."

The cultural hiatus, too, means that while the peasants have lost the old art of enriching their own lives, they often seem to be waiting for others to bring them new commercial entertainment. One Aveyron farmer's wife told me: "Before the war, the families here would group together in the evenings for *entr'aide* work-parties. Now there's just a cinema in the near-by town, and far less real social life." When someone does open a local dance-hall (as a shopkeeper has done in Lacombe's village) it is usually a great success, but such initiatives are rare. Eager people like Lacombe do what they can: he has even drawn up a project for a new social center in his nearest large village, with library, lecture-rooms, etc., and he has had it scheduled in the regional section of the Fifth Plan. But there are not so many Lacombes, and they have other duties, too. What the countryside badly needs, and lacks, are professional *"animateurs culturels."* Early efforts after the war to build *foyers ruraux* (village social and cultural centers) were not very successful. The present Government has a plan to revive the idea, on a large scale; but there is the usual shortage of funds.

It is in education that the farmer feels his isolation and inferiority most keenly. In theory, every village child has exactly the same State education as the most privileged Parisian. In practice, it is not quite like that. In thinly populated areas, many children still have to walk six or eight miles each day, and it is hardly surprising that many of them even fail to finish their primary schooling. A Government system of *ramassage scolaire* has started recently in some places, with buses collecting children for school from lonely farms; but it lacks funds. Moreover, isolated schools often have only one single class spanning the whole age-range, and this holds back the brightest. And the teachers tend to be the dregs of their profession. Not until rural education improves will many of the brighter young couples feel like staying to bring up a family on the farm.

In higher and technical education, however, there have been great strides forward. Hundreds of full or part-time agricultural colleges and evening institutes have been opened in recent years, and France's lag behind Germany or Holland in this field is not as great as it was. The pressure on the Government for these has come, once again, from the Young Farmers, who will often also form their own technical study groups and hire specialists to come and teach them. Some of the pioneering work is rather touching: a Young Farmer's wife in the Aveyron told me of her patient efforts to get a group of ill-educated wives in her commune to study modern techniques of farm management and accounting, tasks that are traditionally left to the women on small farms.

In putting an accent on technical expertise, and the sharing of effort and equipment, the younger generation realize that it may be the only way to save the family farm. Mechanization has spread rapidly since the war, with tractor numbers rising today to over a million. It is true that often the tractors have been badly used, especially by older farmers, who tend to buy them proudly as a status symbol without having large enough fields or the right know-how. A man accustomed all his life to an instinctive *rapport* with oxen or horses will often be unable to run a machine. It breaks down, or incurs heavy running costs, and the farmer grows bitter that his panacea has failed him. This was certainly one factor behind the old guard's riots and protests in the 1950s.

The younger ones have generally gone about things more intelligently. In Normandy, a Young Farmers' leader with a 300-acre cattle and wheat farm, told me: "We formed a group of twenty-two farmers, and bought a silage machine, harvesting equipment, and several tractors in common. We share all costs. It's quite an accepted way of working now, but nearly all of us are young. You'll rarely get the old doing this." Debatisse himself has formed a successful association with two other farmers at Palladuc.

This kind of group farming is entirely new in France, and cuts across deeply ingrained habits of individualism. More than one thousand such groups have been formed privately, and in 1964 they were endorsed by a Government decree granting financial aid to encourage others. Besides helping with costly mechanization, the groups bring other advantages too. Salaried laborers are scarce today, most of them preferring to work in factories; so the groups can provide a pooling of labor for many jobs, and especially the chance of a rota system for milking and minding livestock. This gives the farmer the possibility of taking a weekend off, or even a holiday. The groups also facilitate specialization of produce, increasingly necessary in the new context of the Common Market. Above all, they enable farm units to grow larger and more viable without destroying their family-farm basis or the individual's responsibility.

Some groups have failed and split up, in the Aveyron and elsewhere, either because the older members failed to cooperate; or because the principle of shared decisions was too much for the peasant spirit; or, quite often, because the women kicked against the need for joint accounting. But in one part of this district, a group experiment is taking place that could be of some significance for the poorer regions of France. At Espalion, in the lovely valley of the Lot, a middle-aged farmer called Belières has grouped some twenty small farms into a *Banque du Travail*. This carries the sharing idea a stage farther: each man-hour is set a price, according to the type of work, and if a farmer spends a morning helping a neighbor, or lends equipment, he is credited accordingly in the labor bank. At the end of the season, gains and losses are paid off, like a game of poker. It is a way of getting a group to work together without anyone feeling cheated, and its success at Espalion has led to other banks springing up elsewhere in France. Now Belières has launched a more ambitious scheme: through the local SAFER, the bank itself has bought 320 acres on an empty plateau about thirty miles away, and it plans to grow crops there. Some of the younger farmers have been persuaded to move there, and have had houses built for them in the nearest large village, eight miles from the new estate. This is a first step towards an American-type solution of the isolation problem in a motor age: the farmer lives in town and commutes by car to his fields, like a city worker. Both this and the "bank" itself may seem simple enough notions to Anglo-Saxons or north Europeans; but they represent an unprecedented breach in the French autarchic tradition. Some Aveyron farmers are skeptical: "Will it work? People may not be ready for this kind of thing yet. Farmers are used to living close to their fields and their animals; until recently, they tended to sleep *in* the cowsheds with them."

Although there are bound to be difficulties of this sort, it is certain that group farming will increase. It also seems fairly certain that, within a decade or two, the Young Farmers and the Government will have largely succeeded in their aims of reforming farming structures. Whole areas will have been pulled up towards the level of the big rich farms of the north. The growth in the size of farms, *remembrement,* departure of surplus population, improvement in rural culture and comfort, technical modernization: all this is going ahead steadily, as one generation succeeds another. This battle is half won, and the new leaders are already turning to the next one: the reform of markets, the checking of over-production, the adapting of output to the entirely new and different needs of industrial buyers.

But the Jacist revolution has not touched, and will not touch, the whole of peasant France. There are wide areas where either the soil is too poor or the people too old and backward for much progress to be made. Such areas are the stark hinterland of Brittany, and the ruggedest parts of the Massif Central, much poorer than the Aveyron pasturelands I have described. Only a score of miles from Gourvennec's smiling coastal artichoke plains, you can find grim upland hamlets where no one is left, apart from a few old people. The Lozère (east of the Aveyron), most backward and depopulated of all French departments, is in the same predicament. Here people eke out a living from useless polyculture, that inevitable curse of so much poor-soil farming: a patch of vines for the family's own vinegary wine, a cow or two and some mangy chickens, cabbages struggling to grow on a chalky hillside. Meat is a once-a-week luxury; children, if there are any, are kept from school to help with the chores, and sleep in haylofts. The working day is sixteen hours, and a family's income may be less than £300 a year. Yet the farmer is afraid of getting loans for modern improvements, for this type of peasant fears debt above all else. In a poor part of Brittany I met an old farmer who, rather than spend money on mending the broken gates and gaps in his hedges, made his wife and children stand guard in turns all day, to stop the cattle from straying.

This particular attitude is still common, and this world can only be left to die: it is too late for it to evolve. As the more desolate areas depopulate, their future will lie with afforestation and tourism—such regions are often among the loveliest. In parts of the Massif Central, large-scale planting of new timber forests has begun, partly under the aegis of the State, and is providing employment for some local peasants. In Provence, and in the Cevennes, many hill-top villages are now virtually deserted save for the tourist trade. Here, and in other lonely regions, the Government is now creating national parks, with sports and holiday centers, and wild-life preserves. In this vast and beautiful land of France, as productivity steadily increases in the fertile zones, there will no longer be any need for peasants to scratch at the soil of ungrateful uplands. These can be left, as in the United States, to the splendors of nature.

HUGH SETON-WATSON

The Peasantry of Eastern Europe

THE PEASANT COUNTRIES

The countries of Eastern Europe are predominantly agricultural. The population of most of them is composed in majority of peasants. The proportions for the individual States of 1918 are: Roumania 78 percent, Bulgaria 80 percent; Yugoslavia 75 percent, Poland 63 percent, Hungary 55 percent, Czechoslovakia 34 percent.

OFFICIALDOM AND THE PEASANT

The peasant character of these States has always been stressed by their official spokesmen. They declare themselves proud to be "peasant nations." Official tourist propaganda is backed up by beautifully illustrated pamphlets showing beautiful peasant girls, dressed in beautiful national costumes. The foreign visitor to an Eastern European country is immediately impressed by the enthusiasm of the well-to-do lawyers and business men of the capital for the peasant masses. The peasants, he is told again and again, are the backbone of the nation. They alone embody the stern, sound traditions and virtues that have carried the nation through the difficult past to the glorious present. On them alone can the nation rely in its direst need. Loving care for their welfare is the one permanent principle of the government's policy. If the foreign visitor is fortunate enough to make the closer acquaintance of some well-to-do lawyer or business man, he will be invited to his house, and will be shown his host's daughters dressed up in peasant costumes. And very charming they will look too. After a few days' stay in the capital, the foreign visitor will find the Propaganda Ministry most eager to arrange for him to make a Sunday excursion to a not too distant village, where he will see the peasants come

Hugh Seton-Watson, *Eastern Europe Between the Wars 1918-1941* (Cambridge: Cambridge University Press, 1945), pp. 75-77, 80-84. Reprinted by permission.

out of church in their best clothes. He will be received in a well-selected peasant house with touching hospitality. He will drink several glasses of good local wine. He will admire the rugs and the pottery with which the peasant's house is adorned, and he will have the privilege of watching a number of colorful national dances. The experience is delightful, and is often enough to make the foreign visitor a friend of the country for life, and a staunch supporter, for some years at least, of the good government under which such happy scenes can take place.

Many delightful books have been published in recent years by self-constituted experts on individual Eastern European countries, and few have failed to stress the paternal relation of the various governments to the sound, loyal peasantry. The soundness and loyalty of the peasantry is due to its complete contentment with its condition. Some Eastern European countries have made Land Reforms. In these countries the peasants are contented, because the Reforms have finally satisfied their aspirations, and solved all their social problems. In other countries there have been no Reforms, and the land remains in the hands of big landowners. Here also the peasants are contented, because they devotedly love and admire the landowners, who are true fathers of the peasant family. They are glad to be relieved by them of the responsibilities of land ownership. In both reformed and unreformed countries, then, the peasants lead almost idyllic lives, tilling the soil they mystically love, dancing their ancient national dances, clad in their picturesque national costumes and singing the while their soulful national songs.

Such is the picture presented to the foreign visitor by Eastern European officialdom. But if the foreign visitor stays a little longer in the country, if he leaves the capital for the provinces, and drives and walks a little in the countryside, if he travels sometimes in third-class railway carriages and keeps his eyes open, he will find things that he did not expect. He will see mud hovels, adorned by no rugs or pottery, housing families of seven or eight. He will meet peasants returning from their work in tattered rags that do not recall to him the lovely clothes of his first village. He will notice how the young peasant laborers in the train look at the officials who examine their labor permits. Then perhaps on his return to the capital he will meet some town intellectual, who will express to him opinions very different from those of his hospitable lawyer or business man, and will tell him facts not published in the press or in the Propaganda Ministry pamphlets. Later, they may go together to a village, where he will be introduced to peasants who will put their own views before him. And gradually a picture will form in his mind. The picture will probably be incomplete and a little distorted, but it will be much nearer reality than the flights of imagination of the hard-worked writers employed by the Tourist Department of the Propaganda Ministry. . . .

THE PEASANTS IN THE REFORMED
STATES SINCE 1918

It had been hoped that the Land Reforms would solve the Peasant Problem, and that the masses, socially satisfied, would form a stable basis of the State. These hopes were not justified. The economic developments of the interwar period created new problems, and by 1939 the situation of a large part of the Eastern European peasantry was worse than it had been in 1914.

The new peasant owners lacked technical knowledge. As laborers on the big landowners' estates they had had neither opportunity nor inducement to learn modern methods of agriculture. Having become independent owners themselves, they did not know how to develop their land. Agricultural education was not easily available, and had no social prestige. A peasant's son of ambition who could afford a university education preferred to study law or medicine and then remain in the town. A number of agricultural experts were trained every year, but they were not enough, and although some of them did splendid work in the villages, others did not take their duties very seriously. The governments devoted little money or attention to agricultural education.

The peasants also lacked technical equipment. In the Balkans and Poland there are many places where the wooden plough is still used. Many households had no plough at all. More complicated machines—reapers, tractors etc.—were confined to the remaining big estates. The small holders could not afford them, and their use on these tiny properties would have been uneconomic. The medium holders could have used them if they had collaborated with their neighbors and tilled their lands in common, and if they had had credit facilities for making the expensive initial purchase. But the Governments frowned on communal cultivation, and failed to organize a cheap credit system for the peasants. If they wished to use machines, they had to borrow them from the local landowner, often at great cost. In general the new Governments paid little attention to the improvement of agriculture or the assistance of the peasant owners until the World Depression forced these tasks upon them. But during the ten years of comparative prosperity much of the damage was done, for the backward methods and bad management of these years weakened unnecessarily the position of the peasant owners, and made the subsequent burden of the depression more difficult to bear.

In Eastern Europe it is the custom that the holding is divided on the death of the owner between all his sons. Twenty years of this practice has caused a subdivision of the original holdings of the Land Reforms into a much greater number of tiny plots of land. If a holding consisted of land of different qualities, devoted to different kinds of production, then each son must have a piece of each type. It is arguable that even the original holdings were too small for rational cultivation, but there is no doubt at all of the hopelessly uneconomic nature of the dwarf properties into which they have since been divided. A holding of a few acres may consist of as many as forty small strips, separated from each other by several miles. Large areas of cultivated land were wasted in the form of paths enabling owners to walk from one strip to another. The strips are incapable of efficient production. Even the most casual visitor is impressed by the difference in quality of the crops he sees on a drive through a region such as the Wallachian plain, where small holdings and large estates exist side by side.

The situation of Eastern European agriculture was deeply affected by the competition of overseas cereals in the great European markets. Hungarian wheat, for instance, might compete with American in Vienna, but was undersold in Munich. It was cheaper to transport grain raised on the highly capitalized farms of America by sea from New York or Buenos Aires to Hamburg and Trieste than to bring the products of the less capitalized estates of Hungary, not to mention the uneconomic holdings of the Balkans, a few hundred miles. American competition more than balanced the grain represented by the disappearance of Russian wheat from the world market after the Revolution. It was felt more by the big and medium proprietors than by the small holders, but it influenced directly or indirectly the whole agricultural population of Eastern Europe.

The World Depression struck Eastern Europe in 1929, and its worst years were 1932–34. The price of wheat fell by about one-half in the home markets. Industry suffered too, but the various cartels were able to some extent to defend industrial prices. Thus occurred the "price scissors," the catastrophic disparity between industrial and agricultural prices.

The Roumanian Trade Cycle Research group calculated an index of prices of those industrial goods which are bought by peasants (tools, clothes, town-prepared foodstuffs, etc.) and compared these with the agricultural price index. The respective figures, expressed as a percentage of the 1929 level, are in 1932 47.7 for agricultural and 80.9 for this group of industrial prices; in 1934 44.1 and 82.6. After 1934, owing to government help and to expansion of trade with Germany, agricultural prices began to recover, but they failed to keep pace with industrial prices, which soared to heights unknown for more than a decade. The figures for January 1940 in Roumania are 80 and 159.4.

In Poland the same phenomenon occurred, but the disparity decreased appreciably during the economic recovery immediately preceding the war. The corresponding figures, expressed as a percentage of the 1928 level, are for 1932 48.9 and 81; for 1934 37 and 70.3; and for 1937 49.2 and 66.1.

Throughout Eastern Europe the purchasing power of the peasantry failed substantially to recover from the blow dealt it by this price disparity. The result is a general lowering of the standard of living, which the war has accentuated. In particular, being obliged to spend his reduced cash resources on necessities like clothes, salt, lamp-oil, the peasant cannot buy tools, still less machines. The hope of escaping from poverty by increasing his output through more efficient methods is thus removed.

The reduction of purchasing-power caused by the World Economic Depression has increased other burdens. During the earlier years of comparative prosperity the wealthier peasants had borrowed money, from banks or from individuals, in order to make purchases to improve their lands. The poorer peasants also borrowed money in order to buy food in the critical period of the year, the months before the harvest, when their supplies from the preceding harvest had run out. Borrowing for food was especially common in certain regions, such as Dalmatia, which do not produce cereals, and where the income from other occupations does not suffice for subsistence needs the whole year round. Loans were made at a high rate of interest, particularly those made by individual money-lenders. The rate was often over 20 percent and sometimes amounted to 45 percent. The fall of agricultural prices enormously increased the burden of these debts, since the peasant now received half as much for his products as earlier, while the sum of his debt remained the same. During the thirties agitation for the annulment of debts was widespread in the Balkan countries. In 1934 Roumania passed a Conversion Law, from which 64 percent of the holdings of the country, comprising 58.76 percent of the cultivated land, benefited. The total amount of agricultural debts was reduced by 50 percent, and the rest was to be paid in the form of annuities of 8 percent over a period of twelve years. In Yugoslavia a Conversion Law of the same nature was passed in 1935, which transferred the reduced debt to the State Agrarian Bank. In Bulgaria a number of separate measures were passed during these years, which brought about a similar result. The Conversion Laws relieved the situation, but they still left the peasants with a very considerable burden, and the creditors were unwilling after this experience to make loans. Credit for the peasants remained as difficult as ever.

The same cause increased the burden of taxation. The sums paid in direct taxation by Eastern European peasants seem at first sight very small. But in comparison with the exiguous income of the peasant they represent a very substantial sacrifice. Indirect taxation, mainly in the form of State Monopolies of articles of universal consumption, such as salt, was heavy in the Eastern European States, and weighed most severely on the poorest of the peasants.

These general causes, which operated in all areas of small peasant holdings in Eastern Europe, brought about a striking fall of the standard of living, which had never been high, and at the same time deprived the peasants of the opportunity of improving their condition by more efficient cultivation. . . .

MERLE FAINSOD

Controls and Tensions in Soviet Agriculture

The peasantry, perhaps more than any other element in transitional societies, tends to be distrustful of change. The world of the peasant is bounded by a profound attachment to the land. When he is landless or has only dwarf holdings, his revolutionary aspirations take the form of a hunger for land. When he is established on his own property, he obstinately resists being swept into the anonymity of the collective. Of all the major revolutionary transformations of the Soviet period, none was more difficult to effect than the collectivization of agriculture. Once achieved, the persistent efforts of the peasantry to evade its discipline presented the regime with problems of control and adjustment which have still to be satisfactorily resolved.

In its inception the Communist attitude toward the peasantry represented a curious combination of dependence and hostility. The dependence came from the necessity of appealing to the peasants' land-hunger in order to win and consolidate power in an overwhelmingly agrarian country. The hostility and distrust carried over as an ineluctable legacy from Marx, deriving from the conviction that the petty-bourgeois aspirations of the peasantry made it a natural enemy of any form of collectivism. In Lenin's words, "Small-scale production gives birth to capitalism and the bourgeoisie constantly, daily, hourly, with elemental force, and in vast proportions."

The strange amalgam of hostility and dependence is reflected in Soviet

Reprinted by permission of the publishers from Merle Fainsod, *How Russia is Ruled,* rev. ed. (Cambridge, Mass.: Harvard University Press). Copyright 1953, 1963 by the President and Fellows of Harvard College.

agricultural policy. When the regime feels powerful enough to disregard peasant sentiment, opposition is brushed aside, and the Communist leadership ruthlessly imposes its will on the peasants. When it operates under the necessity of wooing peasant support or holding out greater incentives to stimulate output, concessions to the peasantry are forthcoming. Although the pendulum of policy has swung back and forth with the regime's changing assessment of its own position and needs, its ideological commitment is firmly to collectivism. In the words of the 1961 Party program, "The economic flowering of the collective-farm system creates the conditions for gradually bringing closer together collective-farm ownership and public ownership and in the long run for their merging in a single communist ownership."

THE DEVELOPMENT OF SOVIET AGRICULTURAL POLICY

The course of development of Soviet agricultural policy illustrates this tendency. The peasant revolution of 1917–18, which involved the expropriation of the landlords' estates and their division among independent peasant households, was fully sanctioned by early Soviet legislation. But this was primarily a tactical expedient. As Lenin observed in 1919, "In October 1917 we seized power *together with the peasantry as a whole.* This was a bourgeois revolution, inasmuch as the class war in the rural districts had not yet developed . . . the real proletarian revolution in the rural districts began only in the summer of 1918." In carrying on this struggle, the major enemy was identified as the kulak, or rich peasant, while the major support on which the Bolsheviks relied was the so-called Committees of Poor Peasants. The middle peasants were treated as a vacillating force whom the Bolsheviks could not afford to alienate. Lenin frequently urged his followers to refrain from coercion in dealing with them.

In practice, the pressures of the Civil War drove Soviet authorities to seize grain wherever they could lay hands on it. Little distinction was made among different social strata of the peasantry in carrying out the requisition policy. The response of the peasants to this type of confiscation was what might be expected. Peasants reduced their plantings to meet only their own consumption needs, did their utmost to conceal their reserves from the requisitioning authorities, and occasionally responded to seizures by violent attacks on the food collectors. The catastrophic decline in production caused severe food shortages in the cities as well as in many rural areas. Grumbling mounted as food became increasingly scarce, and the Bolsheviks stood in danger of completely alienating the countryside. The Kronstadt revolt in March 1921 and the peasant rising in Tambov and other provinces in the winter of 1920–21 marked the height of the crisis. Even though the Bolsheviks ruthlessly punished the participants in these disorders, they also concluded that a change of policy was imperative.

The New Economic Policy, which was introduced in 1921 and lasted until 1927–28, marked a reversion to the policy of concessions to the peasantry. A tax in kind replaced compulsory requisitioning, and peasants were free to dispose of their surpluses after satisfying their fixed obligation to the state. Although the title to land remained in state hands, the tenure of the peasant in the land was guaranteed by law. Peasants were permitted considerable freedom in leasing additional land and employing hired labor, practices which had been prohibited under War Communism. The peasant was given an incentive to produce, and a considerable revival in agricultural output soon followed. Peasant home consumption increased substantially, and a general improvement in the living standard of the countryside was visible.

If the concessions of the NEP were received with considerable satisfaction by the peasantry and contributed to its partial reconciliation to the regime, they raised more troublesome problems for the Communist leadership. While Lenin was adamant in justifying the necessity for the NEP, his defense did not extend beyond defending it as a strategic retreat which gave the Soviet regime an opportunity to consolidate its position and to prepare the way for the next leap forward toward socialism. The NEP unleashed tendencies which appeared to challenge the basic premises of Communist ideology and strategy. As Lenin himself observed when the NEP was first introduced, "We must not shut our eyes to the fact that the replacement of requisitioning by the tax means that the kulak element under this system will grow far more than hitherto. It will grow in places where it could not grow before." The entrenchment of a substantial class of independent peasant proprietors could only be viewed with alarm by a Party which had been taught that the kulak was the prime enemy in the countryside and that the nationalization of the land was a prelude to the spread of large-scale socialist agriculture.

The agricultural pattern that crystallized under the NEP raised still other difficulties. As the rural population increased, the average size of peasant holdings declined. The retention of the scattered-strip system of farming and the lack of draft animals and modern implements resulted in inefficient farming. The new peasant farm units placed a smaller proportion of their output on the market, both because home consumption mounted and the scarcity and high price of consumer goods offered peasants few inducements to sell their surpluses. The unfavorable terms of trade between rural and urban areas mirrored the dilemma which the regime faced in dealing with the peasantry. In order to stimulate agricultural output and to entice the peasants to part with a larger share of their production in a free market, it was necessary for the regime to make consumer goods available at relatively favorable prices. If they were not available, the peasants tended to curtail their output, to increase their consumption, and to hoard such surpluses as they accumulated.

The regime's decision to embark on a program of rapid industrialization, with major emphasis on the expansion of heavy industry, greatly sharpened this dilemma. The implication of this decision was clearly that consumers goods would be scarce and high-priced and that the regime would have little to offer the peasants in the way of incentives to increase their output or to dispose of their surpluses. At the same time, it was imperative that a large supply of grain be available at low prices, both to feed the expanding industrial population and to provide exports to pay for imports of machinery and other essential industrial items. With the regime committed to a program of accelerated, large-scale industrialization, it soon became apparent that this objective could not be realized within the framework of the NEP. The ruling group therefore determined to shatter the NEP relationships. Inevitably they were driven toward a revival of the practice of compulsory requisitions which had proved so disastrous during the period of War Communism. The policy of concessions to the peasantry was terminated, and a new era of open warfare loomed.

The first victims were the kulaks, the more prosperous peasants on whom the regime had to depend heavily during the NEP to provide surpluses for urban consumption. The efforts of the kulaks to withhold grain from the government because of their dissatisfaction with the low prices offered by the state were met with what Stalin described as "emergency measures . . . methods of public coercion." In plain language, force was employed to seize the kulaks' stores. As the kulaks fought back, the regime intensified its offensive. In 1929 it launched the policy of eliminating the kulaks as a class. Under the banner of this slogan, approximately a million peasant families were deprived of their farms and property and sent into exile or forced labor.

In order to replace and expand the grain surpluses which the kulaks had produced and to avoid the difficulties which had attended compulsory requisitioning under War Communism, the regime turned confidently to collectivization and mechanization. Soviet agriculture was to be reorganized around two types of large-scale production units, the *sovkhoz,* or state farm, and the *kolkhoz,* or collective farm. Initially, great hopes were placed in the sovkhozes to provide a quick substitute for the kulak output. The sovkhozes were visualized as great grain factories which would be completely mechanized with tractors and combines, which would be operated by skilled agricultural technicians and workers, and which would serve the peasants as socialist models of large-scale farming and advanced technique. Beginning in 1928 a number of huge new state farms were organized on free land in the southeastern, eastern, and southern regions of the USSR. Difficulties quickly developed. The land allotted to the grain sovkhozes was usually semiarid, full of weeds, and sparsely settled. Crop failures were common because of drought. The soil required intensive cultivation and weeding, but seasonal labor to perform these operations was difficult to obtain and was not particularly efficient. Combines and tractors were not effectively utilized. Skilled operators and repair facilities were lacking. Combines became clogged with weeds and were put out of commission. Tractors broke down and could not be mended. Because of the vast expanse of the sovkhozes, supervision was difficult in the best of circumstances, and inexperienced managers had great difficulty in providing the necessary skillful leadership. The grandiose expectations which were centered on the sovkhozes met bitter disappointment. At the Seventeenth Party Congress in 1934 Stalin openly acknowledged the "discrepancy" between "the enormous sums the state has invested in the state farms with the actual results they have achieved to date." The decision was made to subdivide the large farms into smaller, more manageable units, and a halt was called on their expansion. For the rest of Stalin's reign, the state farms receded in importance, and it remained for Khrushchev to provide a new impetus for their expansion.

The original plan for the establishment of kolkhozes contemplated a relatively slow tempo of development. By 1932 the crop area included in collective farms was expected to embrace about 36 million acres, compared with 298 million acres to remain in individual holdings. This relatively modest objective was apparently dictated by the shortage of mechanical power. Until tractors and combines could be provided in large numbers, there appeared to be little advantage in rushing ahead with wholesale collectivization. Meanwhile, the available tractors, combines, and other farm machinery were pooled in the MTS or machine-tractor stations, which were designed to serve the needs of a group of neighboring collective farms and to make possible maximum utilization of equipment.

THE DRIVE FOR COLLECTIVIZATION

Toward the end of 1929 the policy of gradual collectivization was suddenly reversed. In a series of speeches and decrees, Stalin gave the signal for a rapid acceleration of the collectivization program. It was no longer necessary, he claimed, to wait until tractors and combines were produced in large quantities. "A tremendous expansion of the crop area" could be achieved simply by merging individual holdings and by tilling waste land, field boundaries, and virgin soil. The land of the kulaks would be absorbed into the new collective farms, and this additional "sweetening" would serve as an extra inducement to make the poor and middle peasants join.

Behind the move to intensify the rate of collectivization was the realization on the part of the Party leadership that most of the peasants were opposed to the new kolkhozes. As long as the regime relied on persuasive measures and voluntary affiliation, progress was painfully slow. By October 1929 only 4.1 percent of the total number of peasant households had organized themselves into kolkhozes. When the signal came from the Kremlin that speed was essential, the whole machinery of Party and government was mobilized to force the peasants to join.

The use of pressure tactics yielded a quick statistical triumph. The proportion of peasant households enrolled in collective farms mounted to 58.1 percent in March 1930. But as reports accumulated that the peasants were slaughtering their cattle and draft animals in order to avoid confiscation and that the new collective farms were paper organizations to which the peasants refused to contribute their labor, the leaders of the regime began to realize that they had won a Pyrrhic victory. On March 2, 1930, Stalin again reversed course with the publication of his famous article, "Dizziness from Success." In this and subsequent pronouncements, he blamed misguided local Party and Soviet authorities for excesses in forcing the pace of collectivization. Stalin's article was interpreted by many peasants as a laisser-passer entitling them to withdraw from the kolkhozes. The mass exodus which followed reduced the percentage of peasant households in the kolkhozes from 58.1 in March to 23.6 in June 1930. In the central Black Soil region, where 82 percent of the peasants had been reported as collectivized in March 1930, only 18 percent were left in May.

Despite this setback, the campaign for collectivization was resumed in the fall of 1930. This time more subtle means of "persuasion" were combined with the old reliance on force and threats. Discriminatory taxation was imposed on individual peasants, while those who joined the collective farms were offered certain forms of tax alleviation as well as the advantages of sharing in the credits, machinery, seed grain, and other privileges and preferences. The regime was now adamant in insisting on entry, and efforts to avoid collectivization were increasingly hazardous and difficult. By the middle of 1931, 52.7 percent of all peasant households had been collectivized. The proportion increased steadily over the next years, amounting to more than 90 percent in 1936 and 96.9 percent in 1940.

The collectivization crisis of the early thirties exacted a terrible price. The liquidation of the kulaks involved the uprooting and exile of millions of peasants and robbed the countryside of its most efficient and enterprising element. The slaughter of livestock and draft animals inflicted a wound on the Soviet economy from which it took nearly a decade to recover. The disorganization of work in the new collective farms contributed to the disastrous harvests of 1931 and 1932. Despite the drastic decline in crop yields, the authorities were ruthless in enforcing their demands on the countryside, and near-famine conditions prevailed in many rural areas. Motivated by an overriding compulsion to feed the rapidly growing industrial centers and to provide supplies for export, the regime "contracted" with the kolkhozes to obtain grain and other items in amounts determined exclusively by the regime's needs and quite unrelated to the problem of keeping the members of the kolkhozes alive. An unknown number of peasants, variously estimated at from one to several million, died of starvation in these hungry years. The "contracts," by which obligatory deliveries to the state were enforced, were in effect a revival of the compulsory requisitions of War Communism. Although the substitution of a relatively small number of collective farms for millions of peasant households greatly facilitated the state's food collection activities, the large-scale expropriations of the early thirties offered the collective farmers little impetus to produce. The regime again found itself faced with the problem of fashioning incentives to stimulate output.

Beginning in 1933 the procurement system was revised. Fixed deliveries based on acreage planted (or supposed to be planted) were substituted for the largely arbitrary assessments which had previously been made in the guise of contracts. The new system provided inducements to increase production. Since the obligations to the state were definite and any surplus which the kolkhoz accumulated was distributed to its members in proportion to the workdays which they earned, the self-interest of the membership was served by an expansion of output.

As this stimulus took effect and as the disorder of the early days was overcome, the performance of the kolkhozes improved substantially. The harvests of 1933, 1934, and 1935 registered yearly gains. Although there was a sharp drop in 1936 as a result of drought, the 1937 harvest yielded a bumper crop. During the next two years, production declined but still remained above the output of the NEP years.

During the mid-thirties, the kolkhozes went through a process of consolidation and stabilization. After the bitter friction of the first phase of collectivization, the regime succeeded in imposing its controls, and a precarious modus vivendi with the peasantry was arranged. In exchange for obligatory deliveries to the state at very low prices, the collective farmers received certain minor concessions. Each peasant household was granted a small garden plot adjacent to its dwelling and was also permitted to own a few cattle, sheep, and goats, as well as an unlimited number of fowl and rabbits. Any surplus which the collective farmers achieved out of kolkhoz earnings could be sold at prices prevailing in the free market rather than at the low prices fixed for delivery to the state. The principles of remuneration embodied in the Collective Farm Charter of 1935 were designed to reward skill and productivity. The farmers were thus provided with individual incentives to increase their production within the framework of the burden which they collectively shouldered.

While these concessions were welcomed by most of the peasantry, they did not necessarily reconcile them to the collective-farm yoke. The demands of the state were great, and the procurement plan had to be met regardless of whether the harvest was good or bad. In years of poor crops, the plight of the collective farmers bordered on desperation, and even when crops were good the standard of living of the average collective farmer was rarely much above a minimum level of subsistence. Despite the fact that the Collective Farm Charter called for payments to collective farmers which reflected their output, egalitarian tendencies frequently prevailed in the distribution of kolkhoz income, and the incentive to work hard on the collective farm operated with only limited effectiveness. Most collective farmers preferred to pour their energies into their own garden plots. They performed their assignments on the collective farm without spirit and without enthusiasm.

Though the attitude of the peasants toward the collective farms remained largely negative, from the point of view of the regime collectivization marked a triumphant step forward. As an accompaniment of collectivization and mechanization, a substantial migration of rural labor to the new industrial centers was achieved without impairing the output of the countryside. Even more important, collectivization, after overcoming its initial difficulties, provided a greatly improved system for ensuring the urban food supply. The collective farms were an infinitely more efficient food-gathering device than the millions of small farms which they replaced. Instead of trying to collect taxes in kind from twenty-five million peasant households, each with its developed techniques of evasion, the regime could now largely limit its procurement activities to a quarter of a million collective-farm units. From the administrative point of view, this represented a vast improvement and simplification. Moreover, evasion was rendered difficult by the intimate participation of machine-tractor stations in the harvesting of crops of many collective farms. The MTS themselves functioned as procurement agencies, since they collected fees in kind for their services, while they also operated as an unparalleled local intelligence service to check on the performance records of the collective farms they served. The dimensions of state procurement steadily mounted.

As the Soviet authorities consolidated their ascendancy in the countryside, they intensified their demands on the collective farmers. In 1939 a new campaign was launched to tighten control of the collective farms. Investigation revealed that more than two and a half million hectares of land had been unlawfully diverted from the collective farms to private garden plots and that many so-called collective farmers had only a nominal attachment to their kolkhozes and spent most of their time on their own gardens. The joint Party and governmental resolution of May 27, 1939, "On Measures toward Safeguarding the Collectivized Land from Being Squandered," was designed to put an end to these abuses. A survey to check the size of all garden plots was ordered, so that land stolen from the collective farms could be reclaimed. Severe penalties were provided for those farmers found in unlawful possession of such land. A minimum number of workdays was prescribed for each member of the kolkhoz regardless of sex. The USSR was divided into three zones, and the minimum for each was fixed respectively at 100, 80, and 60 labor days. Nonfulfillment of these minima was to be punished by expulsion from the kolkhoz and loss of garden plots. A joint Party and governmental resolution of April 13, 1942, subsequently raised the minima to 150, 120, and 100 labor days and provided a specific allocation of labor days which had to be worked during different seasons of the year.

Meanwhile, efforts were also made to stiffen work discipline and to provide additional inducements for increased productivity. On August 1, 1940, Soviet agricultural authorities were ordered "to put an end to the intolerable practice that in some kolkhozy, MTS, and sovkhozy, kolkhozniki and the workers of the MTS and sovkhozy, instead of starting work at 5–6 o'clock, report for harvesting work at 8–9 o'clock and stop work in the field before sundown." A government degree of December 31, 1940, first introduced in the Ukraine and later extended to other areas, provided a premium system to encourage output in excess of planned goals. Under this system, kolkhoz brigades exceeding their plan were to be rewarded with a certain proportion of the surplus they produced. This was to be made available either in kind or in the form of a cash equivalent.

At the same time, the regime made further demands of the peasantry. In 1940 the basis for computing crop deliveries to the government was shifted from the actual acreage planted to the amount of tillable land in possession of the kolkhozes. This change in the method of assessing compulsory deliveries was accompanied by a substantial boost in the amounts which the collective farms were required to yield to the state. While this measure was probably influenced by the pressure to accumulate reserves against the contingency of war, its effect on the collective farmers was onerous and sharpened their resentment of the burdens which the state imposed on them.

WORLD WAR II AND POSTWAR DEVELOPMENTS

The impact of World War II on Soviet agricultural production was critical. In the first years of the war the Nazis occupied a large part of the richest and most productive land in the Soviet Union. The regime attempted to compensate for this loss by substantially increasing the production of foodstuffs in Siberia and Central Asia, but despite these efforts and the encouragement of urban workers to cultivate vegetable plots, food shortages were frequently desperate. Though the basic needs of the armed forces and essential industry were met by drawing on reserves and Lend-Lease aid, malnutrition accounted for many civilian casualties, and in besieged localities such as Leningrad there were few families whom starvation passed by.

Despite the disorganization of war, the kolkhoz remained the basic form around which Soviet agriculture was organized. In areas occupied by the Nazis, many kolkhozniks hopefully looked forward to the dissolution of the collective-farm system. These expectations were disappointed when the Nazis determined to retain the great majority of the kolkhozes because of their convenience as food-gathering devices. Disappointment was succeeded by complete disillusionment as the Nazi requisitions became increasingly burdensome and many villages began to experience the full brunt of Nazi atrocities. The patriotic sentiment aroused by Nazi brutality led many of the kolkhozniks in occupied areas to identify their fate with the survival of Soviet power. While the Soviet authorities continued to be regarded as oppressors, they were, as some of the kolkhozniks are reported to have remarked, "at least ours." In non-occupied areas, similar patriotic impulses narrowed the gap between collective farmers and the regime. As the armed forces drained the kolkhozes of manpower, the women, old men, and children who replaced them worked all the harder because they were bound to the front by the knowledge that the fate of husbands, brothers, and sons depended on them. The reservoir of patriotism on which the regime was able to draw buttressed the wartime effectiveness of the kolkhoz as a procurement mechanism.

Another effect of the war, however, was to weaken the fabric of kolkhoz controls. In areas abandoned by the Nazis, the kolkhozes usually had been stripped of their cattle and draft animals, and only the most primitive farm implements remained. Collective farmers utilized the general confusion and disorder to enlarge their garden plots at the expense of the kolkhoz. In the reoccupied areas, farms usually had to be reorganized from the ground up, and the shortage of supervisory personnel, draft animals, and mechanical power heightened tendencies toward individual self-help. In nonoccupied as well as reoccupied areas, collective farmers were under a powerful incentive to pour maximum effort into their own garden plots rather than into the communal enterprises of the kolkhoz. With food scarce, prices skyrocketed on the free market. Any surpluses from the garden plots could be readily bartered at advantageous rates for the possessions of the hungry population of the towns. Collective farmers who were in a position to do so used the war emergency to accumulate stores of goods as well as substantial hoards of currency. Within the framework of the collective-farm system, a lively revival of individual enterprise found spontaneous expression. While the war still raged, little was done to curb these tendencies. Indeed, rumors were rife in the villages (and were apparently tolerated by the regime) that the end of the war would see a fundamental revision of the kolkhoz system and a new charter of freedom for the peasantry.

These sanguine expectations met a sharp rebuff. The history of Soviet agricultural policy in the post-World War II period is essentially a record of tightening control over all kolkhoz activities. The opening gun in this postwar campaign was fired on September 19, 1946, with the publication of a joint resolution of the Party Central Committee and the Council of Ministers, "On Measures for the Liquidation of Violations of the Charter of the Agricultural Artel in the Collective Farms." The brunt of the resolution was directed against the "plundering" of collective-farm property which had taken place during the war as a result of illegal enlargements of house and garden plots. Other abuses were also listed. As a result of the inflation of the administrative staffs of the kolkhozes, the resolution charged, "Grafters and parasites frequently hide themselves on useless, artificially invented jobs, avoiding productive work . . . and live at the expense of the labor of those collective farmers who work in the fields and tend the cattle." Local Party and governmental officials were accused of squandering collective-farm property "by forcing the management and the chairmen of the collective farms to issue them, free of charge or at low price, property, cattle, and produce belonging to the collective farms." The principles of the Collective Farm Charter were being violated by excluding collective farmers from "participation in the business of the collective farms." "The matter has reached such a point of outrage," the resolution piously proclaimed, "that the chairmen are appointed and dismissed by the district Party and government organizations without any knowledge of the collective farmers."

A special Council on Kolkhoz Affairs was established on October 8, 1946, to put an end to these abuses and to restore order on the collective-farm front. This council was headed by A. A. Andreyev, a member of the Politburo, and was composed of important Party officials, agricultural administrators, and heads of collective farms. Operating through its own inspection service of controllers, the council reached down from the center through the oblasts, from which is supervised the regular agricultural agencies charged with kolkhoz administration. The Council on Kolkhoz Affairs was given a broad charter. It was to enforce collective-farm rules, to prevent the alienation of collective-farm land or property, to strengthen discipline in the kolkhozes, to regulate the relations between the kolkhozes and the MTS, and to see that the kolkhozes fulfilled their obligations to the state. Subject to the consent of the Council of Ministers, the Council on Kolkhoz Affairs was authorized to issue directives to all governmental agencies concerned with kolkhoz life. As a result of its activity, *Pravda* asserted, some fourteen million acres of illegally appropriated land were restored to the kolkhozes. Measures were also taken to reduce padded administrative staffs. In the two years following the issuance of the September 1946 decree, an official Soviet agricultural organ claimed, some 535,000 members of kolkhozes were shifted from administrative to productive work and another 213,000 were removed from kolkhoz payrolls because they had no real connections with the kolkhozes. Despite this apparently substantial achievement, complaints about bloated administrative staffs continued, and on September 14, 1948, new measures were ordered to deal with this endemic disease of kolkhoz bureaucracy.

While the leaders of the regime utilized the Council on Kolkhoz Affairs to tighten administrative control of the kolkhozes, they also sought to reinvigorate Party controls in rural areas. At the February 1947 plenum of the Central Committee, Andreyev called for a mobilization of Party organizers to strengthen Party authority in the kolkhozes and machine-tractor stations. After the plenum, trusted Communists from urban areas were sent in substantial numbers to serve as assistant directors of political affairs in the MTS. From this vantage point, a vigorous campaign was launched to expand the network of MTS and kolkhoz Party organizations. Despite this effort, Party representation in rural areas remained thin. Although the number of kolkhoz Party units tripled between 1939 and 1949, approximately 85 percent of the kolkhozes were still without primary Party organizations. At the Seventeenth Congress of the Ukrainian Communist Party in September 1952, L. G. Melnikov, the first secretary, reported that only 138,054 members and candidates, or 17.7 percent of the total in the republic, were engaged in agricultural pursuits.

In the postwar years, determined efforts were also made to reduce the private property of kolkhozniks to a minimum and to discourage them from diverting their energies from the kolkhoz to their own private plots. The 1947 monetary reform struck a particularly heavy blow at the hoards of currency which some collective farmers had accumulated. The rate of taxation on income from sources other than the collective farm was substantially increased in 1948 and raised again in 1950 and 1951. Holders of garden plots who owned cows, sheep, and poultry had to deliver increasingly large percentages of their output of meat, milk, eggs, and other products to the state.

At the same time, the system of remuneration within the collective farm was revised to penalize laggards and to reward the productive. The seven-category system of classifying and compensating labor was replaced in 1948 by a nine-category system. Under the new arrangement, income differentials were substantially widened, and a number of less-skilled kolkhoz jobs which had previously been paid at relatively high rates were reclassified into less well-paid categories. Kolkhozniks who exceeded their plans were rewarded with credits of additional workdays in proportion to the percentage of overfulfillment. Failure to reach planned goals was punished by deductions of workdays. Thus, incentives and penalties were combined in order to raise the output of kolkhoz labor.

A somewhat similar scheme was adopted in 1949 in connection with the launching of a three-year plan to increase communal livestock herds on collective and state farms. Collective farms which succeeded in building up their herds to the minima prescribed by the plan were rewarded with a 10 percent reduction in their delivery quota of animal products to the state; those kolkhozes which failed to meet the new requirements were compelled to deliver an additional 10 percent above their normal quota.

The postwar drive to re-establish effective control over the kolkhozes was also accompanied by a campaign to replace the *zveno* (literally, link) or small team by the much larger brigade as the basic unit of agricultural production. During the early and middle thirties, the brigade had been the officially approved form of organizing kolkhoz labor. Toward the end of the thirties, there was an increasing tendency to break down the brigades into *zvenya* or teams of a dozen or so workers who concentrated on working a small plot from the sowing through the harvest. Originally, the zveno was used in connection with technical crops such as sugar beets and cotton where a great deal of hand labor was required, but in the late thirties it spread rapidly to grain farming. At the Eighteenth Congress of the Party in 1939, Andreyev, the agricultural spokesman of the Politburo, strongly endorsed the zveno system. He argued that "the collective farmers working in large brigades are not held personally responsible for the quantity and quality of their work . . . the more the work on the collective farm is individualized, that is, performed by teams or separate collective farmers, and the greater the material encouragement of their labor, the more efficient it will be as regards crop yields and stock raising." During the war and immediate postwar years, the zveno system was widely heralded as the most efficient method of organizing kolkhoz labor. The loss of tractor power during the war and the consequent necessity of relying on hand labor contributed to strengthening the position of the zveno system.

Suddenly, in one of those sweeping reversals in which Soviet history is embarrassingly rich, the zveno system was repudiated. On February 19, 1950, an unsigned article in *Pravda,* entitled "Against Distortions in Collective Farm Labor Organization," explicitly condemned Andreyev for his advocacy of the zveno system, criticized the use of the zveno in grain farming as obstructing the effective use of tractors, combines, and other machinery, reasserted the importance of the brigade as the basic form of organizing kolkhoz labor, and indicated that the zveno system would be retained only temporarily for the cultivation of sugar beets, vegetables, and certain other intensive crops "inasmuch as production of these crops is not yet adequately mechanized." The appearance of this authoritative pronouncement was followed on February 25 by the publication of a letter in *Pravda* by Andreyev in which he confessed his errors and promised "to rectify them in deeds."

This unusual spectacle of the use of a Politburo member as a whipping boy to signal a change in policy pointed to the importance of the issues at stake in this seemingly minor conflict over methods of organizing kolkhoz labor. Behind the attack on the zveno system, as Lazar Volin has indicated, was the apprenhension "that the small zveno unit might eventually supplant not only the brigade but also the kolkhoz itself." As the *Pravda* article put it, "Substitution of teams for brigades would signify the splitting of a single large-scale collective unit into small cells, scattering the energies and reserves of the collective farm, and a return from advanced technology and collective forms of labor to individual, manual labor. It would mean shaking the very foundations of large-scale collective socialist agriculture." The fear of the disintegrative potentialities of the zveno system was reinforced by the difficult control problem which it presented. The zveno system required a much greater number of politically reliable leaders than the brigades, and such leadership was in short supply in rural areas. From the point of view of the regime, the kolkhoz could be more effectively controlled through a few trusted brigadiers who were amenable to Party influence than through a large number of zveno leaders whose interests were identified with the rank-and-file collective farmers.

The replacement of the zveno by the brigade was closely linked with the kolkhoz merger movement which was launched almost simultaneously. On March 8, 1950, Khrushchev, who had succeeded Andreyev as the Politburo's agricultural spokesman, used the columns of *Pravda* to signal the opening of the new campaign. In calling for the amalgamation of contiguous small kolkhozes into larger units, Khrushchev listed a number of benefits which the regime hoped to attain. The mergers, he claimed, would facilitate mechanization and the adoption of the most advanced agricultural practices. They would yield increased production and higher income for collective farmers, greater farm surpluses, and, presumably, larger deliveries to the state. They would also make possible a substantial reduction in administrative expenditures and the selection of outstanding managers and agricultural specialists to direct the new kolkhozes.

One of the paramount objectives of the merger campaign—left unstated by Khrushchev—was the regime's desire to tighten its control over the collective-farm structure. The merger of small collective farms resulted in a substantial increase in the number of kolkhozes with primary Party organizations and an intensification of Party influence. The reduction in the number of collective-farm chairmen meant that those who were retained were likely to be the most politically reliable, as well as technically proficient. The regime appeared headed toward the consolidation of a managerial corps in the kolkhozes which would be increasingly isolated from the rank-and-file farmers and which would function as an effective state instrument to extract maximum output from them.

The merger campaign inaugurated by Khrushchev in the spring of 1950 rapidly gathered momentum. By the end of the year, Minister of Agriculture I. A. Benediktov reported that the number of kolkhozes had been reduced from 252,000 to 123,000. In October 1952 Malenkov indicated that only 97,000 were left. In many cases, however, the amalgamation was "legal" rather than real, and actual unification of operations remained to be carried out. In some areas, including Leningrad oblast, the size of garden plots was substantially contracted, to the consternation of many kolkhozniks.

As the merger campaign intensified, more grandiose aims unfolded. In a speech delivered in January 1951 and published in *Pravda* on March 4, Khrushchev proposed the construction of collective-farm settlements or agro-cities around which the new collective farms would be organized. He also suggested that private garden plots be reduced in size, be located on the outskirts of the new settlements, and be tilled in common.

This apparently authoritative pronouncement, however, was soon repudiated. The next day, March 5, *Pravda* announced that "through an oversight in the editorial office . . . an editorial note was omitted in which it was pointed out that Comrade N. S. Khrushchev's article was published as material for discussion." Soon thereafter, G. A. Arutyunov, the first secretary of the Armenian Party, stated that the proposal to relocate collective farmers in agro-cities was opposed to Party and Soviet government policy. The scheme to reduce private garden plots was also pronounced "unacceptable" and "contrary to the collective farm statutes." At the Nineteenth Party Congress, Malenkov declared:

> Some of our leading workers, especially in connection with the merging of the smaller collective farms, were guilty of a wrong, narrow, utilitarian approach to questions of collective-farm development. They proposed the hasty, mass resettlement of villages to form big collective-farm towns, the scrapping of all the old farm buildings and the farmers' homes and the setting up of big "collective-farm towns," "collective-farm cities," "agro-cities" on new sites, regarding this as the most important task in the organizational and economic strengthening of the collective farms. The error these comrades make is that they have forgotten the principal production tasks facing the collective farms and have put in the forefront subsidiary, narrow, utilitarian tasks, problems of amenities in the collective farms. Amenities are undoubtedly of great significance, but after all, they are subsidiary, subordinate, and not principal tasks and can be solved successfully only on the basis of developed common production.

As this statement clearly implies, the first priority of the regime was to raise collective-farm output and procurement. The heightened control over the kolkhozes which the merger movement made possible was designed to achieve that objective.

Despite all of the forceful measures which Stalin took in the postwar years to bring pressure on the collective farms to increase their production, Soviet agriculture remained backward and stagnant. The full dimensions of the agricultural crisis were not publicly revealed until after his death. . . .

POST-STALINIST REFORMS

The first response of Stalin's successors to this many-sided crisis was tentative and groping but unmistakably designed to meet some of the grievances of the kolkhozniks and to raise their material interest in work. In a speech to the Supreme Soviet on August 8, 1953, Malenkov, then chairman of the USSR Council of Ministers, announced a rise in the procurement price for kolkhoz obligatory deliveries of meat, milk, potatoes, and vegetables and promised higher purchase prices for surpluses of grain, vegetables, potatoes, meat, milk, eggs, and other farm products. There were also important concessions involving the collective farmers' private plots. Cash taxes and norms for obligatory delivery of animal products were substantially reduced; tax arrears were canceled; and collective farmers who did not own cows were offered special relief from taxation for the years 1953 and 1954 in order to encourage acquisitions. In addition, Malenkov stated that the supply of mineral fertilizers and agricultural machinery would be increased, that rural electrification would be extended, that agricultural specialists on the staff of the MTS would be assigned for "steady work" on each collective farm, and that permanent cadres of tractor drivers and machine operators would be established in each MTS. All told, Malenkov estimated that these measures would yield a rise in collective-farm and farmers' income of more than 13 billion rubles over the rest of 1953 and more than 20 billion rubles over a full year.

Less than a month later, a plenary session of the Central Committee assembled to hear a special report by Khrushchev on the agricultural crisis. The line laid down by Khrushchev and approved by the Central Committee followed in the main the program which Malenkov had already announced. In addition to increased reliance on incentives to stimulate output and a substantial rise of capital investment in agriculture, Khrushchev called for an intensive effort to train needed agricultural skills, to redirect agricultural specialists from office jobs to production assignments, and to strengthen administrative and Party controls in the countryside. The training of skilled agricultural personnel was to be advanced by the establishment of new schools and institutes for the mechanization of agriculture and by refresher training for MTS administrative personnel and specialists. Meanwhile, engineers and mechanics from industry were to be reassigned to work in the MTS as directors, chief engineers, and repair-shop managers. By the spring of 1954, a hundred thousand agricultural specialists were to be detached from office assignments and put at the disposal of the MTS, with the expectation that every collective farm would thus be supplied with an agricultural specialist and "each large collective farm with an agricultural specialist and an animal husbandry specialist." In order to strengthen rural administrative and Party controls, fifty thousand Communists were to be dispatched from the cities to district Party headquarters and MTS centers. The post of assistant director of political affairs in the MTS was abolished. Instead a district Party secretary and a group of instructors, operating under the direction of the raikom first secretary, were to be assigned to each MTS, with each instructor serving one or at most two collective farms. Thus, in theory at least, responsibility for every collective farm was concentrated in a full-time Party functionary who could be held accountable for its performance.

The new program contemplated no retreat from the collective-farm system. While higher incentives were held out to encourage increased output on the private plots of collective farmers as well as on the kolkhozes, the September 1953 Central Committee Resolution on Agriculture clearly stated that "the communal economy is central and decisive" and that "the right to have a small, private auxiliary plot" is granted "to satisfy consumer needs until they can be satisfied fully by the communal economy." The spearhead of the initial effort to raise output was the MTS, which was greatly strengthened both in skilled personnel and equipment. Tractor drivers who formerly served the MTS as seasonal employees while retaining their membership in the collective farms became full-time MTS employees, owing their livelihood exclusively to it and compensated at higher rates than they had previously received as kolkhozniks. Concessions to the collective farmers in the form of improved incentives were counterbalanced by tighter and more rigorous Party and administrative controls designed to ensure increased output.

THE VIRGIN-LANDS PROGRAM

In the first year after Stalin's death, the new Soviet agricultural program centered on livestock products, potatoes, and vegetables as critical deficiency sectors. Relatively little attention was devoted to grain, since it was assumed that the problem was well in hand. This turned out to be an incorrect assumption. The sharp drop in the 1953 grain harvest as compared with the preceding year dramatized the failure of grain production to keep up with the demands of the growing urban population. The grain problem now came into the forefront, and in a speech to the Central Committee on February 23, 1954, Khrushchev unfolded a new grandiose program to open up and cultivate so-called virgin lands in Kazakhstan, Siberia, the northern Caucasus, the Volga, and the eastern regions. The program as originally announced called for 32 million new acres; by 1960 it had been expanded to more than 101 million acres, equal to more than one third of all the grain area in Russia in 1953 and considerably in excess of the total wheat area cultivated in the United States. The new lands were seeded mostly with spring wheat and cultivated largely by tractor power. The organizational form chosen to achieve this vast expansion of acreage was the state farm rather than the collective farm.

More than 150,000 workers and technicians—predominantly young people—were initially mobilized to settle on the new lands. Special financial inducements were held out to encourage migration, but these were also reinforced by appeals to sacrifice and by pressure through Party and Komsomol channels to accept virgin-land assignments. The campaign was conducted with great fanfare and excitement. Tens of thousands of students from all corners of the Soviet Union were shipped to the virgin lands to help in the harvests, and the heroic exploits of the new pioneers were widely celebrated and extolled. But a great many of those who volunteered or who were mobilized for service in the virgin lands did not remain there. "In 1960 and 1961," according to *Pravda,*

"103,650 tractor drivers and combine operators were trained [in Kazakhstan] and 53,744 equipment operators arrived from other parts of the country to take up permanent jobs. During that same period, more than 180,000 equipment operators left the state and collective farms." Harsh living conditions and lack of accommodations and amenities led them to abandon their posts on the new frontier. The regime faced the challenge of creating sufficiently attractive conditions in the virgin lands to hold its labor force as the initial wave of enthusiasm and self-sacrifice dimmed. . . .

Thus far, the gamble on the new lands appears to have paid off, despite the bad record in Kazakhstan over the 1959–1961 period. The large additional acreage brought into cultivation has not only operated to lift the average level of total output, but has also served to diversify the risks of Soviet agriculture. To be sure, there remains a real danger that careless plowing up of the dry steppes and a succession of dry years may create dust-bowl conditions and lead to a series of disastrous crop failures. But Khrushchev himself has been inclined to minimize the danger. "Some comrades might ask," he reminded the Twentieth Party Congress, "whether we are doing right in developing virgin lands in areas subject to drought." He answered in the affirmative:

> If in five years we have only two good, one average, and two poor crops, it is possible with the relatively small outlays needed for grain cultivation in these conditions to farm at a big profit and produce grain at low cost.
> The results of our work in virgin-land development make it possible to draw the indisputable conclusion that the line of the Party is correct. This policy assures a substantial increase in grain production within the shortest possible time and with the least outlay of labor and resources.

He should perhaps have added that both human and capital investments in the new land program will have to mount substantially if the fertility of the soil is to be preserved and its future productivity safeguarded. . . .

THE FUTURE OF SOVIET AGRICULTURE

Despite the many shortcomings in the organization of Soviet agriculture and the difficulties which have been encountered in meeting production and procurement goals, it would be a mistake to assume that Soviet agricultural output is destined to stagnate. The scientific and technical potentialities for increasing yields exist, and over time they will probably be exploited to the full.

In many respects, agriculture represents the least developed sector of the Soviet economy. As Khrushchev pointed out in his Central Committee report of March 5, 1962, even on the state farms where mechanization is most advanced, "not more than one fourth of the cows are milked mechanically . . . a large part of the corn for grain is harvested by hand . . . the harvesting of sugar beets and potatoes is not mechanized, and . . . there is extremely little equipment for loading and unloading work." The output of agricultural equipment, mineral fertilizers, and herbicides still falls far short of current needs.

The future growth of Soviet agriculture is likely to depend less on any tinkering with organizational controls than it is on the willingness of the Soviet leadership to improve its incentive system and to make large additional capital investments in agriculture. If resources can be mobilized to increase the stock of agricultural machinery, fertilizer, pesticides, and improved seed varieties, to extend irrigation facilities, to train skilled agricultural personnel, to raise the income of agricultural workers, and to provide them with the equivalent of urban amenities, it can safely be predicted that agricultural output will rise substantially. Until such measures are taken, Soviet agriculture will remain a problem area.

8. FAMILY LIFE IN AN URBANIZED SOCIETY

Some historians now speak of a second industrial revolution, brought about primarily by the chemical and electrical enterprises in this century. These have been of major significance in the development and diversification of heavy industry and of no less importance in the daily lives of the average consumer. Material improvement has been felt to a greater or lesser degree throughout Europe: the common man now lives far better and longer than he ever did. But this is scarcely the whole story of the twentieth century which, after all, has witnessed two of the most terrible wars and one of the gravest economic depressions in history. These events have affected various areas of Europe differently and, as the following excerpts confirm, "progress" has nowhere been achieved without great sacrifices.

Robert Graves and Alan Hodge examine urban life in Britain during the two interwar decades. It was a time when improvements in public housing and sanitation began to ameliorate the conditions of city-dwelling, although this had a problematical concomitant in the form of urban sprawl. The tenement building actually proved to be a boon for countless workers insofar as their material comfort more nearly approached that of the middle classes. Yet, paradoxically, the enforcement of new zoning regulations often segregated them further from the wealthy. Inside the homes and apartments personal habits were changing, too, as more goods became available to a greater number of people. The age of cellophane had arrived, and along with it chain stores, synthetic

278

fabrics, corn flakes, and automobiles. For better and for worse, England was becoming a consumer society.

Jesse R. Pitts attempts a much more abstract analysis of that remarkable and much imitated French institution: the bourgeois family. He untangles the elaborate web of convention which binds father, mother, and child (the nuclear family) with other relatives and in-laws (the extended family). Thus conceived and perpetuated throughout the vicissitudes of this century, the family both afforded security and ensured individuality to its members. Pitts' description, we should note, has relevance not only for millions of middle- and lower-middle-class persons, but also for those working-class people who aspire to material improvement for themselves and their children and look to the middle class for a model. Pitts further expands his discussion to the school, which he sees as an institutional extension and disciplinary complement of the family. He develops the notion of a "delinquent community" to show how French children have learned to cope with authority and peer-group pressure.

Richard Grunberger depicts German family life under the extraordinary circumstances of the Third Reich. His account is, however, of more than episodic interest. Following the First World War, and in part because of it, Germany experienced a serious decline in the birthrate. Although the "cult of motherhood" was a deliberate creation of Nazi racial policy, it was also a response to this general demographic development. A study of the policies and practices of Hitler's regime therefore reveals something of the patriarchal values, the sexual morality, and the status of women and children in modern Germany—all matters of tradition which transcend the attempts of one government, however dictatorial, to deal with them. The overall effects of the Nazi years on German family life, despite the glowing propaganda, were hardly salutary; and the Second World War was in every regard extremely damaging. That they have apparently so well recovered since then, in both West and East, is a credit to the resilience of the German people.

H. Kent Geiger attempts to draft a balance sheet of the Bolshevik Revolution. For the Russian people the twentieth century has been filled with calamities, the effects of which are only now being surmounted. On the debit side Geiger places the appalling loss of life, the broken homes, the religious persecution or discrimination, and the climate of dread engendered during the Stalinist era. These must be weighed against some of the noteworthy benefits of sovietization: an end to the debilitating social injustices of the tsarist rule, a pervasive spirit of renewal and progress, a significant and cumulative material improvement for the vast majority of Russian citizens. There is indication enough that the Soviet people have emerged from their most difficult period and are increasingly able to enjoy the material advantages gained by the astonishing leap to an industrialized society. Geiger insists, however, that this collective achievement has not been possible without taking a psychic toll on the lives of individual Russian families and citizens.

As Bert Brecht once wrote: *"Erst kommt das Fressen, und dann kommt die Moral"* (roughly, "first comes the chow and then morality"). True, much of the history of contemporary Europe consists of national and ideological conflicts. Yet everywhere there has also been an elemental struggle to raise the general standard of living. To a remarkable degree this effort has been successful, so that in the final quarter of the twentieth century all Europeans are enjoying an unprecedented prosperity. Class differences persist, of course, and ideological differences still divide West from East. But on balance the Europeans are probably more alike now in dress and habit and outlook than they have ever been. Slow though it may be, what we are witnessing in our day is the social homogenization of an entire continent.

ROBERT GRAVES AND ALAN HODGE

Domestic Life in Britain

By 1923 building materials had cheapened and the government subsidies granted to urban and rural District Councils were tempting enough to set the housing boom gradually in motion. This boom, which kept a great many trades occupied and benefited the workers themselves by giving them comfortable homes to live in, took another five years to get well under way; but it was a great steadying factor in national life. Builders of houses had to conform to certain specifications of size, airiness and convenience before they could earn the subsidy, and the sites had to be approved by the district surveyor; the result was a great improvement in the general health of the nation, a remarkable decrease in infant mortality, and the elevation of slum-dwellers to lower-middle-class rank by virtue of such amenities as gas, electricity, bathroom, and water-closet. The Conservative papers joked at first about the uses to which these unfamiliar baths would be put, but on the whole the filthy habits of the slums were left behind with the foul air and bugs and the communal earth-closet. Ruffianism in crowded trains and buses, at places of public entertainment, and in public houses, grew most exceptional and if ever it occurred was likely to be put down at once by some strong-armed champion of popular opinion—usually an ex-serviceman. For the habits of discipline and cleanliness learned in the Army and Navy had contributed largely to this improvement in public behavior. Another main cause was a new-found pride of the younger women, who wished everything to conform in cleanliness and respectability to their new domestic standards.

Since London clay, unlike Manhattan Island rock, would not support skyscrapers, a limit was set by the L.C.C. to the height of buildings (it is said that it was first imposed to placate Queen Victoria's fury at having her view of Westminster blocked by the erection of Queen Anne's Mansions). London expanded outwards rather than upwards. In any case, a suburban detached or semi-detached house, with the front door on ground level, and a bit of garden, was what the working classes generally preferred to tenement-flats in the city. Huge housing estates were developed, and new "dormitory suburbs" created by the extension of the Underground and Metropolitan railway systems. The first large extension was in the autumn of 1923, when the Hampstead line was continued from Golders Green as far as Hendon. Sir Philip Lloyd-Graeme, afterwards Lord Swinton, President of the Board of Trade, officially opened the new line by switching on the current with a golden key. His ten-year-old son, wearing a bowler hat, drove the first train, which contained only transport officials, through to Hendon. In 1926 the *Daily Express* headlined the question: "What will London be like in 1930? How soon will the population reach the ten-million mark?" The Morden Underground extension was to be opened that midsummer, and the Southern Railway had recently electrified more local lines. In Morden it was calculated that there was room for eight thousand houses and twenty-five thousand people. Land that three or four years earlier had been sold at £380 an acre was now worth £1,500.

There were similar developments at Edgware. The Underground advertised: "Stake your Claim at Edgware. Omar Khayyam's recipe for turning the wilderness into paradise hardly fits an English climate, but provision has been made at Edgware of an alternative recipe which at least will convert pleasant, undulating fields into happy homes. The loaf of bread, the jug of wine and the book of verse may be got there cheaply and easily, and, apart from what is said by the illustration, a shelter which comprises all the latest labor-saving and sanitary conveniences. We moderns ask much more before we are content than the ancients, and Edgware is designed to give us that much more."

The loaf of bread, the jug of wine and the book of verse were to be obtained from multiple stores which purchased the new shops erected on these estates. These shops were designed to have plenty of depth, though not the cozy back parlors which small traders liked; they were bought up by W. H. Smith's, the newsagents, International Stores and Sainsbury's, the grocers, Dewhurst's the butchers, The Victoria Wine Company, Lord Leyerhulme's immense fish-retailing system, Mac Fisheries, the Express and United Dairy Companies, Burton's and Meaker's the ready-made tailors, the Times Furnishing Company, the Co-operatives, Woolworth's, Marks & Spencer's, the British Home Stores. There was usually a bank and occasionally a branch of one of the Building Societies (which advanced money to the middle classes to buy these estate houses and would also help them to buy and recondition approved old houses), seldom a church or chapel. The roads on the new estates were furnished by the builders: when first made, they looked all that roads should be, but by the time that the houses had been built, and the local Councils took them over, they were usually full of holes and ruts.

Most of the houses put up were of red brick, and the prospective tenants thought the designs "ever so pretty." The problem of the architect was how on a limited expenditure he could give what was called "individuality" or "personality" to a house. People did not care to live in oblong boxes, like the old yellow-brick slum houses, and wanted something "different from the ordinary," with pebbledash, half-timbering, ridge-tiling and unexpected minor features. The houses they were given were not quite so grotesque as the French seaside villas built at the same time—the French likewise wanted personality or "cachet." There was no bright blue paint, no Moorish arabesques and colored tiles: but a tendency to mock-Tudor exteriors. Yet the cost of houses still had to be kept down to estimate: so on a suburban road one could often pass sixteen or seventeen new £1,000 dwellings, each not bad in itself but all precisely alike in their difference from the ordinary—the same unexpected feature of round stair-window, finacled porch, or rough-elm-boarded garage appearing in "Rosslyn," "The Elms," "Mon Abri," "Waratah," "Orillia," "Haytor," "Treen," "Bryn Newydd," and all the rest. These were the houses of people with incomes of £5–£10 a week.

At a later stage the customers of the speculative builder insisted on their houses being not merely distinctive but unlike those of their immediate neighbors. The best contemporary studies of architecture are Osbert Lancaster's *Progress at Pelvis Bay,* a satiric account of the architectural degeneration of a seaside town, and his *Pillar to Post, the Pocket Lamp of Architecture,* both illustrated by himself. In the latter, after giving the characteristics and social explanation of a variety of modern styles, he comes to "By-Pass Variegated."

"As one passes by, one can amuse one's self by classifying the various contributions which past styles have made to this infernal amalgam; here are some quaint gables culled from Art Nouveau surmounting a façade that is plainly Modernistic in inspiration; there the twisted beams and leaded panes of Stockbroker's Tudor are happily contrasted with bright green tiles of obviously Pseudish origin; next door some terra-cotta plaques, Pont Street Dutch in character, enliven a white wood Wimbledon Transitional porch, making it a splendid foil to a red-brick garage that is vaguely Romanesque in feeling. But while he is heavily indebted to history for the majority of his decorative and structural details (in almost every case the worst features of the style from which they were filched), in the planning and disposition of his erections the speculative builder displays a genius that is all his own. Notice the skill with which the houses are disposed, that insures that the largest possible area of countryside is ruined with the minimum of expense; see how carefully each householder is provided with a clear view into the most private offices of his next-door neighbor and with what studied disregard of the sun's aspect the principal rooms are planned."

"It is sad to reflect that so much ingenuity should have been wasted on streets and estates which will inevitably become the slums of the future. That is, if a fearful and more sudden fate does not obliterate them prematurely; an eventuality that does much to reconcile one to the prospect of aerial bombardment."

The poorer classes were given less fanciness in the Council houses; and the new barrack-like tenements built in the cities under the slum-clearance schemes were spared the "gorblimey" trimmings of Portland stone which decorated the middle-class and luxury flats. Lancaster remarked: "They look like pickle factories, but quite good pickle factories." One great blessing of the tenements was that they were provided with wide paved courts where the children could safely play; and another was that, unlike the luxury flats, they were built away from the main streams of traffic and were peaceful enough. Curious class-distinctions were observed in the nomenclature of these new buildings. Working-class flats formed "tenements," and were usually named "So-and-So Buildings"; whereas middle-class and luxury flats formed "blocks," and were usually "So-and-So Court" or "House" or "Close." Neither type, however, could compare in comfort with the new German or Austrian flats: there were few balconies, and these too small for family use, and little storage room on the ground floors, even for prams and bicycles. The classes were, indeed, being increasingly separated by the layouts of new estates. The Town-Planning Act of 1932 perpetuated this cleavage. Until mid-Victorian days there had been a mixed development of new houses, but now there was "zoning"—whole districts were to be developed at the scale of one house to the acre, eight to the acre, or twelve to the acre, thus inevitably segregating families according to their incomes.

The most remarkable outward change of the Twenties was in the looks of women in the towns. The prematurely aged wife was coming to be the exception rather than the rule. Children were fewer and healthier and gave less trouble; labor-saving devices were introduced, especially for washing, cleaning, and cooking—the introduction of stainless plate and cutlery saved an appreciable amount of time daily and this was only one of a hundred such innovations. Provisioning also had become very much easier. The advertising of branded goods was simplifying shopping problems. Housewives came to count on certain brands of goods, which advertisers never allowed them to forget. The manufacturers' motto was: "Swear not by the moon, the inconstant moon, but swear by constant advertising." They made things very easy for the housewives by selling their foods in the nearest possible stage to table-readiness: the complicated processes of making custard, caramel, blanc-mange, jelly, and other puddings and sweets, were reduced to a single short operation by the use of prepared powders. Porridge had once been the almost universal middle-class breakfast food. It now no longer took twenty minutes to cook, Quick Quaker Oats reducing the time to two; but even so, cereals in the American style, eaten with milk, began to challenge porridge and bacon and eggs in prosperous homes, and the bread and margarine eaten by the poor. At first the only choice was Force and Grape-Nuts; but soon there was a bewildering variety of different "flakes"; and grains of rice, wheat and barley "puffed" by being fired at high velocity from a sort of airgun. Bottled and tinned goods grew more and more various and plentiful. When the war ended the only choice was soup, salmon, corned beef, California fruits, and potted meat; but by the Thirties almost every kind of domestic and foreign fruit, meat, game, fish, vegetable could be bought, even in country groceries. Foodstuffs that needed no tin-opener were also gradually standarized: eggs, milk, and butter were graded and guaranteed and greengrocers began selling branded oranges and bananas. Housewives could send or ring up for goods without inspecting them, more and more shops called daily or weekly for orders and delivered free of charge, as light commercial vans displaced the horse and cart. The fish-van brought fresh fish to the door even in inland towns and villages. The cleanest and neatest shops secured the best custom; flies and wasps disappeared from grocers' counters, finding no open pots of treacle or boxes of sugar to attract them, and the butchers began keeping their carcasses in refrigerators out of sight, not suspended bleeding from hooks in the full glare of the sun. By the Thirties cellophane, a cheap wood-pulp product, was coming into general use for keeping dry groceries and cigarettes fresh and clean, and soon also covered baskets of strawberries, lumps of dates, and even kippers and other cured fish.

Woolworth's stores were the great cheap providers of household utensils and materials. There had been a few "6½d. Bazaars" before the war, but the Woolworth system was altogether new. It worked by small profits and quick returns in a huge variety of classified and displayed cut-price goods; some, such as excellent glass and hardware, were even sold below cost price to attract custom. The *Daily Herald* reported in 1924 that the T.U.C. was reviewing complaints about working conditions in Woolworth's—"the well-known bazaar-owners"—and that this was the more serious because the stores were patronized chiefly by the working class. But the firm never had any difficulty in engaging unskilled sales-girls at a low wage; for "the local Woolworth's" was increasingly the focus of popular life in most small towns. And the name of Woolworth was a blessed one to the general public; wherever a new branch was opened, the prices of ironmongers, drapers, and household furnishers in the neighborhood would drop twopence in the shilling. The middle class at first affected to despise Woolworth's goods, but they soon caught the working-class habit and would exclaim brightly among themselves: "My dear—guess where I got this amazing object—threepence at Maison Woolworth! I don't know *how* they do it."

Woolworth's, the Building Societies, and the Installment System made it financially possible for people of small means to take over new houses. The installment or "never-never" system was being applied to all major household purchases, such as furniture, sewing-machines, vacuum-cleaners, gas-ovens, wireless sets. A *Punch* illustration showed a young mother, watching her husband writing out the monthly check to pay off the maternity-home debt: 'Darling, only one more installment and Baby will be *ours*."

The *Daily Mail* greatly assisted in the general improvement of living by its succession of Ideal Home Exhibitions. The British Empire Exhibition of 1924 at Wembley did the same thing in a more grandiose way; it was intended as much for enlarging the domestic market as for encouraging the export trade. The exhibition was advertised as "deriving its interest from its intense realism." The public found, in the first weeks after its official opening by the King, that the roads between the pavilions —named by Rudyard Kipling "Anson's Way," "Drake's Way," "Commonwealth Way," and so on—were as muddy as country lanes. Kiwi Boot Polish patriotically advertised: "Wembley Mud Exaggerated. A little dirt is certainly not going to deter Britishers from seeing this epochmaking exhibition—use Kiwi." As entertainment the exhibition was a great success. The Queen's Doll's House, full of miniature wonders, all done to exact scale, brought in £20,000 for charity. It greatly endeared the Queen to the country, and the King too, who was reported to have roared with laughter at a tiny tin of Colman's mustard on the pantry shelf. Also there was a complete Gold Coast village set up, on the model of the "Assuan" and "Hairy Ainu" villages at the old Earl's Court permanent exhibition. The Empire Pageant, depicting life in different parts of the Empire, past and present, sometimes drew 25,000 people at a time. The military tattoo included a reproduction of the Battle of Balaclava, and air-raids started conflagrations that efficient firemen immediately put out. The Amusement Park proprietors did very well—the Great Dipper was the steepest switch-back railway ever seen in England, and there were flip-flaps, a cake-walk, or rocking-platform, and all the latest American Luna Park thrills. But financially the exhibition was a heavy failure, as almost every such national exhibition had been since Prince Albert's successful Great' Exhibition of 1851.

The great change in women's clothes in the Twenties was mainly due to the development of the artificial silk industry. Rayon (as it was first officially called in 1927) was light, warm and cheap, and took bright colors well. By its use, the weight of clothes that a woman carried was reduced from pounds to ounces and the amount of material for a complete costume from nineteen yards to seven. Underclothes, blouses, dresses, stockings, scarves—all were soon rayon.

Since rayon was not very durable, new clothes were bought more frequently; which shortened the time-lag in fashions between their sale to the well-to-do and their adoption by the poor. It was now at last possible to mistake working girls for titled ladies, if one judged by dress; and since educated speech was a valuable asset in business, and the B.B.C. taught it free, as time went on one could not always judge even by the voice. The American habit of buying cheap mass-produced goods for short use was a novel one to the British: it was gradually extended from clothes to shoes, handbags, and household goods. If the old-fashioned shop assistants still mumbled "I can guarantee this—it will last a lifetime," the modern come-back was "Then for goodness' sake show me something else!"

The general outline of women's dress did not change much in these years, though there was constant variation of trimmings and draperies attached to blouses and skirts; sometimes blouses had square necks instead of pointed ones, and there were fashions in waistcoats and "different" jackets. Each season brought in a "new color," meaning a new name for a hitherto unfashionable shade. The Twenties showed great bravado in names—"Yes, modom, we stock it in all the new shades: Mud, Nigger, Rust, Gunmetal, Old Boots, Dust, and Self."

By 1925 the skirt, after a temporary drop in 1922–3 to just above the ankles, had receded to just below the knees even for women of sixty and seventy, and in 1926 the knee-caps were often free and there was a glint of knickers. Yet bathing-dresses remained modest, with high necks and long sleeves, and after bathing one either wore a wrap or got dressed again. To play tennis without stockings was considered immodest; and as late as 1923 the Underground refused advertisement-space to a French film showing girls wearing backless evening-dresses. In the following year the employers of Birmingham waitresses started a "morality crusade," forbidding their staff to wear short skirts at all.

Short hair did not come into fashion among the well-to-do until 1923, when it was reported that "many men are wearing their hair long and permed at Deauville while women are almost all 'shingled,' as the Americans call the new, very ugly bobbed and shaved haircut." Newspapers mistook this for a passing fashion only and came out with comments such as "Bobbed Hair and Bobbed Love," "Shingle's Blow to Marriage." But the "bob," "shingle," and "bingle" were succeeded in 1926 by the boyish "Eton crop." Heavy make-up was not yet practiced. In 1922 the first Elizabeth Arden advertisements appeared, but they were only for powder and eye-lash dye.

Men's fashions changed far more slowly. Most men still wore shirts with detachable hard collars; the soft collar was only sported by motor-salesmen and similarly advanced business men. Flannel trousers and plus-fours— loose golfing knickerbockers first recorded in 1920 at Oxford—were only for holiday wear. But the heat-wave of 1923 popularized tussore and other light materials and M.P.s dared to appear in the House in something less stuffy than their official black and grey. Mr. John Hodge made Parliamentary history by turning up in a lemon-colored shantung suit, cream socks, and a panama hat.

The immediately postwar interior of a well-to-do sitting-room was something of this sort. Walls of soft bluish-grey distemper—wallpaper had gone out during the war-time paper shortage, and had not yet returned—with, above, a low white picturerail and a dado of faintly blurred lilacs in their natural colors of white and mauve, white woodwork and mantelpiece, a fireplace with pale green tiles and a curb of polished steel, a pale green carpet, lilac-patterned cretonne chair-covers, curtains of lilac-colored silk, and on the walls water-colors framed in dull silver. The furniture was pseudo-Jacobean. This cool effect was disturbed in 1919 with cushions and hangings in startling "jazz" patterns—influenced by Russian Ballet décor—"futuristic" lamp shades, huge ridiculous ornaments to make guests laugh, and a general clutter of "souvenirs." In 1922 came a swing back to sobriety: the mantelpieces and walls grew less encumbered, and jazz-colors were succeeded by pale apple-greens, lemon-yellows, and soft blues. The "arty people" were proving their artistic seriousness by designing their own cushion-covers and curtains, usually using balloon-silk remaindered after the war. They dyed it by the Javanese batik method, which was to cover with melted wax the parts of the silk not intended to take the dye. "Good batik is a joy," the *Daily Mail* approved. In 1923 came the magpie school of decoration—white walls and woodwork, black curtains, black-and-white squared carpet. Then a colored-check period; after which it is difficult to trace any period at all, because "interior decoration" had been discovered as an art. This meant the exercise of ingenuity in a combination of unusual woods, paints, fabrics, and bric-à-brac to express the personality of the owner of the room or the purpose for which it was intended: on the lines of the Continental painting fashion of *collage*—sticking odds and ends to the canvases to enhance an atmosphere. Numbers of interior decorators made large incomes by collecting odd and useless junk from antique shops and giving it a new life in modernistic sitting-rooms in combination with stainless steel, white paint, and plaster imitations of serpentine or malachite. Then "everyone" became his own interior decorator.

This was the age of disguise. Since large houses had given way to flats, space had to be greatly economized and furniture now had a trick of folding away into nothing—or revealing unexpected secondary uses. It was not only a sofa that turned into a bed, but a shelf-full of standard poets was also a telephone container, an easy-chair incorporated a cocktail-bar, a decorative screen opened out into a bridge table. "You never could have guessed if I hadn't shown you." Old period pieces were "vandalized," as the antique dealers called it, by being converted to modern uses: a William-and-Mary commode would be gutted to house a gramophone and records; a Georgian sewing-box repartitioned for cigarettes. In "Stockbroker's Tudor" houses, as Osbert Lancaster noted, exceptional ingenuity was displayed in old-world disguise for interior fittings: "Electrically produced heat warmed the hands of those who clustered round the yule-logs burning so prettily in the vast hearth; the light that showed so cosily from the old horn-lantern was obtained from the grid; from the depths of some old iron chest were audible the dulcet tones of Mr. Bing Crosby."

To save tablecloths, polished tables and mats were used. White painted wooden twin-beds replaced the old mahogany or brass double-bed for married couples. It was the time of glass-topped dressing-tables: buoyant imitation-leather chairs; chromium-plate and glass bathroom appliances; miraculously organized kitchen cupboards with white enamel fittings; lamps and lampshades of degenerately seductive style.

The British motor-car industry had been stimulated by the import duties on American cars and by the system of taxing car licenses according to horse-power—for American cars were in general more powerfully engined than the new British models. The British were suspicious of speed and quick acceleration. In fact, a recurring newspaper theme throughout the early Twenties was an attack on motorists as "road-hogs." Roads in some parts of England were indeed thoroughly unsafe for motor traffic—narrow places, banks and hedges concealing turnings, bottlenecks, restive horses, unattended railway crossings.

The Austin advertisements of 1919 had been headed with the word *Distinction!* "Everything about the new Austin 20 is distinctive and high-class, the graceful streamline from the radiator to the back of the body, unbroken by a flapping, bulging hood, is a feature not to be found in any other car." For the aeronautical word "streamline" was already applied early in the Twenties to objects other than planes and airship-gondolas— in this case to open cars. The use of streamlining as a modern style in domestic objects such as electric irons, floor-polishers, and prams, followed in the middle Thirties. The Ford "Tin Lizzie" was the greatest rival to the popular British family four-seater: even with the tax it was still the least expensive, and though much derided on account of its undistinctive shape—box-like body and diminutive bonnet—was recognized, by country drivers especially, as the most serviceable. It was now manufactured in England, seventy percent of the parts being shipped over from what were termed "mammoth factories" in the United States and Canada. But by 1923 British manufacturers were also using mass-production methods, and though music-hall jokes of the Harry Tate "Motoring" type were still as popular as ever, the performance of cars was becoming reasonably trustworthy: one seldom saw a car drawn up at the side of the road with the boots of the driver sticking out from underneath as he tinkered away with screwdriver and spanner. Soon the Morris-Cowley and Morris-Oxford family cars ousted the Ford. In 1923 cord-fabric was first used as a component of tires, prolonging their lives by five thousand miles. Four-wheel brakes were also introduced, and superchargers to improve acceleration. By 1924 the increasing use of cars by weekenders brought the Baby Car into the market. The "Austin Seven" cost £165. It was described as "The Mighty Miniature," but the popular name was "The Bed Pan." Then came the solid-tired Trojan four-seater at £125, and the Morris Minor.

The many small firms among which British motor-production had been divided were now beginning to amalgamate. Humber, Hillman and Commer, for example, amalgamated in 1929, with Rootes as their distributing agents. This grouping tendency, and the disappearance of many small firms, such as Cubitt's, AC, and Angus-Sanderson, were due to the pressure of mass-production. It was not only the lower price of the mass-produced car that recommended it, but the readiness with which spare parts could be supplied—a car of obscure make which met with a slight accident in some distant country spot might have to wait days and even weeks before the appropriate spare part could be found and fitted. Technical improvements in bodies and engines meanwhile continued, but in small, barely perceptible ways, as in film production. The 1913 25-h.p. Talbot, the first to exceed one hundred miles an hour, was still considered a wonder of engineering, for a recently constructed 300-h.p. Fiat had failed to reach two hundred miles an hour, although its engine was twelve times more powerful. The gearless car and other equally revolutionary productions were constantly prophesied, but never arrived.

Scores of thousands of new drivers, who were given no preliminary tests, brought road accidents into the news. There was hopeful talk of great new road-planning schemes; but for a long time the authorities concentrated on widening and rectifying old roads rather than building new. The Automobile Association and the Royal Automobile Club cooperated by putting up numerous warning signs and providing "scouts" as extra traffic-policemen on difficult crossroads. Country people grew to hate cars, for their noise, smell, danger, and the unconcerned bearing of the drivers, and often encouraged children to pelt them with stones and line the road with glass and upturned tacks to cause punctures. A new division of Britain took place: Motorists and Pedestrians. In most country places the magistrates were at first pedestrians, and imposed heavy fines for the slightest offenses. Their view was that motoring was still not so much a means of transport, as a dangerous form of sport. Motortraps, of policemen with stopwatches, were laid on long, straight, clear roads where motorists might be tempted to exceed the local speed limit; and, since the limit in some districts was fifteen and even ten miles an hour, the courts were crowded. Godalming Bench was the most notoriously pedestrian-minded of all.

Parking was a great problem—there were not enough carparks in any of the big cities—and traffic jams were another. These often lasted twenty minutes and sometimes half an hour; for there was no central control, and a complicated crossing like Piccadilly Circus was managed by several policemen at once. Point-duty and a watch on motorists' offenses were engrossing the attention of the constabulary almost to the exclusion of all other social services. Though hundreds of policemen were employed on the Derby course and its approaches in 1928, the forty thousand cars that appeared caused jams that took hours to sort out. "Safety First" campaigns started in the Press. Pedestrians were advised not to cross roads between meeting trams, not to stoop to pick up parcels in the streets, and not to read newspapers when crossing roads. But the only new traffic regulation adopted in the cities was to limit sidestreets in busy areas to one-way traffic. . . .

JESSE R. PITTS

Continuity and Change
in Bourgeois France

THE BOURGEOIS FAMILY

The French bourgeois family traditionally stressed emotional dependency between the members of the family rather than the formalism and detachment often affected in the "pure" aristocratic family. It is precisely because many aristocratic families in the eighteenth and nineteenth centuries did in fact adopt this emotionality that the bourgeois family became a true integrative institution for French society. The climate of emotionality between the parents and their children was a factor in the abandonment of primogeniture; it became difficult to discriminate in the giving of property, since one did not discriminate in the giving of affection.

Another factor working against primogeniture is the way the "nuclear family" (parents-children) is embedded in the "extended family" (grandparents, uncles, aunts, cousins, great uncles, second cousins, etc.). In France the dominance of the paternal line was not maintained as strongly as in Italy or Germany. We have in France true bilaterality. Both lines of kinship—the father's and mother's—are equally important to the nuclear family. For this reason problems often arise from conflicting loyalties, making it hard for the nuclear family to act as a united group. The French bourgeois family has partially solved this problem by supporting some strong personality in the larger family group who carves out a "patronage" empire and presents an overriding claim for the loyalty of his relatives. Such leaders are usually the richest and most successful members of the kin group; hence the nuclear family which attaches itself to each leader is likely to benefit from its associations. Conflicting claims within the extended family may cause a nuclear family temporarily to

Reprinted by permission of the publishers from pp. 249–59 of *In Search of France* by Stanley Hoffman et al. (Cambridge, Mass.: Harvard University Press). Copyright 1963 by the President and Fellows of Harvard College.

suspend a relationship through the device of the family quarrel. The seat of authority in the extended bourgeois family is never permanently fixed. Some branch is sure to challenge it.

Within the nuclear family, however, the parents try to be omnipresent and undisputed. The child is allowed little initiative—officially. The proper forms of behavior, the *principes,* exist once and for all, and parents require perfect performance before the child is allowed to make his own decisions.

Although parental authority and particularly the father's authority are theoretically unquestioned, the child of six and over soon perceives that there are possibilities for evasion and relief. In the kin group of which the nuclear family is a part there are relatives whose prestige may equal, if not exceed, that of the father's. When these relatives offer the child preferential treatment, he can find oases of relaxation and security from the exacting pressures, particularly those of his father. These preferential relationships are one of the child's main sources of spontaneous and sensual pleasure in a society which prizes pleasure highly. The child is taught both implicitly and explicitly that without knowing how to please (*savior plaire*) one is not *distingué* (refined).

The French child continually attempts, in face-to-face encounters, to create these preferential relationships with extended kin (and sometimes even within his own nuclear family), although he realizes that these demands are somewhat illegitimate. In terms of the aesthetic-individualistic tradition which makes every man the priest of Nature's truth, he has a right to these preferences. In terms of the doctrinaire-hierarchical values upon which paternal authority is based, his demands are illegitimate because they bypass parental authority and because the preferential relationship is part of the power struggle within the extended family. A grandmother seeks a new protégé; an uncle wants an admirer. For the child the new relationship implies guilty secrets and betrayal of his parents. On the other hand, the nuclear family encourages these preferential relationships in the hope that they will lead to increased prestige or property. Thus a strain is felt in the preferential relationship. It is love but also interest, and a change in the interest aspect can challenge the justification for continuing the relationship, for the individual owes his first allegiance to the nuclear family and the second to his own pleasure.

When face-to-face encounters do not result in the formation of a preferential relationship, hostility is likely to follow; the other person is *pas juste* (unjust) and gives a preference to someone else. "Who is not with me is likely to be against me." An elaborate politeness pattern will permit holding down the expression of this hostility and will make it possible to preserve a future in which the rejected of today may became the favorite.

Within the nuclear family, the authority of the father depends on his aloofness. By avoiding intimacy, he can embody justice; he is immune to the attempts a child makes to seduce other members of the family. Only the mother can be intimate with all her children and not be accused of having succumbed to persuasion or wiles. In the formal relationship, especially between the child and his father, the child's need for pleasure cannot be satisfied. Compliance with the rules testifies to the child's respect for authority while he finds pleasure under the secrecy and protection of a preferential relationship. The child realizes that each member of the family is equal on the formalized and authoritarian level; but he also knows that each member is expected to satisfy his needs for pleasure by paying only lip-service to this concept of equality. Thus the French child learns to expect that his need for love will be gratified by some illicit relationship.

We may now ask what are the consequences of these family roles for the future citizen roles the child will be called upon to play. First, the child constructs in his mind two sacred extrafamilial collectivities: the state and the motherland. Though the bourgeois child is very early made aware of God and the Church, these categories tend to dissolve into the two secular collectivities, state and motherland. They correspond to the ideal parental couple. The state is the arbiter, the judge, the source of the *principes* (unconditional rules of conduct) which must govern behavior. The motherland is the *Madone,* loving all equally, that de Gaulle speaks about.[1] Second, the child sees that in the constant struggle for supremacy among the various branches of the family his duty in the struggle is to serve his own nuclear family to the best of his ability. There is not, as in classical Germany, a status order which is immutable. Third, although rules and regulations are sacred, they may be easily bypassed if one has a preferential relationship and a zone of secrecy.

This type of family system allows for much individuality. A French child develops a considerable subtlety and a realistic sense of the intermingling of interest and affection in preferential relationships. Although the same person can represent quite different values depending upon the context in which he or she is viewed, what happens within one context must not be allowed to interfere with what happens in another. The family network of sometimes contradictory objectives and emotions prevents any one obligation or feeling from being pursued to a deadly ultimate. This is an important source of the famous French *mesure.*

At the same time that it respects the individuality of all its members, the French bourgeois family gives them all a high degree of emotional and financial security. For the aristocrat, ownership of property is not

---

[1] Charles de Gaulle, *Mémoires de guerre,* vol. I, *L'Appel* (Paris: Plon, 1954), p. 1.

crucial; an aristocrat ruined is still an aristocrat. But a bourgeois without property is no longer a bourgeois. Property for him is a symbol of family relationships, but it is also the proof of the family's rootedness and the guarantee of its status. Therefore, traditionally, it has been kept safe from the fluctuations of the market. Savings are in gold, land, government bonds, and certain very safe stocks which are usually backed by the state. Everything possible is done to preserve the continuity of the bourgeois family by maintaining it as an island of integrity and order in a disorganized and unprincipled world. The family respects and depends upon the older members to link the generations by bonds of affection and tradition. The bourgeois further protects himself from the threats of the world by favoring those careers where safe revenue is assured. A family firm is managed so as to minimize market risk. A bourgeois investor feels a great responsibility not to lose money, for this would be a crime against his family. If the French bourgeois seems often obsessed with saving, it is because he wants to be freed from the economy just as his aristocratic neighbor appears to be.

Given the high valuation of the family, the destruction of one family by another is considered a heinous offense. The thought that mere business failure, the result of market mechanisms, could wipe out a family, is most distressing to the classical French bourgeois. That an essentially moral force, the family, should be destroyed by events which concern exclusively the material, seems illegitimate. It will happen, but few families will want the blood on their hands. Hence the competition among families, inevitable in the drive to maintain or better one's family position, is moved to the *salon,* where the wounds are not mortal, and to marriage, where the wounds are mortal but where the wounded take a long time to die.

The bourgeois marriage is the great test of the family. This is the moment when all the efforts of one generation can receive their reward. A "poor marriage" is almost a confession of failure, and the family finds it difficult to maintain its social relationships. But if the family has been thrifty and has worked hard, if its representative behavior has been better than average without being showy, it can hope for a good marriage, perhaps even a "brilliant" one. And with the marriage and the new allies, an introduction into a new milieu can be made, more often for the brothers or sisters of the bride or bridegroom, but often also for the parents. Thus we may explain the paradox of the desire of the bourgeois to move up on the social-economic ladder and the respect with which he acknowledges a fixed position on the same ladder (*positions acquises*). Once an improved position is obtained it becames family property and is therefore regarded as sacred.

The French bourgeois family has been admired by many people for many reasons. It is the source of a rich literary and artistic culture. It is an organizational *tour de force*. Despite its strains and weaknesses, in the pantheon of organizations it takes its place next to the Catholic Church, the Roman army, the American corporation, the German general staff, and the British Commonwealth as a great creation of the human mind.

THE DELINQUENT COMMUNITY

In school, the French child gets more of what he has gotten at home. We have seen how the French bourgeois family teaches the child basic attitudes toward authority. He learns to accept an aloof father as the primary source of authority; he expects protector-protégé relationships; he knows the importance of *savoir-plaire;* and he recognizes the fact that in order to protect his individuality he must resort to secrecy and political manipulation. The school experience reinforces these attitudes toward authority and elaborates the ways in which a Frenchman will join with others in formal and informal organizations.

In dealing with the teacher the child will meet a typical implementation of the doctrinaire-hierarchical tendencies in French culture. On the one hand the teacher uses magisterial methods exclusively: there are definite standards of excellence, standards of what a cultured Frenchman should know, how he should express himself. The teacher makes relatively few allowances for the interests and fantasies of youth. Typically, he ignores his students' needs as children. He often talks to pupils of eleven and twelve years old on a level which supposes an intellectual maturity that they are far from having reached. On the other hand the teacher defines the world into a set of clearly delineated principles, and what he wants from the students is easily apprehended by them. In his relationships with students the teacher attempts to maintain aloofness and impartiality. The child will respond by trying to "seduce" the teacher. This can be done by playing on the teacher's pet peeves, his political or stylistic preferences. The child is very sensitive to cues which indicate what the teacher—as a man—wants to hear or read beyond the requirements of the curriculum, and the child will try to please the teacher, to break down his commitment to impartiality by playing on these preferences.

The peer group, like the teacher, is a crucial force for the socialization of the child. However, contrarily to what happens in England or in America, the peer group receives no official recognition and no legitimacy from the school authorities or the student's family. For that matter the family will not encourage attachments to teachers, to peer groups, or to the school as a corporate body. The school is seen as a *facility* where the child must procure the knowledge without which one cannot become a cultured personality. It is a facility to be used, but it is not supposed to compete with the family as a center of loyalty. Though the parochial schools have an enhanced prestige with the bourgeoisie because of the spiritual standing of the priestly staff, even they do not receive from their students (boarders included) the loyalty and attachment that are common among the alumni of English or American schools. In fact the ideal among the French upper classes was to have children tutored at home by private instructors, or even by their mothers; and even in the early 1950s one could find bourgeois mothers who made it a point to teach their children at home the equivalent of the elementary school curriculum.

Hence the peer group operates *sub rosa*. Games and sports are too minor an aspect of French classical school life to provide a legitimate outlet for peer group activities. Every student *as a student* has to recognize the legitimacy of the teacher's demands in homework and formal perfection. On the other hand the teacher's classroom administrative authority will not be taken for granted. On the contrary the teacher will find the peer group engaging in a continual battle against him, a battle which he can never win. The best he can get is a truce; and he gets it by his capacity to punish without pity and without argument. Authority, to be effective, has to be aloof and immune to seduction. A few teachers rule by charisma, but the great majority find aloofness and unilateral decisions the best guarantees of order. Every time they let down the barriers of hierarchy they find the peer group ready to abuse the situation. The teacher who tries to appeal to reason, who attempts to win the responsible cooperation of the peer group in the preservation of order, and who finds the use of arbitary power difficult and fraught with remorse, will be heckled mercilessly.

The peer group thus is in a perpetual stance of delinquency. True, the occasions to realize this delinquent potential do not occur very often, because the administration, taking this stance for granted, attempts to exercise the most rigid supervision of student groups at all times. What is crucial to the peer group, then, is the delinquent potential, rather than immediate success in delinquent actions. And this delinquent potential not only covers the possibility of transforming the *class situation* into occasions for entertainment or for cheating, but also creates a friendly public for the expression of all sorts of deviant fantasies on the part of the individual members. Aggression against parents or teachers, sexual fantasies sometimes close to the "abnormal," smut, slang, make up the essence of the peer group activities. To a certain extent this is true of all student peer groups everywhere, but the French peer group has a much stronger delinquent characteristic than the British or the American. It operates above all as an organization for defending the interests of the individual member—the integrity of his personality in its entirety and particularly in those aspects of the self which find no outlet in the roles encompassed by the legitimate group activities.

On the other hand the peer group, lacking a collective legitimacy of its own (which it might gain through a connection to some adult value), finds it difficult to ask for sacrifices in its own name. Its function is centered on guaranteeing each member the maximum enjoyment of his private interest, which, in the school context, is mainly the freedom to express delinquent feelings through fantasy and verbalization. There is the defense against the school authorities, useful to all, and there are the *copains* (pals) who provide the supportive audience for spontaneity and for the search for forbidden pleasures—the spectators for the delinquent version of prowess.[2] Since the basis of the peer group is supremacy of individual interests, one cannot expect from the members the type of loyalty that the American and especially the British or the German peer group can ask as its due. First, there are the claims of the family which override all others. Second, the systematic delinquent posture of the peer group debunks all official morality, which includes the heroic mandate to suffer for the group's welfare. The peer group understands that the member cannot prejudice his interest position for the sake of the group, since the *raison d'être* of the group is to protect his interest position. There is a general expectation that members will not *cafarder* (play stoolie) on one another; but if the school administration starts putting pressure on an innocent, which it might do out of plan or out of the inevitable arbitrariness of its unilateral decisions, the innocent is unlikely to take punishment for someone else very long. The delinquent "task force" of the moment will collapse, without, however, threatening the peer group in its fundamental structure, since this structure depends more upon a compact of delinquent motivation than upon the achievement of any specific goal.

An interesting aspect of this delinquent community is that it accepts the legitimacy of the teacher's demands for school performance. It is his business to make these demands just as it is the business of the peer group to facilitate formal compliance or evasion, as the opportunities may be. Even though certain teachers have a sort of permanent revolution on their hands, the work will somehow proceed. The peer group does not develop an antiintellectual culture. The teacher thus benefits from a basic legitimacy as bearer of the sacred models. In his priestly quality he is invulnerable. The peer group tries to prevent him from utilizing this priestly quality too often against its own interest, and against the unofficial self—"the flesh," as it were, of each of its members. In this defense the peer group has a sort of "second-order legitimacy," but it is vulnerable at any moment to the teacher's charisma.

The teacher, taking advantage of this vulnerability, can manipulate ridicule as a powerful sanction. If a student makes a crass mistake or an unintentionally humorous one (this will happen frequently in Latin

---

[2] A wonderful example of the delinquent community is to be found in Jules Romains, *Les Copains* (Paris: Gallimard, 1932).

or in French essay writing), the teacher may expose the culprit to the whole class. What happens then is somewhat unexpected (though not altogether unknown) by American or English standards: the peer group will respond to the teacher's action by deserting its own hapless member and siding with the teacher, thus demonstrating its commitment to the teacher's values. The student stands completely alone. To be sure, in this betrayal there may be a good deal of unspoken sympathy, but the victim becomes the *lampiste* (scapegoat), whose sacrifice gives a breathing spell to the peer group. Few experiences can be more devastating to the child. It will help him remember forever the great rule of French life: *faut se méfier.* ("Be on your guard" would probably be a better translation than "don't trust anyone.") One can never predict when the authority figure will be able to call upon the prestige of his connection with ultimate values, or when the balance of individual interests and costs will lead the *copains* to abandon a member who finds himself in an exposed position.

In some ways this process continues the complex game of shifting family coalitions. The family provides a much higher level of personal protection but does not preclude the insecurity of exploitation. The peer group provides a higher level of acceptance to the most idiosyncratic of feelings, so that the individual feels encouraged to search for his uniqueness as long as it does not affect the interest position of other members. The peer group is more sincere, and yet creates the insecurity of abandonment of the individual. It is very efficient in defending the *status quo* where the interest reference of each member is obvious and immediate; in such a situation the intensity of interaction, the flexibility of roles, will be very high. The French peer group, more perhaps than the peer group of other Western societies, requires the cement of opposition to the "outgroup," but an opposition that would be embarrassed by a complete victory. The peer group is more in its element as a consensus of delinquent motivation than as an organization. It has developed a great technique for establishing this consensus and excluding the noninitiates who are insensitive to the passwords, the nuances, the implicit. It gives respect and prestige to the communicators, the articulate ones who deepen the consensus and who elaborate new refinements which quickly make a stranger of the nonparticipator.

The school peer group is the prototype of the solidary groups which exist in France beyond the nuclear and extended family. They are characterized by jealous equalitarianism among the members, difficulty in admitting newcomers, and conspiracy of silence against superior authority. They do not deny authority, however. Indeed they are incapable of taking initiative except in interpreting the directives of superior authority and accommodating themselves to those interpretations. In an effort to create for each member a zone of autonomy, of caprice, of creativity, these peer groups thrive on the unrealism of the authority's directives. The directives testify to the authority's connection to a superior world, and create greater zones of *debrouillardise* (make do). On the other hand any change that is apt to create new ambiguities of status, or restrict the individual zones of autonomy in favor of a systematic and rationalized approach to the problem, will be resisted with all the strength the group can muster.[3]

RICHARD GRUNBERGER

The Family in Nazi Germany

In calling the family the "germ-cell of the nation" the Nazis, for once, did not simply indulge their penchant for pompous verbiage: the phrase actually meant what it said. The regime set out to make the automatic activity of cells—self-multiplication—the conscious motive force behind family life and looked to success in the battle of births as a prerequisite for victory on all other fronts.

Looking back, it attributed Germany's centuries of weakness before unification largely to the decimation wrought by the Thirty Years' War;

From *The Twelve-Year Reich* by Richard Grunberger. Copyright © 1971 by Richard Grunberger. Reprinted by permission of Holt, Rinehart and Winston, Inc.

[3] Michel Crozier (for instance in "La France, terre de commandement," in *Esprit,* December 1957, pp. 779–97) has described, on the basis of what he calls a "horror of face-to-face" authority relations, a pattern of French organization which fits well into our model based upon the juxtaposition of doctrinaire authority to the "delinquent community." The French worship the *idea* of authority and yet cannot endure its incarnation. Even though Crozier ignores the importance of "seductive authority" in French structures, he has pointed out the difficulty the French experience in accepting face-to-face subordination on a purely functional basis. The escape from this situation is found in the recourse to a higher authority (non–face-to-face) as umpire, in letting the situation evolve until *la force des choses* commands a solution, and more commonly by a coagulation of the bureaucratic organization into impermeable castes with little communication between each other. Here the bureaucratic procedures become rituals of membership and semifeudal rights. What was supposed to insure predictability and subordination becomes the guarantee of "in-group" autonomy. In the extreme forms we have the bureaucratic fossils described by Courteline.

looking forward, Hitler, in a secret address to his top brass in 1937, extrapolated a steadily increasing population lead of the Slav countries over the Reich—and resolved to meet this threat by "pre-emptive" war at the earliest practicable moment.

The gradual levelling out of Germany's demographic growth curve had in fact been comparatively recent. At the turn of the century the annual average of births per thousand of the population had been a spanking thirty-three, but this figure was more than halved during the next three decades.

There were various reasons for this decline. Even before the Great War —itself a major check to population growth—the notion of limiting one's family had percolated downwards to the middle strata of society; unionization was spreading awareness of birth control techniques among the workers, and even country folk were becoming acquainted with it. The war familiarized all classes with the use of contraceptives. After the war there was no potential husband for one out of every four women aged twenty-five to thirty, and inflation further aggravated this shortage. It became accepted, moreover, that smaller families enjoyed higher living standards and could give their children a better start in life. But contraception did not operate uniformly throughout the country: it was actively opposed in Catholic areas and had to contend with ingrained traditions in country districts.

The average birth rate in the twenties had been 20.3 per 1,000. This relative decrease—which was to be intensified by the Depression—provoked dire forebodings among nationalists, who simultaneously (and paradoxically) adopted the title of Hans Grimm's novel *People Without Space* (*Volk ohne Raum*) as a summary of the country's postwar ills.

It was this tradition that led the Nazis, while clamoring for *Lebensraum*, to give absolute priority to a growing birth rate. Their concern for the family was motivated by power politics, but dovetailed with wider popular aspirations. "Restoring the family to its rightful place" seemed to be a nonpolitical battle cry round which the yearnings of those in retreat from the complexities of the present could crystallize.

In reality, of course, this slogan was anything but nonpolitical: the pre-1914 family pattern had been male-centered and authoritarian. Those who profited from it saw the postwar liberalization of family relationships and sexual mores as an attack on the foundations of the social order; those who disliked the Republic attributed the increase of juvenile prostitution bred by the Depression to the same cause.

But they saw the concurrent decline in the birth rate as far more crucial. The slump had affected it for two reasons: married couples practiced far stricter family limitation, and job-discrimination in favor of family men, kept bachelors out of work—and wedlock. As a result the birth rate dropped by well over a quarter—from 20.3 in the twenties to 14.7 in 1933.[1] (Marriage was less drastically affected, declining by an eighth from 9.1 per 1,000 to 7.9 in 1932).

The new regime proved its claim to be better protectors of family life by imposing harsh curbs on equality for women, abortion, homosexuality and (conspicuous) prostitution. Beggars—who had proliferated during the slump—were cleared from the streets so that anxious matrons need no longer go in fear of assault. Above all, by a combination of revived economic activity and special eugenic measures it produced a spectacular upswing in the demographic curve; fertility increased and the incidence of marriage grew in the proportion of 2:1.

The baby boom that followed constituted a biological vote of confidence in the regime. Already during its second year the birth rate climbed by over a fifth to 18 per 1,000; with 20.4 (or 1,413,000 live births) by 1939 it both relatively and absolutely exceeded the twenties average. Inevitably there was a falling-off after 1940, but the figure for 1943 (1,124,000) still compared favorably with the all-time low of 1933 (971,-000).

The regime's eugenic measures—apart from the negative one of sterilization—were chiefly of a monetary or propagandist nature. Financial inducements to fecundity were basically threefold: marriage loans, child subsidies and family allowances.

Under the terms of the marriage-loans program newlyweds initially received loans of up to 1,000 marks and the birth of each of the first four children converted one-quarter of that loan into an outright gift. The loan—minus deductions resulting from births—was repayable at 3 percent per month if both parents went to work, and at 1 percent if only the father did so.

Child subsidies were grants of lump sums to parents of large families with limited incomes, to be spent on furniture, implements and clothes. These subsidies were limited to a maximum of 100 marks per child and 1,000 marks per family. To be eligible, the families had to have at least four children under sixteen, but this stipulation did not apply to widows, divorcees and unmarried mothers.

The actual child allowances amounted to 10 marks per month for the third as well as the fourth child, and 20 marks a month for the fifth child.

The figures show a remarkable correlation between the Nazi exchequer's bounty and the upswing in Germany's birth rate. By the end of 1938 a grand total of 1,121,000 marriage loans had been ad-

---

[1] According to the *Statistische Handbuch für Deutschland 1928–44*, Franz Ehrenwirt, Munich, 1949, p. 47, the annual marriage average for the decade 1920–9 had been 575,183, compared with 516,793 in 1932; the annual average of live births was 1,285,902, as against 993,126 in 1932.

vanced since 1933, compared with 980,000 cancellations due to births; this represented an almost 90 percent human yield on the fiscal investment made. In addition, the availability of this public money provided a strong inducement for legitimizing marriage after conception had already taken place.

Propaganda inculcated a philoprogenitive mood by the manipulation of language, rituals and social pressures, as well as by a blueprint for domestic revolution. Exhibitions were staged showing that the world's greatest men had a dozen siblings (or children, e.g. Johann Sebastian Bach) and the term "family" was given aristocratic rarity-value by being officially reserved for parents with four children and over. The highly emotive phrase *Kindersegen* (blessed with children) was used constantly, while the desire for a life unencumbered by children—or even for strict family limitation—was called—a "by-product of the asphalt civilization," as reprehensible as desertion in battle.

A veritable motherhood cult was set in motion. Annually on 12 August (the birthday of Hitler's mother), fertile mothers were awarded the Honor Cross of the German Mother (in three classes: bronze for more than four children, silver for more than six, gold for more than eight). The medals, which had the motto "The mother ennobles the child" engraved on the obverse, were presented at ceremonies conducted by the local Party ward leaders. The prolific German mother was "to occupy the same honored place in the folk community as the front-line soldier, since the risks to health and life she incurs for *Volk* and Fatherland are the same as equal those of the soldier in the thunder of battle." The *Völkische Beobachter* announced: "In August 1939 three million German mothers will be honored; in future all members of the Party's youth organizations will be duty-bound to salute wearers of the Mother's Honor Cross, and thus the young generation will be paying homage to them."

The homage reflex spread beyond the Party ranks. On trams, buses and tubes men would jump up and offer their seats to pregnant women or mothers with small children. Mothers-to-be also received preferential rations and safer air-raid shelter accommodation in the war, when Nazi mother-worship reached its climax in the slogan, "I have donated a child to the Führer."

But what of the wives who had given the Führer no children? They were a sizeable group: one married woman in five; one in three in Berlin.[2] By the mid-thirties a eugenic lobby of Party spokesmen and lawyers was stressing the genetic wastefulness of allowing such marriages to

[2] At the end of 1938, 22.6 percent of Germany's sixteen million married women were childless (cf. *Frankfurter Zeitung,* 24 May 1939). In Berlin, 34.6 percent of 1,126,000 married women had no children. (cf. Kurt Pritzkoleit, *Berlin,* Karl Rauch, Düsseldorf, 1962, p. 15.)

continue, since currently barren partners might successfully cross-fertilize in other combinations.[3] This concern with procreation had all sorts of ludicrous repercussions. Public (and private) employees were liable to be reminded that their duty to the state—or the firm—did not end when they left the office. At one point even the *Schwarzes Korps* registered dismay at the manner in which certain supporting actions for the birth-battle were being fought:

> It is inadmissible for a superior to admonish his subordinate publicly to be blessed with children (*zum Kindersegen*) and when the latter objects that the marriage is not barren through any fault of his, to state: "In that case, you must get a divorce or adopt somebody else's child."

But such unusual delicacy was short lived. When the Dresdner Bank —Germany's largest—published its annual balance sheet (which, characteristically, included data about the incidence of marriage and fertility among its staff) the SS organ expostulated "The figures are alarming! One half of the bank's married employees are childless."

In its preoccupation with the birth-battle the *Schwarzes Korps* produced a blueprint for a revolution in the German home. Since the increased work-burden that large families imposed on women militated against an all-out population growth, the paper, in addition to advocating nappy services, launched a campaign for intramarital equality, backed up by photographs of exemplary (and therefore quite un-German) husbands pushing prams and carrying shopping bags.

Though the wielding of shopping bags or dishcloths by German males remained largely in the realms of fantasy, concrete domestic assistance was made available to mothers by means of the duty-year for girls, by such Party institutions as "Mother and Child," and the *NS-Frauenschaft* as well as through the wartime conscription of "maids" from occupied Europe. A special association—the National League of the German Family (*Reichsbund Deutscher Familie*)—was set up to deal with general family problems; it was a clear reflection of the fragmentation of German social life during the Third Reich that the association established a network of marriage bureaus for eugenically eligible candidates (who, by the way, had to pledge themselves to the principle of massive procreation).

In the matter of arranging marriages many Germans still had recourse to newspaper advertisements. The emphasis on money in this type of advertising had often aroused foreign comment. With the advent of the Third Reich the content of marriage advertisements began to reflect a

[3] Dr Kleeman stated in the *Schwarzes Korps* on 24 December 1936: 'There is nothing absolutely sacrosanct about a childless marriage. This is obviously so where the childlessness is intended, but even involuntary childlessness harms the nation. It is possible that both partners might prove fertile in other marriages.'

subtle change of values; though money remained a consideration, eugenic qualifications now loomed even larger: thus a widowed schoolmaster, in the *Neueste Nachrichten,* who stated no cash requirements, unblushingly described himself as an idealist; and one characteristic advertisement read: "fifty-two-year-old pure Aryan doctor, veteran of the battle of Tannenberg, who intends to settle on the land, desires male progeny through a registry-office marriage with a healthy Aryan, virginal, young, unassuming, economy-minded woman, adapted to hard work, broad-hipped, flat-heeled and earring-less—if possible also propertyless," while another stated, "Widower aged sixty once again wishes to have a Nordic mate who is prepared to present him with children, so that the old family shall not die out in the male line." These two advertisements, incidentally, though steeped in the official breeding dogma, shocked that self-appointed moral tutor to the Nazi public, the *Schwarzes Korps,* which commented testily on the fifty-two-year-old doctor, "He's left it rather late before remembering his eugenic obligations." Of the sixty-year-old widower it wrote, "If he has not yet been presented with a male heir, he will have to forgo one at his age, unless he wants to be guilty of irresponsibility towards a young woman who ought to be more than simply a guinea-pig on whom an old man carries out experiments. Since this advertisement has already been inserted a few times, he must be someone who derives furtive gratification from the sort of replies he obtains."

As these censorious outbursts showed, the implementation of the population policy was beset by problems of its own, particularly those of large families. Eugenic experts stressed the fact that parents practicing no family limitation at all were often of racially inferior stock (cf. the "improvident poor" of Victorian terminology) and that official encouragement of their offspring would contradict the sacrosanct Nazi principle of racial selection. Therefore the authorities awarding marriage loans contacted local health offices, school medical services, welfare agencies for the mentally ill, and so on, before making their grants, in order to ascertain whether applicants were racially valuable; among those whose applications were turned down, half were adjudged either physically or mentally "below par," and one-third consisted of unskilled workers.

The Race Policy Office of the Nazi Party also initiated a national eugenic register, in which "decent" large families were listed separately from the antisocial ones living at public expense.

Next to the anti-Semitic Race Defilement legislation, the regime's chief device for improving racial stock was the law for the prevention of hereditarily diseased offspring. Under its terms, Germans suffering from physical malformation, mental retardation, epilepsy, imbecility, deafness or blindness were compulsorily sterilized. Sterilized persons were not allowed to marry and if they were discovered to have done so, their marriages were judicially annulled. The offspring of "hereditarily diseased persons" who had slipped through the sterilization net could also be legally aborted [4] (as could embryos reputed to be half-Jewish) although abortion *per se* was one of the most heinous crimes in the Nazi statute book.

Immediately after the seizure of power, the advertisement and display of contraceptives was banned (their manufacture and sale, on the other hand, were not limited) and all birth control clinics were closed down. Abortions were termed "acts of sabotage against Germany's racial future," involving commensurately heavy punishment. Whereas in Republican Berlin fines on abortionists sometimes did not exceed 40 marks, Nazi courts imposed jail terms of six to fifteen years on doctors found guilty of abortionist practices.[5] Before 1933 the annual average of abortions was estimated at between 600,000 and 800,000, as against between a million and 1¼ million births per year: a ratio of almost two to three. For the Third Reich, even approximate figures are hard to come by. In 1938 every eighth in 1½ million pregnancies was officially listed as a miscarriage; the preceding four years had seen an increase of 50 percent in prosecutions against abortionists (1934; 4,539 and 1938; 6,983). Positing a 1:100 ratio of detected and indicted abortions as against ones which had actually been committed,[6] we infer that the decline after 1933 was not so much absolute as relative to an increased total of pregnancies.

Another highly publicized method of boosting the birth rate was the official campaign to reduce infant mortality. This achieved a reduction of several tenths of 1 percent during each peacetime year of the regime. (Thus in 1936, 6.6 percent of all babies born died during their first year; in 1938, only 6.0 percent). The war, however, reversed this trend so that by 1943 the incidence of infant mortality in Germany was 7.2 percent as against a British one of 4.8 percent and an American one of 4.0 percent. (In peacetime, too, the Anglo-Saxon record had been rather better than that of the Germans.)

One of the reasons for this comparatively unimpressive performance was the reluctance of German employers and female workers to heed the provisions of the 1927 "law for the protection of mothers" which prohibited their working for six weeks before and after confinement.

---

[4] This required the approval of a commission of three doctors as well as the mother's consent (cf. Wallace R. Deuel, *People under Hitler,* Harcourt Brace, New York, 1942, p. 248).

[5] At Nordhausen a doctor received six years in a penitentiary for four completed abortions and a number of attempted ones (cf. *Frankfurter Zeitung,* 2 September 1937). At Göttingen, a colleague of his was jailed for fifteen years for fifteen completed abortions (*Frankfurter Zeitung,* 16 June 1939).

[6] This is the concept of the so-called *Dunkelziffer* (literally 'dark figure') with which German sociologists—e.g. Wolf Middendorff in *Soziologie des Verbrechens,* Dusseldorf, 1959—operate.

Pregnant employees frequently preferred to work right up to the onset of labor pains rather than incur a pay reduction of 25 percent. For the same reason they nursed their babies for only a few days and then handed them over to somebody else's care. To combat this practice the "Mother and Child" organization set up postnatal convalescent homes and village crêches.

Another aspect of the country's overall demographic situation was the increase of the average expectancy of life by over twenty years, between the Franco-Prussian War and the outbreak of the Second World War. This meant that whereas before 1914 one-third of the population had been under sixteen, during the nineteen-thirties only one-quarter were.

Changes in the relative number of young and old were, however, more than a matter of shifting proportions. Right up to 1933 the Nazis had successfully—and not unjustifiably—presented themselves as the Party of Youth versus Age; upon seizing power they had authoritatively declared the struggle of the generations to be at an end: no divisive issue was to be allowed to mar the internal harmony of the family and the Reich. Actually the regime successfully rejuvenated the heads of both institutions: the average age of members of the Reich Cabinet was about ten years below that of their Republican predecessors (or their Western counterparts), while the average age at which young couples married was reduced by two to three years as a result of the economic revival and the measures to promote population growth.

Undercurrents of conflict between the generations nevertheless continued to affect family life, though in more covert form. Being more susceptible—and, in school and the Hitler Youth, more exposed—to indoctrination, the young tended towards greater conformity (not to say fanaticism) than their elders.

With parents fearful of being denounced by their children or having family talk innocently regurgitated in public, dialogue between the generations dwindled further.

Mother and son relationships were particularly affected. Ten-year-old lads who were awarded daggers not surprisingly entertained vastly inflated notions of their self-importance, and many a mother's patience was sorely tried by a preadolescent "Master in the House" for whom the thought of having to defer to the authority of mere women seemed unnatural.

Another group of women found themselves reduced to a state jocularly described as political widowhood: although their husbands were alive, Party involvement prevented them from using the home for more than bed and board. In certain cases the clash of loyalties between political commitment and domesticity was so great that it constituted a new category of divorce. A Berlin paper wrote in 1937: "It is a husband's duty to participate in National Socialist activities and a wife who makes trouble on this score gives grounds for divorce. She must not complain if her husband devotes two evenings per week to political activity, nor do Sunday mornings always exclusively belong to the family."

Though this sounded reasonable, it was belied by a subsequent court decision: "The accused cannot excuse her refusal to participate in political activity on the grounds that she has been unable to lead the sort of family life she had anticipated when marrying, because the plaintiff had been kept away from home almost every night by Party work. At times of political high tension, German women must make the same sacrifices as the wives of soldiers in the present world war."

Although "political widows" completely outnumbered "widowers," there were occasional instances of the latter phenomenon. A Halberstadt court granted a woman a divorce because her husband had said that membership of the National Socialist Association of Women (*NS-Frauenschaft*) was like belonging to a ladies' coffee circle.

But the explicitly political encroachment on family life (as depicted in the joke about the SA [7] father, *NS-Frauenschaft* mother, Hitler Youth son and BDM [8] daughter who met each year at the Nuremberg Party Rally) was only one aspect of a wider process of erosion. The regime engendered a whole range of additional pressures inimical to family cohesion: the removal of young people for long periods (for military and labor service, Hitler Youth camps or the girls' duty year), the widespread industrial employment of women,[9] the increasing incidence of overtime and shift work, the creation of work places from which employees could only come home at week-ends (or even less frequently), and so on.

Juvenile delinquency figures soon showed the effect of these developments on family life: within the overall context of a decreasing crime rate (the total number of court convictions dropped from almost half a million in 1933 to just under 300,000 in 1939) juvenile criminality showed an increase from just under 16,000 in 1933 to over 21,000 in 1940.

The war, of course, accentuated this trend, and further undermined family relations. The casualty figures made the regime accord even greater precedence to their "population policy" at the expense of conventional morality. The Nazi poet laureate, Hanns Johst, writing of his impressions in a transit camp for "ethnic Germans," mentioned a *ménage à trois* consisting of a farmer, his barren wife and his pregnant maid with every

---

[7] *Sturmabteilung*.
[8] Bund Deutscher Mädchen (German Girls' League).
[9] The female labor force increased by nearly 50 percent between 1937 and 1939: by 1942, it was almost twice as large as it had been before the seizure of power.

sign of approval. The *Schwarzes Korps* publicized a similar situation under the heading, "A private matter—craftsman in childless marriage has child by wife's sister."

The vindication of the eugenic principle at the expense of social taboo was typified by litigation initiated by the forty-two-year-old wife of a grammar-school teacher to prove that she was not the legitimate offspring of her deceased mother's marriage to a Jew. Fortunately for the plaintiff two aged witnesses were on hand to testify that her mother had been of very vivacious disposition and had spent much time in the company of army officers.

Compared to this form of posthumous exoneration, other instances of officially promoted bad taste seemed almost to be innocuous *jeux d'esprit,* one example being the autobiographical details inserted by the playwright Hans Erich Forel in the program of the Dessauer Theatre when his play *Frauendiplomatie (Female Diplomacy)* was performed there. "As the last male scion of my line, I would dearly love to have a son and heir, but all my attempts to date have been fruitless. I have attempted it with two wives, but the result was four daughters. If my wish for a son and heir is not fulfilled, I shall have to give up the race."

If the degradation of family life in the Third Reich thus had its aspect of sick humor—wittily illustrated by such neologisms as *Rekrutenmachen* (producing recruits) for sexual intercourse, *Gebärmaschinen* (childbearing machines) for procreative women and *bevölkerungspolitische Blindgänger* (eugenic duds) for barren women—it could also lead to unmitigated tragedy. Apart from the cast-off wives, there were quite a few cast-off parents, i.e. fathers and mothers whose political or religious convictions led the authorities to take their children away from them. The official procedure was quite simple: if the local Youth Office discovered a child being reared in a nonconformist family atmosphere, it applied to the guardianship court for an order of removal to a "politically reliable" home. Among parental offenses punishable by judicial kidnapping were friendship with Jews, refusal to enroll children in the Hitler Youth, and membership of the Jehovah's Witnesses.

Nazi courts were kept very busy with actions involving family legislation. Maternity proceedings were a case in point. Premarital sexual intercourse was very widespread in the Third Reich (the estimated frequency varying from 51 percent in Saxony to over 90 percent in Munich). In its racially motivated concern to establish the pedigree of every newborn child, the government empowered the authorities in 1938 to require both the mother and all putative fathers to submit to blood tests, after which the child could be removed from its home. Whereas previously a father was only able to start paternity proceedings within twelve months of the child's birth, such a probe could now be undertaken throughout the child's life and even after its death. If a husband tried to cover up his wife's adultery, the state intervened to establish the correct paternity. Since a growing proportion of the Third Reich's biological fathers were below the permitted age for marriage, the authorities instituted a special procedure by which minors were legally declared to have obtained their majority, so that their marriage could be solemnized. A special application form for the award of majority status to men under twenty-one bore this wording:

> I ask to be declared of full age. I have been engaged since . . . to . . . , who has borne a child on the . . . , whose father I am. I want to marry my bride, who is an orderly, industrious and thrifty girl, as soon as possible, so that I can care for her and my child better than I am able to do at the moment. My weekly income is . . . , which means that I can take care of a family. We have/are going to get a flat. I know what marriage means.

When members of the legal profession had to adjudicate on matters of sexual morality, they frequently discovered that the foundations of their own code rested on quicksand. Thus in one and the same year two separate judicial bodies treated cases of adultery in diametrically opposite ways. The Thüringian Disciplinary Chamber (*Dienststrafkammer*) dismissed from his post a forty-five-year-old primary-school teacher who had committed adultery, whereas the Hereditary Estate Court (*Landerhofgericht*) at Celle refused to declare a farmer accused of the same offense as ineligible for a hereditary estate and quoted village opinion in support of its decision.[10]

In the case of the Reich Labor Court, it was one and the same tribunal that handed down mutually contradictory decisions. The court upheld the dismissal of an unmarried shop assistant since "the visibility of her condition might offend customers' susceptibilities," but arrived at an opposite conclusion concerning an industrial employee dismissed on analogous grounds. "Such pregnancy need no longer be regarded as *ipso facto* immoral and reproachable."

Nothing exemplified the internal inconsistency of the Nazi moral code as clearly as the position of women under the terms of the race-defilement legislation of 1935 and the 1938 divorce reform respectively. The race-

---

[10] It was the latter judgement that came increasingly to typify the attitude of the courts, often arrived at in deference to an opinion expressed by the *Schwarzes Korps*. One court actually quoted a *Schwarzes Korps* diatribe in justifying the reversal of a previous decision in which it had defined tolerance by the future parents-in-law of sexual intercourse between an engaged couple as 'procuring' (cf. *Juristische Wochenschrift*, 1937, pp. 2, 387). A Berlin court ruled that living in sin constituted valid grounds for terminating a tenancy only if the couple concerned aroused their neighbors' indignation by unseemly conduct (cf. *Frankfurter Zeitung*, 23 August 1939).

defilement law reflected Hitler's characteristically banal and outdated view of sex as a subject/object relationship with the male cast in a relentlessly active role *vis-à-vis* the helpless playthings of his desires. This resulted in obvious discrimination against male offenders. Race-defilement cases provided the absurd spectacle of Nazi courts favoring Jewish accused at the expense of Gentile ones, but only where Aryans had been male partners in an act of "mixed" coitus. (Incidentally, even the *Schwarzes Korps* was moved to criticize the bias built into race-defilement legislation [cf. *Schwarzes Korps*, 8 December 1938].)

In the sphere of divorce legislation the law tended to be biased in the opposite direction. As far as comparative incidence was concerned, the divorce rate climbed more steeply during the peacetime years of the Third Reich than either the marriage rate or the birth rate. While the total of marriages in 1939 exceeded that of 1932 by a fifth and births had increased 45 percent, there were half as many more divorces; from just over 42,000 divorces in 1932, the number mounted to over 50,000 in 1935 and 1936, dropped slightly in 1937 and 1938, and in 1939 shot up to well over 61,000. It was axiomatic from the very start that certain categories of marriage were ripe for dissolution, i.e. mixed marriages between Aryans and non-Aryans and marriages in which one of the partners was politically obstreperous. With the passage of time, the notion that infertility in marriage was not all that dissimilar from political opposition to the regime gained ground. The official concern with fertility also found expression in a campaign to transform separation into actual divorce, so that separated marriage partners might be enabled to start new families.

These various considerations eventually prompted the promulgation of the 1938 divorce-reform law by the Minister of Justice, Dr. Gürtner.[11] Divorce reform, incidentally, was also connected with the incorporation of Austria, where the Catholic laws that had previously been in operation had condemned thousands of separated individuals to live in sin with their new partners.[12]

The following constituted grounds for divorce under the terms of Gürtner's law: adultery, refusal to procreate, dishonorable and immoral conduct, a diseased mentality, serious contagious infection, three years' separation of marriage partners, and infertility (unless a child had previously been conceived or adopted—even so, the infertility clause was only to be applied in accordance with what Nazi legislators defined as the healthy instinct of the people).

[11] It was the operation of this law that accounted for the sharp increase in divorce figures between 1938 and 1939.

[12] But the 1939 divorce statistics we have quoted exclude the Austrian figures; in Austria the introduction of the new law led to such a flood of divorce applications that new forms had to be printed to ease the strain on the officials concerned (cf. *Frankfurter Zeitung*, 14 August 1938).

The *Frankfurter Zeitung* welcomed the reform for facilitating the *de jure* dissolution of *de facto* broken marriages and forging new marriage bonds. But within three months it announced the supreme court's first decision interpreting paragraph 55 of the new law: "After a three-year separation divorce shall also be granted if the husband has left the wife for the sake of another woman and the wife's conduct has been entirely blameless." Within two years, Gürtner's reform in fact produced 30,000 instances of marriage partners being cast off; 80 percent of such proceedings were initiated by husbands whose wives were completely innocent of the loosening of the marriage bonds. Three out of every five of the cast-off wives were women over forty-five years of age and had been married for twenty years and more.[13] . . .

H. KENT GEIGER

What the Revolution Brought to Russia

A MULTIPLICATION OF CATASTROPHES

There is a homicidal cast to Soviet history. Estimates of the number of untimely deaths are staggering—nine million in the First World War, twenty million in the Second, with additional millions who perished in the Civil War and from famine, epidemics, forced deportation of kulaks, and the persecutions of Stalin's Terror and labor camps. According to one Western scholar, Soviet population losses, if birth deficits suffered during the World Wars are included, come to approximately 100 million in some forty years.

Although all have suffered, most of the victims have been men. The

Reprinted by permission of the publishers from pp. 120–38 of *The Family in Soviet Russia* by H. Kent Geiger (Cambridge, Mass.: Harvard University Press). Copyright 1968 by the President and Fellows of Harvard College.

[13] Under the 1938 law, ex-wives who had been innocent parties in divorce proceedings had to forgo any claim to alimony or maintenance, unless they were old, infirm or had children who were minors.

1959 census shows twenty million more women than men in the Soviet Union and in the age group thirty-two and older almost twice as many women as men. This fact alone demands that two easy stereotypes about the USSR be called into serious question. It is sometimes said that the Soviet Union is a land of youth, but in reality it is more a land of women. The second stereotype, inherited from what now seems, inside the USSR, a distant past, sees the Soviet Union as a land of free love, though in reality it is much more a land of broken families.

These two realities indicate the significant fact that a very great proportion of Soviet families are headed by women. In the village of Viriatino, subjected to intensive study in 1953, a breakdown of the distribution of the 456 families showed that women made up 44.5 percent of the total number of heads of households, and that the modal type (67 families) was a two-person family headed by a woman.

Life itself is of course the most precious possession, but other things are also dear, and catastrophe has visited Soviet families in several guises. The October Revolution itself turned the old social order upside down, and the various other revolutions, both episodic and continuing, have suppressed and actively persecuted entire groupings because of their undesired positions in the social structure. As a sample, one respondent explained that his father, a civil engineer, was arrested "only because he belonged to the bourgeoisie." "He was given the verdict— exile for five years to any of the smaller cities of Russia. They called this punishment "minus five," which meant that he could not live in any of the five largest cities of the Soviet Union. Before his release he asked the judge why he was being punished, and the answer came: " 'Listen, citizen. You are a man of the past, and we don't need people of your kind around. Be glad that the Soviet Government is merciful.' " A detailed accounting of all groups and categories involved would detract from the main theme of this discussion. It is more important to understand the consequences inside the family of the precipitate declines in status that have been so frequent. Two further examples of the categories of families involved include suggestions of what it has meant to the family to be of the "former people" or "alien elements," as they were called.

> My father was refused a passport because he was a kulak. He was required to leave the village and go to some other place in the Kharkov Region 50 kilometers away. He just had to leave; they did not tell him where he was to go. So he left. But he was still persecuted, to the point where he could not talk to his family. He went to live with some comrades who were in the same position as he was. He left us without even telling us where he was going.
>
> My father was the son of a very plain and ordinary priest. This certainly did not help him. He was referred to as a "son of a priest," and the fact that his father had been of very humble peasant stock did not

help him at all. We were disfranchised. We were thrown out of our house and told to go wherever we wanted. We lived in a house that was fit for chickens. We could not do anything. We had no prospect of decent work.

Even when members of such men's families remained alive, they suffered separation, dispossession, and loss of such civil rights as were accorded to the population.

Particularly revealing is the case of the kulaks, who were the main victim's of Stalin's most unpopular reform, the collectivization of agriculture. As has so often been the case, Soviet social reconstruction was paid for in the coin of individual suffering and broken families. In the official language the "liquidation of the kulaks as a class" paved the way for "building socialism in one country," but in the language of the people the Soviet power took their possessions, caused famine, and scattered them and their families to the four winds.

For these peasants family life often simply ceased to exist. Husbands and wives, parents and children were separated from each other as well as from their land. Unable to enter a kolkhoz or to farm other land, and with no occupational skills but those of the farmer, those kulak men who remained alive and free often drifted to newly active construction sites, where they worked at unskilled labor and lived in barracks. Their wives, considered by the regime to be more backward than hostile, sometimes went to the cities to work as servants or at other unskilled jobs and occasionally journeyed to live with relatives. Kulak children were often adopted, taken in by more fortunate relatives or neighbors, or added to the population of homeless children.

The fate of the priesthood has been similarly hard. Heavy taxes, public ridicule, quasi-legal persecution for conspiracy against the state, denial of alternative opportunities for work and for the education of their children, and sometimes physical destruction were the lot of the Russian priest until the Second World War.

These kulaks and clergy have been especially prominent among the groups persecuted, I suspect, because of their social visibility and also their relative inability or unwillingness to adapt to the new Soviet order. The story about the priest continues: "Throughout the entire . . . Soviet Revolution and the Soviet regime he continued his religious work. The peasants loved him . . . At one time, while we were living in that village on the Dniester, someone offered to get my father across the river. My father refused to flee. He said he would stay to face his fate as God had willed it."

As important as these typical catastrophes—the physical destruction or separation of the family members and the radical decline in status with loss of material possessions, civil rights, and opportunities—has been a profound sense of insecurity and, at times, even dread. This pattern, perhaps the most distinctive of all Soviet experiences in daily life, developed early, in the form of efforts to settle accounts with the ruling classes of Tsarist times, became more striking in the drive against the kulaks, and gradually rose to the frenzied destruction and horror associated with the peak of the great purge of 1936 and 1937, the *Ezhovshchina*. By then the term "enemy of the people" was being applied to long lists of loyal party members condemned out of hand by the all-powerful Stalin. The circle of families affected was constantly widened, but for many it was only the culmination of a trend that had begun earlier with the Revolution and the Civil War, events that left the Bolsheviks, party of the minority, in command of a people toward most of whom they felt little sympathy. Since that time Stalinist terror has relented, and has even been "explained" as the time of the cult of personality, but its traces are still to be found, and the reality of fear remains a crucial factor in many Soviet homes.

For many in the population the Soviet period ushered in a sense of protracted conflict with the political rulers—a peculiar type of civil war between the regime and the people. The sides were, of course, quite unequal, but the powers of passive resistance and spiritual independence are great, and it is still true today that many Soviet citizens look upon their government and leaders with aversion and think in terms of "we" (the people) and "they" (our oppressors in the Kremlin). Largely responsible was Stalin's terrorism and the climate of fear it caused. A fifty-six-year-old nurse tells: "We all trembled because there was no way of getting out of it. Even a communist himself can be caught. To avoid trouble is an exception."

Though much of the activity was hidden from the eyes of the outside world, there were some very public signs. For instance, in June and July of 1934 legal measures were introduced which, in effect, converted the Soviet citizen's close relatives into hostages. The laws established criminal liability for members of the family of a "traitor to the homeland" or a deserter from the armed forces. Sentences were meted out even if the treason or defection was not known to those who lived with the traitor or were dependent of him. As law this policy remained on the books for some time after the death of Stalin, apparently until the appearance of new criminal codes in 1958, though Soviet jurists criticized it before then and in 1957 a Western legal scholar was assured by the Deputy Procurator General of the USSR that it was "no longer applied."

Again and again measures that the Soviet rulers regarded as progressive steps toward a better society were experienced by the people as intense cultural deprivation. The two most prominent examples are the reorganization of peasant life on the collective and state farms and the officially sanctioned opposition to the church and religious institutions, both of which were extremely unpopular with the great majority of the population. The response to agricultural collectivization is indicated in the following account by a party member who was also a peasant in 1930: "When we were told of collectivization . . . I liked the idea. So did a few others in the village, men like me. The rest of the village was dead set against it . . . Well, we got going . . . I called a village meeting and I told the people that they had to join the kolkhoz, that these were Moscows' orders, and if they didn't they would be exiled and their property taken away from them. They all signed . . . and felt as though they were being sent to jail." Since that time the Soviet peasants have continued to chafe under the collective farm system, resenting those who forced it upon them, and extreme poverty and economic insecurity have added greatly to the burdens of institutional deprivation. To many, life on the kolkhoz has seemed like forced labor mainly because of its social organization: "Before the Revolution he [respondent's father] was master on his fields. He worked when he wished to. No overseer stood behind his back and pushed him to work like a donkey. Under the Soviet regime we became slaves."

Turning to the other main form of institutional-cultural oppression, the Soviet regime has always been unfriendly to religion as faith and ideology, and to the church as an organization. Though formally church and state are separate, and freedom of religious worship is supposedly guaranteed, in fact churches have been destroyed or withdrawn from use, and continuous streams of antireligious propaganda have been emitted by Soviet agencies and institutions. Every Soviet schoolboy learns that religion is the opium of the people, unscientific and reactionary, and party and Komsomol members are expelled for entertaining religious superstitions or prejudices.

Thus the formal right of religious worship has been made a mockery through action behind the scenes, purportedly at the behest of the toiling masses but in reality through decision by the party at the highest level. A notion of the extent to which the people were deprived of religious facilities in the prewar years can be gained from scattered facts and figures on the number of churches destroyed, withdrawn from use, or not replaced. In 1936, for example, *Izvestiia* reported that some of the fastest growing of the new cities, including Magnitogorsk, Karaganda, and Stalinsk, had no churches at all. Of all the many forces brought to bear in the effort to wipe out religion this elimination of places of worship has clearly been the most destructive. A young worker from a peasant background reports the story in barest outline: "From 1933 to 1942 I never went to church. There was none in the city in which I lived." In Moscow in the year 1942 there were an estimated seventeen churches remaining in use by parishioners, in comparison with a total of at least six hundred before the Revolution. During the postwar era, in connection with the new favor which the church gained, many damaged churches have been rebuilt or repaired, and new ones constructed. As of the late 1950s it was reported that there were twenty thousand to twenty-five thousand churches functioning, about half the number at hand in 1917.

In addition, the party has periodically undertaken campaigns to discredit and obstruct what it contemptuously refers to as the practice of cults, and for a young person, in particular, to be identified as a believer involves a serious stigma in Soviet public life. Similarly, even though the clergy were given legal status equivalent to that of other citizens in the 1936 Constitution, a move said to have been sponsored by Stalin himself, even heavier repressive pressure was simultaneously imposed against individual members of the clergy. The considerable shortage of priests is a problem that continues today.

Eastern Orthodoxy is a faith with little explicit theology, ritual-centered to an exceptional degree. With no church in which to worship and with no priest to administer, for many Soviet people there just has been "no religion." The relevance in the political thoughts of a good many of the Soviet people is suggested by the words of a young man describing the view of his mother: "She thought that the communists were anti-Christ and atheists. She believed that men could not live without God and that people who were against God were against her."

To sum up, Soviet history has brought many traumatic and deprivational experiences into the lives of the people, and a good share of these have been shared as family tragedies and misfortunes. The men—husbands and fathers in families—have been killed, separated, and greatly handicapped by denial of status and opportunity. The women—wives and mothers—have been hard pressed to carry on. Stories of a destroyed family like the following are often heard. The narrator's father was a peasant separated from his family and could neither rejoin nor help support those he left behind. As a result: "My mother had to work very hard; she was employed in excavation for building foundations. For this work she received one half liter of soup—not soup, really, but water—and 200 grams of bread each day. She did not get any money at all. This was not enough to maintain me and my brother, so we had to go to a children's home. All the children there either had no parents—many of their parents had died in the famine—or they were children like myself, whose parents could not feed them or who did not know where their parents were."

In those families where all were able to survive and remain together, the outer society seemed threatening and improvident. In some periods and for some families arrest by the political police represented the ultimate misfortune. It was hard to anticipate calmly the possibility of arrest.

Nevertheless, some provided in advance a dramatic symbol of the people's mood—the packed suitcase, ready to take along if the secret police knocked at the door—and some others thought of the economic security of those who would be left behind. One bookkeeper, relatively affluent, reported that he kept "only small sums" of money in the savings bank in order not to attract attention, but that "we had larger sums at our disposal just in case of trouble—so in case I should be arrested my daughter would have some support. Money was kept at home . . . I was always expecting an arrest and I wanted my daughter to keep the money by her, in case of emergency."

Aside from such practical measures, some reactions were purely individual, like those of a forty-five-year-old mining foreman from a city in White Russia who was described as "very anxious," in constant fear that his former life as a kulak would be uncovered. His mind was chiefly on food, and all his thoughts were directed toward assuring the nourishment of his family. He spoke mostly about eating, for "eating his fill" was for him the most important consideration. Probably the search for gratification from the most accessible sources of human pleasure has been a major response to the hard lot of Soviet daily life. Eating, drinking, and sexual activity have doubtless attained greater general esteem, along with a sense of gratitude for the mere chance to live in a complete family.

Finally, insecurity in the presence of a threatening political environment frequently draws people together, and the evidence suggests that the catastrophic experiences of Soviet life have often had the effect of strengthening the sense of comfort and unity that family members have found in each other. It may even be true that while the suffering imposed by Soviet history has destroyed many specific families, it has also strengthened the family in general. For the family seems to profit from the adversity of the individual, especially when the source of injury is clearly located "on the outside," and the political leadership can be blamed. Thus, the best data available when subjected to statistical analysis suggest that political deprivation of the family (defined operationally as the execution, disappearance, or prolonged imprisonment or exile of one or more family members other than the respondent) increases solidarity among those who remain in the family. On the other hand, deprivation of a purely economic nature seems to have the opposite effect, as if there were a tendency for family members to blame each other. Concretely, of course, the sources of the two forms of deprivation tend to merge, and both have often been laid at the door of the Soviet regime, leading to a district differentiation in the minds of many of the people between the harsh, threatening outer society and the haven of home: "At home we felt secure and safe. At home we wept, we smiled, we criticized or cursed those who made us poor and hungry."

BENEFITS OF THE REVOLUTION

Foremost in the long list of benefits of the October Revolution put forth by the party and government are major institutional innovations. Most important are economic measures, such as abolition of the private ownership of productive property, national economic planning, and an end to wage slavery, economic crises, unemployment, and the exploitation of man by man. New institutions have also appeared in the countryside, where agricultural work was organized into large-scale collective and state farms, eminently praiseworthy in official view because they facilitated the introduction of heavy machinery, scientific method, and coordination of crop assortment and growth on a mass scale. Collateral activities—scientific research and development, training of professional manpower, and even cultural affairs—are directed by plan to the maximum extent feasible. The market as a distributive mechanism is derided and its function restricted as far as possible.

It is claimed that these structural changes have made it possible to organize Soviet society more rationally, that they afford Soviet man a heretofore unavailable opportunity to bring the basic forces influencing his life into conscious control and will ultimately provide him with material abundance, social security, cultural and leisure opportunities—in fact, the chance for all-around self-development of his personality. As the political orators like to say, summing things up with a flourish, the October Revolution and the victory of socialism in the USSR have ushered in a new era in the history of mankind.

These changes and associated claims are of the greatest importance in that they constitute a kind of institutional return to the people, payment extended, in exchange for the sacrifices exacted by the Revolution, and it would be a grave error to dismiss lightly the fact that they have been and are highly valued by many Soviet citizens. Even in the face of dire Stalinist oppression the achievements of the Revolution have found their adherents. In the words of a young refugee who found Soviet life hard but nevertheless had in the main a "positive attitude towards the regime": "I thought that all the difficulties were connected with the sacrifices which were necessary for the building of socialism and that after a socialist society was constructed, life would be better." Moreover, these achievements were not only experienced as promises for the future. The young man continues: "I also felt that there was much that was positive. Even in the present life."

Analyzing the statements of refugees and current members of Soviet society, there seem to be three general classes of benefits that must be taken into account: in general terms, sympathetic identification with communism, status advances, and increments of social justice and security made generally available to the population at large. The first, alluded to above, involves a sense of largesse derived from identification with the accomplishments of the regime. One recent case can be seen as a kind of rehabilitation of pride, corresponding with the end of the cult of the individual. A man, forty-five-years-old, a "minor clerk in an unimportant job" in Moscow, married, father of three children, "just a plain man, neither a saint nor a scoundrel" according to his brother, "decided to join the party after the Twentieth Congress. He told me then that though he wasn't one of those who had destroyed socialism, he would be glad to try and repair it, working together with other people like himself." [1]

Behind such sentiments lie three considerations. Along with a general approval of the desirability of socialism comes the very considerable success of the regime in meeting both the tasks it has imposed upon itself, as in its economic growth, and the challenges visited upon it from without, as in the war with the Axis; to these correspond the readiness to identify with the system and to share the glory of prodigious achievement. The third consideration is a composite of the two preceding, involving the future prospects of the Soviet system and producing a sense of inevitable triumph, in which the party, the government, the people, and their system are "in step with history." This general feeling of confidence and security has been termed by one observer "optimism about progress"—"a trust in the overall development of society, a conception of unceasing, further economic expansion, a sense of power, and national pride."

The sense of certainty and inevitability, seemingly so foreign to the Western world today, is most striking. The author of a recent account asserts that all his informants from the Soviet working class considered the present system not only stable but final, the most common argument being this one: "The USSR came into being as the result of the operation of historical law, therefore nothing can overthrow it. Marx, Lenin and Stalin predicted a long time in advance what would happen, and this always did happen."

The second class of benefit, status advances, is more concrete. The overthrow of the upper classes, the scattering of the kulaks, and similar practices, while probably never equally balanced, found at least some compensation on the scales of justice in terms of advantages gained by other groups. This was, after all, a revolution in the name of the oppressed masses and seemed to many of them to be just that. In its earliest years Soviet history brought status gratuities to the urban proletarians and to the poor peasantry. Because of their spotless class backgrounds, they benefited from a general opening of doors previously closed to them.

---

[1] From *The Future Is Ours, Comrade,* by Joseph Novak. Copyright © 1960 by Doubleday & Company, Inc. Reprinted by permission of the publisher.

In the words of a twenty-six-year-old chauffeur from a peasant background: "Among my relatives . . . there were not any kulaks. My father had fourteen brothers. All were alive . . . Under the tsar they lived very badly. When the Soviet power came, most of them joined the party, more than half . . . They lived in the city as workers under the Soviet power. Because the Soviet power gives life only to those who talk well, who propagandize, and who lived badly under the tsar."

A political career beckoned to those with clean background, and for many brought rapid mobility and psychic satisfaction. A thirty-three-year-old army officer of proletarian background tells of his own life: "Once I had been in the Komsomol, it was the natural thing to move ahead into the party. Besides that, entrance into the party was considered a great honor. The government was showing you its trust and that it considered you to be a man capable of bearing responsibilities and of being an example to other people." Here gratuitous status advance begins to merge with advance through achievement. The latter form has come increasingly to predominate as the Revolution has aged and Soviet society stabilized.

Even today, however, the shortest route to social and economic advance is probably the political, and in a totalitarian system orthodox political attitudes continue to play a major role. In words calling to mind the power of positive thinking, a Soviet citizen explains that "Here, a man can reach the highest positions in society if he is always positive. And he can easily be positive by active work in social and political organizations." At the same time, economic growth and an expanding labor market played a strong supporting role in the rise of the status level of the Soviet masses; here I shall focus mainly upon the politically significant side of status advance.

As a result of the Revolution, the status of ethnic minorities advanced in relation to the Slavic majority, and women were declared equally eligible to participate fully in the life of the new society and to receive a greater share of its rewards. A young woman tells of her desire to exercise her new prerogative to study for an occupational career: "You see, in the Soviet Union that is the way they brought us up. At meetings and at lectures they constantly told us that women must be fully equal with men, that women can be flyers and naval engineers and anything that men can be."

The third category of benefit is perhaps the most important, for it corresponds rather closely with desires held by peoples everywhere. Into this category fall institutional forms according social justice, well-being, and security to the people—all that is signified by the term welfare state. Clear examples are the generous provision to the people of medical services, the growth of the Soviet educational system, and the development of new facilities and opportunities for pregnant women, the aged, young children, and other categories of the population needing special support. Such benefits must be further analyzed according to both the extent to which they satisfy universal human aspirations and the extent to which they are perceived as accomplishing this task in a fashion morally superior to that of the Tsarist past or the capitalist outside world.

The valuation of distributive justice seems quite prominent in the informal culture. Indeed, an early and continuing source of support for the Revolution has been found in the degree to which privilege, opportunity, material wealth—all the things to which the general label "benefit" has been attached—have been distributed impartially, irrespective of ascribed social characteristics. Immediately after the Revolution this source of gratification was perhaps at its strongest. In the words of a woman who compares the old times with the new, in the simplest possible terms: "In the old times a peasant could not get a higher education. Now he could and he could also do some better work. People were very happy to see that the old families now had to go to work just as they did."

It is quite likely that most Soviet citizens still think of their country as the world's leader in defending the poor and oppressed, and as the place where ethical universalism finds its highest expression and staunchest defense. Such thoughts reflect propaganda as well as reality, for the Soviet leaders lose no opportunity to publicize the equal status of Soviet women, the privileges of Soviet children, the absence of racial discrimination and animosity, and the brotherly solidarity of all Soviet citizens. Indeed, the last party Program claims that equal distribution of the total social product increases in and by itself the resulting total utility. In the future, "Soviet people will be more prosperous than people in the developed capitalist countries even if average incomes will be equal, because in the Soviet Union the national income is distributed fairly in the interest of all the members of society." Probably this unproven claim is accepted on faith by the great majority of the population.

The dispensation of benefits has affected the Soviet family primarily by accelerating the process of adaptation inside the family to the changing circumstances of the outer society. Such a link applies, of course, most strongly in the case of those families whose members profited most and who expressed in their own lives the acceptance of the Revolution. Both the connection between societal changes and family change and the role of status advance as the activating mechanism are expressed in the words of a young man: "My father, of course, was very much in favor of my joining the party. He felt we were living like the new family of a new society."

ADAPTING TO SOVIET REALITY

The foregoing may serve to suggest two prominent goals of the Soviet family: to avoid catastrophe, or to survive or diminish it if it could not be avoided, and to profit, so far as possible, by the more attractive features of the new society. Both adaptations have been strongly and explicitly held and in combination have fed back into the larger society behavior that adds up to a profound change in the nature of that social system.

The point is well-illustrated in terms of ideological orientations. Virtually all sources agree that the past forty years have seen a decline in religious faith in Russia. No statistics on the distribution of religious believers have been made public since 1937, but at that time Iaroslavski, head of the League of Militant Atheists, estimated that about two-thirds of the urban adult population over sixteen called themselves atheists, and that in the countryside from one-half to two-thirds were believers. A recent estimate by a prominent Western observer has it that at least half of the Soviet population has broken with religion, and the best study of the question with refugee opinion data revealed a striking generational trend toward the weakening of religious faith.

A trend of opposite direction has been observed in respect to the Revolution and the Soviet regime, but acceptance of the Soviet system, while generally upward, has had sharp declines. It has probably taken the form of a W-shaped curve, with the high points in the 1920s, during World War II, and at the present moment. The feet of the W are mired in the forced collectivization, purges, and forced labor camps of the 1930s and in the postwar years, when Stalinist policy tightened things up again after the wartime relaxation.

These, of course, are very broad trends and, while important, they obscure almost as much as they reveal about Soviet family life. The avoidance of catastrophe and the acceptance of the various benefits offered have not been equally possible for all. If members of some families felt they were marching in step with the times, others felt like the auto mechanic whose father had been a kulak—"We were different from others because we lived in eternal fear because we were considered to be of an alien class"—or like the Jewish couple of more recent times who were sensitive to an increase in Soviet antisemitism. They, reports the observer, "were very close to each other, in part because of the feeling they shared of constant threat from society."

The social and cultural milieu itself has played a significant role in determining variations in change inside the family. In the villages, for instance, the old faith is still alive. In Viriatino in the mid-1950s, almost every peasant hut had its icon, and the words of a peasant woman, "I don't want people to come into our home and find no icon," suggest that its display was socially mandatory. In the cities icons can also be found, but the atmosphere is much less receptive. A young worker reports quite differently: "My mother was a very devout woman, but religion was forbidden in the Soviet Union. My mother kept an icon in one corner. There were many intelligentsia living around us and of all of our neighbors, none of them had any icons, and they- laughed at us for having one . . . I do not have any religious feelings. I saw how the neighbors were laughing at us."

Contrasting cultural predispositions and social milieus add to the differentiating force of the direct actions of the regime itself. The result is a rich proliferation of spiritually distinctive families. One person says, "My family was very religious . . . My father went out of his way to be religious," while another explains that in his family "the question of religion, as of something archaic, did not come up," and in still another the parents are vigorous "practicing atheists." The same can be said for political attitudes and other indicators of the family's cultural atmosphere.

Alongside the trend of change itself, then, must be ranged an extended array of different types and patterns in family life, many of which suggest change in process or show signs of the strain associated with rapid change. The diversity exists in several forms. First there are many families with abnormal membership composition. Occasionally, the Soviet family approaches a caricature, as in those rare cases when the children are quickly after birth turned over with no regret to the state, or when there is a remarkable amount of make-do involved. A Ukrainian, reared as a peasant, tells how his wife, father, and two youngest children died in a famine, leaving him with an eleven-year-old daughter. He was an unskilled laborer, and took his daughter to live with him in a barracks filled with men of similar occupation: "Well, I just asked the manager of the barracks to give me a bed in the corner, so she slept in the upper bunk and I slept down. I hung up a sheet between the corner and the rest of the barracks . . . A daughter with no mother. What should I do with her? . . . They proposed sending her to a children's home. But it was terrible there. There was no order . . . so a comrade said to me, 'It is better if your daughter stays with you. We will help a little bit and it will be better than sending her away.' . . . (Was it bad for the child to be with a lot of men?) Yes. Very. They swear a lot, like workers will. But there was no other way out. I was absolutely unable to get a family home." Secondly, since religion does not disappear all at once, but in a lingering and dissociated way, there are a great number of families in which religious orientations, images, and practice occur in various muted and distorted forms. Thus, Soviet religion today often seems quite restricted, episodic, and makeshift. Although refugees often reported religious faith among the members of their families, accompanying qualification nullified the effect of their statements. A young coal miner says of his mother, a collective farmer: "My mother believed in God and she never said anything against Him, but she had not completely surrendered to the priests." A restricted quality is also suggested by the extent to which the higher status groups fail to allow their religious orientations to exert influence on other aspects of their lives. In white-collar and intelligentsia families, for instance, attitudes toward religion seem to bear little relation to "attitude expressed inside the family toward the Soviet regime," whereas in worker and peasant families, where religious faith is generally stronger, the association between a positive attitude toward religion and disapproval of the Soviet regime is quite pronounced. The acme of such "religion-in-transition" is reached in the cases of party members who secretly baptize their babies at night, or in the peasant families where the portrait of Lenin and the holy icon stare at each other from opposite corners of the room. A peasant woman explains: "Lenin is for this life; the saints are for the other. Lenin gave bread to the people, but only God can give peace."

The significance of religion is always greatest at the time of the major events of family life. Although there is no church in the village of Viriatino, virtually all infants are baptized and the dead given Christian burial. Indeed, the investigators concluded that one of the main reasons religion continues in the village is the service it renders to these "great moments" of family life. They were especially impressed with the "extraordinary vitality" of rites connected with death.

On the other hand, the Soviet ethnographers were intensely interested in ritual behavior the meaning of which none of the peasant villagers could explain, behavior that seemed to have little religious significance, patterns that were followed "just by habit." A typical example, in the words of a villager: "We consider faith outmoded. But we observe the [religious] holidays with food and rest from work." The makeshift quality of Soviet religious practice is seen most clearly in the patterns resulting from the shortage of facilities for worship and ceremony. A bookkeeper, of peasant origin but urban residence, tells of a substitution: "I was compelled to have my children baptized by a Lutheran priest even though I myself am Orthodox. This was more convenient since there wasn't any Orthodox priest around."

Similar admixtures can be found in political sentiments: both belief and doubt, partial and episodic enthusiasms, formal patriotism with substance, and loyalty in the midst of anti-Soviet anecdotes—in short, all the muted tones, combinations, and contradictory elements found in religion. Analogous to the icon of the religious family are the political portrait, the statuette of Lenin, or the writings of Marx in the pro-Soviet family. And corresponding to the view that religion is archaic, with the occasional Sunday afternoon visit to the museum of science and atheism, is the phenomenon of political alienation, and the anti-Soviet anecdote, that peculiarly effective device by which the people hold at a distance the absolute demands of totalitarian rule. Political opinions are a more private concern of the family than are religious beliefs. They ordinarily are kept from neighbors, for they expose to danger, and even within the circle of close relatives political attitudes are not to be taken lightly. A young woman whose father was a Kiev physician and whose uncle was an army officer and a staunch partisan of the regime observed: "We could never tell an anti-Soviet anecdote in his presence. Not that he would report on you, but simply that he would tell you you were not politically conscious enough."

Close examination reveals occasional scraps of evidence to suggest that political faith may be suffering some of the same transmutations that can be observed in Soviet religious life. For example, one man attempts to explain why, like so many of his fellow Soviet citizens, he has faith in Soviet justice even though he is also very conscious of its defects: "A man is only a man. He must have faith in the justice of the authority under which he belongs. If we doubt this, what is left? How will we live without this faith? Do you really believe that faith in injustice helps you in life better than faith in justice, even if you don't think everything is right and proper?"

These various combinations and contrasts permeate the family, and indeed all of Soviet life, for they reflect a poorly integrated social system. Outer social and cultural developments have been so rapid and often so coercive in their effect that the different parts of less complex units and structures have changed at markedly differing rates. This is true not only of the family, but also of informal groups and cliques and of the individual personality.

One need not search far to find dissonant elements in the psyche of Soviet man. The individual's reaction to the Soviet scene frequently has been political disaffection, certainly a normal response to much of what has occurred but one which has also been a liability, which has brought various subsequent mechanisms of coping and defense into play. One example can be seen in the life of a thirty-seven-year-old widow who was living with two children and her mother and working as a construction engineer. This attractive, energetic woman, a party member, had "critical feelings": "Since she was conscious of her critical feelings, she lived in constant fear of the MVD and forced herself to exhibit the utmost reserve in her dealings with all persons . . . This fear also led her to assume a certain mask; she was a party member, zealous and emphatically interested . . . She was also a very hard worker in her job, [but] . . . She felt insecure in the city, and also in her party position."

Similar signs of rapid, stressful change in the larger society can be seen in informal social groups, the clique of friends and circle of acquaintances. One of the most alarming aspects of social life under Stalin was the extent to which people could not trust each other, together with the general feeling that such relations, which are particularly appreciated in the traditional culture, had been spoiled. Of course, the fact that different persons held varying political viewpoints accounts for some aspects of the problem, but more important was the degree to which Stalin's police were "secret." Too frequently the *seksot,* the "secret worker" or informer, was used as a means of political control, and the threat of betrayal for a chance remark supported the view that friendship was somewhat dangerous. The feeling that one had to be very careful about new acquaintances also led to a Soviet brand of "gallows humor": A man telephoned the local secret police representative. "My wife and I want to give a party tomorrow night and thought we should notify you in case you want to send someone out." The official asked, "How many will be there?" The man answered, "Fifteen." The official replied, "Don't worry. In any group that large there's bound to be someone working for us."

The nature of informal organizations in Soviet social life reveals much about what has happened in the country's history. One refugee respondent perhaps summed it up more accurately than he realized when he compared two different types of social stratification. Things really were not too different after the Revolution, he felt, for "In Tsarist times there were the rich and the poor; under the Soviet power there were the party members and the nonparty members."

Social stratification in the USSR has always had a strong economic basis, but it is also important to remember the extent to which it has a political foundation and to realize that political stratification is a keen reflection of rapid societal change, expressing the diversity of fortunes associated with it. In the Soviet political class system there have always been two extremes. At the top the most highly placed party families form a social stratum whose subculture is reinforced by social distance from the rest of the people. A Soviet common man, a fifty-year-old Ukrainian supply worker, sees the life of party members and their families this way: "They got full legal and actual rights to rule the country. As a mode of life they have to keep apart from the rest in order not to compromise the party. They must be loyal instruments of the party policy. They have to live in a circle of their own. They form a caste behind a little iron curtain."

At the other extreme is the milieu of the déclassés, the dispossessed, and the alienated. Between the two, the political middle class is comprised of the masses who are ambivalent, apathetic, perhaps too tired, too fearful, or too busy to think. A working-class woman tells of her attitude toward the Soviet system: "I gave no special thought to such questions in the USSR and did not concern myself with it. I only knew that it was necessary and that I had to work."

Political beliefs also function as a poignant indicator of changing times inside the family. Typically, for example, children are less religious and more admiring of the Soviet regime than their parents, and men more than their wives. The following description, offered by the young army officer quoted earlier, was probably quite characteristic inside many Soviet families for some time after the Revolution: "[My father] brought me up in the Soviet spirit, teaching me that the Soviet Union had opened the road to opportunity for the Russian worker and peasant . . . My mother on the other side was a religious woman, and so was always against the regime."

In brief, a look inside the family reveals the same marks of rapid change that can also be found in other parts of Soviet society and in the Soviet personality structure. There are indications that accepting the new and forsaking the old has not been easy: the changes in religious orientation, political attitude, and so on which have taken place have produced a surprising proliferation of contrasting types and poorly integrated structures. Such developments have tended to destroy guidelines for the individual's conduct of life, and Soviet informal social life sometimes can be not too inaccurately characterized by the phrasing of a former participant—"a consciously created chaos." The challenging fact is that underneath the totalitarian façade of order and control lies a quite different world.

9. THE CULT OF YOUTH

The demographic revolution of this century is such that more persons under twenty-five years of age are alive today than ever before. The renewal of the European population since the end of the Second World War has been an extraordinary phenomenon which has altered the entire composition of society. Nor is this a matter of sheer numbers. The attitudes and values of youth have become a political factor with which the ruling elders of every European nation must contend. To contain the energy and to harness the potential of young people has required that their ambitions be honored, not just guided. For this reason it seems appropriate to identify the cult of youth as one of the characteristic features of contemporary European society.

Walter Z. Laqueur probes the background of the German youth movement (*Wandervogel*), explaining why conditions in Germany were somewhat different from elsewhere and how the First World War came as an exhilarating shock to the young. Then intensity of the war years was followed by a pervading sense of disillusionment in Germany and, along with it, a desire to change the "mechanistic society" which seemed so antithetical to the ideals of youth. In these terms Laqueur defines the origins of the Hitler Youth which placed its trust in the Third Reich.

Paul Wilkinson explores the parallel in England, hoping thereby to show why it was that the youth organizations there remained relatively apolitical in orientation. He narrates how the English Scouts were "mobilized" in the First World War and how their learned skills were put to use in the war effort. But, as in Germany, a certain disillusionment was not long in coming. The English youth leader, Robert Baden-Powell, was nonetheless able to hold scouting securely within the political consensus and to maintain an idealistic and indeed chivalric ethic. Other youth groups came and went, each with its special appeal. Yet the Boy Scouts remained the quintessential English form of youth organization until the Second World War.

John Ardagh portrays the postwar change of climate in France where there are now twice as many youths as in the final years of the Third Republic. After 1945 a whole new generation arrived, seemingly with their own dress, moral values, and life style. But Ardagh suggests that much of the innovating wind has gone out of their sails. Instead, France was swept in the 1960s by an emotional (and commercial) movement known as *Salut les Copains* which generated at most a kind of subculture composed of rock, slang, and Coca-Cola. If Ardagh is correct, most young French radicals continued to be guided by a certain formalism taught in the schools and by basically bourgeois values inherited from the home. In his view, the wild spectacle of student revolt in May 1968 was therefore largely episodic and did not signal a fundamental change.

Ralph T. Fischer, Jr., attempts to define the model which Soviet youths have been encouraged to emulate. The programmatic ideals expounded by the official communist youth organization (*Komsomol*) sound not dissimilar to those of the Boy Scouts insofar as one finds the same exhortations to courage, resourcefulness, honor, and love of country. But there is also, as once in the Hitler Youth, a frank political orientation tinged with xenophobia: hence the themes of "ideological purity" and "vigilance." Fischer claims that the Soviet goal has indeed been to produce a generation of "eager robots," even though some allowance has necessarily been made for "small groups" which chafe at party discipline from time to time. Thus the reality of youth, in the Soviet Union as elsewhere, does not always conform perfectly to the expectations of elders.

Galia Golan denies that the liberal reform movement in Czechoslovakia, abruptly throttled by the invasion of Warsaw Pact troops in 1968, was the product of a generational conflict. Yet her article demonstrates that much of the impetus to reform did, in fact, originate with youth groups or youthful critics of the Czech communist party. The problem which authorities faced was not so much a generation gap as the potential union of youthful dissidents with their liberal elders. The champion of such an alignment was Alexander Dubcek, the man who eventually led the reform wing and who was, with many of his colleagues young and old, purged in the wake of the invasion. Thereafter the only alternatives—short of the desperate act of self-immolation by Jan Palach—were passive resistance or dutiful accommodation.

It is more than a truism to say that the future of European society depends on its youth. At no other time in history has their number been so immense or their opinion so solicited. Nor have their possibilities ever seemed so bright. Europe has more to offer the young in terms of material prosperity and social mobility than at any time in the past. Whether the opportunity will be seized to create a more generous and more equitable society, no one can tell. The jury is still out and Everyman must judge for himself.

WALTER Z. LAQUEUR

Young Germany

ROMANTIC PRELUDE

. . . Europe had made unprecedented economic and technical progress between 1860 and 1900. While standards of living rose faster than ever before, not all classes benefited equally and strong social tensions were generated. But in most European countries the working class could view with satisfaction and confidence the constant growth of its political influence, as well as its economic and social achievements. There had been no major war in Europe for several decades, and there was every reason to expect another long period of peace, progress, and general well-being.

But serious symptoms of cultural decline were not lacking in that world of growing plenty and rapid technical advance. It would be interesting to speculate about the psychological sources of the discontent, the sense of emptiness and general dissatisfaction that found its expression in a *fin de siècle* mood even in a country like Russia, which faced more urgent political and social problems than the West. Why did so many people throughout Europe welcome the outbreak of the First World War as a "liberation?" Such an investigation might show that man has often found it difficult to suffer serenely a prolonged period of tranquillity

From *Young Germany: A History of the German Youth Movement,* by Walter Z. Laqueur. © 1962 by Walter Z. Laqueur. Published by Basic Books, Inc., Publishers, New York. Also by permission of C. A. Watts & Co. Ltd., London.

and well-being. When no major problems exist, minor problems tend to take their place. We tend to look back on the world that ended in 1914 with a nostalgia mixed with a certain amusement. It is true that the great crisis of 1900 seems somewhat unreal, if not artificial, in comparison with the problems of the twenties and thirties. But for those who lived then, the cultural crisis was real enough; it turned some towards socialism, others towards an attitude of aristocratic disdain of the masses and hostility to bourgeois society and its culture or lack of culture. Politically, this rejection of society and its values could lead to either left- or right-wing extremist solutions. . . . The German youth movement was an unpolitical form of opposition to a civilization that had little to offer the young generation, a protest against its lack of vitality, warmth, emotion, and ideals.

The angry young men of 1900 were found among the more articulate sections of the younger generation throughout Europe. Some developed a new cult of youth in an attempt to bring fresh air into the stale and musty atmosphere surrounding their elders. The writings of "Agathon" in France, and of the early Italian Futurists, are evidence of this trend. The *Wandervogel* was one of the specific German forms of protest. It was and remained unique in many respects, since Germany's situation in Europe was different from that of other countries. The triumph of liberalism in France, Britain, and the United States had never extended to Germany; the "bourgeois revolution" had never been completed; the middle classes were not fully emancipated. Capitalism had indeed prevailed in Germany and industrialization had made rapid strides, but in many sections of the population a medieval, antiliberal, and anticapitalist mentality survived because the people themselves had not taken a prominent and active part in these developments, which had frequently been initiated from above or from outside. . . .

THE FIRST WORLD WAR

A prodigious wave of enthusiasm swept over German youth at the outbreak of the world war in 1914. "We had not known the reason of our existence . . . youth had seemed to us a burden and a curse," wrote Ina Seidel, in her poem ending: "O holy fortune, to be young today!" [1] Those who had previously found no dominant aim in life now felt that they knew the meaning of their destiny—total identification with the Fatherland in its hour of uttermost peril. "How stupid it is to ask what is our attitude to the war! Anyone who finds time to think about it shows

[1] *Führerzeitung,* November 1914, p. 205.

that he does not know how to feel with his people, and is shutting himself up against the blessing that fate intended for him." [2] If any explanations were needed, they were to be found in the first appeal by the *Wandervogel* leader Neuendorff; the war had come "because the other peoples could no longer hold their own in peaceful competition with German power, German industry, and German honesty . . . they perfidiously sought to defeat Germany by brute force and weight of numbers." [3]

But German youth had been hearing for years past how jealous enemies and rivals begrudged the German people its rightful place in the sun. When the storm broke, it should not have found them altogether unprepared. Yet it struck them like a bolt from the blue, for despite all the warnings and the mounting tensions of the preceding months, there had been a general, persistent belief that everything would somehow at the last moment be settled.

To the members of the youth movement, war was so incredible as to seem unreal; their world had been one of carefree rambling, dreaming and singing—a joyful world of utter peace, in the greatest contrast imaginable to the ravages of war. To many, as to Rupert Brooke in England, the sense of liberation, of an awakening out of torpor, was the most memorable experience of those days of high patriotic emotion. But this was a reaction against spiritual emptiness and material frustrations that was perhaps more acutely felt by those outside the *Wandervogel* than by its members. For the youth movement was one of active idealism, in less need of an external moral stimulus; at any rate, it was so in the Reich, though conditions in Austria and the German regions of Bohemia were different. There, the possibility if not the desirability of a world war had been loudly discussed for years past.[4] The youth movement in those parts had also been much more involved in politics; more than once it had been said at their conventions that they were fighting a losing battle against Slavonic encroachment. Many of them seemed to think that the only way to stem this tide was a victorious war in alliance with Germany, leading to the eventual emergence of a *Grossdeutschland* in which foreign elements would be put in their place.

Many group leaders were called up in the very first days of the war, others volunteered, and the girls put themselves at the disposal of the Red Cross. Some of the younger ones feared that the war would be over before they saw any fighting, and a few even tried to reach the front line without having enlisted. Meanwhile groups of younger boys and girls went to the countryside to help with the harvest. Regular youth

---

[2] *Wandervogel*, I. Kriegsheft, p. 259.
[3] *Ibid.*, p. 257.
[4] Luise Fick, *op. cit.*, deals at considerable length with conditions in Austria before 1914.

movement activities, needless to say, were disrupted for many months: some members, assuming that the war would soon be over, argued that no particular effort should be made to resume normal activities, that all energies should be directed towards the war effort. Others thought the time had come for a *rapprochement* with other youth organizations such as the Boy Scouts and the para-military *Jung Deutschland*.

As the months went by, however, and a certain wartime normality was established, the meetings and outings were resumed, albeit on a smaller scale. Girls frequently took over the leadership of groups, and after a few months were reinforced by soldiers who had been wounded and invalided out of the army.

In 1915 the youth movement resumed its longer expeditions despite the strict rationing of food and clothes; there were now enough prisoners of war to help with the harvest.[5]

One of the most important tasks was to maintain contact with those serving in the forces. The soldiers related their adventures and impressions in long letters that often were published, while the groups sent greetings and parcels to their leaders and members on the field of battle. Gradually an organizational network was established in the various army units; there were unofficial clearing houses, and eventually the *Wandervogel* soldiers even had their own circular letters and little newspapers on both the Western and Eastern fronts, and in other major theaters of war. Two hundred of them held a convention in Brussels at Whitsuntide 1917, and there were other, smaller meetings elsewhere.[6]

How did the individual *Wandervogel* soldier face up to the great patriotic challenge? In the first immense wave of national enthusiasm all petty quarrels were forgotten; all that was best in that generation was demonstrated: unselfishness, comradeship, the readiness to sacrifice. They had not the slightest doubt of the rightness of the cause they were fighting for, and the first great victories appeared to promise an early triumph. "We are chasing the enemy like a herd of sheep," —Johannnes Ilgen wrote on 2 September 1914 from Chalons-sur-Marne. But the German advance was soon halted, and the writer of the letter was killed the very same month; what then followed was grim-visaged war unrelieved by any great advances or triumphs, or by the hope of an early victory. At Langemarck in November 1914 thousands of German students, including many members of the youth movement, stormed the enemy lines and were mown down in swathes, singing "Deutschland, Deutschland über Alles;" the lists

---

[5] *Wandervogel,* 5, 1916, p. 98.
[6] There is a vast literature on the *Feldwandervogel*. See for instance *Rundbrief* on the Eastern front; R. F. Heiling, *Feldpachanten* (Glogau, 1918); *Zwiespruch,* the *Wandervogel* organ at the Western front; 'Cölner;' 'Der Feldwandervogel' in *Wandervogel,* 12, 1929; J. H. Mitgau, 'Der Feldwandervogel,' in Will Vesper (ed.) *Deutsche Jugend,* Berlin, 1934.

of "Fallen for their country" became longer and longer. Different under-tones began to appear in letters from the front: "The war is not beautiful. I would thank God if it were over today, and if I could return home un-scathed." [7] It was not only the war itself that was ugly; it soon transpired that the *Wandervogel* soldier had often to face serious difficulties within his own unit. After the first flush of excitement had ebbed away, there was not much left of the comradeship and understanding that he had expected. Max Sidow had been one of the most enthusiastic during the first weeks of war,[8] but five years later he wrote about the *Fronterlebnis* in a very dif-ferent vein: "One was alone among the many. The uneducated hated every cultured soldier. Every conversation began and ended with ob-scenities." [9] Another wrote of the "sad days and the heavy nights among vulgar and mean people, the first terrible impressions, and the great ideas of fatherland and world history that made their impact only much later—and sometimes not at all." [10] What had caused the shock and disappoint-ment? Rudolf Piper thought the assumption that the youth movement had really come to know "country and people" during its perambulations had been no more than an illusion. On such excursions they had seen only the best side of their people. Even the provincial inns, for instance, had been outside their experience; hence their "terrible disappointmnt in the army barracks." [11] Robert Oelbermann, an army lieutenant and future leader of the *Nerothers,* said that "horror seized us. Were we human beings? Or animals? Duty alone upheld many of us until the end." [12]

In the early days of the war it had been commonly assumed that its moral effect would be that of a great purifying fire; it would destroy every-thing that was rotten and decaying. But gradually it became apparent that the war was bound also to destroy many real values and achievements; that it was bringing in its train a general brutalization which could be nothing less than an immense cultural and moral catastrophe.[13] . . .

THE "WHITE KNIGHT"

For a long time the Boy Scouts had been regarded as the poor relations of the youth movement: led by adults, and specializing as they did in para-military education, they were somewhere on the periphery, outside the main stream of the movement. In contrast to the *Wandervogel,* the Scouts were not strictly selective in the recruitment of their members.

[7] *Wandervogel,* 11/12, 1914, p. 284.
[8] See his poem in *Wandervogel,* 9/10, 1914, p. 259.
[9] *Krieg, Revolution und Friedeutsche Zukunft* (Hamburg, 1919), p. 27.
[10] *Wandervogel,* 2, 1916, p. 35.
[11] *Ibid.,* 10/11, 1916, p. 211.
[12] *Ibid.,* 6, 1919, p. 156.
[13] See for instance Johannes Müller in *Grüne Blätter,* quoted in *Freideutsche Jugend,* 7, 1917, pp. 223–4.

After the war the Scouts underwent a minor revolution analogous to that which occurred elsewhere in the movement; the adult leaders were deposed and younger members took over. But, unlike what happened in the *Wandervogel,* their revolution did not stop there. New forms of activity and new ideas were developed which were to have a decisive influence upon the whole German youth movement and, in effect, to shape the whole course of its development between 1919 and 1933.

At their first postwar meeting in Schloss Prunn there were discussions very much like those that went on among the *Freideutsche* and the *Wandervogel:* should the Scouts become the organization of an élite, or should they on the contrary try not to lose contact with the masses? Was a nationalist orientation to prevail, or should internationalist views be given wider currency? What about the place of religion in the life of the *Bund?*

Deliberations went on for some time, and in 1920 the reformers seceded and founded their own group, the *Neupfadfinder,* led by the so-called Regensburg circle (F. L. Habbel, Ludwig Voggenreiter and others) and a young parson from Berlin, Martin Voelkel. The Regensburg leaders were down to earth, mainly interested in education, and they provided some new ideas about "tribal education"—the tribe (Stamm) was to replace the group as the basic unit. Voelkel, the ideologist, provided the notions of the "Reich," the "knight," and the "holy grail," with their specific meaning for the young. But at the very center was the idea, and the reality, of the *Bund.* The former scouts found their way into the youth movement; it could be said that they took it over during an interregnum, and under their influence it was to change its character.

In its second, *bündische* phase the youth movement became much more ambitious. The very name suggested a new trend. Whereas rambling had been the central activity before the First World War, in the new era it became only one of several activities, and not necessarily the most important. The *Wandervogel* had been critical of society, but had never assumed that it had a mission to change the world. This was just what the *Bünde* tried to do; it was a romantic attempt to cope with realities. In the *Wandervogel* the group had been a comparatively loose association; the emphasis had been on the individual and his own development; there had been no specific plans for the future of its members, who were expected gradually to grow out of the youth movement. People belonged to a group because they liked it, there was little reflection and no sense of a purpose beyond this activity. But in the *Bund* created by Voelkel and his friends the collective mattered more than the individual; there was stricter discipline, and it was envisaged as an all-embracing bond making total demands upon the individual [14] for the rest of his life. One belonged to a group to serve a cause, and under the surface of all its activities there were magic formulas, or implied hints pointing to the cause itself. After an initial struggle girls had entered the *Wandervogel,* and although all its leading figures were male, it is impossible to think of the *Wandervogel* as exclusively a boys' movement. The *Bund*, on the other hand, had no mixed groups; it was a male society *par excellence*. Illogically enough, many of the *Bünde* included separate girls' groups, but these were merely subsidiaries and played no great part in the movement; there was too much talk about fighting, struggle, and battle, and it was difficult to imagine a female knight. Generally speaking the lyric romanticism of the *Wandervogel* had been replaced by something tougher—a romanticism that had been decisively affected by the First World War. Freedom and unrestraint had been sacrificed to duty and service in voluntary subjection to a greater whole. Whereas the ideal figure of the *Wandervogel* had been the itinerant scholar, an anarchist if not a democrat, the aristocratic tendencies of the *Bünde* were reflected, not only in the exemplary image of the knight who set himself a rule of conduct in deliberate contrast to that of the multitude, but also in a strict hierarchy within the *Bund*.[15] . . .

PANORAMA OF THE BÜNDE

It is impossible to generalize about associations so conspicuously devoid of a common denominator. Some of the *Bünde* pursued definite purposes of a political, social, or religious character; others were, or at any rate aspired to be, purposeless, free of any tie to the world of adults, spontaneous, united only by the bond of comradeship. A *Bund* might be favored simply as an educational means or as the form of organization most attractive to youth itself and most efficacious from the point of view of its sponsors—the churches, for instance. Others considered the *Bund* to be an end in itself; some thought of it in terms of a life-brotherhood, while others took a more realistic view of the limitations of the youth movement and understood that the *Bund*, like youth itself, was only a transitional stage.

All this was based on the tacit assumption that life in a group, in intimate association, was vastly preferable to life in interest-motivated, atomistic, impersonal society.[16] The *Bünde*, and the youth movement in general, thought that the group was a deeper, more immediate and organic way of living together than that provided by "mechanistic society." Such views

---

[14] Including, according to their draft constitution, the duty to obtain the leadership's consent to marry. The constitution remained a dead letter.

[15] These observations refer mainly to the first heralds of the *Bund*, the *Neupfadfinder*. There was a variety of form and content throughout the youth movement, and a more realistic approach generally prevailed in the late twenties, but there was hardly a single group that was not affected to some extent by early *bündische* ideology.

[16] The youth movement was influenced by the school of German sociologists that made the famous division between *Gesellschaft* (society) and *Gemeinschaft* (com-

were very common, and not seriously challenged, either in the youth movement or in German sociology at the time, but since then they have come in for serious criticism.[17]

The youth movement wanted, like Rousseau, to return to nature, to enter into a life free from the restraints of civilization, warmer, more vital and more spontaneous. To justify this aspiration, it unduly idealized primitive society, completely unaware that it is in fact hag-ridden by fears and taboos, and anything but free. Equally unfounded was the assumption that human beings in groups were more sincere and spontaneous than as individuals; for is it not precisely within a group that people learn to adopt mask-like patterns and attitudes? To think and act as exclusively in terms of group and community as the youth movement tried to do is an impossible undertaking, an attempt to cheat the devil out of his share in this world.[18]

This is legitimate criticism, for the youth movement not only committed excesses, especially during its *bündische* period; there was something mistaken in its basic approach. The mistake of most of the *Bünde* was that they wanted to remedy the discontents of modern society by reverting to the irrecoverable past, instead of seeking by trial and error for new forms of life within modern civilization. For that purpose, the group itself was neutral, neither good nor bad. Whether people were better or worse for belonging to a group is a question impossible to answer. Whether they became more or less sincere in a group likewise depends upon such a multitude of factors as to defy generalization. Psychoanalysts, who as a rule are more interested in the individual than the group, have nevertheless come to adopt group analysis and therapy in many cases, which suggests that they do not necessarily find that people behave less sincerely in groups than as individuals. Group education has its distinct advantages; what the *Bünde* frequently failed to realize was that group life was no panacea, and no absolute value; the deification of the group (or the *Bund*) always had unfortunate results.

The *Bünde* chose to ignore sexual problems; in this respect the *Wandervogel* and the *Freideutsche,* with all their half-baked ideas on the subject, had been more mature in their attitude. The existence of exclusive boys' and girls' groups was probably a necessity during puberty, but the attempt to delay the meeting of the sexes beyond the age of seventeen—to create

---

munity). The *Bund* did not fit into the scheme since it was willed, whereas the community, in theory at least, was organic and free of any ulterior purpose. It followed that a new sociological category had to be created to accommodate the *Bund* in sociological theory.

[17] Cf. the summary of a lecture by Prof. René König in *Erkenntnis und Tat,* VI, 4, n.d. (ca. 1956), pp. 4–6.

[18] *Erkenntnis und Tat,* quoting H. Plessner.

an exclusively male *Jungmannschaft*—was doomed to failure and, in individual cases, caused or aggravated sexual maladjustments later on. What were the achievements of the *Bünde*? At their best, they did succeed in finding new and promising forms of community life. The visionaries who thought in terms of a community for life, with all-embracing demands upon the individual, were the least successful. But the less ambitious, who were aware of the limitations of the group, *Bund,* and youth movement, made steady if inconspicuous progress, turning more than one difficult corner before the general disaster overtook them. . . .

IN HITLER'S SHADOW

The Hitler Youth adopted many of the outward trappings of the youth movement, but differed from the *Bünde* in essential respects. It adopted their uniform and organizational structure (group, tribe, and *gau*); it had its banners, sang many of the movement's songs (as well as some of its own), and played war games. But whereas the primary concern of the *Bünde* was with group life and the education of individual character, the Hitler Youth was mainly a training center for future members of the S.A. or the S.S. While the *Bünde* retreated into the seclusion of woodlands, or went on long and adventurous journeys abroad, the principal task of the Hitler Youth was to impress the public by ostentatious parades through the streets of big cities. The youth movement engaged in mock fights and war games; a knife was part of the scout's equipment, but it was not to be used to wound or kill. The Hitler Youth, on the other hand, took part in frequent street fights in which weapons were freely used. Opponents were attacked and sometimes killed in these brawls, which occasioned some casualties among the Hitler Youth themselves, including the twenty-one "martyrs" of the "years of struggle." The overwhelming majority of *Bünde* members were high-school students, whereas, according to their own statistics, only twelve percent of the Hitler Youth were from secondary schools; the bulk of them were of working-class origin and many were unemployed.[19] Middle-class youth who joined Hitler's party were more likely to have belonged to the National Socialist *Schülerbund,* and some of them were group leaders in the *Jungvolk,* the junior section of the Hitler Youth for those between ten and fourteen years of age.

The leaders of the Hitler Youth were greatly irritated by what they regarded as a patronizing attitude in those circles of the *bündische* youth which professed *sympathy* with National Socialism. These sympathizers

---

[19] Günter Kaufmann, *Das kommende Deutschland* (Berlin, 1943), p. 19. There are no means of checking these figures, but there is good reason to believe that a fairly high proportion came from lower middle-class families who had been 'proletarianized' during the years of inflation and economic crisis.

were always saying that the Hitler Youth were of course doing a useful and necessary work, but that it was "not our work." [20] Other *bündische* critics even deplored the Hitler Youth's total involvement in politics and its utter submission to the party, and one of them cast doubt upon the party's dogmatic omniscience, quoting Cromwell's remark that "he who knows not whither he goes, goes furthest." [21] They accused Gruber and von Schirach of trying to destroy the *Bünde,* and blamed them for the bodily violence practiced against their members.[22] But what infuriated the Hitler Youth most of all was the calm expectation of the right-wing *Bünde* that the key positions in the coming Third Reich would be theirs by right, for had they not paved the way and trained an élite for the new dispensation?

There were leaders of the *Bünde* who went over to the Hitler Youth in the twenties; but not all of them stayed the course, and some came to grief in the Third Reich.[23]

The Hitler Youth undoubtedly had its share of misguided idealists, but the boys who were induced to join it (there were very few girls in it before 1933) had neither the makings nor the aspirations of the "ideal *bündisch* type"; it therefore attracted comparatively few of the members of the *bündisch* élite, who looked upon it as a collection of uncouth upstarts.[24] It appealed most of all to mass organizations on the fringe of the youth movement, such as the gymnasts and the Protestant youth groups. Leopold Cordier, one of the leading figures in the Protestant youth movement, estimated that in 1931 about seventy percent of the members of the "Bible Circles" were already under National Socialist influence, and an even higher figure was put forward by another Protestant observer. Many leaders of the Protestant *Bünde* attempted to resist the rising flood, but were soon swept aside, and the groups which tried to oppose it by declaring that membership of the Hitler movement and of their own confessional body were incompatible had as little success.[25]

It was National Socialism, not the Hitler Youth, that made such a powerful appeal to young Germans, above all by its activist character.[26] In vivid

[20] W. Fabricius in *Die Kommenden,* 13 December 1929.

[21] G. Rebsch, *ibid.,* 28 March 1930.

[22] W. Müller, *ibid.,* 19 July 1929.

[23] According to a National Socialist source, 400 members of the *Bünde,* and 300 former members of the Socialist and Communist youth organizations (including the former secretary of the Communist youth), joined the Hitler Youth in 1929. *N. S. Monatshefte.* 5, 1930, p. 59. These figures cannot, of course, be checked.

[24] The chief exception was the *Junabu,* some sections of which went over to Hitler in 1930.

[25] Leopold Cordier in the *Evangelische Jugendführung,* 3, 1931, p. 70; Manfred Müller, quoted in M. Priepke, *op. cit.,* p. 17.

[26] 'The *Jungmannschaft* of almost all the *Bünde* and the Protestant youth are in their majority either members of the NSDAP or its storm troops and youth sections, or about to join the party' (Werner Kindt in *Das junge Deutschland,* 12, 1932, p. 397).

contrast to the interminable discussions of the *Bünde,* elaborating ideals that were to be realized in some indefinite future, Hitler affirmed that the hour had already struck; the day of national salvation had arrived. The *Bünde* had wanted their members to understand that all the different aspects and facets of the political problem had to be studied, each from its own angle, before a political judgement could be valid and comprehensive. Commendable in itself, this relativistic approach was also their weakness, and made them an easier prey to the fanaticism and one-sidedness of National Socialism. While the *Bünde* were talking about sacrifice, their rivals were demanding, and getting, immediate action.[27] Facing the rising tide of National Socialism, more and more of the *bündische* youth feared that history would pass them by, and felt incapable of remaining inactive. The cry for political engagement awakened a profound response in such a period of disarray and desperation. It must be remembered that the middle classes were hardly less seriously hit by unemployment than the working class; everything seemed undermined by the general economic decline and the specter of academic and white-collared poverty was becoming a grim reality. Choosing Hitler was not an act of political decision, not the choice of a known program or ideology; it was simply joining a quasi-religious mass-movement as an act of faith. Rational misgivings about the relevance of Hitler's professions to the solution of Germany's real problems cannot have been entirely absent from the minds of many, but they were perfectly willing to surrender their own critical judgement. It meant abandoning democracy and freedom as impotent and discredited ideas and trusting the Führer, who would know best what to do.[28]

[27] For a critique of the relativism of the *Bünde's* thinking as the source of their weakness in confrontation with National Socialism, see G. Rebsch, quoted in *Wille und Werk,* 1, 1930, pp. 6–7.

[28] A leading member of the *Bünde* complained bitterly about the 'shocking lack of independence among our older members' who preferred to be fellow travelers rather than to think for themselves. 'They trust one man who is to be in charge of everything' (*Der Bund,* 12, 1932, p. 169). Erik H. Erikson, an American psychoanalyst of German origin, touched the very kernel of the problem, observing several years later that Hitler had replaced the complicated conflict of adolescence with a simple pattern of hypnotic action.

PAUL WILKINSON

English Youth Movements

A recent survey [1] using a national sample has shown that 34 percent of males born between 1901 and 1920 claimed to have belonged to the Boy Scouts, and that a further 14 percent claimed membership in the Boys Brigade. Even allowing for a small amount of dual membership, it is reasonable to assume that around 40 percent of all men in this age group have, at some stage in their lives, been brought into touch with one of the two predominant youth movements in Britain. The popular impact of these movements has been enormous, yet they have received scant attention in historical writing, which is all the more surprising given the abundance of colorful material on their early history available at their national head-quarters.[2] Still more colorful, often bizarre, are the histories of the small woodcraft movements, the Order of Woodcraft Chivalry, the Kibbo Kift Kindred and the Woodcraft Folk, that attempted to create a new kind of youth movement in England in the 1920s. One is forced to conclude that they have been ignored because of their essentially Fabian and pacific role, because they eschewed involvement in extremist political movements, and because of the very success and social acceptance of the established movements, the Scouts and the Brigades.

The interesting thing about the English movements, in contrast to the continental, is why they did *not* become vehicles of overt political protest or instruments of party political manipulation. It is temptingly simple, but misleading, to suggest as the reason the relatively stable conditions in English society: even in the midst of depression the degree of economic

Paul Wilkinson, "English Youth Movements, 1908–30," *Journal of Contemporary History,* vol. IV, no. 2, pp. 3–4, 14–23. Reprinted by permission of George Weidenfeld and Nicolson, London.

[1] The survey was carried out by Mass Observation in Spring 1966, using a sample of 2000 adults. 59 percent of all men interviewed and 52 percent of all women said that at some time they had belonged to one or more of the uniformed youth movements.

[2] Archives of a fairly comprehensive nature (minute books, administrative memoranda, complete sets of early publications, etc.) are held at the headquarters of The Scout Association, The Boys Brigade, and The Church Lads Brigade. It is from their reports and files that the figures in this essay have been taken.

or social dislocation was not intolerable; in war the country was neither defeated nor humiliated; the general willingness of successive governments to introduce piecemeal social reforms. One would then have to explain the reasons for this stability. Young and adult alike clearly experienced the tensions and pressures that crowded in on their everyday lives, whether in sustaining an exhausting and costly war, or fighting for their personal or national economic survival.

What then were the moral and psychological resources within English society, and in particular within the young generation, which helped them to take these strains? I suggest that the mass youth movements were themselves important agencies in the creation of these resources. They fulfilled this role by a series of imaginative and original responses to the demands and pressures on the young generation. The simple model of a rebellious, nihilistic youth standing against adult values and institutions does not fit the English case. There was a far more complex and subtle intergenerational dialectic of pressure, response, leadership, and collaboration. The ambiguities and inner contradictions of the movements are illustrated in their history and in that of some of their less well known competitors. . . .

The outbreak of war in 1914 gave the Scouts and their leaders an opportunity to show their value as a patriotic and enthusiastic auxiliary national service. Baden-Powell, keen for his boys to show their worth Mafeking style, issued a Mobilization Order and listed the task they could undertake under the direction of Chief Constables; these included guarding against sabotage, messenger duties, organizing relief measures, and establishing first aid, dressing or nursing stations, refuges and soup kitchens.[3] Some of their duties on the home front, such as giving air raid warnings and sounding the all clear on their bugles, could often expose them to danger. In other roles, such as working as bellboys on Birmingham's trams and helping with the flax harvest, they released large numbers of men for more urgent tasks and for military service.[4]

Many ex-Scouts and Brigade members, of course, volunteered or were conscripted into the armed forces. Many, like Jack Travers Cornwell, the ex-Scout who won the V.C. at Jutland, were entered on the agonizingly lengthening roll of honor. Many more, like John Hargrave (who has described how he had to teach his own officer how to orient a map[5]), proved the value of Boy Scout resourcefulness and practical training, loyalty and dependability. They formed the backbone of the citizen armies.

[3] See *B-P's Scouts*, 73, and circular letter in Scout Association Archives, Vol. 3, Ref. 68.
[4] Cf. Asa Briggs, *History of Birmingham*, II (London, 1952), 209; Scout Association archives, Vol. 3A, Ref. 29.
[5] John Hargrave, *Suvla Bay Landing* (London, 1965), Chapter 2.

While some of the boys were held spellbound by accounts of the fighting and worshipped the young officers as heroes,[6] many of the soldiers at the front were experiencing a change in attitude. The frustration, disgust, and anger expressed in Graves's *Goodbye to All That* and Sassoon's *Memoirs of an Infantry Officer* reflected the feelings of legions of less articulate cannon-fodder. Baden-Powell was sufficiently imaginative and responsive to grasp the change in the national mood, the revulsion against the war, against the sacrifices it had exacted, and against a social system that, it was widely felt, had somehow been responsible both for Britain's involvement in the war and for the disastrous losses. As early as September 1914 he had written: "the lessons of this war . . . should not then be thrown away and forgotten; they should give urgent reason for a more effective education in the brotherhood of man . . . with the dawn of peace . . . our Scout brotherhood may take a big place in the scheme of uniting the nations." [7]

Imperialism was cast aside in favor of the League of Nations idea, and in the 1920s and 1930s Scouting was notable for its well publicized international jamborees, and its phenomenal growth into the largest youth movement in the world. At the same time Baden-Powell stressed that peaceful reconstruction and advance at home could be achieved only by preserving class unity and avoiding the infection of bolshevism:

> Reconstruction after the war may bring about the best democratic government with ultimate prosperity—and peace for all: at the same time it may not, unless we are very careful. . . . There are men who, through their orators and their literature, preach class hatred and down with everything. . . . It is simple mad Bolshevism such as might bring about not merely the downfall of capitalists but the ruin of the great mass of quiet steady-going citizens and wage-earners.[8]

Baden-Powell knew that he was expressing the views of the great mass of steady-going citizens; they followed him in his League of Nations internationalism and his firm antibolshevism. Scouting had placed itself shrewdly and securely at the liberal center of the British ideological spectrum. Only the minority on the extreme left showed real hostility to Scouting in the interwar period—the Young Communist League described

---

[6] See, for example, The Earl of Lytton, *Antony: A Record of Youth* (London, 1935) 20–21, for an account of Antony Knebworth's experience as a schoolboy scout. An ex-Scout Commissioner, Captain Roland Phillips, visited the school and told 'lovely yarns about the front.' Antony (aged 13) wrote: 'We have got a God in the room. . . . He is talking so well that he makes you think you are in the trenches.'

[7] 'The War,' in *The Scouter* (September 1914), reprinted in *B-P's Outlook* (London, 1941).

[8] Baden-Powell, *Scouting towards Reconstruction* (London, 1918), 12.

it as an "anti-working-class organization." [9] Such denunciations were not taken seriously by the general public. For them Scouting had proved itself politically safe and reasonably adaptable; one of the mistakes its rivals made in the 1920s was to underestimate the extent to which Scouting could adapt its image to meet new conditions. The climax of Scouting's interwar internationalism was reached at its coming-of-age Jamboree in 1929 held at Birkenhead. At this vast tented camp of over thirty thousand scouts, contingents from forty-two nations represented a two-million-strong movement. In his address to the Jamboree Baden-Powell proudly proclaimed: "We alone have the universal ear of the young. Let us set about teaching that the highest virtues are friendliness and good-will. And there will be no more war." [10]

In the United Kingdom Scouting also expanded its appeal by catering for a wider age range. The original scheme was aimed primarily at boys between eleven and fifteen. The Wolf Cub sections for the younger boys were started in 1914. The problem of the older boy remained. When he reached the age of fifteen, the average boy scout had left full time schooling and was anxious to leave the world of smaller boys and short trousers behind him: it was difficult to retain any but the keenest among them. To meet this need, Rover sections were developed in the 1920s and in 1923 Rover Regulations, stipulating a minimum age limit of seventeen, and laying down the procedure for Rover scout tests, were issued by Headquarters.[11] Baden-Powell wrote *Rovering to Success* (1922), prescribing a chivalric code of service to the community, patriotism, and "clean living" for the Rover. Despite these efforts, Rover sections had only a minor share in the enormous expansion of Scouting in Britain in the 1920s. Although total membership almost doubled between 1920 and 1930, from 232,758 to 422,662, in the latter year Rovers were still outnumbered by scout leaders.

By the mid-twenties the predominant position of Scouting as a British mass youth movement was apparently unshakable. Attempts to form a new type of youth movement had no chance of displacing it. Their origin, and the ideas and methods they advanced, are worth examination.

In the autumn of 1909 the rift between Baden-Powell and Sir Francis Vane, County Commissioner for London, reached breaking point. Vane was dismissed from his post in November, and complained that Scout Headquarters had behaved in an "antidemocratic" manner. It was not until March 1910 that a fuller account of his differences with the Scout leadership emerged from a newspaper interview he gave:

[9] Young Communist League circular dated 19 October 1927, signed by William Rust, then national secretary.
[10] Scout Association archives, Vol. 13, Ref. 17.
[11] *Policy, Organization & Rules*, Boy Scouts Association (1923).

Its [Scouting's] controllers were distinguished soldiers who, he felt sure, did not love the horrors of war, yet, as trained military men . . . it is as a field of recruiting the Territorials they regard it, and not in its universal spirit. Personally I do not fear a physical invasion of England by Germany as I fear an intellectual invasion from the same quarter.[12]

Vane announced the formation of his own Peace Scouts which were intended to avoid the errors of militarism. He claimed there were 85,000 potential members, and Carl Heath of the National Peace Council and the Rev. Carey Bonner of the Sunday School Union lent their support.[13] The venture failed to make any dent in the Scout movement and soon fizzled out.

A more distinctive and durable venture was the Order of Woodcraft Chivalry (OWC), founded in 1916 by Ernest Westlake, the natural scientist, and his own son Aubrey. Ernest (1856–1922), the son of a wealthy Quaker businessman, studied under Huxley at London University and developed his interest in evolutionary theory through work in geology and anthropology. He became interested in the wider ramifications of the theory, particularly in the American Stanley Hall's theory of recapitulation and the Scottish sociologist Patrick Geddes's work on natural education. Westlake saw the 1914 war as a threat to the survival of civilization; his diagnosis was that in highly industrialized countries man had got too far away from his origins and "the primitive sources of primal social energy." [14] What was needed was an educational method to supplement book learning by recapitulating the vital primitive stages of human learning and self-discovery. With the interested support of the Council of Guidance,[15] he set about the formation of a youth movement which would implement his program of evolutionary education.

Westlake's son, Aubrey, had been a scoutmaster while reading medicine at Cambridge. This, combined with attempts to implement OWC ideas at the Quaker school of Sidcot and among slum children in east London, convinced the Westlakes that their method could be successfully applied. Proof was found when it was used at the Le Glandier refugee center, in northern France, which was full of "dejected, pathetic" Belgian refugee children who were "living in a state of anarchy." [16] Aubrey Westlake and several colleagues of the Friends' War Victims' Relief Committee were

---

[12] *Sunday School Chronicle and Christian Outlook,* 17 March 1910.

[13] *Daily News,* 1 April 1910.

[14] Ernest Westlake, *The Forest School and other papers* (London, 1919).

[15] The original Council members included Mrs. Maud Sharpe, G. Alston Watson, Mrs. Beatrice Norman, Frank Moreton, Professor Patrick Geddes, George Lansbury, Mrs. Margaret McMillan, Dr Alfred Salter, and Professor J. Shelley.

[16] Aubrey Westlake, 'Le Glandier Experiment,' private MS in author's possession.

astonished at the response of these children, and the effect it had of creating among them a spirit of community and service.

Though the Order never had more than 1500 members in Britain it has survived (present membership approximately 300) and spread to Ireland, Belgium, and New Zealand. It has maintained an extremely high reputation for the quality of its woodcraft training and the impressive and colorful ritual and ceremonial of its camps at its beautiful home in Hampshire. It is this movement which Ernest Thompson Seton recognized as the truest British version of his own woodcraft training ideas, and he became its honorary Grand Chieftain in 1923. Like Seton's own movement, it remained purely educational and avoided all political alignments, although Aubrey Westlake tried unsuccessfully to persuade the Order to involve itself in the British Social Credit campaign of the mid 1930s which he and his wife enthusiastically supported.

A more ambitious and potentially more dangerous threat to scouting was the Kibbo Kift Kindred,[17] founded by John Hargrave in the early 1920s. Hargrave had a particularly magnetic appeal as a youth leader.[18] He had been an active scout with a great enthusiasm for woodcraft lore and tribal symbolism of the Thompson Seton type. He made great use of his talent as an illustrator and newspaper artist in his work as a scout leader and publicist; he became Headquarters Commissioner for Camping and Woodcraft, and wrote a regular column for *The Scout* under his woodcraft name, White Fox. His appeal as a leader of youth was enhanced by his sense of style and ritual, his knowledge of the romantic and exotic primitive origins of woodcraft lore, and his insight into the symbolism of exotic civilizations.[19] He was moreover, a hero, a veteran of the Suvla Bay landing in which he served as a stretcher-bearer. There is no evidence that Baden-Powell or Headquarters resented Hargrave's personal following among many of the older scouts, but there is no doubt that there was tension between him and the more orthodox leaders. This was due to Hargrave's stress on woodcraft, the primitivist cult, and tribal training, which went considerably beyond the *Scouting for Boys* ideas. Hargrave's warrant as HQ Commissioner was cancelled in 1920: he was then free to promote his own ideas which he had outlined in *The Great War Brings It Home* (1919).

He argued, in a similar vein to the Westlakes, that the war had demonstrated the bankruptcy of industrial civilization. Mankind had become rotten and sick by neglecting to provide a balanced natural and evolu-

[17] Kibbo Kift was derived from Anglo-Saxon and was intended to signify 'proof of great strength.'
[18] 'Hargrave always spoke as though possessed of an absolute and even insolent certainty of where he was going and what he was doing. That carried immense reassurance with it.' Leslie Paul, *Angry Young Man* (London, 1951), 54.
[19] John Hargrave, *The Boys' Book of Signs and Symbols* (London, 1920).

tionary education. Borrowing ideas from Hall's recapitulatory theory, he set down a scheme of youth training which would enable the individual, from infancy to manhood, to recapitulate the primitive phases of human development; exploration, hunting, conflict, invention and so on. The idea was that a new elite, drawn preferably from the "children of the slain," would be created which would be physically and mentally superior to its predecessors.

The idea of a New Samurai had fascinated H. G. Wells, as it had many other utopian socialists. For the utopians it was a prerequisite of any socialist educational movement that was to promote true mental fitness that its youth should be brought up free from any taint of reactionary ideas. The destructive influences of nationalism, militarism, imperialism, capitalism were to be counteracted by teaching the new elite to desire and work for a new world, united under a world government, for democracy, peace, and distributive justice. The new world was to be free of the hatreds, superstitions, and prejudices of the old. How far Hargrave himself shared these vague utopian aims is uncertain, but they did figure prominently in the Covenant of the Kibbo Kift which was drawn up by the founding group at a meeting in the Pethick-Lawrences' house in August 1920.[20] Many of Hargrave's old admirers in the Scout movement, particularly those inclined towards the political left, followed him into the Kift, and a number of Labor and Co-operative youth groups in the South London area also joined, but despite this hopeful start the Kift failed to create the powerful left Scout movement which many of its sponsors had hoped for.

In truth Hargrave did not have his heart in the scheme: he preferred to run the movement himself rather than through any genuinely democratic structure. In 1924 the Kift split when Gordon Ellis, Leslie Paul, and the London Labor groups withdrew after unsuccessfully challenging Hargrave's authority on a relatively minor organizational issue, and after this the movement became increasingly exclusive, elitist, and secretive, with its own exotic language of occult symbolism which Hargrave elaborated in *The Confession of Kibbo Kift* (1927). It became almost impossible for an outsider to penetrate the obscurities of the movement's ideology and methods, and in the late 1920s when Hargrave became a convert to Major Douglas's Social Credit theory, those who wished to remain in the Kift had to accept the "New Economics." By the early 1930s it had been assimilated into the Social Credit movement, on the fringe of British political life.[21]

The withdrawal of the Labor groups from the Kift in 1924 was followed by another attempt to set up a working-class youth movement, the

[20] *Angry Young Man*, 54.
[21] For an account of the Social Credit phase see George Thayer, *The British Political Fringe* (London, 1965).

Woodcraft Folk. Though, like the Kift, it confronted the entrenched positions of the Scout movement, and was not sufficiently well endowed or supported to become a mass movement, it did succeed in developing a woodcraft education program (drawing on Hall, Seton, and Baden-Powell) which had a carefully thought out socialist content.[22] Like the Kibbo Kift and the OWC, it devised an attractive costume and symbolism, rejected religious orthodoxy, and was proudly coeducational.

In 1925 Leslie Paul was elected Headman of the Woodcraft Folk which was formed by the federation of four London Woodcraft fellowships with a total membership of seventy. The London groups remained the strongest element in the movement, but, with some financial help from the Royal Arsenal Co-operative Society, and later the National Co-operative Society, the Folk grew until it had an active membership of approximately five thousand by the mid 1930s,[23] and still survives as an activity of the Co-operative education movement.

The Folk avoided the romantic and exotic excesses of the Kibbo Kift in its terminology and literature. Working-class history, co-operative and trade-union development, were given a large place in their educational program. The Wellsian enthusiasm for internationalism, which had soon faded out of the Kibbo Kift movement, was constantly stressed in its journal, *The Pioneer;* it was affiliated to Max Winter's Socialist Educational International and exchanged camp delegations with other social-democratic youth movements such as the Czech Sokols and the Austrian Red Falcons. Yet despite the political interests of the movement and the fact that Leslie Paul and some of his older colleagues were diverted into left-wing political journalism and campaigning in the thirties, the appeal of the movement, as its founder has admitted, was fundamentally due to its mixture of woodcraft, comradeship and "the longing to live a kind of poetry." [24]

All these colorful movements clearly had a strong appeal for their small bands of devotees, but none of them developed into a working-class alternative to scouting. At least part of the explanation can be found in their rejection of orthodox Christian beliefs as a basis for ethical guidance, which discouraged much potential adult support, and in the 1920s coeducational camping for children was regarded by most parents as morally dangerous. Nor did any of these movements attract strong support from powerful interest or political circles. Even the Woodcraft Folk was denied official help from the Labor Party, and had to wait several years before receiving limited financial help from the Co-operative movement. Pre-

---

[22] The programme was published in Leslie Paul, *The Child and the Race* (London, 1926), and in more elaborate form in his *The Training of Pioneers* (London, 1936), and the Woodcraft Folk handbook, *The Folk Trail* (1930).
[23] Leslie Paul, *The Republic of Children* (London, 1938), 54.
[24] *Angry Young Man,* 67.

cisely because the leaders of these movements tended to be more politically conscious than the leaders of the mass movements, they were drawn into adult political activity, leaving their youth movements with inadequate direction. Confronting them all was the massive expansion of Scouting, which, far from retaining its pre-1914 outlook, turned itself into a more formidable movement through its ability to adapt to changes in public opinion.

The successful English youth movements were not simply movements of protest by the young. Rather they were carefully designed attempts to respond to their needs and demands, to harness their energies for great causes approved by their adult leaders—imperial defense, national defense, international cooperation, national efficiency, and so on. As educational movements they had no need to challenge the political status quo. They brought about improvements in training and recreational facilities, physical fitness (and incidentally increased opportunities for social advancement) on behalf of the less privileged. Tactically they were restricted to the pace permitted by their patrons among the political, ecclesiastic, and military elites. They should therefore be regarded as movements not of protest, but of peaceful reconstruction and reform. Through their agency many demands of the young were contained, absorbed, and redirected, with astonishing success. It is no exaggeration to say that Kitchener's New Army depended on a boy-scout spirit and resourcefulness for its morale, and on the dissemination of public school loyalties and values among lower middle-class and working-class men. This had been, to a large extent, accomplished by the patriotic youth movements. As a result, loyalty among volunteers and conscripts alike withstood even the criminal negligence of the generalship in that war, though inevitably it wilted as the terrible cost in life mounted.

In comparison with the established movements, the small experimental woodcraft movements that arose in the 1920s were both romantic and utopian. They regarded Scouting and the Brigades as too authoritarian, establishment-minded, and hidebound. They rejected the orthodox Christian doctrines which the established movements had always treated with reverence and respect, and claimed to be working for the realization of a new model society. In the case of Kibbo Kift and the Order of Woodcraft Chivalry the aim was a more mentally and physically fit society. In the case of the Woodcraft Folk there was, in addition, the aim of a more egalitarian society. Yet they all worked for their "revolutions" in a typically English manner, in a spirit that Robert Owen, William Morris and Edward Carpenter would have endorsed. Education was to be the road to Utopia. Not for them the dangerous confrontation with the established political order, or the risks of violence. Their rejection, their protest, took the form of a temporary escape to the open air, to the campfire circle, a new religion of the senses. It is true that the Woodcraft Folk put politics into its program, which drew heavily on its socialist and Co-operative background, and that the Kibbo Kift ultimately became a section of the Greenshirt Social Credit Party. Nevertheless, in the 1920s the real appeal of the English woodcraft movements for a small band of devotees derived from their heady mixture of natural freedom, romance, and escape.

JOHN ARDAGH

French Youth with a Dusty Answer

It was in the corridors of the new Préfecture building near the Bastille, one day in 1965, that I had my own Gibbonian moment of awareness of the rise of a huge new generation in France. Usually one expects French public offices to be filled with shuffling, elderly bureaucrats and messengers, spun about with the cobwebs of the Third Republic, and nothing is more typical of this than the old Préfecture in the Hôtel de Ville. Suddenly in this new annex, as the clock struck noon for lunch, I was besieged by hundreds of chattering clerks and typists, few of them over thirty. Visibly I saw confirmation of the statistics: there are more than twice as many people under twenty-five in France today as in 1939, although the population has risen only 15 percent. In many offices the old *huissiers* with their stained suits and sad faces are being replaced by sleek young *hôtesses* with public-relations smiles; and it is easy to find scores of other symptoms, too, of France's demographic facelift and of the new national emphasis on youth.

Every Frenchman today professes his faith in *la jeunesse*. *Une France jeune—soyez jeune—il faut l'esprit jeune*—the phrases tumble daily from the mouths of politicians and the pages of glossy magazines, as though youth were synonymous with virtue. In a country previously dominated by the prerogatives of age and hierarchy, this marks a striking change of

From pp. 306, 339–49 ("Mais que . . . as they are."). 462–63 ("For a few . . . or his aims."), and 470–74 ("The most . . . new hope.") Copyright © 1968, 1969 by John Ardagh. By permission of Harper & Row, Publishers, Inc. and Martin Secker & Warburg Ltd., London.

heart. "*We* may have failed—but *les jeunes,* they are serious, they are made of good stuff, they will do better than us": this a comment you sometimes hear from older people still ashamed of the defeats of recent decades. Often this kind of sentiment seems to be based more on hopeful thinking than on reason: few older people, even parents and teachers, claim to know what this reticent and elusive new generation is really like. But at least they are given more public attention than ever before. In their name a great national debate on education is now raging, and the highly traditional structure of French schools and universities is being remodeled to an extent unparalleled since Napoleon.

LA JEUNESSE: *NOT SO MUCH REBELS, MERELY CHUMS*

'*Mais que pensent les jeunes?*' ask the headlines in a constant stream of magazine articles: '*Nos jeunes, qui sont-ils?*' And few of them can find an easy answer. What are they like, this mysterious new generation, for whom all the educational crusades are being fought? Ostensibly, they are following much the same paths as modern youth in other Western countries, though less aggressively than in Britain. They have their own powerful new consumer market for music, clothes, and cars; their own world of young singing idols like Johnny Hallyday and Françoise Hardy, their own fringe minorities of delinquents and beatniks with hair-styles imported from London. All, or nearly all, have far more freedom from parents than cloistered French youth had before the war. Many are conscious of the gulf between their own morality and that of the older generation.

And that older generation in turn has become aware of youth as never before. *La Jeunesse* is now a slogan, a doctrine of faith in the future, a symbol of France's recovered vitality. For more than a century this used to be an adult-dominated country, where teenagers were treated as small-scale adults and were not expected to exist as a national group in their own right. Now the grown-up world has woken up, as it were, to the existence of a neglected minority in its midst, with its separate values and needs. Youth is solicited, analyzed, indulged (except by its teachers). But this parental lip-service to the new cult of youth is not always accompanied by actual understanding of individuals. And in some ways the youthful revolution *à l'anglaise* is more apparent than real in France; or at least, it has not yet found proper expression.

In the first decade or so after the war, many of the most important changes in France were due to a new generation rising against the standards of its elders—from the young farmers of the JAC to the cinema's *nouvelle vague*. And other phenomena (St. Tropez, Françoise Sagan, the early existentialists) gave the world a popular image of French youth in open revolt. Today, in the late '60s, that image has become strangely deceptive. As often as not, older people nowadays complain, "But the young, they're so docile, so conformist." While Britain's youth have now leapt ahead in precocious emancipation, the French are still, relatively, under the shadow of school and parents. Seduced by prosperity and placated by adult acceptance, many of them seem to be tamed into a listless submissiveness, or else into a feeling of impotence.

The climate of 1945 was very different from today's: more austere, but also more adventurous. The upheavals of wartime had broken down some of the barriers that previously kept youth in its place, and an idealistic new generation was able gradually to make lasting inroads into the *positions acquises* of the age-hierarchy. It happened most strikingly in agriculture, and in the civil service and industry where some older men emerged discredited from the Occupation and young ones took their place. It is remarkable how youthful many of the postwar pioneers were at the outset: Leclerc was twenty-three when he began his cut-price campaign in Brittany, and Planchon founded his Villeurbanne theatre at twenty-one. Today the impetus of this generation is still driving forward, in nearly every field; and many of its leaders, now around forty, are in key national positions. But their successors, now in their twenties, born into an age of greater ease and acceptance, have seldom shown the same innovating spirit. This has been even more apparent in the intellectual world. After the Liberation, many young people flocked excitedly around Sartre and Camus at St.-Germain-des-Prés, eager to revolt against their bourgeois backgrounds and help to forge a better world. This existentialist climate has since gradually dissipated. The Sartrian disciples of those days have mostly settled down and become prosperous, and many are now leading the bourgeois lives they once denounced. Their young successors either find money-making, fast cars and hi-fi more appealing than philosophy; or else they are cynical and dispirited at the antibourgeois rebellion's failure to create a new society.

In the mid 1950s a few isolated and much-publicized events, vaguely influenced by existentialism, managed to sustain the impression of a generalized youthful revolt. In 1954 the eighteen-year-old Françoise Sagan, daughter of an industrialist, published her first novel, *Bonjour Tristesse*. Her sophisticated world of whisky and wealth was some steps away from the severe, intellectual *milieu* of the true existentialists; but her heroine's cool disillusion and rejection of social morality sounded a note that seemed to borrow something, however ill digested, from the ideas of Sartre. Two years later the young director Roger Vadim took a little-known actress to a modest Riviera fishing-port and there made on location *Et Dieu créa la femme*. And God-knows-who created Bardot and St. Tropez. Thousands from *une certaine jeunesse* rushed there at once. France and the world were amazed. Was this what French youth was like? Was Sagan's free-living heroine typical of French girls of eighteen? The next year, in 1958, the veteran director Marcel Carné made a film, *Les Tricheurs,* that seemed to confirm the picture. He described a *milieu* of young Parisians, bohemian "intellectuals" and idle bourgeois students from good homes, united in the same anarchic dissipation, breaking up their parents' smart flats with wild parties, stealing and cheating and casually fornicating. According to Carné, everyone in this *milieu* is a *tricheur* (cheat) and honest feelings are taboo: in the climax of the film, bohemian slut and weak rich *fils-à-papa* do genuinely fall in love, but dare not admit it to each other and this leads to tragedy. The girl, trapped in her own depravity, cannot take the strain any more, drives off into the night in a stolen car, and crashes to her death. Another character (a nice one, a sort of Greek chorus) then blames it all on society. As you can see, a sensational and contrived film, hardly a great work of art; but it did carry a certain veracity, and Carné claimed that he knew this world intimately and had drawn his portraits from life. The film caused more of a stir than any other in France for years: many pressure-groups tried to ban it, and *l'Express* gleefully published a twelve-page supplement, 'Qui Sont les Tricheurs?' Some people thought that the film's portrait was out of date and related to a St.-Germain-des-Prés of the late '40s, to the phony existentialists who mistook liberty for license. Others felt it was still true, of a minority. There are still some *tricheurs,* even today, just as the early Sagan novels were clearly based on experience and the crowds around the bars and beaches of St. Tropez are patently no fiction. The *tricheurs* borrowed from existentialism its permissiveness without its responsibility and took it as a cue to do just what they liked: when the young bohemian Mephistopheles of Carné's film goes into a shop to steal a record that he does not want, he claims he is performing the perfect Gidean or Sartrian *acte gratuit.* This muddled intellectual self-justification has underlain a good part of the fringe rebellions among postwar French youth—though one can hardly claim that every St. Tropez lay-about is motivated by such philosophical principles.

The St. Tropez phenomenon has had plenty of postwar counterparts, in Chelsea, California, and elsewhere. What is remarkable here is its intensity in one small, picturesque seaside location. The whole affair was hardly Vadim's fault, or Bardot's: the publicists of *Paris-Match* and other such papers pounced on them while they were filming, and somehow managed to inspire a popular cult that answered a youthful need. Bardot was built into a symbol of sensualist emancipation—and the young crowds came, some innocently and some less so, to find and to worship their goddess. Of course they simply drove her away: she had bought a villa just outside St. Tropez, where she still spends part of each year, but she was soon forced to build a high wall round it, and neither she nor any other star today dares to be seen in the streets or cafés of the town, through fear of being mobbed by adoring fans. Yet the crowds still come, from every part of the world, impelled by the new religion of glamour and stardom, or simply by curiosity. I met a Dominican priest in St. Tropez who told me, "This place is a kind of Lourdes. Young people feel a lack in their lives today, they want to be cured of their desolate yearnings, so they come here to be touched by magic and reborn. But they go away disappointed. All they find is each other." Many of the most vicious elements in St. Tropez today are foreign, not French—the hordes of young German thugs and paederasts, the Chelseaites, the Swedes, the American beats. But the French are still there too in plenty; the girls of little more than sixteen who arrive from Paris without a penny and see how far their charms can carry them. Any summer night you can see them by the score, wide-eyed popsies with gaudy jeans, bare midriffs, and Bardot hairstyles, hanging around the modish bars like l'Escale, waiting for the next well-heeled pick-up who will let them sponge and stay a few more days.

Many of the boys and girls of this kind of milieu, in Paris or St. Tropez, come from cultured, conventional homes and have broken with their families. But they are not typical, totalling perhaps a few thousand. Many other young people today, especially students, seem to have managed to extricate themselves from old-style bourgeois morality in a less irresponsible manner; and if they are discreet, even while still living at home they can practice a good deal of Sartrian "sincerity" in their private lives. Girls have become readier to undertake affairs before marriage, but without ceasing to be *sérieuses*. As one Parisian student told me, "It's not that we're trying to set up counter-conventions like the *tricheurs*. We're not against our parents' morality, we ignore it. The basis of our behavior is rejection of constraint, and within this framework we are very moral."

Among the less intellectual teenagers, the archetype today is not a *tricheur* but a *copain*—the word means "chum" or "pal." And in the 1960s it is the extraordinary pop movement of the *copains,* innocent and mildly charming but vapid, that has given a new brand-image to the whole of French youth and pushed the precocious cynicism of Sagan firmly on to the sidelines. A new generation, sipping its Coca-Colas, looks less to Bardot the sex-kitten than to Sylvie Vartan, chirpy little chum and elder sister, or to Françoise Hardy huskily leading all-the-boys-and-girls-of-her-age-hand-in-hand.

This movement began in 1959 when Daniel Filipacchi, a young disc-jockey and former *Paris-Match* photographer, launched a jazz program on Europe Number One radio and borrowed the title of a song by Gilbert Bécaud to call it *Salut les Copains.* Instantly it was a smash-hit with teenagers, who were tired of sharing Brassens and Trenet with their elders and wanted something swinging and modern of their own, like the Americans had. Soon the program was running for two hours nightly, using mainly American material.

Around the same period an obscure bar near the Opéra, the Golf Drouot, turned itself into a kind of teenagers' cabaret and so provided a breeding-ground for the first of France's own young pop singers. There a boy of sixteen with fair curly hair and an ugly mouth made his hesitant *début* under the name of Johnny Hallyday, singing American rock 'n' roll tunes in French. Filipacchi took him up—and a whole generation chose Johnny as their idol and self-image. French pop was born. He was followed by scores of others—besides Sylvie and Françoise (surnames are taboo among *copains*), the best known have been Richard Anthony, Claude François, Adamo, Sheila, France Gall. And in 1962 Filipacchi astutely complemented his radio show with a glossy magazine also called *Salut les Copains,* which reached and has held a sale of a million copies a month and gets 10,000 fan letters a week. Its rather similar sister monthly for girls, *Mademoiselle Age Tendre,* sells 800,000—both of them astoundingly high circulations for France.

At first the movement was highly derivative, much more so than its Liverpool equivalent. Not only did the stars borrow American tunes; many of them found it smart to adopt Anglo-Saxon names like Dick Rivers and Eddy Mitchell; Hallyday's real name is Jean-Philippe Smet. Gradually, however, the *copains* have acquired a certain French style of their own, less virile and inventive, more romantic and sentimental, than either Beatledom or American folk and rock. Some of them, including Johnny and Françoise, compose and write many of their own songs, and today probably about half the *copains'* material is home-grown and the rest imported and translated. The whole affair is basically a shrewd commercial operation by Filipacchi, who by now is one of the richest men in France. But he and his young stars can afford their mink and Ferraris just because they have managed to provide millions with an outlet of self-identification they were looking for. The tradition of modern popular songs is much older and stronger in France than in Britain, but it has, therefore, belonged to an older generation, from Piaf through to Aznavour. Teenagers resented these as their parents' idols. But their own Johnny, singing ingenuously about being sixteen and its problems, was themselves and the boy next door. At his concerts, children wave and shout hallo: "He's young, he's gay, he's just like us," said one girl of fourteen, "and not at all like a real music-hall star. So we love him." Idols and fans are all equally *copains* together, and all are *tu*: this is the carefully fostered principle of their success, and if any idol breaks the code and behaves like an aloof Hollywood star, he is finished.

Parents at first were a little anxious, as gramophone-record sales shot into scores of millions and Hallyday became the most-photographed male in France after de Gaulle. Their concern reached its height after the night of 22 June 1963, when Filipacchi staged a "live" open-air broadcast from the Place de la Nation in Paris, and 150,000 boys and girls, twisting and rocking, surged into the square and brushed aside the police. It was the first time in French history that teenagers had displayed their solidarity in public, on this scale. Some observers saw it as a political portent, comparing it with the mass-hysteria of the Nazi rallies. A few arrests were made and an enquiry was ordered. A little damage had been done to cars and windows, but this was due simply to the weight of the crowds, and to the presence among them of a handful of hooligans. Once the fuss had blown over, it became clear that the famous *Nuit de la Nation* was really quite innocent: the kids had simply wanted to dance, and to have a look at their heroes.

Parents soon came to see there was nothing much to worry about. Filipacchi, in fact, has always been shrewd enough to steer the *copains* away from rebellious paths that might have got him into trouble. Their revolt has been purely one of music and rhythm, not of morals. The very phrase *Salut les Copains* ('Hello, Chums!') gives some idea of the *Boys' Own Paper* or *True Romance* spirit of the thing; and so harmless is the magazine that the Catholic Church has felt safely able to copy it with its own rival monthly for the teenage faithful, *Formidable,* a bit more varied and a bit less artfully glossy but otherwise much the same. Filipacchi's editor-in-chief, Raymond Mouly, a young man in black leather jacket and side-whiskers, told me: "I suppose we've simply created a new conformism, inevitably. But there's still something zippy and fresh about us—and we needed a change from Yves Montand. What we're really doing is to prolong the age of innocence, the *âge tendre.* Life is easier than in 1945, and people have more time to live their youth."

This belongs to a typically French romantic tradition that seems to hark straight back to Gérard de Nérval and *Le Grand Meaulnes:* adolescents playing at love, sometimes touched by melancholy and *ennui* but not by cynicism or social indignation. Browse through the brilliantly edited pages of *Salut les Copains* and you will see what these idols are like, or at least how they are presented to be. Huge snazzy color photos in the manner of *Un homme et une femme* show the various stars wandering hand in hand through autumn woodlands or lazing on Mediterranean beaches. Photo-articles forty pages long proclaim *Tout tout tout sur Sylvie* and *Tout tout tout sur Johnny:* that Sylvie dislikes celery and likes colored candles, that Johnny likes hot-dogs and dislikes umbrellas. Johnny, philistine and petit-bourgeois, mad about cars and motor-bikes, is in reality much as he is made to seem; he is the perfect modern folk-hero and looks exactly like any French youth you see hanging around the streets with his *vélo* on a Sunday. Sylvie, Bulgarian by birth, is more intellectual: she used to read philosophy on the Métro before she became famous, and is known as *la collégienne du twist*. But with her tulip-mouth, her long ash-blonde curls and sturdy little figure, she projects the perfect image of the jolly bobby-soxer who's become a star by mistake; and when she bounces on to the stage of the Olympia music-hall as if it were an end-of-term concert, to trill *Ce soir, je serai la plus belle pour aller danser,* every *midinette* in the audience identifies with her. In 1965, after a long engagement, Johnny and Sylvie became Mr. and Mrs. Smet: two hundred photographers were present, yet it seemed much closer in spirit to a typical middle-class wedding than, say, to aloof Bardot marrying some foreigner in Las Vegas.

Not all the *copains* conform quite so closely to this tame bourgeois ideal. Françoise Hardy, ex-student of German at the Sorbonne, tall and languid with a spoilt, sulky temperament, has even brought a note of Grecoesque sorrow and self-doubt into some of her recent songs; there is more than a touch of Garbo about her, and she is one of the very few *copains* to have much following among maturer people as well as teenagers. But she does keep roughly in line with the Filipacchi ethic, and her *mystère* does not simmer into actual revolt. However, an intruder of a much more violent sort, calling himself Antoine, did manage to burst into the *copain* world briefly in 1966: his hair was far longer than Lennon's or Jagger's (shocking by most *copain* standards), and, instead of sweet love-lyrics, the songs he wrote and then growled at the audience were full of a bitter, socially-conscious nihilism that any intellectual beatnik might have envied. His clamorous success indicated that some French youth, at least, hankered for a stronger diet than chummery. But Filipacchi was against him, so was French adulthood; and he fizzled out.

And what will happen to the *copains?* After tiffs and reconciliations that filled all the headlines, the Smets are now parents in their twenties, growing away fast from their teenage equals. '*Adieu les copains!*' wrote *l'Exprèss* after their wedding; 'Johnny and Sylvie were *copains*. Mr. and Mrs. Smet will try to remain stars. And they will have lots more little Ferraris!' Others no doubt will take their place, but the movement may well change or fade. The *copains'* appeal has always been mainly to the less sophisticated middle teens; older or more alert ones have often preferred a more robust nourishment such as Bob Dylan or English pop. A youth in Filipacchi's office who had spent some time in London told me, "I admit your young singers are more mature and original than ours; a group like The Animals, for instance, seem to have firm ideas about modern society. Your youth as a whole is more aggressive, creative, and non-conformist than ours. But they get more freedom."

On its credit side, the *copain* cult may have fostered a kind of sweet romantic comradeship among French youth. Like British pop it has certainly helped in the struggle against delinquency; and unlike British pop it is seldom crudely hostile to real culture. Its idols have undeniable puppy-charm; and, for all the commercial wire-pulling, there has been something spontaneous and infectious about their appeal to French youth in a voice it could recognize as its own. But that voice has not proved a very inspiring one: insipid, somewhat effeminate, content to idolize a safe world of glamour and niceness. Even the melodies are not very exciting. Parents, in fact, can safely look on the *copains* as a harmless way of keeping the children out of mischief. The young things are now being allowed to throw a party on their own; but Mummy and Daddy are on the *qui-vive* upstairs.

Under this discreet parental eye, France's six million teenagers have been elaborating their own semi-private world with its own crazes, conventions, and slang—a world that is largely innocent but difficult for a noninitiate to grasp at first. Here are some examples of their slang. *Chouette, formidable* and *terrible* all mean "super" or "smashing"; *vachement* or *terriblement* mean "very"; *ça chauffe* means "things are getting hot"; *c'est du folklore,* "it's stupid, out of date"; *dans le vent,* "with-it"; *moins de vingt dents,* a pun meaning "the old"; *croulant* ("crumbling"), an "adult," a word in vogue about ten years ago but now only used by *croulants* about themselves. The notorious term *yé-yé* more or less means "pop," and derives from French attempts to pronounce "yeah! yeah!" in their songs. Adults often apply it pejoratively to the whole *copain* generation; teenagers themselves use it rarely, except to denote, also pejoratively, their own more *outré* elements.

When teenagers give parties on their own, they are usually informal *surprise-parties* which may sometimes develop into wilder *surboums* if *tricheurs* are around or parents well out of the way. Generally French teenage parties are noticeably sedate by London standards, at least when given (as usually happens) in parents' homes. Outside the family foyer, however, things *chauffent terriblement,* notably at one or two new Paris nightspots catering for really switched-on youth. One of these is La Locomotive, a vast rock 'n' roll club below the Moulin Rouge, banned to over twenty-fives, where the young parade their latest fashions and sit on a floor of purple glass listening to English and American rhythms. English influence is strong also at the fantastic Bus Palladium, near Place Pigalle: this was a seedy old strip-joint for tourists which in 1965 decided to get with-it by importing an English pop group and appealing to a new clientèle. Its success was unprecedented. Smarties and beatniks, typists, students, and celebrities, all flocked along to this one large darkened room where bodies swayed and jerked through the night to the strident music. The baroque church-like décor, with frescoes, aisles, and Byzantine pillars, reinforced the impression of being present at some religious rite—and several of the pale-faced, long-haired acolytes could hardly have looked more biblical. Few reporters failed to comment on this: "It's a midnight mass in full oecumenicism," said the *Nouvel Observateur;* "The priest sucks his micro, the communicants sip their Coca-Cola." But reporters have also noted how extraordinarily innocent and unerotic it all is.

La Loco and the Palladium are in the *avant-garde,* and so are some British fashion imports. Beatle haircuts still tend to be laughed at in public and thought effeminate, but are beginning to spread more widely. Mini-skirts and trouser-suits made a belated but successful invasion from London in 1966, and the various new Paris shops catering for teenage fashion (Vog, Dorothée Bis and the Gaminerie) are all heavily influenced by London. Young Parisians interested in this kind of with-it-ness know that Paris can no longer make great claims to originality, and most of them are keenly aware of what is going on in London. But they get a little bored by Londoners who come and tell them how old-hat and derivative they all are.

One characteristic feature of French teenage society since the war has been the rise of the band or group. No longer expected to spend so much time with parents or relatives, young people nowadays often choose to go around in little groups of six or more, boys and girls together; frequently the relations remain platonic and fairly uncommitted, and there is less splitting into couples or "dating" than in many Western countries. Of course, this trend has provided fertile soil for the spreading of the *copains* cult.

As for adult-organized youth activities, teenagers mainly show no great enthusiasm for them, though boy-scouting is quite popular and some of the Church movements do well. The national chain of youth clubs (*Maisons des Jeunes*) might attract far greater numbers if they were better organized and had better amenities. Not that French youth moves to the opposite antisocial extreme: there is less delinquency, and certainly less drug-taking, than in many countries. Juvenile lawlessness appeared comparatively late in France, in 1959, with warring gangs of leather-jacketed youths known as *blousons noirs.* After they had swiped their bicycle chains at a number of innocent passers-by, they were severely repressed by the police, and today the gangs have largely split up and been succeeded by small groups of young professional thieves, or by sporadic hooliganism and pilfering.

Whereas in postwar Britain youth has often channeled its energies into violent self-expression, destruction or creative, in France the dominant impression left by all the varying tendencies is of a kind of docile listlessness. I do not wish to exaggerate this contrast, for the youth of the two nations also have much in common. But it does exist. The *copains* may have provided a generation with a new self-awareness, yet they seem unsure quite what to do with it. One answer to the puzzle lies in the influence of parents and school. It is true that French parents are less strict than they used to be, and are much readier to let sons and even daughters go out on their own; it is true that they have grown more aware of their children's enthusiasm and needs *as children,* instead of treating them as minor adults. Often they are indulgent with pocket-money. But their offspring remain curiously under their sway.

In Parisian upper-class society, parents in recent years have resorted to various ingenious devices to keep their teenage children in check. One of the most remarkable of these is the *rallye,* a kind of exclusive dancing-club for girls of fifteen to nineteen and their carefully chosen escorts. There are some dozen of these *rallyes* in Paris today; and a boy or girl who is entered for one by his or her mother must expect to spend from four or five years in a steady round of formal parties and dances, under close parental supervision. It helps to steer the young things towards suitable marriages, and to keep them out of mischief. And astonishingly, most of the young things appear to accept this discipline, as teenagers rarely would in London.

Another reason for the French teenager's submissiveness is purely practical: the housing shortage. Emancipation from parents is not so easy when cheap furnished flats or rooms are still such a rarity: three in four of sixteen-to-twenty-four-year-olds live at home until marriage, including 54 percent of young men of twenty-two to twenty-four. Yet even if there were no housing shortage, the picture might not change so radically. It is still considered the "norm" to live with your parents; and very many young people, even when they do have the means to move away, prefer not to do so. This is changing, but not fast. A rich young girl I knew in Paris, who could easily have found and afforded a small flat of her own or with girl-friends, told me just before her wedding at twenty-six: "Now at last I can get away from my mother." In such cases, children are suffering from parents' emotional blackmail; but in millions of other cases it is simply that young French, far more than young Anglo-Saxons or Nordics, seem to remain tied to their parents by psychological cords that they find hard to cut, even when there is no parental pressure. They are still often in the grip of the kind of obsessive child–parent relationships that are such a recurring theme of modern French literature. Perhaps this is why, when they do revolt—against parents or against society more generally— the gesture is all the more extreme, just because it has cost them so much of their inner selves.

Young people will often profess unconventional or progressive ideas in abstract, but in practice when faced with concrete situations will defer to the lead and authority of their elders. I met a twenty-year-old Sorbonne philosophy student, living with his parents in Paris, who delighted me with his mature and profound ideas about modern society and his own destiny, then surprised me by saying, "A few young friends of mine and I have formed a local dramatic club. Luckily, my father runs it for us. You see, without him, none of us would have the right authority, we'd just quarrel." I refrained from replying that, in England, boys much younger and stupider than he were often in charge of the discipline of large schools. But it is plain as daylight that the French school system has a large influence here. It fails to provide any training in group initiative or responsibility, and so throws the child back on parental discipline. It presses him towards an intellectual precocity that is basically conformist. And the severe and formal approach of teachers outwardly inculcates docility, while inwardly producing a kind of frustrated resentment. Perhaps it is reaction against the severity of school, or against the shadow of parents, that makes so many French teenagers behave so very badly when they escape to a different setting. In English towns such as Brighton, where they come *au pair* in the summer, they have a worse reputation for trouble-making than any other nationality. It is often hard to decide whether they are spoilt little brats or sadly deprived.

Two recent opinion surveys of teenage attitudes both give a somewhat discouraging picture. The first, carried out in 1961 among *lycéens* and apprentices by a psychologist, Yann Thireau, and an educationist, Georges Teindas, showed them as "interested above all in securing an easy life, with lots of money." The heroes they admired most were scientists, sportsmen, world leaders—but they seemed to envy them less for their qualities than for their style of life: "Prince Rainier, he's got money and he's happy," "Churchill, he's rich," were two replies. The second enquiry was carried out in 1962 by the Institut Français d'Opinion Publique, among a wide range of boys and girls between sixteen and twenty-four. Asked what they valued most in life, the vast majority put health and money well ahead of love, freedom, or religion. They laid immense stress on the home, mainly as a symbol of material security; they were anxious above all to secure good, well-paying jobs, and they were confident that they would be much more prosperous than their parents. They cared little about French politics—less than a third were able to cite the names of more than two Gaullist Ministers—but they showed even less concern for old-style patriotism and *la gloire*. What mattered more to them was the Common Market and the idea of Europe. Few expressed much desire to change the basic order of society; or, if they did, they sensed a kind of powerlessness. The portrait that emerged was of an orderly and bourgeois generation, modern-minded and technocratic, anxious to feather its own nest, and idealistic mainly towards practical ends. The survey concluded: "Rarely have we discovered signs of revolt; more often docility, or even passivity. The young accept the institutions of the adult world as they are." . . .

POSTSCRIPT, JULY 1968

For a few weeks in spring, half of France went joyfully and creatively mad. There were many diverse elements in that madness, and it is still too soon to assess their real significance. On the one hand, I think one should not overlook the purely theatrical element. Although with a part of themselves the French are conservative and attached to security, they also enjoy drama and action and a relief from the boredom of papa-knows-best government; and although the students and *lycéens* were certainly in earnest about their frustrations and injustices, they would not have been human had they not also relished the dramatic break from routine. One American observer has sceptically dismissed the euphoria of May as "the Club Méditerranée on a nation-wide scale," a kind of irresponsible holiday. I would not go nearly as far as that; but I think it is important for foreigners to remember that the ideal of "revolution" has a very special and romantic appeal in France. And during the crisis many a Frenchman's instinct was to rally emotionally to the challenge of Cohn-Bendit without necessarily sharing his views or his aims. . . .

EDUCATION

The most astonishing aspect of the May crisis is the new visage it has uncovered of French youth. We thought them docile and conformist, or frivolously *yé-yé;* we knew that a number were serious and idealistic, but most of these were frustrated by a sense of impotence and felt isolated not only from society but from each other. Among those who felt this isolation, and this impotence, were the little group that met around Cohn-Bendit at Nanterre on March 22. Two months later, half the nation was at their side. It needed only this detonator, the Sorbonne revolt of May 3, for French youth to come out of its reserve and discover a solidarity and a force that were always latent but never before expressed. Across France, young people who for years had been nourishing certain hopes, certain feelings, became aware of each other for the first time. This was genuinely a kind of revolution, and French youth and French society will never be quite the same again.

But this is not to say that all French youth, or even a majority of it, shares the views of Cohn-Bendit and Jacques Sauvageot. The small extremist element in the revolt rallied wide sympathy for a while because of its daring and because of the stupid police repression against it; but in itself, it contained many unpleasant and negative aspects of nihilism, violence and irresponsibility. I met many serious students in Paris who at first were delighted by the seizure of the Sorbonne and the outburst of free debate, but later felt that the whole thing had turned sour. This is not very surprising; but if some of the revolutionaries went too far and spoilt their own cause, it does not invalidate the importance of the nation-wide movement as a whole. Youth rose up not only against the archaic and muddled education system but also against its own parents, their paternalism, and their strange mixture of over-indulgence and sheer lack of understanding. Family crises broke out "on a scale the nation has not seen since Dreyfus," as one paterfamilias put it. This breach in traditional French parent-child relations carries many dangers, as does any new vacuum; it also carries hope. Exactly as in industry, much will depend on how "les chefs de famille" react.

The education system, too, has been torn apart, and cannot be patched together into the same shape as before. Whereas the Fouchet reforms touched on exams and cycles of study, now there will have to be a much more profound overhaul of methods of teaching, student-teacher relations, centralized bureaucracy, and so on—the fundamental and difficult problems, structural and psychological, that the Fouchet reforms barely tackled. But the crisis has left behind it such chaos that the application of any new measures will be harder than ever—like trying to rebuild a city that is still suffering from epidemic and incendiarism. While the factories in June went quietly back to work, the educational world was still seething, having witnessed amazing scenes that none could have believed possible in this staid milieu. Not to mention the barricades and the burning cars, there was the spectacle of the "desanctified" Sorbonne like a cathedral in the hands of joyous pagans, with red flags and Maoist slogans stuck all over the venerable statues of the gods of French culture, Molière and others. In colleges and faculties throughout France, the same thing happened. Professors and students who in the past had hardly exchanged a word sat around in groups in sunlit courtyards discussing their joint future, or created special assemblies to declare their universities "autonomous" in defiance of Paris. In the academic world, this was 1789. There was also the spectacle in July of *agrégatifs* committing professional hara-kiri by refusing to sit for their *agrégation* rather than compromise with the hated "system."

Even more surprising than the university revolt was what happened in the *lycées,* among schoolchildren, usually so quiet and orderly. A national action committee of *lycéens* (CAL) proved every bit as militant as the students. Teachers no longer dared sit at their rostra, but either fled their classrooms, or, the more liberal of them, sat for hours each day on the benches beside their striking pupils, discussing school, politics, sex, careers, life. "I never knew my girls before, except as minds; now I know them as people," one young woman teacher told me. *Lycéens* suddenly discovered in themselves a political and social awareness that before had been barely latent; and although many reacted stupidly, some showed a remarkable maturity. Parents, invited to take part in the *lycée* debates, were in some cases astonished to hear thoughtful and persuasive public orations from their own sons and daughters—how the babies had grown up! Other parents, worried above all that the *bac* might not take place and a precious career be jeopardized, sometimes hit back brutally. "When some parents entered the *lycées,* we teachers had physically to prevent them from setting on their children and beating them up," I was told in one school. Finally the *bac* did take place, in a sort of way, and the holidays began. Some *lycéens* went off quietly to the seaside with their parents, but others, filled with a new fire, embarked on strange projects—I met several, one of them only fifteen, who planned to spend the summer touring round France spreading the gospel to peasants and workers, just like the Bolsheviks after 1917! My favorite anecdote comes from a girls' *lycée* in Paris at the moment of its "liberation" by a crowd of male invaders from a nearby boys' *lycée*: the main foyer was filled with excited schoolboys calling the girls out on strike, and in their midst was the Directrice, a tiny, round, elderly figure, totally bewildered, clutching at the jacket of a *lycéen* leader, a wild "hippie" figure towering above her, and imploring him desperately, "Mais non, Monsieur, je ne refuse *pas* le dialogue! Je ne le refuse pas!"

Let us hope she means what she says. It was the hostility and conservatism of the teachers that blocked some of the positive aspects of the Fouchet reforms, and reforms needed today will not succeed unless a majority of the teachers is prepared to accept them. Certainly, the crisis will have helped to change their attitudes. In many cases, it has broken the barriers of formality and aloofness that existed between students and even many of the more liberal teachers; it was as if each were afraid to make contact with the other, and now crash, bang, the contact has been forced upon them. Everywhere, pupils and professors have been discussing their problems together. But of course, there has also been a back-lash. Many professors, especially the older ones, denounced the strikes, dug their heels in, and are now struggling to redress the situation. What is even more dangerous is that many of the liberal reformist professors, who had been patiently trying for years to persuade their colleagues of the need for change, have now been abruptly *depassés sur leur gauche* by the more extremist student leaders who condemn them as "softies." It is the dilemma of any revolutionary situation: the liberals are squeezed in the center. But as passions subside, it is possible that the more moderate approach will gain ground again. And it will be the task of the Government to find the right "interlocuteurs valables" among these elements.

In every college and university, during the crisis and just after it students and teachers set about drawing up projects for reform. Millions of words were written, thousands of resolutions were passed, much of it wild and woolly verbiage; but, as the eminent educationalist Jean Capelle told me in July, "If only one percent of it is of any value, that will be an immense success." Certain themes recurred in these projects: *co-gestion,* autonomy, reform of exams and curricula, and of teaching methods, especially the *cours magistrale.* The idea of *co-gestion,* whereby like workers in industry students would have a say in the running of affairs, has already been enshrined *de facto* in *commissions paritaires* in most institutions: committees created by the students and teachers themselves with equal representation for both. They do not yet have any official status, but the Government might find them hard to abolish and could usefully build on them. It is recognized—except by the more extremist students— that there are some matters, essentially academic and financial ones, that should be left to the teachers and executives; but there is a wide move for giving the students much more regular voice in such questions as the shaping of curricula, study methods, and career orientations.

Autonomy is an even more important problem. At the height of the crisis, de Gaulle himself intimated that individual universities would now be given more freedom and that constricting Napoleonic centralization would be modified. Various unofficial projects are in the air, for a national federation of universities, for giving the universities organic links with their regions, even for abolishing the Ministry of Education. There seems to be wide agreement that, even if the finance still comes from Paris, the universities should have far more individual control over how they spend their funds and how they direct their studies and methods of selection. Linked with this is a movement, led by men like Capelle, to break down the "ivory tower" tradition of French universities and put them into closer touch with local life. Some practical progress had already been made here, notably at Nancy and Grenoble, but it is slight by Anglo-Saxon standards. Why not, suggests Capelle, put professors on the boards of local industrial firms and *vice versa?* But teacher opposition to this trend is still very strong.

Projects for reform of studies and exams revolve round the students' desire, shared by many younger teachers, to do away with the didactic *cours magistrale* and the formal dissertation, and to have more group study and seminars. Fine: but where is the money to come from, short of a much more rigorous system of university entrance which the students likewise oppose and on which teachers are still very divided? There is also a move to modernize and liberalize studies such as psychology and sociology which are very badly taught in France. One younger professor told me, "We should like to see far more interdisciplinary penetration, as you now have in Britain—but that's still taboo in France."

In July the Ministry of Education began to send "quaestors" around France to collect these projects, to study them, and possibly to use them as a basis for its own proposals. As I write, the Government has revealed its own intentions much less clearly here than in some other fields, such as industrial or regional reform. It is true these problems are more intractable and need more thought; but they are also more pressing. The Government faces not only the continued wariness of most teachers, as it did in the Fouchet period, but also a much more militant student opposition than before. The extreme Left-wing students represent only a small minority of the total, but they are influential because of the leading part they played in the revolt, and they want to go much farther than the Government or any teacher body. They seem deliberately to have overlooked many issues, and their policies have many contradictions. They want to abolish exams, but they have not suggested what should be put in their place to ensure that merit and hard work are fairly assessed. They want wide and easy entrance to universities, but do not say where the money will come from when student numbers swell to a million. They are indignant about lack of suitable career outlets and lack of vocational training; they also want the university to be "une finalité culturelle" that does not worry itself with practical ends. Many of them are quite simply set on anticapitalist revolution at all costs, and would probably boycott any reforms.

The problem for the Government therefore is to try to isolate this minority, and the diehards among professors, by appealing to the rest of the students and the more moderate teachers. I repeat: this will require more tact than any Gaullist Ministry has shown hitherto. The appointment of Edgar Faure as the new Minister of Education is possibly a hopeful sign; for although he is no great reformist, he is a skilful politician with more horse-sense than many of the younger Gaullist technocrats; and his particular qualities may be more important in the academic world than they were in his previous post, as Minister of Agriculture. Several liberal teachers told me, "We shall accept no imposed solution. But if the Government plays fair with us, we shall try to help." And this dialogue is having to take place at a time of acute physical crisis, when the faculties will be flooded with those who never took their exams in the summer, and when passions and divisions are still acute after the revolt. But *now or never* is the opportunity to tear French education once and for all from its encrusted feudal encasements and reshape it to the needs of a modern society, a technological society but also a human and a just one. Something *will* happen. In education, more than anywhere, people are saying, "I am deeply pessimistic about the short term, but for the longer term I now have new hope."

RALPH T. FISHER, JR.

The Soviet Model
of the Ideal Youth

In this essay, "youth" refers to those between the ages of fifteen and the middle or late twenties—that is, those roughly within the age group of the Communist League of Youth, or Komsomol. The "Soviet model" is that constructed by the top Soviet leaders in their public expressions and actions. This abstraction combines the ideal images appropriate to the countless social roles demanded of Soviet young people. It is a model that is important because it has been propagated by the immense educational and coercive resources of the Soviet state. This model bears no necessary similarity to those that have actuated the leaders in their own lives. Nor is it the only model that has influenced Soviet youth. Certainly there are widely differing models of youth in operation for many of the subcultures within the conglomerate of Soviet society. The coexistence of other models must be kept in mind as we study the most conspicuous ones.

There have obviously been changes, through forty years of the Soviet regime, in what might be called the external appearance and functions of the Soviet model of the ideal youth. Some of these changes reflect shifts in the composition of the Soviet population. For example, the composite model youth of today is better educated and less "proletarian" than his counterpart in the early postrevolutionary years.[1] Other changes

Reprinted by permission of the publishers from Cyril E. Black, ed., *The Transformation of Russian Society* (Cambridge, Mass.: Harvard University Press). Copyright 1960 by the President and Fellows of Harvard College.

[1] For relevant statistics from the congresses of the Komsomol, see *S"ezd IV*, 325–331; *S"ezd VI*, 299–302; *S"ezd VII*, 489–491; *S"ezd VIII*, 546–547; *S"ezd IX*, 405–406; *S"ezd X, II*, 399–404; *Komsomol'skaia pravda* (hereafter abbreviated *KP*) (April 1, 1949), 2; (March 23, 1954), 2. (Note that in 1949 and 1954 the proportion of "workers" was no longer given at all.) The abbreviation *S"ezd* followed by a Roman numeral will be used here to designate the stenographic report, in book form, of one of the first ten Komsomol congresses (held in 1918, 1919, 1920, 1921, 1922, 1924, 1926, 1928, 1931, and 1936). All were published in Moscow, and the dates of editions used here are as follows: I (3rd ed.)—1926; II (3rd ed.)—1926;

reflect the major stages in the development of the Soviet regime. Whereas the model of the Civil War years had a military cast, the model youth of the NEP was waging mainly ideological battles, and each succeeding period left its distinctive imprint. Within each area of Soviet life the detailed functions associated with the model have changed. If in the countryside the ideal youth of 1918–1920 was confiscating grain and recruiting soldiers; under the early five-year plans he was collectivizing the farms and wiping out the kulaks. If in the educational realm the ideal youth of the early 1920s sneered at conventional schools and tried to combine education with factory work, the ideal youth of the 1940s was actively reinforcing discipline under the command of the authorities within the regular school system. But a survey of these changes in the multiple roles of youth in each area of Soviet life would involve the whole history of Soviet youth since 1917, and cannot be undertaken here.[2]

Granting these changes in the shell of the model, we must focus our attention on the central core of traits demanded. We want to see what kind of personal character the regime has been trying to produce in its youth and whether the kind of character has changed significantly in the course of the past forty years. To learn this we may first examine the model that characterized the full bloom of postwar Stalinism, after the "abnormal" eras of the Great Purge and World War II, and then proceed to determine how far this model differed from that of the early years of the Soviet regime and that of the post-Stalin era.

The essential features of the ideal youth of postwar Stalinism emerge from the authoritative proceedings of the Komsomol congress of 1949, published at length in the Soviet press for the guidance of those who were training Soviet youth. For example, the letter sent to the Komsomol congress from the Central Committee of the Communist Party declared:

> The Komsomol must bring up, among our youth, fighters who are fearless, cheerful, buoyant, confident in their strength, ready to overcome any difficulties—fighters for the freedom and honor of our Homeland, for the cause of the Party of Lenin and Stalin, for the victory of Communism.[3]

This passage was often repeated during the congress and and was incorporated with little change into the revised regulations of the Komsomol.[4]

III—1926; IV—1925; V—1927; VI—1924; VII—1926; VIII—1928; IX—1931; X (2 vols.)—1936.

[2] For further details on the specific functions demanded of young people at various periods see Ralph Talcott Fisher, Jr., *Pattern for Soviet Youth: A Study of the Congresses of the Komsomol, 1918–1954* (New York, 1959).

[3] *KP* (April 1, 1949), 1.

[4] *Rezoliutsii i dokumenty XI s"ezda VLKSM* (Moscow, 1949) [hereafter abbreviated *Rez. i dok.*], 50.

Another typical characterization appeared in the letter sent by the Komsomol congress to Stalin:

> We vow to you, dear Comrade Stalin, warmly to love our socialist Homeland, mortally to hate her enemies, not to know fear in the struggle, patiently to endure hardships and misfortunes, to display determination and persistence in reaching the goal that has been set. The young generation of our country is ready to carry out all your instructions and all the instructions of the Communist Party and the Soviet Government. We promise you always to be watchful, ready to deliver a crushing rebuff to the imperialist aggressors, ready to give all our strength and, if necessary, our lives in the defense of our socialist Fatherland.
>
> You teach Soviet youth perseveringly to master knowledge, culture, science, and technology.
>
> We vow to you, Comrade Stalin, to carry out with honor these instructions of yours. . . .
>
> Love of you and loyalty to the Fatherland is the life and the spirit of the youth of our country![5]

From those statements and many other like them, one could draw up a list of traits sought in youth—patriotism, loyalty, courage, vigilance, honesty, persistence, industriousness, optimism, initiative, cheerfulness, idealism, obedience, militancy, ideological purity, and many others.

The central theme that gave the above traits their meaning was that of absolute devotion, respect, and subservience to the leadership represented in the trinity—Stalin, party, and government.[6] Although the worship of Stalin was then near the peak of its extravagance, even the gaudiest panegyric[7] illustrated that the cult was of Stalin as the leader of the party and, hence, of the people and their government; when the ideal youth was told to regard Stalin as the incarnation of everything good, the recipient of vows, and the source of inspiration and strength, these demands only reinforced the demand for loyalty, respect, and obedience to the party leadership.[8] Komsomol orders were an extension of party orders for the young. The Komsomol regulations declared that "the strictest observance of Komsomol discipline is the first obligation of all members of the Komsomol" and went on to say that each member "must faultlessly carry out the decisions of party, soviet, and Komsomol bodies."[9]

[5] *KP* (April 10, 1949), 1.
[6] For some of the many possible illustrative statements, see *Rez. i dok.,* 3–5, 13, 50, 51, 55; *KP* (March 30, 1949), 1, 2; (March 31, 1949), 3; (April 1, 1949), 1, 2; Tamara I. Ershova, *O rabote komsomola v shkole* . . . (Moscow, 1949), 31.
[7] See the chant of praise at the end of the above-mentioned letter in *KP* (April 10, 1949), 1.
[8] For illustrative statements, see *KP* (March 30, 1949), 1, 2; (March 31, 1949), 3; (April 1, 1949), 2, 4; (April 2, 1949), 3; (April 3, 1949), 1; (April 6, 1949), 2; (April 7, 1949), 2; *Rez. i dok.,* 6, 8.
[9] *Rez. i dok.,* 62.

Not only the reference to discipline [10] and to unity and solidarity,[11] but the whole conduct of the congress, including the nature of the discussion and the always miraculously unanimous votes, made it clear that the party leadership was exercising very tight control and that eager acceptance of this "guidance" was a distinguishing feature of the ideal youth.

It was in that context alone that all the other traits demanded in the ideal youth could be interpreted. Words like patriotism, courage, daring, heroism, self-sacrifice—these were applicable only to those who fought for the party's cause.[12] "Vigilance" concerned the security of the party and the Soviet state; "honesty" concerned the observance of principles laid down by the leadership.[13] Persistence, industriousness, all-out effort, the constant striving for perfectionist goals, the refusal to be satisfied with what one has attained—such qualities were of course related to the "building of Communism," that is, the tasks enunciated by the party leaders.[14] Virtuous conduct in personal life was inseparable from political life.[15] "Initiative" must follow strictly the commands of the party.[16] The cheerfulness that was part of the ideal did not preclude some satisfaction with the present, but was essentially based upon optimism regarding the promised future.[17] One might conceivably argue that it was that future —the long-range goal, Communism—to which the ideal youth was subordinating himself, rather than to the leadership of the party. When, however, one takes into account the persistent vagueness of all descriptions of that ultimate goal,[18] as well as the leaders' assumption that only they knew how to reach it, then one is bound to conclude that, while references to the goal were used to justify the immediate demands of the leadership, those demands themselves were the essential guideposts for the ideal youth.

The Soviet model of the ideal youth in 1949 was, in short, the "eager robot"—inwardly so complete a tool of party leadership as to be devoid of a genuine self, yet outwardly seeming to possess such human attributes as will and judgment and enthusiasm.

[10] *Rez. i dok.,* 27–28, 31; Ershova, 8; *KP* (March 30, 1949), 2, 3; (March 31, 1949), 3.

[11] For example, *KP* (April 1, 1949), 3; *Rez. i dok.,* 5; V. N. Ivanov, *Izmeneniia v ustave VLKSM* . . . (Moscow, 1949), 3. For sample references to party guidance see *Rez. i dok.,* 13, 51; *KP* (March 31, 1949), 3.

[12] *KP* (March 30, 1949), 2; (March 31, 1949), 1, 2, 3; (April 1, 1949), 2; *Rez. i dok.,* 9.

[13] For example, see *Rez. i dok.,* 51–53.

[14] For illustrative passages, see *KP* (March 30, 1949), 2, 3; (April 1, 1949), 2; April 3, p. 4; April 8, p. 2; April 10, p. 1; *Rez. i dok.,* p. 7; Ershova, 13; Ivanov, 19.

[15] *KP* (March, 31, 1949), 2 (Mikhailov speaking).

[16] *Rez. i dok.,* 7; *KP* (March 30, 1949), 2; (March 31, 1949), 4.

[17] *Rez. i dok.,* 8; *KP* (March 31, 1949), 4; (April 2, 1949), 2; (April 3, 1949), 2, 3; (April 8, 1949), 3, 4.

[18] The nearest approach to a description at the congress of 1949 was by Mikhailov, in *KP* (March 30, 1949), 2.

With this ideal youth postwar Stalinism in mind, we can now return to the early Soviet period when Stalin had not yet added his impress to the mold. Although there was in those days very little glorification of any leader, including even Lenin,[19] subservience could nevertheless be demanded. How subservient was the ideal youth?

When the Komsomol, which ostensibly embraced the best young people, held its first congress, in October 1918, the assembled delegates agreed virtually unanimously that while the League was to be "solidary" with the Bolshevik Party it was at the same time to be "independent."[20] It was to safeguard "the principle of the spontaneous activity of youth."[21] In April 1919, however, a plenary session of the Komsomol's central committee "requested" that the Komsomol be brought more closely under the party's direction,[22] and soon (August 1919) the two central committees jointly declared that the Komsomol must be "directly subordinate" to the party from top to bottom.[23] While the Komsomol continued to be called "autonomous" (as well as *samostoiatel'nyi* or "self-standing"), the word "independent" dropped out of use and by 1920 was already stigmatized as typical of the dangerous "counterrevolution of the left."[24]

The direct subordination of the League to the party was evident in deed as well as in word. Some of those whom the first and second congresses elected to the League's central committee were unceremoniously removed from their posts by the party.[25] Already by 1920 the top officials of the League, although ostensibly still elected by the Komsomol congress, were in fact designated by a "Communist faction" operating behind the scenes and subject to party orders.[26] Pronounced tendencies toward authoritarian rule from the side of the party were evident in the conditions of deliberation and criticism in the early Komsomol congresses, in the admission and expulsion of members, and in the organizational structure.[27] When some especially zealous Komsomolites launched satellite groups designed to influence and guide the broad masses of Soviet youth, the party stopped them, evidently fearing to let Komsomolites gain

---

[19] For illustrations of the treatment of top party leaders at the Komsomol congresses of 1918, 1919, and 1920, see *S"ezd I*, 38–39, 62, 95; *S"ezd II*, 33, 67, 121–125, 154–155; *S"ezd III*, 26, 236–237. For a discussion of this point, see Fisher, 36–37.

[20] *S"ezd I*, 75, 97, 98.

[21] *S"ezd I*, 74.

[22] *S"ezd II*, 183–184; *Bol'shaia sovetskaia entsiklopediia*, supplementary volume *SSSR* (1948), cols. 645–646 (hereafter abbreviated *BSE, SSSR* (1948).

[23] *S"ezd II*, 45–47, 168, 183–184; *VKP(b) o komsomole i molodezhi: sbornik reshenii i postanovlenii partii o molodezhi, 1903–1938* (Moscow, 1938), 77–78.

[24] *S"ezd III*, 101.

[25] *S"ezd II*, 57; *VKP(b) o komsomole*, 80–82; *S"ezd III*, 34ff.

[26] For significant episodes, see *S"ezd I*, 43, 89–91; *S"ezd II*, 112, 117–118; *S"ezd III*, 102, 235.

[27] For amplification of these points, see Fisher 28–39.

too much influence over auxiliary youth groups until the Komsomol itself was more firmly under party domination.[28]

In that early institutional setting the personal quality most insistently demanded in youth was discipline. This discipline was to spring from acknowledgment of the Communist goal and was to be conscious, self-willed, and self-enforced, rather than imposed from without in an "authoritarian spirit." [29] Thus it was theoretically not in conflict with the parallel demands for initiative and spontaneity. But it must produce unity and solidarity—in Lenin's words, "a single will" for all the millions of workers and peasants.[30] It must be manifested in strict obedience to higher authority.[31] Said Shatskin at the Komsomol congress of 1920:

> There are some comrades among us who say that there is one discipline in the party and another in the League. They say that since our organization is an educational one, we can somewhat loosen the reins with which the leading bodies must hold their subordinate Komsomol organizations in check. This opinion must be refuted root and branch. . . . We must finally establish the most unconditional unquestioning subordination of all active workers to the leading bodies of our organization, and the personal responsibility of each responsible official for each member of our League, for that work which these members are performing.[32]

The same congress in closing issued to all members "an appeal for the greatest self-control and discipline." After describing the perils they faced, it proclaimed that

> In such conditions, there stands before the whole proletariat and also before proletarian youth first of all the task of preserving, developing, and strengthening iron discipline in the ranks of their organizations. Only with such discipline, consolidating the proletariat into an impregnable granite rock, can it resist the crowd of enemies and the loose petit-bourgeois element.
>
> The Third Congress appeals for the preservation of such iron discipline in our ranks. May the ranks of our League be invincible battalions of young proletarians storming the old world.

[28] Relevant to this generalization are the issues of the "Young Proletarian Homes," the "Youth sections affiliated with the trade unions," the Dunaevsky dispute, and the "Ukrainian Opposition." For sample passages from the sources, see *S"ezd I*, 48–49, 70, 75, 77–78, 90–91, 94–95; *S"ezd II*, 34–38, 56, 60, 74, 108–110, 141–147, 179–181, 188, 195; *S"ezd III*, 98, 186, 195, 198–200, 212–240, 247–248, 257–276, 300, 302; *VKP(b) o komsomole*, 80–82. For an account and analysis of these issues, see Fisher 17–28.

[29] See *S"ezd I*, 64; *S"ezd II*, 123, 171–173; *S"ezd III*, 31, 37, 242, 243, 305.

[30] *S"ezd III*, 11. Preobrazhensky and Bukharin echoed the same thoughts (III, 31, 37). See also *S"ezd II*, 125; *S"ezd III*, 33–37.

[31] See, for example, *S"ezd I*, 99; *S"ezd II*, 55–56; *S"ezd III*, 100, 242–243.

[32] *S"ezd III*, 242–243. Lazar' Shatskin was one of the top Komsomolites of the League's first decade.

Long live our militant front!
Long live the victorious proletariat!
Long live revolutionary proletarian discipline! [33]

Other traits much in demand included self-sacrificing bravery for the Communist cause,[34] alertness and vigilance against hostile forces,[35] confidence in the victory of Communism,[36] a sense of responsibility, and such qualities as toughness, dexterity, precision, and industriousness.[37] Those and other demands—to learn Marxism, to set an example, and to avoid dogmatism and pride [38]—were expressed in harmony with the overriding insistence on conscious discipline and strict obedience. The Soviet ideal youth in 1918–1920 was above all a good follower.

Thus the models of 1949 and 1918–1920 appear highly similar. Although in the early Soviet ideal there was probably a shade more independence than in the Stalinist version, the characteristics of the eager robot were already predominant.[39]

One might protest, quite logically, that the conditions of the Civil War would have produced the eager-robot ideal, no matter what had been the Communists' original intent. It is therefore pertinent to examine briefly the prerevolutionary Bolshevik model of the ideal youth, as revealed in the writings of the chief prophet of Bolshevism.

Lenin left no finished portrait of his ideal Bolshevik, young or old, even though his program called for remaking man and society. But as a revolutionary leader he demanded and appreciated certain traits in his followers. He especially prized worker and student youth for their turbulence, daring, and revolutionary potentialities,[40] and considered young people suited to play the semisacrificial role of a vanguard or skirmishing force which could be sent into battle without committing the main body of the party.[41] Apart from such notions, however, Lenin's image of the ideal

---

[33] *S"ezd* III, 305.

[34] For a few of the many references to bravery and self-sacrifice, see *S"ezd I*, 62, 68; *S"ezd II*, 16, 19 (an especially colorful passage by Trotsky), 20–21, 30–31, 66; *S"ezd III*, 29, 31.

[35] *S"ezd I*, 40, 62; *S"ezd III*, 18, 277, 306–307.

[36] *S"ezd I*, 39–40, 97; *S"ezd II*, 14, 28, 65–67; *S"ezd III*, 61–63.

[37] *S"ezd II*, 12–13, 103, 146, 171; *S"ezd III*, 6–22, 139, 141.

[38] *S"ezd II*, 157; *S"ezd III*, 7, 18, 20, 29–30, 36–37, 244–245, 300.

[39] In the light of this predominance, steps were soon taken to ensure that the deterministic side of Marxism could not furnish an excuse and refuge for the nonconformist. See Raymond A. Bauer, *The New Man in Soviet Psychology* (Cambridge, Mass., 1952).

[40] V. I. Lenin, *Sochineniia* (2d ed., Moscow, 1927–1932), V, 79 (March 10, 1902), 347 (August 15, 1903); XXI, 319–320 (October 21 [8], 1917).

[41] Lenin, VIII, 294 (October 17 [4], 1905), 325–326 (October 16, 1905); XII, 336–341 (October 16 [3], 1908).

youth was roughly equivalent to his image of the ideal Bolshevik, for he considered his party to be the party of youth.[42]

Lenin conveniently divorced his model from customary ethical standards by labeling those standards either "feudal" or "bourgeois" [43] and by asserting that the proletariat—whose will he considered himself uniquely fitted to interpret—would establish the moral code of the future.[44] Proletarian ethics admitted all methods. Lenin declared that "Social Democracy does not tie its hands . . . it recognizes all means of struggle so long as they are suited to the available forces of the party and afford the possibility of gaining the greatest results attainable under the given circumstances.[45]

Lenin insisted that his followers exhibit "partyness," by which he meant allegiance to his Bolshevik faction of the Russian Social Democratic Workers' Party and observance of party discipline.[46] In his view a truly nonpartisan approach was impossible.[47] When some of his disciples intimated that partyness was a negation of freedom within their own group, Lenin retorted that partyness constituted "freedom from bourgeois-anarchist individualism." The principle of freedom of organization, he declared, gave the party the right to exclude those who insisted on being individualistic.[48] Lenin was not above declaring support of his own tactics to be a criterion of partyness.[49] But when he was accused of using partyness as a mere cloak for his own political demands, he argued that his policy was that of "the majority of class-conscious Marxist workers participating in political life." [50]

He did not always sound completely authoritarian. For example, he could say:

> Precisely in order not to become too outspoken and . . . harsh regarding "anarchistic individualism" we must, in our opinion, do everything possible—even to the point of some retreats from the pretty diagrams of centralism and from an unconditional submission to discipline—in order to grant these little groups freedom to express themselves, in order to give the whole party the possibility of weighing the profundity or insignificance of disagreements, and to determine just where, in what, and *on just whose side* there is *inconsistency.* . . . We must have more faith in

---

[42] Lenin, X, 188 (December 20 [7], 1906).

[43] Lenin, I, 261–262, 292 (late in 1894).

[44] Lenin, I, 94 (1894).

[45] Lenin, IV, 58–59 (December 1900).

[46] The Russian word is *partiinost'*. See Lenin, IX, 390 (July 14 [1], 1906), and XX, 419 (June 6 [May 24], 1917).

[47] Lenin, VIII, 400–401 (December 1 [November 18], 1905), and VIII, 302 (October 17 [4], 1905).

[48] Lenin, VIII, 386–390 (November 26 [13], 1905).

[49] Lenin, XV, 202 (1911).

[50] Lenin, XVII, 25–26 (October 30 [17], 1913).

the independent judgment of all the masses of party workers. They, and only they, can soften the excessive vehemence of schismatically inclined groupings; can, with their gradual, imperceptible, but all the more persistent influence, inspire these groups with "good will" toward the observance of party discipline; can cool the ardor of anarchistic individualism.[51]

But this semi-tolerance toward "little groups" within the party was exhibited late in 1903, after the party had split and Lenin had lost his fight to control the party organ, *Iskra*. In other words, it was at a moment when he had reason to fear that he and his followers might for a time be one of those "little groups"—that is, until they could fight back to a position of power.[52]

Lenin's view of personal relationships fit into the framework of partyness and centralism. He condemned clannish or cliquish relations—which included personal loyalties to individuals other than himself—on the ground that they obstructed party discipline.[53] Comradeliness had for him a special meaning: "We acknowledge the duty of comradeship, the duty of supporting all comrades, the duty of tolerating the opinions of comrades." "But," he went on, *"for us the duty of comradeship stems from the duty to Russian and to international Social Democracy, and not vice versa."* Comrades were comrades, he said, "only because and insofar as they toil in the ranks of Russian (and, consequently, also international) Social Democracy."[54] While Lenin appealed for initiative,[55] this merely complemented his demand for discipline. A reminder on discipline could be used to bring into line comrades who did something wrong, while a request for more initiative could stimulate those who were merely not doing enough of what was right.

Plainly underlying Lenin's concept of the ideal Bolshevik was his preoccupation with fight and struggle. For him there was no possibility of a peaceful compromise. "The question," he said, "can be posed *only this way*: bourgeois or socialist ideology. There is no middle ground." "Therefore," he went on—in a phrase that has since become a Communist slogan —*"any* belittling of socialist ideology, *any deviation* from it means the same thing as a strengthening of bourgeois ideology."[56]

This by no means exhaustive survey of Lenin's prerevolutionary desiderata suggests strongly that the eager-robot ideal of 1949 and 1918–1920 was already well developed early in the twentieth century.

[51] Lenin, VI, 120–121 (December 8 [November 25], 1903).
[52] For a fuller account of this period in Lenin's life, see Bertram D. Wolfe, *Three Who Made a Revolution* (New York, 1948), chaps. 14 and 15, especially 255. For the colorful conclusion to Lenin's article, see Lenin, VI, 122–123.
[53] Lenin, VI, 354 (August 1904).
[54] Lenin, II, 541–542 (1899).
[55] Lenin, IV, 383 (1902), and VII, 149 (March 8 [February 23], 1905).
[56] Lenin, IV, 391–392 (1902).

The ideal did not die with Stalin. In 1954, at the first Komsomol congress after Stalin's death, the leadership called for a revival of "criticism from below," observance of the collective principle in leadership, and wider democracy within the League.[57] But the congress itself, in its discussion, criticism, and voting, gave no hint of genuine relaxation.[58] Soviet literature was still said to be failing to depict lifelike heroes who could serve as models for the young.[59] Although the Stalin cult was gone, the cult of the party and its Central Committee provided ample occasion for the same extravagant expressions of devotion. In their letter to the party's Central Committee the delegates said:

> The young men and women of the land of the Soviets have boundless love and loyalty for the Communist Party. Their most cherished thoughts and hopes are bound up with the party; they are obligated to it for all the happiness and joy of their lives. . . . In all its activities the Leninist Komsomol senses the daily, fatherly care of the Communist Party and its Central Committee. . . .
> The Communist Party is the wise teacher and mentor of youth. For the Komsomol, the word and deed of the party come before all else.[60]

And when that letter was read at the final session, all delegates reportedly rose "in a united transport of boundless love for their own Communist Party" and gave a "tumultuous ovation," shouting "Glory to the Communist Party!" [61]

Since 1954 there has been no clear sign of change. The Komsomol central committee in February 1957, while calling for more democracy in the League, insisted also, in the very same sentence, on the need for stronger discipline, and the attitude toward the party leadership was just as subservient as ever.[62] In July, when Khrushchev's victory over Malenkov, Kaganovich, and Molotov was announced, the accompanying editorial—studded with references to monolithic unity, discipline, and obedience to party directives—was in the Stalinist tradition.[63]

The Soviet model of the ideal youth—the model expressed by the party leadership—has had, then, an almost unvarying core. Changes have occurred in the external appearance and functions of the model,

---

[57] *KP* (March 20, 1954), 3, 4; (March 24, 1954), 1; (March 26, 1954), 2; (March 27, 1954), 3; (March 30, 1954), 2.

[58] *KP* (March 20–30, 1954), *passim.*

[59] *KP* (March 20, 1954), 3; (March 24, 1954), 2; (March 25, 1954), 3; (March 26, 1954), 4.

[60] *KP* (March 27, 1954), 1.

[61] *KP* (March 27, 1954), 2.

[62] *KP* (February 28, 1957), 1, trans. in *Current Digest of the Soviet Press* (April 17, 1957), 16–18.

[63] *Pravda* (July 3, 1957), 1, trans. in *CDSP,* (July 17, 1957), 7–8.

but these have not significantly affected the continuity of the eager-robot ideal—the ideal of utter loyalty to the party chiefs, iron discipline, self-sacrificing bravery, incessant vigilance, burning enthusiasm, unshakable conviction, and uncompromising militancy. While many of those qualities suggest a military figure, the ideal youth, unlike a soldier, is never off duty. There are no areas of human knowledge, appreciation, or action in which he can exercise full freedom and imagination.

The persistence of the eager-robot ideal reflects the continuing importance of doctrine for the Soviet regime, the regime's reliance upon an atmosphere of crisis, and the regime's totalitarian and authoritarian character. The official ideal as treated here could not change significantly without considerable changes in the nature of the regime.

But the answer to the question of continuity and change in the Soviet model of the ideal youth must be termed incomplete. We are driven back to the difficulties suggested earlier, which stem in large part from our lack of free access to Soviet society. We lack the means of penetrating very far beyond the formal or official or external model, but we can perceive that it does not monopolize the scene. To the extent that it appears too harsh and uncompromising, to the extent that it fails to *live* for Soviet citizens, it encourages other models to flourish. The Soviet system, never completely authoritarian or totalitarian despite its aims and its dictatorial excesses, can inspire models of careerism, of apathy, of compromise, of opposition. The cynicism of the leaders vitiates the official model, while beyond the circle of political chiefs there are other model makers who play significant but not easily appraisable roles in establishing operating images of the ideal. Thus there is the possibility that, while "the Soviet model" remained the same, other models, without being formal or official, nevertheless could alter significantly the orientation of Soviet youth.

GALIA GOLAN

Youth and Politics in Czechoslovakia

It would be inaccurate to see the "revival" in Czechoslovakia in terms of a conflict of generations, or to attribute to this the radical changes of those startling eight months, for the issues were not specifically generational; more important, the forces in the struggle for power and leadership were not the young versus the old. Such a characterization was vigorously denied by Ota Sik in an interview immediately after the crucial central committee meeting which brought the liberals to power.[1] He pointed out that many of those who pushed hardest for change were among the oldest members of the party, including people like Frantisek Vodslon and Frantisek Kriegel. Indeed it was actually some of the youngest men in the Czechoslovak party such as Lenart, once regarded as promising "new blood," who stood by Novotny in many of the presidium and central committee battles. This is not to say that there was no generational problem in Czechoslovakia, or that it played no role in the movement for democratization. The problem was complex and constantly changing both in importance and function, and for his reason may be more easily understood within the context of three different periods: the pre-1968 liberalization; the period of the "revival," i.e., January to August 1968; and the invasion and postinvasion period.

Following the twelfth congress of the Czechoslovak Communist Party in December 1962, destalinization was at last undertaken in Czechoslovakia. This period, from early 1963 until 1967, might be called the prerevival revival, during which certain elements within the party—principally liberal intellectuals, economists, and Slovaks—struggled to introduce thoroughgoing reforms, and when almost every area and aspect of Czechoslovak society came under scrutiny. One of these was the gap between the gen-

Galia Golan, "Youth and Politics in Czechoslovakia," *Journal of Contemporary History*, vol. V, no. 1 (1970), pp. 3–22. Reprinted by permission of George Weidenfeld and Nicolson, London.

[1] Prague radio interview, 21 and 26 February 1968, reported in *Bratislava Pravda*, 29 February 1968.

erations and the youth problem, though it must be added that only gradually did the youth emerge as anything of a force or issue with which the
party had to contend.

Czechoslovak youth in the early 1960s was a disillusioned and generally
speaking apathetic group, ashamed of its elders because of the Munich
capitulation, and repelled by the regimentation, authoritarianism, and de-
ceptions of the communist regime. It was precisely this apathy, or more
accurately, this political indifference, which was of concern to the regime,
as the liberals again and again pointed to the party's failure to win over
the youth.[2] One survey concluded that among the students interrogated
only some 11.4 percent considered themselves politically active, while 47
percent considered themselves politically neutral, 6.6 percent passive, and
3.5 percent "did not know." [3] Another study showed that only 11.3 percent of the students who were members of the party joined out of "inner
conviction"; 27.6 percent joined for material advantage, 4.4 percent under
the influence of their environment, and 44.2 percent for "other reasons,"
among which material motives and environment were predominant.[4] Still
another study revealed that Czechoslovak youths were pacifists, uninter-
ested in the army, and so desirous of peace that they "underestimate the
motives of the enemy." Of the group polled, 20 percent believed that the
United States arms because of its desire for peace, and over 30 percent
said the United States arms for reasons other than war. Moreover, an
astonishingly high percentage of nineteen year old boys were unaware of
the existence of the Warsaw Pact (no doubt this figure has now declined).[5]
In addition to these phenomena, juvenile delinquency was becoming a
problem and young people were increasingly seeking pastimes, in groups
or individually, outside the framework of the associations established and
designed by the regime to organize their leisure time in the interests of
the party. According to Vladimir Koucky, then a member of the Presidium,
the institutions of higher learning had become hotbeds of "petty-bourgeois
weeds and anti-Marxist attacks . . . new formations of technocratism,
managerialism, mysticism, pro-Djilas pamphlets, the apotheoses of bourgeois democracy, and philosophical irrationalism." [6] Presumably to com-

---

[2] One article highlighted the dilemma of a teacher forced to present a new line
every day, and the damage done to the young because "we tore down the old morality and left a vacuum." V. Kvardova, in *Kulturny Zivot*, 16 February 1963.
Another article complained of the distortions fed the young and emphasized that
they would not tolerate "the big lie." V. Zykmunt, in *Plamen*, 1963, 134. The failure
to replace religious principles by anything constructive in the course of atheistic education was pointed out by V. Gardovsky in *Veda a Zivot*, February 1966, 65–70.

[3] M. Schneider, in *Zivot Strany*, March 1966, 13.

[4] Unsigned article in *Student*, 19 January 1966.

[5] *Smena*, 28 December 1965.

[6] *Rude Pravo*, 24 October 1964: report by party ideological commission chairman
Vladimir Koucky to the central committee. A conference on the growing problem

bat this, the party decided early in 1965 to establish party university committees, even though (or perhaps because) only 5 percent of students were party members. The party admitted, however, that the problem was not limited to young intellectuals; Koucky pointed out that a poll of a provincial agricultural secondary school had revealed unsatisfactory attitudes towards work, lack of drive, and insufficient social responsibility.

While the party sought to solve these problems in a number of ways, including educational reform,[7] it placed the greatest blame for the situation on the Czechoslovak Youth Union (CSM), the organization designed to stimulate and direct youth and to shape its political activity. The CSM had been conceived as a unified youth organization designed not only to educate its own members, but also to exert an influence on the youth outside its ranks. In this it clearly had failed, as it became increasingly apparent over the years that instead of an organization for and of the youth, the CSM was a regime agency over the youth. Because of the fluid nature of its membership and the small number of communist members, it had by 1958 become the only mass organization under *direct* party control, instead of the usual indirect control exercised through communist members in an organization's leadership. In 1966 it covered 1,055,000 young people from the ages of fifteen to twenty-six, that is, about 50 percent of those eligible for membership. Most of these were pupils and students, a reflection perhaps of the fact that CSM membership was one factor in admission to higher studies or other educational benefits.[8] Only 25 percent of factory youth were CSM members and the percentage was even smaller among agricultural youth.[9] In the three years from 1963 to 1966 CSM membership had dwindled by almost 400,000, from 1,418,783 to 1,055,000.[10] Membership had in fact become a largely formal matter, allegiances only superficial. Many a youth left the CSM as soon as he felt that membership was no longer necessary to his career. It was in part to correct this state of affairs that the party instigated a "Party Talks to Youth Campaign" in 1965 and called upon the CSM to reorganize and reform itself.[11]

---

of juvenile delinquency was held as early as 1963: Prague radio, 2 December 1963. In that year juvenile delinquency rose by 12 percent: Bratislava radio, 8 March 1964.

[7] In 1964 and 1965 reforms were introduced in the primary and secondary school system, and the higher educational system respectively. Among other things they provided for greater differentiation within the educational system, more attention to the humanities, less time in production, entrance examinations for the academic secondary schools, an end to the cadre system for admission to the university, election of Rector and Deans, and student representation in the university scientific councils (senate).

[8] Prague radio, 27 May 1966; cf. *Rude Pravo*, 23 July 1965; *Mlada Fronta*, 25 April 1963.

[9] *Prace*, 24 April 1966.

[10] *Mlada Fronta*, 24 April 1963; Prague radio, 27 May 1966.

[11] CTK, 13 January 1966.

The party's reaction was in fact a response to more than the situation in the CSM; it was an effort to stifle pressures which were beginning to gain dangerous momentum, from the party's point of view. The youth had been the first, perhaps the only, group outside the party to grasp early on the importance and possibilities of the campaign for reform launched within the party. Young workers as well as students had tentatively joined these forces by turning the traditional May Day outdoor poetry readings into political demonstrations.[12] In response to the liberalization in the cultural world, there appeared a new "generational" literature, numerous *avant-garde* satirical theatrical groups among the young, jazz and poetry-reading clubs, and a new, highly controversial journal for young writers called *Tvar*.[13] Moreover, in conjunction with the intellectuals' pressure for changes in such organizations as the trade unions, and the creation of genuine interest groups with an effective role in society, the youth, particularly the students, began to press for changes in their own organization, the CSM. After months of discussion and warnings from the party,[14] the most radical of the proposals for CSM reform was presented at the national conference of university students in Prague, 18–19 December 1965, by Prague Technological Institute student Jiri Mueller. His plan outlined changes in both the function and the organization of the CSM.[15] He suggested that the union be broken down into a loose federation of autonomous professional groups, i.e., a students association, a young workers association, and an association of young farmers, each to be subdivided by

[12] The most striking of these were the May Day demonstrations of 1965 and 1966. In 1965 the regime permitted the students to hold their traditional Majales Festival for the first time since 1956, when 'revisionist' and 'anti-party' slogans in the student parade had led the regime to prohibit the event. The posters in 1965 in Prague and Bratislava carried such slogans as: 'Whoever cannot read or write can always quote,' 'Criticize only the dead,' 'As you grow older you will have to alter what you learned as a youth.' In Prague the students brought the day to a climax by electing visiting beat poet Allen Ginsberg Majales King. One week later Ginsberg was expelled from the country for propagating 'bourgeois attitudes' and corrupting the youth, since he was both a drug addict and a homosexual. Cf. *Rude Pravo,* 17 May 1965, speech by Novotny; *East Europe,* July 1965, 40; *Mlada Fronta,* 2, 22 May 1965; Prague radio, 14 May 1965. In May 1966 students and young workers held a demonstration in Prague carrying such slogans as 'We want freedom, we want democracy,' 'A good communist is a dead one,' and for the police 'Gestapo! Gestapo!' Twelve youths were arrested and received five to ten months sentences by a Prague court on 24 May 1966. J. Ruml, in *Literarni Listy,* 21 March 1968.

[13] Some of this literature is discussed in J. F. Brown *The New Eastern Europe* (London, 1966). The "generational literature" of such writers as Jan Benes, Milan Uhde, Ivan Klima, Jaroslava Blazkova, Ales Haman, and Milan Hamada came under severe party criticism, as did the satirical theatres. Cf. S. Vlasin in *Nova Mysl,* November 1964. The journal *Tvar* became the center of a controversy within the Czechoslovak Writers Union and between the union and the regime in late 1965. It was finally shut down and its editor-in-chief expelled from the party. Cf. *Literarni Noviny,* 4 December 1965; V. Uhler, in *Zivot Strany,* April 1966, 17.

[14] Cf. for example Koucky's speech to the party central committee, *Rude Pravo,* 24 October 1964.

[15] *Student,* 26 January 1966.

age. These structural changes were designed for one purpose and one purpose only: to make the CSM a legitimate, independent representative of the youth by serving as a platform for its ideas and supporting them vis-à-vis the decision-making powers of the country. Mueller claimed that the CSM, as it stood, was a political organization (i.e., serving the party's interests and preparing the youth for the party) "without any possibility of acting as such." To act as such, Mueller argued, it must truly express the views of its members even to the extent of opposing the party if necessary. Concretely, he demanded an effective role for the CSM in the National Front, representation in all state bodies and in the National Assembly. In essence he was advocating the formation of a genuine political party.

The conference was favorably impressed by this proposal and set up an eleven-man committee under Lubos Holacek to look into its feasibility.[16] This marked the beginning of a controversy which was destined to make the youth issue one of the elements in the liberals' campaign against Novotny. The party's immediate reaction was to condemn Mueller's ideas as wrong or confused, arguing that there was no need for an opposition when there already existed ample opportunity for frank discussion within the party and CSM and between them.[17] Nonetheless certain liberals and moderates in the party recognized the importance of taking the students seriously. The then moderate Martin Vaculik, a rising star in the party hierarchy but still the liberal leader he had been in his earlier posts in Brno, pointed out that "a youth organization cannot merely imitate the organizations of the adults; it must find contents and forms of work which correspond to the needs, interests, and thinking of the young." [18] A later article in the party daily admitted that the young did not feel themselves part of a system they had merely inherited rather than created themselves: it was just this absence of "an active political relationship" to the system which had led to their apathy, opposition, and criticism. Implicitly criticizing direct tutelage by the party, the article concluded with the suggestion that a way be found to make the CSM "an authoritative and attractive component of our political system." [19]

Interestingly enough, it may not have been that Novotny feared that a serious generational gap had been or would be caused if the CSM were reorganized; rather it appeared that he was concerned with precisely the opposite, i.e. that the youth would join forces—were already doing so— with their elders among the liberals, who were at that time demanding

[16] *Mlada Fronta,* 27 January 1966.
[17] *Rude Pravo,* 22 December 1965.
[18] M. Vaculik, in *Nova Mysl,* 11 January 1966.
[19] *Rude Pravo,* 8 April 1966.

such things as an opposition (within or outside the party), "integrated criticism," and so forth.[20] For this reason, apparently, Novotny acted to bring the movement to a halt. Addressing a young workers delegation in the spring of 1966, he strongly denounced Mueller's proposal. The conservative majority of the CSM leaders heeded this warning and also condemned the proposal as "one-sided and politically wrong." [21] The question was left for the CSM national congress in 1967, but before that meeting the party took stronger action. In December 1966, one year after the Mueller proposal, Jiri Mueller and Lubos Holacek were expelled from the CSM and from the university and drafted into the army.[22] After this move it was only to be expected that the June 1967 CSM congress did not concern itself with liberalization. These actions, together with other repressive measures introduced by Novotny in 1966 and 1967, irreparably alienated the students and set the stage for a showdown.[23] The Slovak party, at least, seemed to grasp the potential danger of the situation, for its daily organ published an article by Academician and party theorist Miroslav Kusy and journalist Juraj Suchy which once again urged that attention be paid to youth as a distinct group. Without referring directly to the CSM, the reform of which now appeared unlikely, the two liberals argued that the youth must have some political outlet and some way to produce their own "generational program." A program devised by the older generation should not be forced on them; they should be allowed to propose their own solutions to their problems, to determine their own way of life in socialism, as well as the goals which they, as a generation, wished to achieve. "The youth which has no generational program of its own," Kusy and Suchy argued, "cannot have positive aims and thus, as a generation, it must disintegrate; one part takes over the generational program of the "fathers" and becomes a conformist appendage, offering at most passive resistance, while the other part keeps to itself . . . slowly sinking into a position of criticism for criticism's sake, protesting against

[20] Space does not permit an excursion into this subject. The reference is to a discussion conducted on these topics by intellectuals such as Zdenek Mlynar, Julius Strinka, Andrej Kopcok, Miroslav Kusy, Michal Suchy, and Michal Lakatos. Some of these ideas are discussed in an article by M. Schwartz in *Problems of Communism,* January–February 1967.

[21] Prague radio, 18 April 1966; *Rude Pravo,* 20 May 1966. It was typical of Novotny to deliver this warning to a delegation of workers rather than to the students themselves, for he had long played upon worker distrust of intellectuals in the hope of setting them one against the other, and thereby defeating the intellectuals' proposals while preventing the emergence of a potentially dangerous worker-intellectual alliance.

[22] Cf. *Reporter,* 6 March 1968, 'The Case of Jiri Mueller.'

[23] After weathering the crises of 1963 and 1964, Novotny gradually regained control and began to obstruct or even revoke many of the concessions he had been forced to grant under pressure from the liberals. The moves against the youth must be seen in this context.

everything that exists." They concluded, as others had before them, that youth must be made equal political partners rather than mere political objects in society.[24]

This warning apparently went unheeded, coming as it did in August 1967 just when the regime was fully preoccupied with the faltering economy (and with complaining economists), as well as with recalcitrant intellectuals and demanding Slovaks.[25] The regime may well have thought the issue closed by the neutralization of Mueller and Holacek and the conservative trend of the June CSM congress. This was, however, a miscalculation, for just as the party central committee was meeting in what turned out to be the first of the three plenary sessions which brought the liberals to power,[26] the showdown came. A purely nonpolitical demonstration became the occasion for student demands differing little from those of the party liberals. It is not unusual for demonstrations, particularly student demonstrations, as we have seen them in the 1960s, prompted by purely material motives, even by minor grievances, to change their character, broadening out to include grievances against the political or socio-economic nature of society itself. Czechoslovak students and young workers had on previous occasions turned peaceful gatherings into anti-regime platforms, but in the early winter of 1967 the atmosphere was such—and the regime's reaction was a reflection of this atmosphere—that the student outburst was to be of great significance.

On the night of 31 October residents of the Prague Technological Institute's Strahov hostel took to the streets in protest against conditions in the hostel. Their peaceful candlelight march was dispersed by the police who even entered the hostel and indiscriminately beat up anyone found there.[27] This police brutality enraged the students (of many faculties and in other cities), who responded in the following days with meetings, demands, and threats of repeated demonstrations. Party conservatives realized the political nature of the student outburst and blamed it on western

[24] *Bratislava Pravda,* 2 August 1967.

[25] The economists were discouraged by Novotny's interference in and obstruction of the economic reforms; the intellectuals' rebellion at their June congress is well known; the Slovaks found their voice again when Novotny belittled their national aspirations by referring to nationalism as 'reactionary.' Novotny also moved against the young writers by the trial and imprisonment of Jan Benes, former editor of *Tvar,* in the summer of 1967.

[26] These are the meetings held at the end of October 1967 to discuss the role of the party, in December to discuss the splitting of the top government and party positions, and early January to elect a new first secretary. The move to get rid of Novotny crystallized at the October plenum.

[27] *Smena,* 19 November 1967. The candles were deliberate; one of the complaints was against electricity failures. Indeed the students went into the streets because that very evening, during one of their many sessions with youth officials (from *Mlada Fronta*) about the situation, the electricity failed again. *Rude Pravo,* 14 November 1967; *Prace,* 2, 3 November 1967.

anticommunist propaganda, especially that of Radio Free Europe, and on the banned Writers Union weekly *Literarni Noviny*.[28] In response to the students' demands, an investigation was begun and the police were found guilty of "unduly harsh measures." The Interior Ministry was ordered to look into the affair, but the matter was left more or less in the air pending resolution of the crisis which had already reached an acute stage in the party's central committee.

The youth became something of an issue, and a relatively important one, as a result of the 1967 demonstration. The Strahov affair (as it came to be called) impressed upon the regime the need to look upon the youth as a stratum of society to which it would have to answer. Alexander Dubcek acknowledged that "among all the questions facing us today, that of the youth holds a special position." [29] Indeed the youth themselves took advantage of the impact of the Strahov affair to form themselves into something of a vanguard of the "revival." They organized a great many rallies and meetings to which they invited leading political, cultural, and economic figures to answer their outspoken questions.[30] They did not restrict themselves to their own concerns, but put forward a list of comprehensive demands including freedom of the press, freedom of association, freedom of travel, re-establishment of a constitutional court, separation of powers within the government, investigation into the death of Jan Masaryk, solidarity with Polish students, and even changes in foreign policy (relations with Israel, equal status vis-à-vis the USSR, and so forth).[31] Nor was this activity limited to students; the students themselves sought to counter the conservatives' efforts to drive a wedge between workers and intelligentsia, sending letters to factory workers explaining their demands and arranging joint meetings and discussions.[32] The rallies themselves were by no means exclusively student affairs, any more than earlier May Day demonstrations had been composed exclusively of students, or, as *Prace,* the trade union daily pointed out (10 March 1968), any more than *Literarni Noviny* had lacked a large number of readers among the working youth. To aid the students in their efforts to cement their ties with young workers, *Prace* condemned the attempt to paint the Strahov affair as

---

[28] F. Kolar, in *Kulturni Tvorba,* 16 November 1967. Kolar also said that the police were just young workers trying to do their job. For this, students accused him of trying to drive a wedge between them and the workers; they even threatened to bring him to court. *Frankfurter Allgemeine Zeitung,* 22 November 1967.

[29] *Rude Pravo,* 23 February 1968.

[30] One of the largest and perhaps most interesting of these was held in Prague on 20 March. Some 6000 young people crammed the hall to question Smrkovsky, Sik, Goldstücker, and others. Prague radio, 20 March 1968; *Rude Pravo,* 22 March 1968.

[31] Ibid. See also *Reporter,* 3 April 1968, 'Manifesto of Prague Youth'; Unsigned, *Student,* 29 May 1968.

[32] *Mlada Fronta,* 13 March 1968.

a class battle (young intellectuals against young workers, i.e., the police) and pointed out that most of the students were children of workers or party officials.

At this time there was some discussion of the generational aspect of the youth issue. On the most simplistic, perhaps vulgar, level, one indignant party member castigated the young for condemning past party actions: "it is true that we then proceeded harshly [in collectivizing agriculture]. You, the young, can now easily speak of the law and its sanctions. But at the time the towns had nothing to eat. If we had not been hard you would not be sitting here at all, or you would be crippled with rickets." [33]

While such an attitude (not an isolated phenomenon), sought to reduce the issues pressed by the youth to this type of oversimplification of a difference between generations, others feared that the attacks on the past might result in a wholesale rejection by the young of everything and everyone connected with the older generation. It was for this reason that the party made efforts to demonstrate that political age or youth, such as that demonstrated at the crucial party sessions, had nothing to do with chronological age.[34] Dubcek for his part urged party members not to fear such accusations but to prove their "political youth" by adopting the healthy skepticism and initiative of the young. That a problem nonetheless existed was pointed out by many who were disturbed by the distrust and disillusionment of the youth vis-à-vis the older generation. As one journalist put it: "they do not believe us, they do not believe that these changes are permanent"; or as another put it: "they saw at each step that practice was different from what was preached. And at the time of the exposure of the so-called personality cult the youth ceased to believe even the teachers." [35] The liberal writer Jan Prochazka sarcastically explained: "The young people's instinct made them understand that we usually do not believe what we say. And then we were surprised to realize that they have been losing their respect for us!" More specifically he added: "For the more intelligent boys and girls, it was hard to understand that in the history of other nations it was possible and permitted to pay homage even to tsars and tyrants, while in our own country there was no place in history for the man who was the founder of our democracy, who was neither a usurper nor the murderer of his own children, but an educated, democratic, and highly moral man, and this does not refer to T. G. Masaryk alone." Prochazka considered it foolish to think that young people believed all the lies they had been told or accepted the dogma uniformly presented them in schools: "It is an artificial pyramid. One day the wind will blow

---

[33] *Bratislava Pravda,* 8 March 1968.
[34] Cf. *Rude Pravo,* 29 January 1968.
[35] J. Ruml, in *Reporter,* 24 April 1968; *Prace,* 10 March 1968.

it down and the young people educated all these years in love of the USSR will one night go out into the streets and rejoice at an ice hockey victory in a manner which makes it clear even to the most uninformed that this does not concern ice-hockey alone." [36] Goldstücker echoed these sentiments when he told an Italian communist journal that "in general the young people are disillusioned by the evolution of Czechoslovakia." [37]

As these comments indicate, there was indeed a conflict between generations: the young distrusted the old, especially the party members, and found few people they could believe in since so many of even the liberals had Stalinist or opportunist pasts. There was little they could admire among their elders, for their aversion to the communists' mistakes, distortions, and terror had an earlier counterpart in the shameful sell-out at Munich, blamed on the leaders of the First Republic. But probably the greatest gap existed between the generations of communists, for among the noncommunists at least the parents could and did maintain contact with their children by educating them (despite the influences outside the home) in the principles of the First Republic. A gap existed even here too, however, for the end of the First Republic and of the postwar Benes regime, plus the nature of the society which emerged after 1948, undermined any respect for authority and dispelled any interest in ideologies among the youth. There were no pat answers, no messianic solutions, and their ambivalence towards their elders, bordering on cynicism, was aptly expressed when Lubos Holacek said at a mass rally that student support for the progressives should not be taken as something assured. If, he explained, the "political monopoly of the Communist Party" failed to secure the activity of the masses, the students would have to seek another system.[38]

Though the gap indeed existed, the youth were well aware that their position could be improved only in the context of a general political change, and their demands were not limited to strictly youth needs; indeed, they were warned by one of their mentors, the philosopher Ivan Svitak, not to "solve only the narrow generational problems of youth." They should realize "that the decisive problems are the common human ones. You cannot solve them by advancing the demands of the young; you must grapple urgently with problems of all people." [39] In fact there was little or no conflict between the demands of the youth and those of the liberals. Even such ideas as federalization of the republic, urged by the older generation of Slovak communist nationalists, were sincerely shared by the

[36] J. Prochazka, in *Ucitelske Noviny,* 7 March 1968.
[37] *Rinascita,* 19 April 1968.
[38] Prague radio, 20 March 1968.
[39] Ivan Svitak, in *Student,* 13 March 1968. Youthful scepticism extended even to Svitak from time to time; many students questioned his sincerity.

Slovak youth whose nationalism appeared to be as strong as that of their elders.[40] Yet many students were to point out that while the words might be the same, and the slogans shared, there was a wide gulf between the generations as to the meaning of the words they used, such as democracy, rights, and so forth. This was one reason why they so sharply questioned their elders, demanding at every step actions rather than words.[41] Nonetheless, it may be said that the youth accepted Svitak's advice, for whatever their inner reservations about almost all the country's leaders, liberal or otherwise, they did their utmost to support them in the democratization struggle, serving as a rallying point for people of all ages, speaking out and agitating for mass participation in and support of the process.

However, they did not intend to lose their identity as a specific stratum; they operated as a pressure group, maintaining and indeed demanding enough independence to be an effective force. This was perhaps the greatest difference between their role in the prerevival liberalization struggle, and in the revival period itself. So long as the struggle remained within the party, they joined in, for outside it they could not play a part of any importance. The best they could do, and this they did with varying degrees of success, was to attempt to awaken their own ranks and make sure that their own demands (for changes in the CSM or changes in the educational system) were included among those of the party liberals. When the process became a public affair, when the party turned to the public for support and participation, the youth found that they had room within which to operate. As the best informed and best organized group outside the party—one of the few (if not the only) nonparty groups to have grasped from the outset the possiblities of the pre-1968 struggle—they were natural leaders of the hitherto uninformed, uninvolved, or unconsulted masses, and a natural bridge between them and the party liberals with whom they had collaborated in the past. In this new capacity the youth were indeed a force, and both they and the new regime had to consider how best this force might be institutionally constituted and exercised.

The party was naturally concerned that the political activism of the young people should not be used *against* the party but rather *for* it, and an editorial in *Rude Pravo* (22 March 1968), urged communists to go among

[40] *Rolnicky Noviny,* 29 April 1968, pointed with pride to the mass march of youth commemorating the youth march 123 years earlier led by Slovak nationalist hero Ludovit Stur, noting that today, too, Slovak youth wanted a free Slovak state, i.e., a federated CSSR.

[41] It is in this context that one must see the efforts by students to introduce a second candidate into the Presidential election of the spring of 1968. Student leader Ivan Hartel has said privately that he suggested the candidacy first of Smrkovsky and then of Cisar not out of any opposition to Svoboda, but in the interests of democracy.

the youth, talk to them, and try to win them over by deeds as well as words in the spirit of the post-January program of revival. Dubcek had a clear grasp of the problem: "I do not think we can win over the youth simply by constantly telling them or even throwing constantly in their teeth all that has been successfully achieved . . . their enthusiasm and ardor cannot be exhausted by merely praising what has been realized. They want to create themselves, to implement their longings and ideals themselves— precisely as the older generation wanted to do when they were young and when the revolution provided them with the possibility. They must not get ready-made things, gifts, or achievements, but scope for their own initiative, for their ideas, for arranging their own future life so as to accomplish their tasks." [42] He urged that conditions be created to permit the youth to express themselves, and it was to these conditions or, more specifically, the institutional framework within and through which youth could operate, that attention was turned in the effort to cope with this new force.

Thus once again the question of the structure and role of the CSM was raised. At this point, however, the organization was almost disintegrating, for group after group was demanding autonomy. The most important, or at least most controversial, of these groups was the students. After the Mueller and Strahov affairs, and all that had happened in the first few months of 1968, the earlier demands appeared conservative. The students would no longer be content with a federal CSM but demanded independence, and a bitter struggle ensued between them and the CSM. While the CSM met, temporized, argued, introduced personnel changes, and tried to keep things under its control, the students took matters into their own hands. Student Academic Councils, originally started in December 1967 in response to the failure of the CSM to support student demands in the Strahov affair, began to spring up in various faculties with the CSM representatives in many cases resigning in their favor. From this a student union began to emerge which was organized as a federation of separate Slovak and Czech associations, outside the CSM. The new organization's program was based on the United Nations Declaration of Human Rights and proposed such things as support for the progressive forces in the party, personnel changes in the party, rehabilitation of the victims of past injustices, legal guarantees of civil rights, postponement of the national elections pending amendment of the electoral law, and shorter military service for students. There was even talk of running candidates for the National Assembly. They rejected the idea of any solution or arrangement within the CSM: it was a moribund organization, membership in which had become a mere formality; in any case it had lost the confidence of the stu-

[42] *Rude Pravo,* 23 February 1968 (22 February speech).

dents. They wanted student self-government at the lower levels, working up to a national union of students, on a truly voluntary and elective basis.[43]

The regime's reaction to this movement was perhaps influenced by the rapid appearance of similar demands for independence from (or within) the CSM; young workers held a state-wide meeting in Prague to consider the formation of a Union of Working Youth; young Slovak agricultural workers demanded their own organization; the Hungarian minority demanded their own youth and Pioneer organizations, while the Pioneers themselves demanded autonomy. The Junak (Boy Scouts) were rehabilitated, also as an independent organization, and youth groups began splitting off from another mass organization, Svazarm. Young soldiers spoke of forming their own organization and secondary school pupils decided to set up an independent union. With the founding of a preparatory committee for an Association of Socialist Youth there was even the possibility of a direct rival or replacement for whatever would be left of the CSM.[44]

Despite certain sympathetic comments,[45] the party did not look favorably on this involuntary dissolution or undermining of the CSM. While it was ready to concede the need for an independent federated youth movement as an effective component of the National Front, it was not willing to see the CSM lose its monopoly as the only youth organization. While this was in direct contradiction to the party's Action Program (which called for freedom of association), the party presidium, meeting 21–22 May 1968, declared its opposition to any youth organization independent of the CSM.[46] The democratization process being what it was, however, most groups went on setting up independent organizations in the hope that the law on freedom of association, for which the liberals and youth were together campaigning, would resolve the issue and force the government to license them. Indeed, more than ten different youth associations were

[43] The course of events can be followed in the reports over Prague radio, and in *Student,* 31 January, 7 February, 6 March, 26 June 1968; *Prace,* 29 February 1968; *Mlada Fronta,* 1, 15 March 1968, *Svobodne Slove,* 1 March 1968. Mueller and Holacek were reinstated by the CSM and readmitted to the university. Eventually the students submitted the following demands to the National Assembly's education committee: 1. Democratic legislation on civil rights; a. new concept of the political system in the CSSR, b. open debate, c. speedy justice, d. freedom to travel and stay abroad, e. freedom of internal movement, f. right to demonstrate; 2. Strict observance of laws; 3. Acceleration of the federalization of the State; 4. Retirement of persons involved in past errors; 5. Return to the rule of law. *Student,* 24 July 1968.

[44] Prague radio, 1, 24 March 1968; Bratislava radio, 15 January, 23 March 1968; CTK, 26 March 1968; *Uj Szo,* 15 March 1968; *Mlada Fronta,* 3, 5 April 1968. The Association of Socialist Youth was described as designed to appeal to members and nonmembers of parties to provide "an open dialogue between equal partners and . . . a source of progress and a guarantee of democracy."

[45] Cf. Smrkovsky speech to the April central committee plenum (*Rude Pravo,* 4 April), or Sik at the same plenum (*Rude Pravo,* 7 April).

[46] *Rude Pravo,* 10 April, 24 May 1968. The programme specifically condemned monopoly by one social organization.

founded in the months before the invasion. The youth defied the party on this issue and on many occasions prodded the regime to act more swiftly and resolutely in accordance with the Action Program, at the same time expressing their solidarity with the party in face of the pressure and threats from the other communist countries.[47]

Despite the profusion of youth organizations and the disintegration of the official movement, solidarity among the young enabled them to maintain their leadership role even in the confused days of the invasion. Their reaction was spontaneous rather than organized, but it demonstrated a genuine solidarity, not only among themselves but with their elders, in which the generational gap was temporarily forgotten. At the same time the natural generational differences were reflected in the greater activity of the youth, who assumed in some degree a leadership role among the public second only to the communications media (which actually carried on the role of the legal government). While for the most part they displayed during the invasion the same degree of discipline as did their elders, and at all times proclaimed their complete support for the country's abducted leaders, the situation did produce conflicting feelings among the young and their elders. The young had been raised in an atmosphere of shame and even contempt for the capitulation of 1938, and it was little comfort that the students had heroically resisted the occupation of Czechoslovakia in 1939; in 1968 the young people were intent upon *not* repeating the shameful mistake of the past. Their open and courageous defiance in the days of the invasion may be seen in this light, and indeed many older Czechs felt that the young people's behavior had restored their pride. In these days the youth did *not* necessarily feel that their elders had voluntarily abandoned the aims and ideas of the "revival"; on the contrary they joined the party in large numbers to demonstrate their continued faith and solidarity. Nonetheless, as the initial shock wore off, more and more of them began to wonder if the country's leaders had been equal to the tasks confronting them, if the conditions agreed to in Moscow were legitimate, and if indeed they, the youth, had in fact acted any differently from their elders. In retrospect 1968 appeared to many of them as a capitulation no less shameful than that of 1938, no matter how it was rationalized. As one of the protest songs written by and circulating among the youth in 1969 put it, this generation was not much better than its predecessors.[48]

The issue of the generation should not, however, be oversimplified, for from the early days of liberalization in 1963 on through the invasion and after, a certain alliance existed which cut across age differences. It was

[47] E.g. *Student,* 24 July 1968, on the Warsaw letter.
[48] 'Pasazova revolta,' by Karel Kryl.

the primary task of the conservatives to break this alliance; their success as far as one can tell has been only partial, and it is not yet clear just how much the youth feel they are now on their own, as the population becomes resigned to its fate, threatening the return of the pre-1968 mood of apathy and alienation. At a two-day plenary session of its central committee 19–20 September 1968, the CSM decided to set up a preparatory committee for a new youth union which would be a loose federation of the independent associations set up before the invasion.[49] This in fact led to the creation, on 19 December, of a new Czech Association of Juvenile and Youth Organizations. The member organizations were to remain independent and autonomous; the Association was to assume only co-ordinating functions, and to act as representative of the member organizations. It did not claim to speak in the name of all youth and did not assume responsibility or jurisdiction for nonmembers. Nor did it cover Slovakia. The Slovak section of the CSM had decided at its meeting on 22 November to create a separate Slovak Union of Youth for the Slovak organizations. In addition the Czech Student Union itself insisted upon emphasizing its independence (and was therefore banned in June 1969). While in one respect this comprehensive organization (although there were now two) was what the party had all along sought, the new associations and the refusal of at least the Czech union to fulfil the former functions of CSM suggest that the youth were still asserting their independence. More important, the new Czech association demonstrated its intention to stand by the preinvasion program by conferring an award on the Czechoslovak radio for its performance during the invasion, to declare Dubcek, Smrkovsky and Cernik Heroes of the CSSR, and to recommend that Svoboda be given the country's highest honor, accorded till then only to T. G. Masaryk.[50] The Czech association also stood by the youth dailies, *Smena* (Slovak) and *Mlada Fronta* (Czech), which had come under attack from the Soviets and the conservatives. These attacks continued throughout 1968 and into 1969, but the papers remained defiant. Both gained popularity outside youth circles and according to the organ of the journalists union (*Reporter*, 6 February 1969), the Slovak youth daily became the most widely read daily in Slovakia.[51] After the invasion the student journals voluntarily ceased publication, refusing to be bound by the Moscow-imposed restric-

---

[49] These included the University Students Union, Pioneers, Junak (Boy Scouts), Military Youth League, Campers Union, Council of Farm and Countryside Youth, Council of Secondary School and Apprentice Youth, Union of Youth Clubs, Union of Working Youth, and the Union of Polish Youth. Prague radio, 21 September.

[50] Prague radio, 21 September, 19 December 1968; Bratislava radio, 22 November 1968.

[51] *Smena* was reprimanded by the Slovak Office for Press and Information for "articles inconsistent with internal and foreign policy." The paper refused to accept the reprimand. *Smena*, 28 November 1968.

tions. In their place a Czech student weekly, *Studenske Listy,* appeared in January 1969—and a Slovak student fortnightly, *Reflex,* in April 1969. Both journals continued in the liberal spirit of their predecessors and, as a result, *Studenske Listy* was banned on 6 May and *Reflex* suspended.

By way of action and agitation the youth organized a demonstration on the fiftieth anniversary of the Czechoslovak Republic, which included a sit-in in front of the Soviet Embassy in Prague, as reported in the western press, and a three-day strike throughout Czechoslovakia in protest against the party's November central committee decision which in effect placed serious restrictions on the Action Program.[52] Together with lecturers and instructors, students peacefully occupied university buildings and conducted seminars and meetings on the situation in Czechoslovakia. They were entertained by outside groups such as a chamber orchestra which played on the premises of the Philosophy Faculty of Charles University, and food and cigarettes were brought in by people of all ages. During the strike, regular visits were exchanged between the universities and factories. The students produced a ten-point program specifically based on the Action Program. As before, their demands were not limited to student or even youth issues; they included demands for worker self-government and for the civil rights promised in the preinvasion period. The significance of the strike was summed up by one journal thus: "By their action, which took its course in a peaceful and orderly manner, the students have proved that they are a force which must be taken into consideration both now and in the future, that they are people who have their own views and who can defend them." [53]

If indeed the students were a force, some of them decided that they must make use of this to prevent the greatest threat to the ideals of the revival, that of a general relapse into resignation and indifference. It was to startle the people out of this, as well as to bring pressure on those in

---

[52] *Rude Pravo,* 19 November 1968, carries the text of the controversial resolution.

[53] *Lidove Demokracie,* 21 November 1968. The ten points were: 1. The Action Programme adopted by the April 1968 plenum of the Communisty Party of Czechoslovakia is the basis of our policy; 2. There will never be a policy from behind closed doors. In particular, the flow of information in both directions between the citizen and the leadership will be renewed; 3. The introduction of censorship in the mass communication media is temporary and will not last longer than six months; 4. Freedom of association and assembly must not be encroached upon; 5. Freedom of scientific research and of literary and cultural expression will be guaranteed; 6. Personal and legal security of citizens will be guaranteed; 7. Those who have lost the trust placed in them and have never sufficiently explained their attitude will not remain in important posts; 8. The establishment of enterprise councils of the working people as organs of self-administration will continue; 9. Freedom of travel abroad will be guaranteed; 10. In the area of foreign policy, we must never participate in actions which are contrary to the feelings of the Czechoslovak people, the UN Charter, and the general declaration of human rights.

the government who still regarded the people's wishes as binding, that a small group chose what was an act of desperation: self-immolation. For the orderly, rational Czechs the use of such a symbol—associated with the martyrdom of Jan Hus as well as with the more recent protest over Vietnam—by a young philosophy student was bound to come as a deep and grievous shock. The honor paid throughout the country to the self-immolated student Jan Palach, the massive attendance at his funeral, the spontaneous attempts in Czechoslovakia (and elsewhere in eastern Europe) to emulate his act, and the hesitancy of the regime to take a stand against it, all demonstrated the efficacy of the deed. Whether it had any lasting effects is another question. That it represented a new weapon in the struggle against the increasingly repressive regime was in fact denied by student leaders. Student and youth leaders were not prepared to make such tragic demands on their followers or themselves, and with the passing of the regime from the hands of Dubcek to Husak there seemed to be few left among the country's leaders who would be impressed or influenced by such pressure from below.

Since April 1969 the sense of frustration among all ages has been growing in Czechoslovakia. It would not be true to say that the younger generation has been broken, for it continues to organize protest wherever and however it can. The alliance between young workers and students has held, as has the broader alliance of youth with the liberals in the older generation. Yet today the younger people understand, in a way they may never otherwise have done, the meaning and nature of their elders' failures, particularly those of 1938. Today they are learning the techniques of passive resistance their parents mastered long ago; yet there are signs that they still consider themselves a generation with an important role to play— if, as some have pointed out, they do not permit themselves to be intimidated as were those before them by the overwhelming pressure to accommodate themselves and to compromise.[54]

[54] P. Pithart, 'Words, Words, Words . . .' *Listy,* 21 November 1968.

SUGGESTED READINGS

A. THE AGONY OF INDUSTRIALIZING (1750–1850)

EVELYN ACOMB & MARVIN BROWN, eds. *French Society and Culture Since the Old Regime* (New York: Holt, Rinehart & Winston, 1966)

FREDERICK B. ARTZ. *Reaction and Revolution 1814–1832* (New York: Harper & Row, 1934)

ALFRED COBBAN. *The Social Interpretation of the French Revolution* (Cambridge: Cambridge University Press, 1964)

PHYLLIS DEANE. *The Frst Industrial Revolution* (Cambridge: Cambridge University Press, 1965)

JOHN L. HAMMOND & BARBARA HAMMOND. *The Skilled Laborer, 1760–1832* (New York: Longmans, Green & Co., 1920); *The Town Laborer, 1760–1832* (New York: Longmans, Green & Co., 1917); *The Village Laborer, 1760–1832* (New York, Longmans, Green & Co., 1911)

JÜRGEN KUCZYNSKI. *The Rise of the Working Class.* tr. by C. T. A. Ray (New York: McGraw-Hill, 1967)

GEORGES LEFEBVRE. *The French Revolution.* tr. by Elizabeth M. Evanson, 2 vols. (New York: Columbia University Press, 1962)

BARRINGTON MOORE, JR. *The Social Origins of Dictatorship and Democracy: Lord and Peasant in the Making of the Modern World* (Boston: Beacon Press, 1966)

JOHN W. OSBORNE. *The Silent Revolution: The Industrial Revolution in England as a Source of Cultural Change* (New York: Scribners, 1970)

R. R. PALMER. *The World of the French Revolution* (New York: Harper & Row, 1971)

PRISCILLA S. ROBERTSON.   *Revolutions of 1848: A Social History* (Princeton, N.J.: Princeton University Press, 1952)

JEAN ROBIQUET.   *Daily Life in France Under Napoleon,* tr. by VIOLET M. MACDONALD (New York: Macmillan, 1963)

ALBERT SOBOUL.   *The Sans-Culottes* (New York: Anchor Books, 1972)

E. P. THOMPSON.   *The Making of the English Working Class* (New York: Random House, Inc., 1966)

WAYNE S. VUCINICH, ed.   *The Peasant in Nineteenth Century Russia* (Stanford, Calif.: Stanford University Press, 1968)

B. ACCELERATION AND SOCIAL CONFLICT (1850–1914)

ROBERT C. BINKLEY.   *Realism and Nationalism 1852–1871* (New York: Harper & Row, 1963)

PAULINE GREGG.   *A Social & Economic History of Britain, 1760–1970* (London: George G. Harap & Co., 6th ed., 1970)

THEODORE S. HAMEROW.   *Restoration, Revolution, Reaction: Economics and Politics in Germany 1815–1871* (Princeton, N.J.: Princeton University Press, 1958)

THEODORE S. HAMEROW.   *The Social Foundations of German Unification, 1858–1871* (Princeton, N.J.: Princeton University Press, 1969–72)

ORON J. HALE.   *The Great Illusion, 1900–1914* (New York: Harper & Row, 1971)

CARLTON J. H. HAYES.   *A Generation of Materialism, 1871–1900* (New York: Harper & Row, 1941)

E. J. HOBSBAWM.   *Bandits* (New York: Delacorte Press, 1969)

E. J. HOBSBAWM & GEORGE RUDÉ.   *Captain Swing* (London: Lawrence & Wishart, 1969)

CHARLES M. MORAZÉ.   *The Triumph of the Middle Classes: A Study of European Values in the Nineteenth Century,* tr. by PETER WAIT & BARBARA FERRYAN (London: Weidenfeld & Nicholson, 1966)

ROGER PRICE.   *The French Second Republic: A Social History* (Ithaca, N.Y.: Cornell University Press, 1972)

GUENTHER ROTH.   *The Social Democrats in Imperial Germany: A Study in Working-Class Isolation and National Integration* (Totowa, N.J.: The Bedminster Press, 1963)

JEREMY SEABROOK.   *The Unprivileged* (London: Longmans, Green & Co., 1967)

PETER N. STEARNS.   *European Society in Upheaval: Social History Since 1800* (New York: The Macmillan Co., 1967)

EDITH THOMAS.   *The Women Incendiaries,* tr. by JAMES & STARR ATKINSON (New York: George Braziller, 1966)

J. J. TOBIAS.   *Crime and Industrial Society in the Nineteenth Century* (New York: Schocken Books, 1968)

C. BRAVE NEW EUROPE: 1914 TO
THE PRESENT

WILLIAM S. ALLEN. *The Nazi Seizure of Power: The Experience of a Single German Town, 1930–1935* (Chicago: Quadrangle Books, 1965)

MARGARET SCOTFORD ARCHER & SALVADOR GINER, eds. *Contemporary Europe: Class, Status and Power* (London: Weidenfeld & Nicholson, 1971)

RONALD BLYTHE. *Akenfield: Portrait of an English Village* (New York: Pantheon Books, 1969)

T. A. CRITCHLEY. *The Conquest of Violence: Order and Liberty in Britain* (New York: Schocken Books, 1970)

RALF DAHRENDORF. *Society and Democracy in Germany* (Garden City, N.Y.: Doubleday & Co., 1967)

ARTHUR MARWICK. *The Deluge: British Society and the First World War* (New York: Norton, 1965)

JOHN B. MAYS. *The Introspective Society* (London: Sheed & Ward, 1968)

HENRI MENDRAS. *The Vanishing Peasant* (Cambridge, Mass.: MIT Press, 1970)

EDGAR MORIN. *The Red and the White: Report From a French Village*, tr. by A. M. SHERIDAN-SMITH (New York: Pantheon Books, 1970)

GEORGE L. MOSSE, ed. *Nazi Culture* (New York: Grosset & Dunlap, 1966)

JÜRGEN NEVEN-DU MONT. *After Hitler: A Report on Today's West Germans* (New York: Pantheon Books, 1970)

DAVID SCHOENBAUM. *Hitler's Social Revolution: Class and Status in Nazi Germany, 1933–1939* (New York: Doubleday & Co., 1967)

RAYMOND J. SONTAG. *A Broken World, 1919–1939* (New York: Harper & Row, 1971)

GORDON WRIGHT. *Rural Revolution in France* (Stanford, Calif.: Stanford University Press, 1964)